# THE ROLE OF CIRCUIT COURTS IN THE FORMATION OF UNITED STATES LAW IN THE EARLY REPUBLIC

While scholars have rightly focused on the importance of the landmark opinions of the United States Supreme Court and its Chief Justice, John Marshall, in the rise in influence of the Court in the Early Republic, the crucial role of the circuit courts in the development of a uniform system of federal law across the nation has largely been ignored. This book highlights the contribution of four Associate Justices (Washington, Livingston, Story and Thompson) as presiding judges of their respective circuit courts during the Marshall era, in order to establish that in those early years federal law grew from the 'inferior courts' upwards rather than down from the Supreme Court. It does so after a reading of over 1800 mainly circuit opinions and over 2000 original letters, which reveal the sources of law upon which the justices drew and their efforts through correspondence to achieve consistency across the circuits. The documents examined present insights into momentous social, political and economic issues facing the Union and demonstrate how these justices dealt with them on circuit. Particular attention is paid to the different ways in which each justice contributed to the shaping of United States law on circuit and on the Court and in the case of Justices Livingston and Thompson also during their time on the New York State Supreme Court.

# The Role of Circuit Courts in the Formation of United States Law in the Early Republic

## Following Supreme Court Justices Washington, Livingston, Story and Thompson

David Lynch

·HART·
OXFORD · LONDON · NEW YORK · NEW DELHI · SYDNEY

HART PUBLISHING
Bloomsbury Publishing Plc
Kemp House, Chawley Park, Cumnor Hill, Oxford, OX2 9PH, UK

HART PUBLISHING, the Hart/Stag logo, BLOOMSBURY and the Diana
logo are trademarks of Bloomsbury Publishing Plc

First published in Great Britain 2018
First published in hardback, 2018
Paperback edition, 2020

Copyright © David Lynch, 2018

David Lynch has asserted his right under the Copyright,
Designs and Patents Act 1988 to be identified as Author of this work.

All rights reserved. No part of this publication may be reproduced or
transmitted in any form or by any means, electronic or mechanical,
including photocopying, recording, or any information storage or
retrieval system, without prior permission in writing from the publishers.

While every care has been taken to ensure the accuracy of this work, no responsibility for
loss or damage occasioned to any person acting or refraining from action as a result of any
statement in it can be accepted by the authors, editors or publishers.

All UK Government legislation and other public sector information used in the work is
Crown Copyright ©. All House of Lords and House of Commons information used in the
work is Parliamentary Copyright ©. This information is reused under the terms of the Open
Government Licence v3.0 (http://www.nationalarchives.gov.uk/doc/open-governmentlicence/
version/3) except where otherwise stated.

All Eur-lex material used in the work is © European Union,
http://eur-lex.europa.eu/, 1998-2020.

A catalogue record for this book is available from the British Library.

Library of Congress Cataloging-in-Publication Data

Names: Lynch, David (Judge), author.
Title: The role of circuit courts in the formation of United States law in the early Republic: following
Supreme Court Justices Washington, Livingston, Story, and Thompson / David Lynch.
Description: Oxford [UK]; Portland, Oregon: Hart Publishing, 2018. | Includes bibliographical references and index.
Identifiers: LCCN 2017049615 (print) | LCCN 2017048784 (ebook) | ISBN 9781509910861 (Epub) |
ISBN 9781509910854 (hardback: alk. paper)
Subjects: LCSH: Circuit courts—United States—History. | Law—United States—History. |
United States—History—1783–1865. | United States. Supreme Court—Officials and
employees—History. | Washington, Bushrod, 1762–1829. | Livingston, Brockholst,
1757–1823. | Story, Joseph, 1779–1845. | Thompson, Smith, 1768–1843.
Classification: LCC KF8750 (print) | LCC KF8750 .L96 2018 (ebook) | DDC 347.73/24—dc23
LC record available at https://lccn.loc.gov/2017049615

ISBN: HB: 978-1-50991-085-4
PB: 978-1-50993-947-3
ePDF: 978-1-50991-087-8
ePub: 978-1-50991-086-1

Typeset by Compuscript Ltd, Shannon

To find out more about our authors and books visit www.hartpublishing.co.uk. Here you
will find extracts, author information, details of forthcoming events and the option to
sign up for our newsletters.

# ACKNOWLEDGEMENTS

I extend my very special thanks to those academics who guided my steps through the thesis which forms the basis of this volume. My Director of Studies, Dr Colin Harrison has given me constant support, countless insightful suggestions and much-needed reassurance throughout the entire research process. I also express my gratitude to my second supervisor Professor Glenda Norquay for her many pointers on structure and style and to my third supervisor, European Law specialist Dr Carlo Panara, for his long-range legal analysis from Germany where his current research has led him. I have been very fortunate to have as an external supervisor an American who is also a United States Supreme Court specialist. Dr George Conyne of the University of Kent at Canterbury has been invaluable in ensuring that my facts are accurate, that I prove my arguments and consider both sides of Federalist and Republican philosophy.

I would also like to thank the librarian and staff of The Honourable Society of Middle Temple for the use of the *United States Reports,* the Institute of Advanced Legal Studies in London for permitting access to the 30 volumes of *Federal Cases* and the Archive Section of the Liverpool Central Library for the prolonged use of their microfilm readers. I am also grateful to Denise Minde and Sheena Streather of Aldham Robarts Library, Liverpool John Moores University for their assistance in helping me to obtain original material from the Library of Congress and the Massachusetts Historical Society.

Circumstances prevented my spending many months in the United States examining the papers of Justices Washington, Livingston, Story, and Thompson. I am, therefore, heavily indebted to the librarians and staff of the following institutions who came to my rescue by delivering to me photocopies and microfilm reels of the justices' papers. Their enthusiastic support eased my task considerably: Harvard Law School, Library of Congress, Massachusetts Historical Society, Mount Vernon Ladies Association of the Union, New York Historical Society, New York State Library, Princeton University and William L Clements Library at the University of Michigan.

I am grateful to the following people at Hart Publishing for their editorial and production skills which have assisted me greatly: Bill Asquith, Anne Flegel, Rosamund Jubber and Francesca Sancarlo. I also appreciate the professionalism of my copy editor, Paula Divine and of Maureen MacGlashan who prepared the index and table of cases.

Finally, I thank my wife Ann who has lived with this and other research projects over far too many years. Her patience has been remarkable for one who believed retirement to mean something completely different.

# TABLE OF CONTENTS

*Acknowledgements* ........................................................................................v
*Table of Cases* ............................................................................................. ix
*Introduction* ..............................................................................................xix

1. **The Supreme Court Justices and the Circuit Court Experiment** ..................1
   A Team Effort ....................................................................................7
   Why Washington, Livingston, Story, and Thompson? ...............................15

2. **The Federal Circuit Courts: Shaping Local and National Justice for an Emerging Republic** ..................................................................23
   The Politics of Federal Law................................................................23
   The Grand Jury Charge: A Bond between Government and Citizen ........32
   The Circuit Court Discourse in the Constitutional Ratification and Senate Debates .........................................................................37
   The Jurisdiction of the Federal Circuit Courts....................................39
   'A Certain Uniformity of Decision in United States Law' ....................41
   Conclusion........................................................................................48

3. **Bushrod Washington: The Role of Precedent and the Preservation of Vested Interests**............................................................................51
   A Federalist's Journey from Revolutionary Virginia to the Supreme Court .............................................................................52
   Justice Washington and the Role of Precedent in the Federal Legal System ..................................................................................56
   Property Rights and Commercial Law on Circuit................................66
   States' Rights, the War of 1812, and Slavery......................................73
   Conclusion........................................................................................83

4. **Henry Brockholst Livingston: Consolidating Mercantile Law** ..................86
   The Early Years: Political Allegiances: From Federalist to Republican ......87
   Commercial Law for New York State .................................................91
   A Republican on a Federalist Supreme Court ....................................96
   Maritime and Commercial Law for the United States .......................104
   Conclusion......................................................................................109

5. **Joseph Story: Admiralty Expertise and the Importation of Common Law** ...........................................................................111
    A Modernising Influence on Law and Procedure on the First Circuit....121
    Admiralty and the Enforcement of Embargo Laws................................125
    Consistency Through the Sharing of Expertise........................................138
    The Supremacy of Federal Law ..............................................................143
    The Protection of Minority Groups........................................................147
    Importing Common Law into the Federal Legal System ........................151
    Conclusion.............................................................................................153

6. **Justice Smith Thompson: Promoting Commerce, State Sovereignty and the Protection of the Cherokee Nation** ................................................157
    State Supreme Court: Statutory Interpretation and New York 'Hard Law'........................................................................................159
    Contractual Obligations on the Second Circuit and on the Court ........166
    'What is to be Left to the States?'..........................................................171
    The Cherokee Nation and the African-American Slave........................175
    Conclusion.............................................................................................180

**Conclusion**...................................................................................................183

*Appendix A: Reversal Rates* ..........................................................................195
*Appendix B: Majority Opinions Delivered by the Justices* .............................198
*Appendix C: Legal Education and Prior Judicial Experience of United States Supreme Court Justices 1801–1835*............................................................202
*Bibliography*..................................................................................................206
*Index* .............................................................................................................219

# TABLE OF CASES

*The Active*, 1 F Cas 69, Conn, April 1809, ................103, 110:
  see also Ross v The Active; United States v Bright, 24 F Cas 1232, 1809
Adams v Story, 1 F Cas 141, New York, April 1817,................ 47, 98, 100, 101, 109
The Aeolus, 16 US 392 (1818), ................106
Albee v May, 1 F Cas 134, Vermont, May 1834, ................168
The Alexander, 1 F Cas 362, Mass, May 1823, ................133
The Alligator, 1 F Cas 527, Mass, 1812, ................128
The Amistad, 40 US 518 (1841), ................149, 177, 178–9, 181
The Ann, 1 F Cas 926, Mass, May 1812, ................126
The Ann, 13 US (9 Cranch), 289 (1815), ................146
The Argo, 1 F Cas 1100, Mass, May 1812, ................124, 125
Armroyd et al v Williams et al, 1 F Cas 1132, Penn, April 1811, ................78
Arnold v United States, 13 US (9 Cranch), 104 (1815), ................146
Balfour's Lessee v Meade, 2 F Cas 543, Penn, April 1803, ................68
Bank of Alexandria v Swann, 34 US 33 (1835), ................170, 181
Bank of Columbia v Lawrence, 26 US (1 Pet) 578 (1828), ................170, 181
Bank of the United States v Halstead, 23 US 51 (1825), ................175, 180
Bank of the United States v Northumberland Union and Columbia Bank,
  4 Peters 108, 1821, ................47
Barker v Jackson, 2 F Cas 811, New York, October 1826, ................167–8, 193
Barnes et al v Billington et al, 2 F Cas 858, April 1803, ................43, 60, 61, 83
Barnewell v Church, Caines' Reports, vol 1, 230, August 1803, ................164–5
Baudy et al v Union Insurance Co, 2 F Cas 1039, Penn, October 1809, ................72
Baxter v New England Ins Co Inc, 2 F Cas 1058, Mass, October 1822, ................130
Bayard et al v Massachusetts Fire & Marine Ins Co, 2 F Cas 1065, Mass,
  October 1826, ................130, 154
Beach v Woodhull, Trenton, New Jersey, April 1803 in Peters, Reports of the
  Third Circuit, 1803–1818, vols 1, 2, ................62
Beardsley v Torry 2 F Cas 1188, Penn, October 1822, ................59
Bell et al v Davidson, 3 F Cas 100, Penn, April 1818, ................65
Bell v Morrison, 26 US (1 Pet), 351 (1828), ................136, 189
The Betsey v Duncan, 3 F Cas 308, Penn, October 1808, ................73
Blair v Miller, 4 US 21 (1800), ................201
The Blairau, 6 US 240, ................63
Bleeker v Bond, 3 F Cas 687, Penn, October 1819, ................69–70
Bobyshall v Oppenheimer, 3 F Cas 785, Penn, October, 1822, ................60, 83
The Bolina, 3 F Cas 811, Mass, 812, 1812, ................46, 128
Bond v The Cora, 3 F Cas 838, Penn, 1807, ................63, 83
Borden v Fitch, Johnson's Reports, vol 15, 139, January 1818, ................165

The Boston, 3 F Cas 925, Mass, October 1812, ...................................................126, 153
The Bothnea: The Janstoff, 3 F Cas 962, Mass, May 1814, ...........................127, 153–6
The Bothnea 15 US 169 (1817), ...........................................................................127
Boyce & Henry v Edwards (1830), ...............................................................170, 181
Brandt v Ogden, Caines' Reports, vol III, 10, May 1805, ................................95, 110
Brewster v Gelston, 4 F Cas 82, New York, April 1825, ................................168, 181
The Brig Struggle, 13 US (9 Cranch) 71 (1815), ................................................106
Brown v Maryland, 25 US (12 Wheat) 419 (1827), ...................................173–4, 180
Burrill v Phillips, 4 F Cas 832, Rhode Island, November 1812, ..........................133
Burton et ux v Smith, 4 F Cas 876, Penn, October 1826, .....................................61
Butler v Hopper, 4 F Cas 904, Penn, October 1806, .............................................79
The Cadmus v Matthews et al, F Cas 977, New York, December 1830, ..............167
Calbraith v Gracy, 4 F Cas 1030, Penn, April 1805, .............................................60
The Caledonian, 17 US (4 Wheat.), 100 (1819), ................................................146
Calhoun v Vechio, 4 F Cas 1049, Penn, April, 1812, .............................................65
Campbell et al v Claudius, 4 F Cas 1161, Penn, October 1817, ............................61
Carpenter v Butterfield, Johnson's Reports, 1799–1803, vol 3, 145, July 1802, ......163–4
Carver v Jackson, 29 US (4 Pet) 1 (1830), ..........................................................123
Casey v Brush, Caines' Reports, vol II, February 1805, 295, ......................94, 109–10
Charles River Bridge v Warren Bridge, 36 US 420 (1837), ................................66–7
Cherokee Nation v Georgia, 30 US 1 (1831), ......................... 12, 148, 174, 175–7,
  182, 192, 199, 229
Childs v Corp, 5 Cas 622, Vermont, October 1810, ...............................105, 109–10
Citizens Bank v Nantucket Steamboat Co, 5 F Cas 719, 1811, ................44, 45, 124
Cloutman v Tunison, 5 F Cas 1091, Mass, May 1833, ........................................129
Cobb v Haydock, 5 F Cas 1132, Conn, 1810, ..................................................104–5
Cochrane v Swartout, 5 F Cas 1144, New York, 31 October, 1834, ....................168
Codwise et al v Gleason et al 5 F Cas 1167, Conn, April 1808, ...............104, 109–10
Cohens v Virginia, 19 US 264 (1821), ................................................................198
Coles et al v Marine Insurance Co, 6 F Cas 65, Penn, April 1812, ........................71
Consequa v Willings, 6 F Cas 336, Penn, April, 1816, ..........................................65
Corfield v Coryell, 6 F Cas 546 (1823), ...........................................74, 84–5, 141, 193
Corfield v Coryell, 6 F Cas 551–552, Penn, April 1823, ....................................75–7
Corser v Craig, 6 F Cas 601, Penn, April 1806, ....................................................70
Craig, Trenton, New Jersey, April 1803 in Peters, Reports of Third Circuit Cases,
  1803–1818, vol 1, 1, ......................................................................................61, 83
Craig v Brown 6 F Cas 723, Penn, October 1819, ...........................................71, 84
Crawford et al v The William Penn, 6 F Cas 781, New Jersey, October 1819, ....60, 62
Cross v United States, 6 F Cas 892, Mass, May 1812, ....................................126–7
Croudson v Leonard, 8 US 434, 1808, ........................................................59–60, 83
Cruder v Pennsylvania Ins Co, 6 F Cas 921, Penn, October 1809, ........................71
Dartmouth College, Trustees v Woodward, 64 New Hamp 473 (1817), ......108, 189
Dartmouth College, Trustees v Woodward, 17 US (4 Wheat) 518 (1819), ......66, 81, 144, 198
Davidson v Seal-Skins, 7 F Cas 192, 194, 1835, ....................................................46
Delancy v M'Keen, 7 F Cas 371, Penn, April, 1806, .........................................64, 83
Delaware Insurance Company v Hogan, 2 Peters 4, Penn, April 1807, ............71, 84
Delovio v Boit et al 7 F Cas 418, Mass, October 1815, .........................131–2, 154, 189

Denniston et al v Imbrie, 7 F Cas 485, Penn, April 1818, ....................................................71
Doe on the Demise of Elmore v Goymes, 26 US (1 Pet), 469, .........................................48
Dugan v United States, 16 US 172 (1818), ..................................................................107
Dusar v Murgatroyd, 8 F Cas 140, 1803, ........................................................................45
Edwards v Percival & Paulding (1827) (unreported), ................................................160n18
The Elizabeth, 8 F Cas 468, New York, April 1810, ..............................................103, 110
The Elizabeth v Rickers et al, 8 F Cas 470, New York, December 1831, ........................167
The Emily and The Caroline, 22 US (9 Wheat) 381 (1824), ......................................177–8
The Emulous, 8 F Cas 704, Mass, October 1832, ..........................................................130
The Enterprise, 8 F Cas 732, 736, 1810, .........................................................................47
The Estrella, 17 US (4 Wheat) 298 (1819), ...................................................................106
Evans v Hettick, 8 F Cas 861, 1818. Affirmed, 7 Wheat (20 US) 453, Penn,
  October (1822), .................................................................................................46, 61–2
Evans v Jordan, 3 US (9 Cranch) 199 (1815), .................................................................82
The Experiment, 21 US (8 Wheat), 261 (1823), ............................................................146
Fales et al v Mayberry, 8 F Cas 970, Rhode Island, November 1815, ............................133
Ferguson v Zepp, 8 F Cas 1154, Penn, April 1827, ...................................................60, 83
Field v Joel Gibbs et al, 1 Peters 155, New Jersey, October 1815, ....................................61
Finlay v King's Lessee, 28 US 346 (1830), .................................................................160n18
Fisher v Harnden, 9 F Cas 129, New York, April 1812, .........................................100, 109
Fitzsimmons et al v Ogden et al (1812) 7 Cranch 2, ..............................................13, 201
Fletcher v Peck, 10 US 87 (1810), ..........................................................69–70, 118, 198
Foot v Tracy, Johnson, vol 1, 46, February, 1806, .........................................................166
Gallagher v Roberts, 9 F Cas 1089, Penn, April 1808, ....................................................70
Gammell v Skinner, 9 F Cas 1142, Mass, May 1814, .....................................................124
The George, 10 F Cas 196, Mass, October 1814, ..........................................127, 153, 154
The George, 10 F Cas 205, Mass, May 1832, .......................................................129, 193
Gibbons v Ogden, 22 US (9 Wheat) 1 (1824), ...................................... 103, 172, 198
Ex parte Gilchrist, Federal Cases no 5420, ................................................................97–8
Gill v Brown, Johnson's Reports, vol 12, p 386, October 1815, .....................................162
Girard v Ware et al, 10 F Cas 441, Penn, April 1815, .....................................................73
Glass v The Sloop Betsey, 3 US 6 (1794), .....................................................................201
Glidden v Manufacturers' Ins Co, 10 F Cas 476, Mass, October 1832, ...................130, 154
Golden v Prince, 10 F Cas 542, Penn, April 1814, .........................................................70
Goodyear v Matthews (Case No 5576, F Cas), .........................................................46, 62
Gordon v Holiday, 10 F Cas 798, Penn, April 1805, ................................................69, 84
Gordon v Kerr et al, 10 F Cas 801, Penn, October 1806, ...............................................68
Goyon v Pleasants, 10 F Cas 891, Penn, April 1814, .....................................................71
The Grand Turk, 10 F Cas 956, 1817, ...........................................................................45
Grant & Swift v M'Lachlin, Johnson's Reports, 1806–1823, 39, February 1809, ............164
Green v Beals, Caines' Reports, vol II, November 1804, 255, ...........................94, 109–10
Green v Biddle, 21 US (8 Wheat) 1 (1823), ............................................................81, 146
Green v Watkins, 19 US (6 Wheat) 260 (1821), ........................................................123–4
Griffith v Tunckhouser, 11 F Cas 42, Penn, April 1817, ...........................................69, 84
Griswold v Hill, 11 F Cas 60, New York, September 1825, ...........................................169
Harden v Gordon et al, 11 F Cas 480, Maine, October 1823, ..............................129, 154
Harding et al v Wheaton et al 11 F Cas 491, ...............................................................123

Harrison v Rowan, 11 F Cas 663, New Jersey, April 1820, .................................65–6, 83, 95
Hatch v Ellis, 11 F Cas 806, Mass, May 1812, ................................................................124
Henderson v Brown, Caines' Reports, vol I, 92, May 1803, ......................................162, 181
Henderson v Brown, Caines' Reports, vol I, 94, May 1803, ................................................94
Hills v Ross, 3 US 184 (1796), .........................................................................................201
Hodgson v Dexter, 5 US 345, 363 (1803), ........................................................................162
Hodgson v Marine Insurance Co of Alexandria, 9 US 100 (1809), ...................................201
Hogan v Jackson, Cowp. 299, ...........................................................................................60
Hohn v United States, 524 US 236, 251 (1998), ................................................................58
House v Mayo, 324 US 42 (1945), .....................................................................................58
Houston v Moore, 18 US 1 (1820), ..................................................................................139
Hudson & Smith v Guestier, 10 US (6 Cranch) 281 (1810), ..........................................107–8
Hudson v Guestier, 11 US Reports, 1 (1812), ..................................................................201
Huidekoper v Burrus, 12 F Cas 840, Penn, April 1804, ...............................................68–9, 84
Humphreys v Blight's Assignees, 12 F Cas 875, Penn, April 1803, ..............................70, 84
Hunt v United States, 12 F Cas 948, Mass, May 1812, ...............................................128, 169
Hurst v Hurst, 12 F Cas 1028, Penn, April, 1803, ..........................................................43, 83
Hurst v Hurst, 12 F Cas 1031, Penn, April 1807, ...............................................................63
Hurst v Hurst, 12 F Cas 1031, Penn, April 1803, ...............................................................61
Hylton v Brown, 12 F Cas 1122, Penn, October, 1805, .......................................................43
Hylton v Brown, 12 F Cas 1123, Penn, October 1806, .......................................................61
Hylton v Brown, 12 F Cas 1129, Penn, April 1806, ............................................................64
Imlay v Sands, Caines' Reports, vol 1, p 572, February 1804, ..................................162–3, 181
The Industry, 13 F Cas 35, Mass, May 1812, ...................................................................128
Insurance Co v Dunham, 78 US (11 Wall) 1, 77, .......................................................132, 154
Jackson, ex dem Van Vechten et al v Sill et al, 11 Johnson's Reports,
    201, 220 (1814), ....................................................................................................160–1, 181
Jackson v Horton, Caines' Reports, vol 3, 202, August 1805, .............................................92
Jackson v Munson, Johnson's Reports, vol 1, 283, May 1806, ............................................92
Jackson v Porter, 13 F Cas 235 New York, September 1825, .............................................175
Jackson v Sill, 11 Johnson 201, NY, August 1814, ............................................................181
Jackson v Sprague, 13 F Cas 253, New York, September 1825, .........................................168
Brig James Wells v United States, 11 US 22 (1812), ..........................................................201
In the Matter of Jeremiah Ferguson, a Soldier in the United States Army, Johnson,
    vol 9, 241, (August 1812), ...........................................................................................173
The Jerusalem, 13 F Cas 564, Mass, May 1815, ...............................................................131
Johnson v M'Intosh, 12 US 571 (1823), ...........................................................................175
Johnson v M'Intosh, 21 US 543 (1823), .......................................................................147–8
Johnson v Phoenix Insurance Co 13 F Cas 782, Penn, April 1806, ......................................72
The Joseph Segunda, 18 US (5 Wheat) 338 (1820), ..........................................................107
The Julia, 12 US (8 Cranch), 181 (1814), ....................................................................146–7
Keene v United States, 9 US (5 Cranch) 304 (1809), ........................................................105
Ketland v Lebering, 14 F Cas 433, Penn, April 1808, .........................................................73
King v Delaware Ins Co 14 F Cas 516, Penn, October 1808, ..........................................61, 65
Kingston v Kincaid et al 14 F Cas 590, Penn, April 1806, ..................................................61
Kirkpatrick v White et al, 14 F Cas 685, Penn, April 1826, ...........................................59, 83
Koning v Bayard Jr et al, 14 F Cas 843, 845, ......................................................................48

## Table of Cases

Krumbaar v Burt et al, 14 F Cas 872, Penn, October 1809, ..................................................61
Lambert's Lessee v Payne, 7 US (3 Cranch) 97 (1805), ..............................................80–1, 83, 201
The Langdon Cheves, 17 US (4 Wheat), 103 (1819), ...................................................146
Lanning, Lessee of v London, 4 Peters 332, Penn 1822, ................................................79
Lanning v London et al 14 F Cas 1123, Penn, October 1821, .........................................61
Lee v Lee, 33 US 44 (1834), ........................................................................178
Lee v Munroe & Thornton, 11 US (7 Cranch) 366 (1813), .............................................107
Lennox v Prout, 16 US 3 Wheat. 520 (1818), .........................................................110
Leroy v Lewis, May 1803, Caines' Reports, 175, ..................................................93, 109
Livingston & Gilchrist v Maryland Insurance Co. 11 US (7 Cranch), 506 (1813), .............88
Livingston v Delafield, Caines' Reports, vol III, 53, ..................................................93
Livingston v Van Ingen, 9 Johns Report 507 (1812), ..................................................172
Livingston v Van Ingen, 15 F Cas 697, New York, April 1811, ...............................103, 180
McConnell v Hampton, Johnson's Reports, vol 12, 235, May 1815, .............................165
McCulloch v Maryland, 17 US (4 Wheat) 316 (1819), ........................................144–5, 198
McCutchen v Marshall, 33 US 220 (1834), ..........................................................177
McDonough v Dannery, 3 US 188 (1796), ...........................................................201
McFadden [aka McFaden or McFaddon] v The Exchange, 16 F Cas 85, Penn,
 October 1811, ........................................................................62–3, 84, 99
McGregor v Insurance Company of Pennsylvania, 16 F Cas 129, Penn, April 1803, .....71, 84
McMurtry v Jones, 16 F Cas 312, Penn, April 1813, ..................................................70
McMurtry v Jones, 16 F Cas 312, Penn, April 1913, ..............................................70, 84
Mandeville v Riggs, 27 US (2 Pet) 482 (1829), ....................................................124
Mandeville v Welch, 18 US (5 Wheat) 277 (1820), ................................................147
Marbury v Madison, 5 US 137 (1 Cranch) (1803), ..................20, 27–8, 49, 143–4, 187, 198
Marine Insurance Co of Alexandria v Tucker, 7 US 357 (1806), ...............................201
Marine Insurance Co of Alexandria v Wilson, 7 US Reports, 187 (1805), ..................201
Marshall v Beverley, 18 US (5 Wheat) 313 (1820), ..........................................108, 110
Marshall v Delaware Ins Co, 16 F Cas 838, Penn, April, 1807, ..............................60, 61
Marshall v Union Ins Co, 16 F Cas 849, Penn, October 1809, ...................................72
In re Martin, 2 Paine 348; 16 F Cas 881, 884, ...................................................180
Martin v Bank of the United States, 16 F Cas 885, 1821, ........................46, 62, 81, 83
Martin v Delaware Ins Co, 16 F Cas 894, Penn, October 1808, .................................71
Martin v Hunter's Lessee, 14 US 304 (1 Wheat) (1816), ........................141, 143, 144, 155
The Mary, 16 F Cas 938, 941, .................................................................47–8
Mason v Haile, 25 US (12 Wheat) 370 (1827), ................................................80, 83, 174
Mellish v Arnold, Bumb 51, ..................................................................95, 110
The Mentor, 17 F Cas 15, Mass, October 1825, ...................................................129
The Merino, 22 US 391 (1824), ................................................................81–2
Milligan v Dickson et al, 17 F Cas 376, Penn, April 1817, ..............................68, 84, 193
Mills v Duryee, 11 U.S (7 Cranch) 481 (1813), ...................................................143
The Monte Allegro, 22 US (9 Wheat) 616 (1824), .........................................170, 181
Mossman v Higginson, 4 US Reports, 12 (1800), ................................................201
Mott v Maris, 17 F Cas 905, Penn, April 1808, ...........................................61, 63–4, 83, 188
Mumford v M'Pherson, Johnson's Reports, 1806–1823, vol 1, 417, August 1806, .......164
New Jersey v Babcock, 18 F Cas 82, New Jersey, April 1823, ..................................59
The New York, 16 US (3 Wheat) 59 (1818), .......................................................106

*Table of Cases*

Ninety-five Bales of Paper v United States, 18 F Cas 266, New York, April 1820,.......102, 110
The Ship Octavia, (Nicholls et al, claimants), 14 US 20 (1819),....................................146–7
Odlin v Insurance Company of Pennsylvania, 18 F Cas 583, Penn,
    October 1808,.................................................................................................62, 84, 98–9
Ogden v Saunders, 25 US (12 Wheat) 213 (1827),.......................................59, 60, 64, 82, 83,
                                                                                                101, 158, 173, 180, 198–9
Orne v Townsend, 18 F Cas 825, Mass, October 1827,................................................130, 154
Osborn v The Bank of the United States, 22 US (9 Wheat) 738 (1824),....................175, 180
Otis v Watkins, 13 US (9 Cranch) 339 (1815),.............................................................. 106–7
Parker v United States, 18 F Cas 1179, Penn, October 1809, ........................................78, 84
Payne v Tennessee, 501 US 808 (1991),...............................................................................58
Peisch v Ware (1808) 8 US 347,..........................................................................................14
Pendleton v Evans, 19 F Cas 140, Penn, October 1823,.....................................................61
Penhallow v Doane, 3 Dall (3 US) 54 (1795),................................................................. 74–5
Penn v Klyne et al, 19 F Cas 166, Penn, April 1817,..........................................................60
Penny v New York Insurance Company, Caines' Reports, vol III, August 1805, 157,........93, 109
The People v The Utica Insurance Co, 15 Johnson's Reports, 380–81 (1818),..............161–2
Perry et al v Crammond et al, 19 F Cas 277, Penn, April 1804,.................................. 70, 84
The Phoebe v Dignum, 19 F Cas 530, Penn, April 1803,....................................................73
The Pizarro, 15 US (2 Wheat) 227 (1817),.................................................................123, 138
The Plattsburgh, 23 US (10 Wheat) 133 (1825),...............................................................149
Potts v Gilbert, 19 F Cas 1203, Penn, April 1819,..............................................................61
Priestman v United States, 4 US 28 (1800),.....................................................................201
Prigg v Pennsylvania, 41 US 539 (1842),.....................................................121, 149–50, 191
Ramdulollday v Darieux, 2 F Cas 211 Penn, April 1821, .................................................61
Randolph v Ware, 7 US 503 (1806),................................................................................201
Renner v Bank of Columbia, 22 US 581 (1824), ......................................................170, 181
Rhinelander v Insurance Company of Pennsylvania, (1807) 8 US 29!, ...........................14
Rhoades et al v Selin et al, 20 F Cas 631, Penn, October 1827,........................................60
Ricard v Williams, 20 US 59 (1822),...............................................................................147
Ridgway v Underwood, 20 F Cas 760, New Jersey, October 1821,...................................61
Riggs v Lindsay, 11 US (7 Cranch) 500 (1813),......................................................108, 110
The Robert Fulton, 20 F Cas 869, New York, April 1826,...............................................173
Robinson v Hook, 20 F Cas 1017, Maine, October 1826, .....................................128, 153
The Rosalie and Betty, 2 C. Rob Adm. 343,.....................................................................127
Ross v The Active, 20 F Cas 1231, Penn, October 1808,...................................................72:
                                                                                        see also The Active
The Rugen: Buhring, Claimant, 14 US 62 (1816),..........................................................106
Rust v Low, 6. Massachusetts Reports, 90, .....................................................................114
Rutherford v Moore, F Cas 12174, C.C.D.C. 1807, ................................................. 135n135
The St Lawrence, 13 US (9 Cranch), 120 (1815),............................................................146
The St Lawrence, 21 F Cas 180, New Hampshire, October 1813,....................................126
The Sally, 12 US (8 Cranch), 382 (1814),........................................................................146
The Sally, 21 F Cas 243, Mass, 1813,........................................................................... 125–6
The Santa Maria, 20 US (7 Wheat) 490 (1822), .............................................................106
The Schooner Exchange (McFadden [aka McFaden or McFaddon] v The Exchange),
    16 F Cas 85, Penn, October 1811,................................................................... 62–3, 84, 99

## Table of Cases

Scriba v Insurance Co of North America, 21 F Cas 874, Penn, October 1807, ............59, 83
Seamen v Patten, Caines' Reports, vol II, February 1805, 314, ............94
Seixas v Woods, 2 Caines' Reports, 48, New York, 1894, ............163, 176, 181
The Short Staple, 22 F Cas 23, Mass, May 1812, ............126, 127, 153–4
Ex parte Simmons, 27 F Cas 151, Penn, October 1823, ............79
Sims v Jackson, 22 F Cas 183, Penn, April 1806, ............73
Six Hundred and Fifty-One Chests of Tea v United States, 27 F Cas 253, New York, April 1826, ............167
Slaughterhouse Cases, 86 US 36 (1873), ............78
Slocum et al v Hathaway, 22 F Cas 339, 1820, ............45
Smith v Barker, 22 F Cas 454, Conn, April 1809, ............104
Smith v Barker, 22 F Cas 454, Conn, September 1808, ............45
Smith v Cheetham, 3 C.R. 57, ............110
Smith v Chetham, Caines' Reports, vol III, May 1805 p 58, ............95
Smith v Jackson, 22 F Cas 576, 577–578, 1825, ............46
Smith v Smith, 2 Johnson's Reports, 241 (1807), ............163
Sperry v Delaware Ins Co (Penn, October 1808), ............61
Spurr v Pearson, 22 F Cas 1011, Mass, October 1816, ............129
Stevens v Columbian Insurance Company, Caines' Reports, vol 3, 46, May 1805, ............164
Stuart v Laird, 5 US 299 (1803), ............20, 49, 187, 199
Sturges v Crowninshield, 17 US (4 Wheat) 122, 1819, ............58–9, 83, 100–1, 108, 144
Swift v Tyson, 41 US 1 (1842), ............152–3, 154, 192
Talbot v Simpson, 23 F Cas 644, Penn, October 1815, ............61
Ten Hogsheads of Rum, 16 F Cas 932, Mass, October 1812, ............126, 153
The New York, 16 US (3 Wheat) 59 (1818), ............105
Thurston v Martin, 23 F Cas 1189, Rhode Island, June 1830, ............132–3
Tidmarsh v Washington Fire & Marine Ins Co, 23 F Cas 1197, Mass, October 1827, ............130, 154
Tillman v Lansing, 4 Johnson's Reports 45 (1809), ............162, 181
Torrey v Beardsley, 24 F Cas 65, Penn, April 1818, ............69, 84
Treadwell et al v Bladen, 24 F Cas 144, Penn, October 1827, ............46, 62, 83
Tryphenia v Harrison, 24 F Cas 252, Penn, October 1806, ............78–9, 85
Tuttle v Beebee, Johnson's Reports, 1806–1823, vol 8, 154, May 1811, ............164
Two Hundred Chests of Tea, US 430 (1822), ............147
United States v Allen, Cas 772, 1810, ............47
United States v Ashton, 24 F Cas 873, Mass, May 1835, ............129
United States v Astley et al 24 F Cas 875, Penn, October 1819, ............61
United States v Barker, 24 F Cas 987, September 1816, ............105, 109
United States v Barker et al 24 F Cas 985, Mass, October 1829, ............129
United States v Bass, 24 F Cas 1028, New York 1819, ............102
United States v Battiste, 24 F Cas 1042, Mass, October 1835, ............133
United States v Bright, 24 F Cas 1232, 1809, ............57, 74, 75, 76–7, 83, 84, 85, 193: *see also The Active*
United States v Bryan & Woodcock, 13 US (9 Cranch) 374 (1815), ............107
United States v Burr, 25 F Cas 30 (1807), ............193
United States v Charles Stephens (1827) (unreported), ............160n18
United States v Clark, 25 F Cas 441, Mass, October 1813, ............152, 154

## Table of Cases

United States v Colt, 25 F Cas 581 Penn, April 1818, ................................................................61
United States v Coolidge, 14 US 415 (1816), ..............................................................152, 154
United States v Coolidge, 25 F Cas 622, Mass, May 1815, ...............................................133
United States v Dixey et al, 25 F Cas 871, Penn, April 1811, .......................................78, 84
United States v Five Packages of Linen (no citation found), ............................................110
United States v Freeman, 25 F Cas 1208, Mass, October 1827, .......................................130
United States v Giles, 13 US (9 Cranch 212) (1815), ........................................................107
United States v Halstead, 23 US 51 (1825), ................................................................... 174–5
United States v Hamilton, 26 F Cas 93, Mass, October 1818, ..........................................129
United States v Haskell et al, 26 F Cas 207, Penn, October 1823, ................................66, 83
United States v Hatch, 26 F Cas 220, New York, April 1824, .................................167, 193
United States v Hoxie, 26 F Cas 397, Vermont, October 1808, ........................................102
United States v Hudson and Goodwin, 7 Cranch 32 (1812), .................................151–2, 154
United States v The James Wells, 26 F Cas 585, Conn, September 1808, ...............102, 110
United States v Kelly, 24 US 417 (1826), ............................................................................82
United States v Kelly, 26 F Cas 700, Penn, October 1825, .................................................82
United States v Kennedy et al, 26 F Cas 15524, Ill1843, ............................................135n135
United States v La Coste 26 F Cas 826, Mass, October 1820, ...........................................133
United States v La Vengeance, 3 US 297 (1796), ..............................................................201
United States v Lawrence, 3 US Reports, 42 (1795), ........................................................201
United States v Lee, 26 F Cas 15586, C.C.D.C., 1834, ............................................... 135n135
United States v Lowry et al, 26 F Cas 1008, Penn, April 1808, .........................................75
United States v Mann, 26 F Cas 1153, New Hampshire, October 1812, ..........................124
United States v Mantor, 26 F Cas 1157, October 1820, ....................................................128
United States v Marchant & Colson, 25 US (12 Wheat) 489 (1827), ................................146
United States v Morgan et al, 26 F Cas 1315, Penn, April 1811, ..................................78, 84
United States v Morris, 23 US (10 Wheat.) 246 (1825), ............................................... 170–1
United States v Morrow, 26 F Cas 1352, Penn, October 1827, ...........................................65
United States v Moses, 27 F Cas 5, 1827, .....................................................................46, 62
United States v Nine Packages of Linen, 27 F Cas 154, New York, April 1818, .............102
United States v Parmele, 27 F Cas 415, Conn, April 1810, ...............................................104
United States v The Paul Sherman, 27 F Cas 467, New Jersey, April 1815, ............... 77–8, 84
United States v Perez, 27 F Cas 504, New York, September 1823, ..................................168
United States v Phelps, 27 F Cas 526, Connecticut 1810, .................................................102
United States v Rice, 17 US (4 Wheat), 246, (1819), ........................................................146
United States v Ross, 27 F Cas 572, Mass, October 1813, ................................................129
United States v Ruggles, 27 F Cas 912, Rhode Island, November 1828, ..................130, 154
United States v The Schooner Little Charles, 26 F Cas 15612, Virginia, May 1818, ...... 138–9
United States v Sears et al, 27 F Cas 1006, October 1812, ...............................................128
United States v Sixteen Packages, 27 F Cas 1111, Mass, October 1819, ..................126, 128
United States v Skinner et al, 27 F Cas 1123, New York 1818, ........................................102
United States v Slade, 27 F Cas 1125, Mass, May 1820, ................................... 136, 188–9
United States v Smith, 18 US (5 Wheat) 153, 164–83 (1820), .................................102, 147
United States v Smith, 27 F Cas 1166 (1816), ...................................................................129
United States v Smith, 27 F Cas 1167, Mass, October 1820, ............................................133
United States v Smith, 27 F Cas 1247, Penn, October 1819, .........................................72–3
United States v Sturges et al, 27 F Cas 1358, 1362, 1826, ...................................... 47–8, 169

United States v Tillotson (1823) (unreported), ................................................................ 160n18
United States v Webber 28 F Cas 507, Mass, May 1813, ....................................................... 126
United States v White, 28 F Cas 580, Mass, October 1826, ............................................. 135–6
United States v Williams, 28 F Cas 608, New York, April 1826, ........................................... 169
United States v Wonson, 28 F Cas 745, Mass, May 1812, ..................................................... 122
United States v Worrall, 2 Dallas 384 (1798), ......................................................................... 151
Vale v Phoenix Insurance Co 28 F Cas 687, Penn, April 1805, ......................................... 72, 84
Van Ness v Pacard, 27 US (2 Pet) 137 (1829), ................................................................ 136, 151
Vermont v The Society for the Propagation of the Gospel, 28 F Cas 1155, 1827, ........ 43, 188
Wakefield v Ross, 28 F Cas 1346, Rhode Island, November 1827, ................................. 134–5
Walden v Chamberlain, 28 F Cas 1353, Penn, April 1814, ..................................................... 72
Walker v Swartout, Johnson's Reports, vol 12, 445, October 1815, ............................. 162, 181
Walter v Perrin, Case no 17121 in F Cas, ................................................................................. 62
Ward v Arrendo, 29 F Cas 167, New York, April 1825, ......................................................... 173
Watson v Delafield, Caines' Reports, vol II, 224, November 1804, ...................... 93, 109–10
Wheaton v Peters, 33 US (8 Pet) 591, 668 (1834), ..................................................... 172–3, 180
Williams et al v Armroyd et al 7 Cranch (11 US) 423, ............................................................ 78
Williamson v Kincaid, 4 US 20 (1800), .................................................................................. 201
Willings v Consequa, 30 F Cas 55, Penn, October 1815, ........................................... 63, 78, 99
Willis v Bucher et al 30 F Cas 63, Penn, April 1818, ......................... 65–6, 69, 83, 84, 95, 181
Worcester v Georgia, 31 US (6 Pet) 515 (1832), ........................... 12, 148–9, 176–7, 192, 199
Young v Grundy, 11 US (7 Cranch) 548 (1813), ......................................................... 108, 110

# INTRODUCTION

I make it plain from the outset that this volume is not a legal, political, economic or constitutional history of the Early Republic. Its object is to record the results of my research into the part played by four prominent United States Supreme Court Justices in the development of United States law through their work in the circuit courts during the Chief Justiceship of John Marshall.

Having been involved in the study of English law for over 60 years, my life has revolved around guideline cases of the House of Lords and Court of Appeal with only a passing interest in United States law. It was whilst, after retirement, having commenced a Master of Research degree which included a dissertation on 'Cherokee Removal Discourse in Jacksonian America' that my interest in the early days of the United States Supreme Court began. I read the Court's Native American opinions and, in particular, those affecting the rights of Cherokees. Having been impressed by the measured dissent in favour of the Cherokee Nation by Justice Smith Thompson, joined in by Justice Joseph Story, in the 1831 case of *Cherokee Nation v Georgia*, I was interested in a closer examination of the contribution of both justices to the growth of United States law.

Whilst aware of the Supreme Court justices' role when sitting together in the nation's capital, further investigation revealed the significant impact they had on the development of federal law when sitting on circuit at first instance or by way of appeal from a district judge. Having reviewed the modern scholarship, it quickly became clear that much time and effort had been properly paid to the role of the Supreme Court in the formation of federal law, but the workload of the early 'inferior' federal courts had received scant attention despite calls by several scholars to examine the place of the circuit courts in United States legal history.

Frankfurter & Landis (1928) were alert to the need for detailed studies of the circuit and district courts for a better understanding of the nation's history.[1] Scholars have examined different aspects of their suggested research. In a 1970 exploratory essay on Justice Story's time on the First Circuit, Newmyer, when referring to the circuit courts, observed that 'there has been no comprehensive effort to understand their operation or assess their influence on society and on the development of American law and legal institutions'.[2] Tachau (1978) also appreciated

---

[1] Felix Frankfurter and James M Landis, *The Business of the Supreme Court: A Study in the Federal Judicial System* (New Brunswick: Transaction Publishers, 2007), 52–53, n 174. Originally published in 1928 by The Macmillan Company.

[2] R Kent Newmyer, 'Justice Joseph Story on Circuit and a Neglected Phase of American Legal History' (1970) XIV *The American Journal of Legal History* 112–35.

the need for further circuit court research when examining the cases of District Judge Harry Innes, the federal district judge of Kentucky between 1789 and 1816, who exercised circuit court jurisdiction in Kentucky until the appointment of Supreme Court Justice Thomas Todd to the 7th Circuit in 1807.[3] In 1997, Johnson was another who felt that the justices' work on circuit 'deserves far more attention than it has been given in the past'.[4] He began the task of remedying that neglect in a book chapter on 'The Circuit Courts and the Projection of Federal Power'.[5] In a 2009 essay on Justice Bushrod Washington, Johnson, when referring to the justices' circuit work, declared that 'It is in this multitude of cases that Washington and his fellow justices made their greatest contribution to the advancement of federal justice in the young republic', pointing to the 30 volumes of the *Federal Cases* as a starting point, in the case of Washington, to prove his worth as a judge.[6]

More recently, Graham (2010), citing Frankfurter, Landis and Tachau, noted that 'legal historians have focused on the significance of the Supreme Court, its decisions, and its justices', complaining that 'not only have the lower courts been ignored, their significance has even been questioned'.[7] Graham has furthered the scholarship on the 'inferior courts' by a detailed study of the circuit and district courts of Rhode Island, a constituent part of the First Circuit, between 1790 and 1812. La Croix (2012) is another who writes of the tendency of historians 'to focus on the on the Supreme Court alone, to the exclusion of the lower federal courts'. She observes that those who have devoted attention to the lower federal courts 'have largely neglected the history of how those courts developed beyond the early moments of the Constitutional Convention and the First Congress'.[8] LaCroix's paper does not seek to examine the workload of the circuit courts. Rather it is a penetrating insight into the Federalist view that extending judicial power to the 'inferior' federal courts was key to national supremacy.[9]

The nature and extent of the research referred to above will be developed in greater detail in later chapters. Here I have given only a brief outline to justify a

---

[3] Mary K Bonsteel Tachau, *Federal Courts in the Early Republic: Kentucky. 1789–1816* (Princeton, New Jersey: Princeton University Press, 1978). Tachau records the arrival on circuit of Justice Todd but does not examine his circuit work as her focus is on District Judge Harry Innes. Her pupil Glenn Forrester Taylor continued this aspect of research in a 1989 MA thesis at the University of Louisville entitled, 'Jurisdiction in the 7th Circuit, District of Kentucky, 1807–1817'.

[4] Herbert A Johnson, *The Chief Justiceship of John Marshall, 1801–1835* (Columbia: University of South Carolina Press, 1997), 6.

[5] ibid, 112–37.

[6] Herbert A Johnson, 'Bushrod Washington' (2009) 62(2) *Vanderbilt Law Review* 447–90 at 488–89.

[7] D Kurt Graham, *To Bring Law Home: The Federal Judiciary in Early National Rhode Island* (Dekalb: Northern Illinois University Press, 2010), 5. Graham's reference to the questioning of the value of circuit court opinions stems from the unreliable statistics of the number of successful appeals from circuit opinions which Charles Warren took from *Niles Register* of 10 April 1830 and used in his *A History of the American Bar* (Boston: Little Brown, 1911), 406.

[8] Alison L LaCroix, 'Federalists. Federalism, and Federal Jurisdiction' (24 February 2010) Final revised edition of 8 November 2012 in (2012) 30 *Law and History Review,* 205–44 at 206. University of Chicago Public Law Working Paper No 297. Available at SSRN: https://ssrn.com/abstract=1558612.

[9] ibid, 207.

response to the calls for further research into the role of the early circuit court in the development of United States law. Whilst using several sets of reports, I followed Johnson's suggestion of the *Federal Cases* as the basis of any investigation into the value of the justices' time on circuit. I extracted, read and noted up the 1377 reported circuit court opinions of the 14 Marshall Court associate justices. Having taken the view that scholars of legal history have focused on Chief Justice Marshall and that his associates had received comparatively scant attention, I decided not to examine the opinions of the Chief Justice but those of his brethren.

As an analysis of the circuit opinions of the Chief Justice and all 14 justices was clearly beyond the scope of a doctoral thesis, I decided to read those of four prominent associates (Washington, Livingston, Story and Thompson) who sat in busy commercial centres and whose tenures, taken together, spanned the era of the Marshall Court. Those circuit court opinions were key to ascertaining how the circuit experience shaped Supreme Court attitudes and the Chief Justice's opinion assignment choices. I also explored, at a time when there were few federal statutes and Supreme Court opinions to guide them, the sources upon which the justices drew to establish a body of federal law and how they attempted to achieve a consistent approach to federal law and procedure across the circuits. Today's judges have the advantage of law reports immediately available online or on disc and an experienced colleague within easy reach to help resolve a difficult point of law or procedure. Not so in the early days: a justice might find himself on circuit without a law library requiring assistance with an unfamiliar branch of the law when support from colleagues was only available through an extremely slow and sometimes unreliable exchange of letters.

An outline of some of the political and economic events of the period is given only to background the many issues which fell to the justices to determine to establish an in-depth examination of a large number of representative opinions and to show how vital the circuit work of these four justices was in the shaping of United States law in those very early years.

# 1

## The Supreme Court Justices and the Circuit Court Experiment

My main purpose was to decide the extent to which the opinions of Supreme Court justices, presiding over circuit courts, individually and collectively, shaped federal law to meet the political and economic challenges facing the emerging Republic. Although this chapter touches upon the development of federal law from the inception of the national courts in 1789, its focus is on the period 1801–1835, the tenure of Chief Justice John Marshall, at a time in American legal history when the most defining and far-reaching foundations of federal law were laid.

A number of issues faced the Supreme Court justices. They were tasked with riding the circuit with few federal statutes or Supreme Court opinions to guide them and had to decide which sources of law to use to achieve a uniform federal justice system when dealing with both criminal and civil disputes. There was also an important political dimension to their circuit visits as they strove to ensure that the novel concept of federal justice and the notion of a national government was well-received regionally.

My investigation led me to question the premise that the early Supreme Court rose to prominence, in the main, through its landmark decisions by examining a factor in the development of the federal court system which has remained largely unexplored. Scholars covering the crucial early years of the Republic have concentrated on Chief Justice John Marshall and the major constitutional Supreme Court opinions. Those opinions, which asserted the power of judicial review, involving the right to strike down as unconstitutional federal and state legislative acts, have deservedly commanded academic interest because of the part they played in the Court's rising influence.[1] However, such a focus on the Court's history ignores the role of the justices on circuit in the emergence of federal law; this can only

---

[1] The major works on the Supreme Court are: Charles Warren, *The Supreme Court in United States History*, 2 vols, Revised edition (Boston: Little Brown & Co, 1926); George Haskins and Herbert A. Johnson, *History of the Supreme Court of the United States, vol II, Foundations of Power: John Marshall, 1801–1815* (New York: Cambridge University Press, 2010), originally published by Macmillan Publishing in 1981; G Edward White, *History of the Supreme Court of the United States, vols III–IV, The Marshall Court and Cultural Change, 1815–1835* (New York: Cambridge University Press, 2010), originally published by the Macmillan Publishing Company in 1988. The most complete coverage of the earlier Jay and Ellsworth Courts is to be found in Julius Goebel Jr, *History of the Supreme Court of the United States: Antecedents and Beginnings to 1801* (New York: The Macmillan Company, 1971). A wealth of

be ascertained by examining the disputes which fell for resolution in the circuit courts and the manner in which the justices determined the issues. I have, therefore, concentrated on the legal principles established by the large number of cases dealt with at circuit level at a time when the Supreme Court had very little business to conduct. Henderson (1971) calculates that between 1790 and 1801 about 10,000 cases were decided nationwide in the federal lower courts.[2] Domnarski (1996) puts it well when he writes, 'the lower federal courts are where the action is'.[3] Whilst he refers to modern times, he accurately represents the position of the Early Republic.

I also addressed the effect on the development of federal law of the political tensions between the Republican-led Congress and the judicial nationalism of a Federalist-dominated Supreme Court; its struggle for the sole right to interpret the spirit and meaning of the United States Constitution and for the power, on the grounds of uniformity, to review federal and state legislation and state court decisions. I also investigated the effect these ideological differences had on the justices' circuit opinions.

Novak (1966) refutes the myth of American statelessness advanced by those scholars who support the view that the essence of nineteenth-century government was its absence. He does so by using over 1,000 cases, statutes and regulations to demonstrate the 'pivotal role played by public law, regulations, order, discipline, and governance in early American society'.[4] By analysing over 1,800 opinions, my study builds upon Novak's work by establishing the far-reaching effects of the emerging body of federal law on the personal and business affairs of American citizens.

Federal law was shaped, in the first instance, by the many disputes dealt with at circuit level which were subject to appeal to the Supreme Court by way of writ of error. As so few circuit opinions were appealed, they were generally regarded as final resolutions and, therefore, shaped that branch of law for the circuit and, if followed by other justices, for the nation. Interstate and international commerce, the prohibition of international slave trade, embargo and neutrality breaches arising from European conflicts and the War of 1812 with Britain, and the delicate positioning of state sovereignty within the powers of central government were all issues which featured heavily in circuit court dockets. However, slavery was so much a part of American life, and endorsed by the Constitution, that the plight

---

primary material is contained in Maeva Marcus (ed), *The Documentary History of the Supreme Court of the United States, 1789–1800*, 8 vols (New York: Columbia University Press, 1985–2007), and in Herbert A Johnson and Charles F Hobson (eds), *The Papers of John Marshall, 1773–1835*, 10 vols (Chapel Hill: University of North Carolina Press, 1974–2006).

[2] Dwight F Henderson, *Courts for a New Nation* (Washington DC: Public Affairs Press, 1971), 19.

[3] William Domnarski, *In the Opinion of the Court* (Urbana and Chicago: University of Illinois Press, 1996), 90.

[4] William J Novak, *The People's Welfare: Law and Regulation in Nineteenth-Century America* (Chapel Hill: University of North Carolina Press, 1996), 1–6.

of the African-American already held to slavery within the United States did not feature often either at circuit or Supreme Court level.

The justices chosen for the core of this research are, in order of appointment, Bushrod Washington, Henry Brockholst Livingston, Joseph Story, and Smith Thompson. They were selected because, whilst there are some similarities in their jurisprudence, each demonstrates a distinctive contribution to the development of federal law: Washington's dependence on legal precedent; Livingston's advancement of commercial law; Story's admiralty expertise and championing of common law; and Thompson's states' rights stance and promotion of the Cherokee cause reveal how each, in his own way, shaped American law. The four justices chosen were amongst the most prominent contributors; had long tenures on the Court; and from whom there is sufficient primary material available to reach meaningful conclusions.

The federal circuit and Supreme Court opinions of all four justices and the New York State Supreme Court opinions of Livingston and Thompson were examined to ascertain the sources on which they drew, the expertise they developed in particular branches of law, and the effect that expertise had on Chief Justice Marshall's opinion assignment process. Any changes of jurisprudential direction—from presiding in circuit court to sitting as one of seven justices in the Supreme Court—also received scrutiny.

In its first decade, from 1789, the United States Supreme Court delivered only 38 opinions compared to the 10,000 that passed through the lower federal courts.[5] This fact alone speaks to the importance of the circuit courts in the overall picture. The grand jury charges delivered by the justices at the beginning of each circuit session, designed to forge a bond between citizen and government, are further evidence of the significance of the local courts in the reception of federal justice. The use of a certificate of division of opinion, when a justice sat with the district judge, enabling the circuit courts to choose which cases were sent to the Supreme Court for definitive rulings was a further device used in the search for uniformity. Crucially, the circuit courts were the forums in which the justices gained expertise or honed skills gained earlier at the Bar or on the State Bench which lent to their Supreme Court opinions a confidence and authority stemming from collective circuit experiences. This supported the contention that, in the early years, rather than feeding down from the Supreme Court, the successful development of the national court system actually fed up from what the Constitution described as the 'inferior' circuit courts.

Graham (2010) is critical of scholars who have focussed on Marshall and the Supreme Court to the detriment of the circuit and district court where he finds, in early Rhode Island, most of his federal judicial activity took place. He argues, 'it was the daily operation of the federal courts in each of the states, rather than the efforts of a single individual or even the results of a series of Supreme Court

---

[5] *United States Reports,* vols 2–4.

cases, that allowed the judiciary to emerge as an equal branch of government'.[6] I seek to reinforce Graham's research and to ascertain whether his finding in one constituent part of the First Circuit between 1790 and 1812 can be supported over a much wider geographical area for a longer period. Despite the fact that Graham's research ends in 1812, it is extremely valuable because it highlights the significance of the grand jury charge and supports the view, taken here, that the political element of the charge began to disappear after its misuse by Justice Chase which led to the impeachment proceeding against him in 1805. Graham's examination of Justice Story's 1812 charges reveals only instructions to the jury on the law.[7] One can see the force of Graham's further argument that the Rhode Island federal courts were a powerful nationalising force in supporting the federal government and the interests of the local merchant class when he cites the remarks of Story's predecessor, Justice Cushing, in his 1794 grand jury charge, that the court would harness the power of the community to compel dishonest men to perform their contracts. This is a fine example of judicial rhetoric designed to persuade the local people that they had a stake in government.[8]

Johnson (1997) also spells out the importance of the associate justices as a body; he regards the circuit courts as 'the training grounds' for Supreme Court justices. He argues that the circuit duties of the justices brought them into contact with the grass roots of American life and gave them, when sitting on the Supreme Court, 'an insight into the difficulties facing trial judges'.[9] In a 2009 essay he recommends that the individual experiences of justices be examined to see how their circuit work shaped their personal perspectives as well as their approach to constitutional questions.[10] I respond to that call for further research, but do so by examining their approaches to all manner of issues, not just those bearing on the Constitution.

In a 1970 essay dealing with the circuit courts, Newmyer remarks that 'there has been no comprehensive effort to understand their operation, or assess their influence on society and on the development of American law and its institutions'.[11] He confines his attention to Justice Story's activities on the First Circuit dealing principally with his ties to the local people and his working relationships with both district judges and the legal profession. He does not seek to analyse Story's opinions but focuses on the acceptance by the local people of circuit court opinions

---

[6] Graham, *To Bring Law Home*, 6. However, in 1819 Story entered the political arena by roundly condemning slavery in his charges to grand juries in Boston and Providence, Rhode Island. (WW Story, *Life and Letters*, vol 1, 335–47).

[7] Graham, 106.

[8] ibid at 14. Cushing's charge appears in Marcus, Maeva, (ed), *The Documentary History of the Supreme Court of the United States, 1789–1800; The Justices on Circuit*, vol 2 (New York: Columbia University Press, 1988), 491–96, 491 and 492.

[9] Herbert A Johnson, *The Chief Justiceship of John Marshall* (Columbia: University of South Carolina Press, 1997), 137.

[10] Herbert A Johnson, 'Bushrod Washington' (2009) 62(2) *Vanderbilt Law Review* 490.

[11] R Kent Newmyer, 'Justice Joseph Story on Circuit and a Neglected Phase of American Legal History' (1970) 14 *American Journal of Legal History* 112.

and those of the Supreme Court knowing that regional needs would be advanced in Washington by their circuit justice. Recognising the crucial role of the circuit courts in American legal history, he writes, 'Each circuit has its own possibilities and each judge his own opportunity and should be studied on their own merits', concluding that Supreme Court law 'will not be fully understood until we know more, individually and collectively, about the circuit courts'.[12]

Relying on the correspondence of Justices Story and Baldwin, expressing satisfaction that so few of their circuit opinions had been taken to the Supreme Court, Newmyer rightly deduces that 'decisions of the circuit court were in the most instances final, binding the parties and establishing law for the circuit'.[13] This is further support for the argument that those circuit opinions were more important than the few handed down by the Supreme Court. Because circuit cases were tried by Supreme Court justices, their directions on law were more readily accepted by the parties, more so than an opinion delivered by a local district judge however competent.

Most other scholarly references to the circuit courts are restricted to describing the physical and emotional hardships of circuit riding and the justices' repeated efforts to end the duty.[14] That focus has meant that the importance of circuit jurisprudence has been largely ignored. Save for the scholars mentioned above, all attention has centred on the importance of the Supreme Court landmark cases and John Marshall. The calls for further research into the role of the circuit courts in the development of federal law have yet to be met. This research begins that process by an in-depth examination and analysis of 1,255 circuit and 325 Supreme Court opinions of the four chosen justices in order to ascertain the influence of the circuit court in American legal history.

The justices were obliged to wait for the end of circuit riding until the Evarts Act of 1891; this abolished the courts to which they had travelled for so many years. They had fought hard to end the duty from the very beginning of the federal court system.[15] In 1792, Chief Justice Jay and Justices Cushing, Wilson, Blair, Iredell, and

---

[12] ibid, 112–35, 134–35.

[13] ibid, 113–14. Letter, Story to McLean, 25 May 1838 in *McLean Papers*, Library of Congress; Letter, Henry Baldwin to District Judge Joseph Hopkinson, 20 February 1840 in *Hopkinson Papers*, Pennsylvania Historical Society.

[14] For a recent appraisal of the burdens of circuit riding see Dale Yurs, 'The Early Supreme Court and the Challenges of Riding Circuit (2011) 36(3) *Journal of Supreme Court History* 181–92.

[15] Several justices resigned after a short time on the Court, all citing the physical rigours of circuit riding and long periods of separation from family. John Blair Jr resigned in 1796 after five years; Thomas Johnson in 1793 after only 15 months; and Alfred Moore in 1804 after three years. (*The Supreme Court of the United States: Its Beginnings & Its Justices, 1790–1991* (Washington DC: Commission on the Bicentennial of the United States Constitution, 1992), 64, 68 and 76. Thomas Johnson echoed the feeling of all justices on the hardship of circuit riding in his letter of resignation to President Washington when he said 'I cannot resolve to spend six months in the Year of the few I may have left from my Family, on roads at Taverns chiefly and often in Situations where the most moderate Desires are disappointed' (Marcus, *Documentary History*, vol 1, 80). His pessimism was not borne out as he survived a further 25 years after his resignation.

Thomas Johnson complained to Congress that, 'we cannot reconcile ourselves to the idea of existing in exile from our families, and of being subjected to a kind of life, on which we cannot reflect, without experiencing sensations and emotions, more easy to conceive than proper to express'.[16] The Southern Circuit proved to be particularly burdensome to the justices.[17]

Notwithstanding the extreme hardship, Congress had seen the wisdom of establishing local federal justice in the major cities of each circuit, using the justices to cement relationships between citizen and federal institutions. I agree with Morris (1987) that, without the justices' circuit riding, the reception of federal law would have been infinitely more difficult and the justices much less informed about local conditions. Morris puts it well describing the justices as 'conduits for communication' between the capital and the states, writing,

> An itinerant justice had the opportunity of meeting everyone who was anybody on his route—from state governors, to the president of Yale, to inventors, and even local beauties ... swap political and other gossip, visit fledgling industries and generally make himself "enormously knowledgeable about the progress of manufacturing, the condition of farm crops and cattle."[18]

Whilst United States justices have not ridden circuit for almost 125 years, in England and Wales, High Court justices still travel the country to administer justice, a practice originated by Henry II in the 1166 *Assize of Clarendon*. Darbyshire (2011) asked 26 senior English judges for their opinions on judges riding circuit. They favoured the system for a number of reasons. Some cases were so serious as to require the attention of a High Court Judge and it was thought that their presence

---

[16] Letter, 9 August 1792, Supreme Court Justices to Congress (*George Washington Papers* via Mount Vernon Archives).

[17] Justice Iredell calculated that he travelled 1,900 miles to complete just one circuit and he had to ride the Southern Circuit twice each year. He wrote to his wife: 'I scarcely thought there had been so much barren land as I have passed though.' Letter, 10 May 1790, James Iredell to Hannah Iredell in Maeva, *Documentary History*, vol 2, 65–66. The effect a lengthy separation had on the family is well expressed by Hannah Iredell when writing to her husband: 'My anxiety about you is very great. I have not had a line from you since you left Eden House in early October ... I can never think of your Journey, the distance and the risk you run without shuddering almost'. Letter, Hannah to James Iredell, 11 November 1790, cited in Wexler, p 59. In 1791, President Washington proposed a journey through the Carolinas; Iredell was invited to comment, from his circuit experiences, on the quality of roads and taverns. He described the roads as generally poor and accommodation ranging from extremely respectable and hospitable or tolerable, but too many were either very indifferent or wretched. Memorandum of James Iredell concerning the route through North and South Carolina in *The Papers of George Washington Digital Edition* (Charlottesville: University of Virginia Press, Rotunda, 2008). Original source: Presidential Series (24 September 1788–31 March 1795), vol 7 (1 December 1790–21 March 1791; via Mount Vernon Archives). Iredell put it well when complaining to his wife from Salisbury, North Carolina that: 'It has been this time very much crowded indeed—I suffered very much the first night, having to sleep in a room with five People and a bedfellow of the wrong sort, which I did not expect.' Letter, October 1791 cited in Wexler, p 87.

[18] Jeffrey B Morris, *Federal Justice on the Second Circuit: A History of United States Courts in New York, Connecticut, and Vermont, 1789–1987* (New York: Second Circuit Historical Committee, 1987), 19. The quote within a quote is drawn from Richard B Morris, 'The John Jay Court, An Intimate Profile' (1979) 5 *Journal of Contemporary Law* 163 at 175.

on circuit from the capital would deter local practices.[19] Acknowledging the function of a Marshall justice as more akin to a campaign to develop and win acceptance for a new concept of law and government, whereas the English High Court judge's circuit duty is to police a long-established centrally controlled justice system, there are parallels in the search for uniformity. Further, the English High Court judges, when sitting as judges of the Court of Appeal reviewing cases from the lower courts have (as had the Marshall justices) a better grasp of local problems and difficulties facing provincial circuit and district judges.

## A Team Effort

While the emphasis is on the period between 1801 and 1835, it is necessary to examine the federal legal system from its establishment in 1789 in order to understand the Court's transition from virtual obscurity, at the time of Chief Justice Jay's resignation in 1795 and his later refusal to return to the office in 1801, to an institution playing a much more effective role in government by the end of Marshall's tenure 40 years on.[20] This research examines the factors which enabled the Court's rise in influence, despite deep political opposition to the concept of federal justice; it does so by focusing on the circuit courts' role in that transformation.

Until recently, biographers of Chief Justice John Marshall have taken the line that he achieved prominence for the Court because he dominated fellow justices and persuaded them to his point of view by the sheer force of his drive and personality. In the first comprehensive account of his life and works, from 1916, the admiration which Albert J. Beveridge had for his subject is evident from each of the four volumes.[21] His description of Marshall as a 'king on a throne' gives

---

[19] Penny Darbyshire, *Sitting in Judgment: The Working Lives of Judges* (Oxford & Portland Oregon: Hart Publishing Ltd, 2011), 315.

[20] When declining an invitation to return as Chief Justice in 1801, Jay expressed an unwillingness to take part in a system which treated the justices' opinions on circuit riding with 'neglect and indifference'. He felt that the Supreme Court did not have the standing to support the national government or command the respect of the public. Letter, John Jay to President John Adams, 2 January 1801 in Maeva Marcus (ed), *The Documentary History of the Supreme Court of the United States, 1789–1800*, vol 1, part 1 (New York: Columbia University Press, 1985), 146–47. The reasons for Jay's lack of enthusiasm are developed in Matthew Van Hook, 'Founding the Third Branch: Judicial Greatness and John Jay's Reluctance (2015) 40(1) *Journal of Supreme Court History* 1–19, 4–6. Jay had been unhappy with the status of the Supreme Court for some time. When appointed Envoy to Great Britain in 1794 he wrote to President Washington that, 'If the judiciary was on its proper footing, there is no public Station that I should prefer ...' Letter, 30 April 1794, John Jay to George Washington (Papers of George Washington, Mount Vernon Archives). For a recent appraisal of Chief Justice Jay see Jude Pfister, 'The Legacy of John Jay' (2016) 38(4) *Supreme Court Historical Society Quarterly* 6–10. For Jay's collaboration with Alexander Hamilton in the writing of the *Federalist Papers*, see, Jude Pfister, *Charting an American Republic: The Origins and Writing of the Federalist Papers* (Jefferson, North Carolina: McFarland & Co, Inc, Publishers, 2016).

[21] Albert J Beveridge, *The Life of John Marshall*, 4 vols (Cambridge, MA: Riverside Press, 1916).

the flavour of his adulation.[22] Beveridge makes repeated references to Marshall's dominant personality and unparalleled influence over his associates.[23] Similarly, Corwin (1919) begins his biography of the Chief Justice by pronouncing him 'the Hilldebrand of American constitutionalism', and ignores the contribution of the associate justices.[24] Decades later, Baker (1974) wonders how the United States might have developed without Marshall's decisions, despite acknowledging that the Court consisted of six associates, whom Marshall led, but did not control.[25] Thus, the works of Beveridge, Corwin, and Baker suggest that Marshall's associates were mere thin echoes of the Chief Justice's voice.

In his distinguished biography of Justice Story in 1985, Newmyer describes the composition of the Court in 1812 as 'less than awesome', pointing to Marshall as the 'only proven jurist'. He asserts that the remaining justices comprised a 'confusion of specialities and a disparity of talents that threatened to weaken the Court as an institution'. Newmyer bases this view on 'Marshall's lack of expertise in maritime law, Todd's usefulness extending only to Virginia/Kentucky land disputes, and Duvall having no particular specialisation'.[26] Whilst Newmyer acknowledges that all of the justices, save for Marshall, Washington, and Story, had sat as State Supreme Court justices, he does not emphasise that, by 1812, as well as their Supreme Court sittings, the three justices had had the invaluable experience of presiding over busy federal circuit courts: Washington for 13 years, Johnson for eight years and Livingston for five. Not all members of the Court made the same contribution to its rise and influence, but this research questions the suggestion that by 1812 there were insufficient men of intellect, learning, and experience in post to advance the Court to a prominent position in government. In any event, whilst the Court was composed of great jurists such as Marshall and Story, one needs to consider whether its real strength lay in the collective wisdom of all of its justices.

In more recent times scholars have acknowledged that Marshall relied heavily on his associates. Hobson (1996) accepts that, although the Court often spoke through Marshall, 'the opinion was the product of collaborative deliberation, carried on in the spirit of mutual concession and accommodation'.[27] However, as his book is an account of Marshall's jurisprudence, it does not cover the specific nature of the support he received. Ten years later Hobson went further, writing

---

[22] ibid, vol 4, 82.

[23] ibid, vol 4, 59–60.

[24] Edward S Corwin, *John Marshall and the Constitution: A Chronicle of the Supreme Court* (Akron, Ohio: Summit Classic Press, 2013), 2, a reprint of the 1919 first edition).

[25] Leonard Baker, *John Marshall: A Life in the Law* (New York: Macmillan Publishers, 1974), 540–41 and 767–68.

[26] R Kent Newmyer, *Supreme Court Justice Story: Statesman of the Old Republic* (Chapel Hill: University of North Carolina Press, 1985), 80.

[27] Charles F Hobson, *The Great Chief Justice: John Marshall and the Rule of Law* (Lawrence: University Press of Kansas, 1996), 16. In 2006, Hobson completed the editing of the magnificent 12-volume set of *The Papers of John Marshall*, begun by Herbert A Johnson in 1974 (Chapel Hill: University of North Carolina Press, 1974–2006).

that 'scholarship has long exploded the myth of a heroic Marshall who dominated the Supreme Court by the sheer force of his individual genius and will'.[28] He argues that Marshall's 'intellect, learning, and personality' enabled him to achieve success in 'molding [the justices] into a collective entity which spoke with a single authoritative voice'.[29] He further considers his willingness to compromise to achieve unanimity as 'useful in managing his "family" of brother Justices'.[30] His references to 'molding' and 'managing' associates merely mean that Marshall was able to persuade his colleagues, during the infancy of the Court, of the need to speak with one authoritative voice and in no way undermines Hobson's acknowledgement of the contributions of the associates individually or collectively to the single opinion

Whilst Newmyer highlights Story's considerable contribution to the Court, Johnson (1997) is the first scholar to recognise the important influence of the associates as a body and regard the circuit courts as 'the training grounds for Supreme Court justices'.[31] He seeks to strike a balance between those academics whom he describes as 'impassioned Marshall advocates' and those who believe that the contribution of the associates was 'of greater significance and quality'.[32] Johnson was able to give only a brief overview of the role of all of Marshall's associates in a work directed to his life and work.[33]

Robarge (2000) is another who believes that Marshall's success was attributable to his 'personal dominance over the Supreme Court for much of his tenure'. He cites with approval, insofar as it related to the first ten years of the Chief Justice's tenure, President Jefferson's criticism that Marshall craftily manipulated 'lazy or timid associates' to his point of view'.[34] Whilst Robarge acknowledges that Marshall did require help from his colleagues from time to time, he suggests that he was merely demonstrating his open-mindedness and a desire to let the associates feel they were contributing to decisions. He regards the requests as part of a technique to obtain justices' future votes.[35] I contend that Marshall's letters to his colleagues are simply cries for help from a Chief Justice who really did need assistance, not for any ulterior motives. His letter to the senior associate, Justice William Cushing, concerning the trial in 1807 of former Vice-President Aaron Burr for treason is a worried and urgent plea for advice. He wrote: 'It would

---

[28] Charles F Hobson, 'Defining the Office: John Marshall as Chief Justice' (2006) 154(6) *University of Pennsylvania Law Review* 1421–61 at1421.

[29] ibid, 1423.

[30] ibid, 1424.

[31] Herbert A Johnson, *The Chief Justiceship of John Marshall* (Columbia: University of South Carolina Press, 1997), 137.

[32] ibid, 3–4.

[33] ibid, Chapter 1, 'The Chief Justice and his Associates', 21–50.

[34] David A Robarge, *A Chief's Progress: From Revolutionary Virginia to the Supreme Court* (Westport, Conn: Greenwood Press, 2000), 253–54. Letter, Thomas Jefferson to Thomas Ritchie (Republican journalist), 25 December 1820 in Merrill D Peterson (ed), *Thomas Jefferson: Writings* (New York: Library of America, 1984), 1446.

[35] Robarge, 255.

have been my earnest wish to consult with all of my brethren on the bench ... Sincerely I do lament that this wish cannot be completely indulged'. Expressing his doubts and fears, he continues, 'I must anxiously desire the aid of all of the judges [on] the doctrine of constructive treason'.[36] This was not the device of a Chief Justice who wished to make his associates feel wanted; it was the letter of a judge faced with an intricate and politically sensitive trial in desperate need of the advice and support of his colleagues. Other letters from Marshall requesting help from Justices Washington and Story are not expressed in such urgent tones, but it is apparent from their content that he needed assistance on topics with which he was unfamiliar.[37]

Save for a reference to Joseph Story's 'powerful and exuberant intellect', Robarge is dismissive of the associates, referring to Todd and Duvall as 'ciphers', Samuel Chase as 'a boorish Federalist', McLean as a 'decorous Jacksonian' and William Johnson as 'contentious', which is most likely a reference to his propensity to dissent.[38] In his chapter on Marshall's tenure on the Court, Justices Livingston and Thompson do not rate a mention, flattering or otherwise and the entire chapter pays little attention to the associates. When Robarge acknowledges the importance of circuit work generally, he does so to argue that Marshall 'shaped the contours of nineteenth-century America through his circuit opinions'. He asserts that Marshall's individual circuit contributions were a strong force in transforming the federal courts into a true national judiciary because the Fifth Circuit was one of the busiest and his circuit opinions involved more points of law than any other justice.[39] He downplays the circuit contributions made between 1801 and 1835 of the 14 associates, some of whom presided over equally busy circuit courts in New York, Boston, and Philadelphia and whose expertise in admiralty law Marshall was unable to match. The inference is that, Story apart, the influence of the associate justices was small when compared with that of the Chief Justice and disregards the positive influence of a number of significant justices.

Scholars, therefore, differ in their interpretation of the respective parts played by the Chief Justice and his associates in the Court's rise in prominence, but the suggestion that Marshall did it alone has not completely disappeared. More scholars are beginning to accept that the role of the associates in the Court's transformation was substantial. However, the focus of any book or essay on Marshall will not permit an in-depth consideration of the individual or collective contributions of associate justices. What is required for a better understanding of the emergence of an effective federal court system is an examination of the link between the circuit work of a group of major associate justices and the growth in influence of the Supreme Court. This study seeks to end the myth that Marshall was the Court.

---

[36] Letter, John Marshall to William Cushing, 29 June 1807 in *Papers of John Marshall,* vol VII, 60–62.
[37] In all, ten letters from John Marshall requesting help from his associates have survived to *The Papers of John Marshall*. A selection appear in ch 2, dealing with consistency of opinions across the circuits.
[38] Robarge, 255.
[39] ibid, 261–62.

By a detailed examination of the work of these four justices on the Court, but more so on circuit, it seeks to position them as significant contributory factors in the success of the federal court system.

The changes in how the Supreme Court delivered its opinions reflect the struggle to establish its authority. During the Chief Justiceship of John Jay (1789–1795) the few opinions were generally delivered *seriatim* with the junior justice speaking first even though the justices were agreed upon the result. Chief Justice Ellsworth (1796–1800) was the first to prefer the practice of a single opinion preceding rare dissents. In his absence, the justices resorted to seriatim opinions.[40] To counter repeated attacks by Republican supporters, a problem not faced by the first two Chief Justices, Marshall felt it necessary not only to present to the nation a united front by the almost exclusive use of the single opinion, but also by delivering the majority of the opinions himself which, as will be shown, infuriated President Jefferson.[41]

The apparent unanimity behind the single opinion is part of what Johnson described as the 'small group dynamics' of the Marshall Court, concluding that the justices were able to hide their differences and produce an opinion acceptable either to all or to a majority. This, he argues, was made possible by the harmonious collegial residence in the same lodgings, and the need of a small, mainly Federalist, body to present a united front in the face of repeated challenges from a Republican administration who opposed what they considered to be an overly strong federal judiciary.[42] It is, therefore, likely that this close harmony also engendered mutual support on circuit.

Johnson develops his 'small group dynamics' theory in a 2000 essay comparing the Marshall Court with the European Court of Justice and the need of each higher jurisdiction to be sensitive to the demands of their component states. He argues that the dynamic might develop from the sharing of tasks and exchange of specialised knowledge or the introspective or internal bonding which occurs when a small group is opposed by a larger outside body.[43] This is another aspect of decision making which this research will address.

---

[40] William R. Castro, *The Supreme Court in the Early Republic: The Chief Justiceships of John Jay and Oliver Ellsworth* (Columbia: University of South Carolina Press, 1995), 110–11.

[41] For a history of the shift from *seriatim* to the single opinion of the Court and the rise in dissenting opinions see Peter Bozzo, Shimmy Edwards, and April A Christine, 'Many Voices, One Court: The Origin and Role of Dissent in the Supreme Court (2011) 36(3) *Journal of Supreme Court History* 193–215. The authors, citing Joshua M Austin, 'The Law of Citations and Seriatim Opinions' (2010) 31 *Northern Illinois University Law Review*, 19–36, record that as early as 1778, Edmund Pendleton, Chief Justice of the Virginia Court of Appeals 'delivered unanimous opinions of the Court after the judges convened to discuss the case in private', a practice 'roundly condemned by the Republican party, most prominently by Thomas Jefferson'. Spencer Roane, a disciple of Jefferson and a constant critic of the Supreme Court, replaced Pendleton in 1794 and resumed the practice of seriatim opinions.

[42] Johnson, 'Bushrod Washington', 449–50.

[43] Herbert A Johnson, 'Judicial Institutions in Emerging Federal Systems: The Marshall Court and the European Court of Justice' (2000) 33(4) *John Marshall Law Review* 1063–1108 at 1067.

During his 35-year tenure as Chief Justice, Marshall delivered 537 of the Court's 1,236 opinions and orders for directions.[44] Kelsh (1999) has analysed the opinion delivery practices of the Court in its early years, observing that between 1790 and 1800, 71 per cent of the cases reported in the *United States Reports* were simply noted as being 'by the Court' with no justice named. Twenty-four per cent of the opinions were recorded as *per curiam* after *seriatim* opinions by individual justices.[45] However, after Marshall took office and the single opinion of the Court became the norm, he dominated the delivery of opinions; however, towards the end of his tenure, justices felt free to deliver concurrences or dissents.[46] He delivered the opinions on all constitutional issues save for those cases in which he had a personal interest when he recused himself. This was not unusual as, throughout the history of the Court, Chief Justices have delivered many of the landmark opinions. However, the difference now is that Marshall also wrote the Court's opinion in a vast proportion of mundane cases.

Whilst accepting, at that time, the use of the single opinion as a defence mechanism, the compromise of strongly held views to produce a unanimous opinion had the obvious disadvantage of stifling different standpoints and inhibiting public debate. To understand the value of dissent, one need look no further than Justice Thompson's powerful dispute with the majority in *Cherokee Nation v Georgia* which effectively formed the basis of the Court's majority opinion in *Worcester v Georgia*, the following year.[47]

The single opinion, delivered invariably by Marshall, is the basis of the widely held view that he was the Court. Without wishing to detract from his fine leadership and political acumen, an examination of case reports and contemporary correspondence reveal that this was not the case. It is clear that the opinions he delivered in many occasions have benefitted from the assistance he received from his associates rather than being entirely the product of his own research. This is so because of the extent and quality of the majority opinions, concurrences, and dissents of the associates evident in the remaining 699 opinions. The letters from Story and Washington to Marshall, examined in chapter three, helping him resolve points of law in his circuit and Supreme Court opinions further support associate participation.

Two justices throw light on the exchange of views in those early Supreme Court conferences held at the house in which all of the justices lodged during their term in Washington. Story, writing to a friend in 1812, informed him, 'We moot questions as they are argued, with freedom, and derive no inconsiderable advantage from the pleasant and animated interchange of legal acumen'.[48] In another

---

[44] *United States Reports*, 1801–1835.
[45] John P Kelsh, 'Opinion Delivery Practices of the United States Supreme Court, 1790–1945' (1999) 77 *Washington University Law Quarterly* 137–52 at 140.
[46] ibid, 143.
[47] There is a detailed discussion of both cases in ch 6.
[48] Letter, Joseph Story to Nathaniel Williams, 16 February 1812 in WW Story, *The Life and Letters of Joseph Story*, vol 1 (London: John Chapman, 1851), 214.

letter, Story proffered further insight into the decision-making process: 'My familiar conferences at our lodgings often come to a very quick, and I trust, a very accurate opinion, in a few hours'. He went on to express his delight at the successful outcome of the first opinion he had been assigned to write, remarking, 'My own views were those which ultimately obtained the sanction of the whole court'.[49] It would appear that his draft opinion had been revised after consultation with the other justices.

Further evidence of the collaborative decision-making process appears in an undated letter from Justice John McLean who served on the Court from 1829 to 1861. He described the scene thus:

> Before any opinion is formed by the Court, the case after being argued at the Bar is thoroughly discussed in consultation. Night after night this is done, in a case of difficulty, until the mind of every judge is satisfied, and then each judge gives his views of the whole of the case, embracing every point in it. In this way the opinion of the judge is expressed, and then the Chief Justice requests a particular judge write, not his opinion, but the opinion of the Court. And after the opinion is read, it is read to all the judges, and if it does not embrace the views of all of the judges, it is modified and corrected.[50]

McLean does not draw a distinction between the practice during his six years with John Marshall and the 24 years he served subsequently with Chief Justice Roger Taney. Had Marshall behaved in the dictatorial fashion suggested by Domnarski it is surprising that McLean did not touch upon it. These contemporaneous accounts support the more recent view that, individually and collectively, the justices did not merely sit back and leave it all to their Chief.

Domnarski does not appear to accept those contemporaneous accounts of the mechanics of decision making because he writes: 'But for Marshall, getting the work out quickly rather than accountability was the goal. Often, drafts of the Court's opinions were not even circulated to the brethren, which meant that they had no say in the reasoning.'[51] Clearly, opinions had to be delivered within a reasonable period otherwise the Court would be swamped by outstanding business. However, the idea that Marshall simply handed down opinions without a majority consensus is inconceivable and Domnarski cites no authority for this assertion. One can understand why a justice would not write out six extra copies of his draft, but it does not follow that his copy was not circulated or, as Justice McLean records, read out to the justices for their comments. The accounts of Justices Story and McLean of how the justices debated and decided cases do not support Domnarski's argument that often the associates had no say in the reasoning of opinions. If further proof is required, Justice William Johnson aired

---

[49] ibid, 215–16. Letter, Joseph Story to Samuel Fay, 24 February 1812. The opinion Story referred to was *Fitzsimmons et al v Ogden et al* (1812) 7 Cranch 2.
[50] Undated letter, Justice McLean to a Methodist newspaper, McLean Papers, Library of Congress, box 18, cited in John F Frank, *Justice Daniel Dissenting: A Biography of Peter V. Daniel, 1784–1860* (Cambridge MA: Harvard University Press, 1964), 174.
[51] Domnarski, *In the Opinion of the Court*, 32.

many complaints in a letter to former President Jefferson in 1822 about the lack of ability of certain justices and the disappearance of *seriatim* opinions in favour of the single opinion of the Court. At no stage did he suggest that an opinion of the Court was delivered without his knowledge of its content.[52] The accounts of Story and McLean and the absence of criticism by Johnson establish full consultation in the Marshall Court's decision-making process.

There is further criticism of Marshall's leadership by Turner, Way and Maveety (2010) in a preliminary examination of the history of concurrences in the Supreme Court from its founding to 1921. The authors assert that 'Marshall may have cowed his colleagues into agreement' and they wonder 'how many potential concurrences are lost to us due to Marshall's domineering approach'.[53] This assessment of the Chief Justice is based on Marshall's writing the opinion of the court in *Rhinelander v Insurance Company of Pennsylvania*, where he states that one justice supports the decision but for different reasons.[54] Their complaint is that Marshall identifies neither the justice in question nor his reasons, which suggests to the authors that such disagreements may have been viewed as unimportant by the Marshall Court or at least by Marshall himself. It is correct that the justice is not named, but a full reading of the case reveals that Marshall did outline the difference of view when he wrote, '... and the judge who doubts respecting it (the majority reasoning) is of the opinion that, in this case, countersecurity having been refused by the underwriters, the question of freight is yet suspended'.[55] Without citing any particular cases the authors write of 'majority opinions in which Marshall speaks of unanimous agreement, only to have another justice speak up and say he disagrees'.[56] Finally, Marshall is censured for including in his opinion, in some cases (although only one, *Peisch v Ware*, is cited) the reasons used by other unnamed judges for deciding the case and concluding that 'they acquiesce, however, cheerfully in the opinion of the majority of the court'.[57] An examination of the report of *Peisch v. Ware* shows that the Chief Justice outlined the reasoning of two justices; set out shortly why they agreed, but for different reasons and, finally, referring to the three justices who disagreed but went along with the majority, writing that they 'express their dissent from that opinion, solely for the purpose of preventing this sentence from having more than its due influence on future cases of salvage'.

It is clearly preferable for named justices to write comprehensive concurrences when they reach the same conclusion as the majority but for different reasons and

---

[52] Letter, Justice William Johnson to Thomas Jefferson, 10 December 1822 cited in Donald G. Morgan, *Justice William Johnson: The First Dissenter* (Columbia: University of South Carolina Press, 1954), 181–82.

[53] Charles C Turner, Lori Beth Way, and Nancy Maveety, 'Beginning to Write Separately: The Origins and Development of Concurring Judicial Opinions' (2010) 35(2) *Journal of Supreme Court History* 93–109 at 98.

[54] (1807) 8 US 29, 46.

[55] ibid.

[56] Turner, Way, and Maveety, 98.

[57] *Peisch v Ware* (1808) 8 US 347 366; Turner & Ors, 98.

dissents when in the minority. However, one must never forget the perilous position of the Court in these very early years. It was under constant attack from the executive and a Republican majority in Congress. It was, therefore, essential that the Court present a united front to the nation and not reveal discord; the only realistic way of achieving this was the single opinion. Bearing in mind that there is no record of any of Marshall's 14 associates, and in particular Justices, Johnson, Story and McLean, complaining of having their views overridden by the Chief Justice, I am far from convinced that the matters complained of even begin to fix John Marshall as a domineering figure who cowed his associates into submission.

This research also looks at participation in decision making which shaped United States law as a result of the Chief Justice's opinion assignment practice. The majority opinions assignments were not distributed equally as some justices were much more active than others. For example, the *United States Reports* reveal that Justice Todd who sat with Marshall for 20 years delivered a meagre 12 majority opinions and Justice Duvall in 23 years handed down the same number.[58] At the opposite end of the scale, Justice Story who spent 24 years with Marshall, wrote 183 opinions. That disparity is the reason why this study examines the effect of circuit expertise on the Chief Justice's opinion assignment practice. Analysis of the circuit and Supreme Court opinions of a particular justice will reveal a particular speciality and explain why a certain type of opinion was assigned to him. A good example of the assignment of an opinion and the changing views of a justice whilst the draft opinion is in preparation is contained in a letter from Bushrod Washington to Joseph Story which has no year but is likely to be about 1827 because of the reference to Mr Justice Trimble and the date of the opinion.[59]

## Why Washington, Livingston, Story, and Thompson?

The decision to focus on these four justices was made after all the opinions of all associate justices in the 18,000 cases contained in the 30-volume set of

---

[58] Although Duvall was virtually silent on the Court, he fully supported Marshall's efforts to have the justices speak with one voice. There has been a recent reappraisal of Duvall by Andrew T Fede who argues that his career at the Bar; as state court judge, legislator, US Congressman, and US Treasury Comptroller ought to be placed in the balance. See, Andrew T Fede, 'Not the Most Insignificant Justice: Reconsidering Justice Gabriel Duvall's Slavery Opinions Favoring Liberty' (2017) 42(1) *Journal of Supreme Court History* 7–27. My own correspondence with members of the Duvall Society reveals that he is greatly revered in Maryland.

[59] Washington writes, 'The Chief Justice informs me that you are to draw the opinion in *Bell v. Wilkins*. I stated to him that a night's reflection had induced me to change my opinion as to the Kentucky decisions … the view that Mr Justice Trimble takes of the doctrine as settled and understood by the Supreme Court of his State is, as it ought to be conclusive with me … I should be very sorry if the settled construction of a Statute of one State should be unsettled by the S. Court of the U.S.—you may therefore consider me as uniting with Mess Trimble, Duvall and yourself on that point. I shall not be at Court today, being afraid of the weather.' Letter, Washington to Story, 18 February, Massachusetts Historical Society, Joseph Story Papers.

*Federal Cases, 1789–1880* and from volumes 2–33 (1790–1835) of the *United States Reports* had been extracted and examined. These two sets of reports were central to the research, constituting the most important sources of primary material. There were 1,255 circuit opinions and 699 Supreme Court opinions.[60] The four justices contributed 1,445 opinions (1,120 circuit and 325 Supreme Court). In addition, the New York Supreme Court opinions of Justice Livingston (149) and Justice Thompson (250) were analysed which means that 1,854 Supreme Court, circuit court and state supreme court opinions form the basis of this research.

The first step was to determine those justices with sufficient opinions from which to reach meaningful conclusions. It should be noted that whilst all Supreme Court opinions were recorded, the absence of law reporters on certain circuits meant that many early opinions were not recorded because some judges did not commit them to paper (although the more assiduous advocates would note it for future use). The second, and more important, step was to reduce the candidates to those whose reports best reflected events and issues facing the nation; revealed distinctive approaches to the resolution of their caseloads; and showed how they shaped United States law. Having considered those matters, it was clear that Justices Washington. Livingston, Story, and Thompson were prominent associates who each made significant contributions in different ways to aspects of United States law. I had considered Justice Henry Baldwin for inclusion in the study as 48 of his circuit opinions were reported in *Federal Cases*. However, I decided against his inclusion because he sat with Marshall for only five years; his opinions showed no consistent pattern of jurisprudence; and contemporary accounts are strongly suggestive of mental disorder.[61]

Dealing with the justices in order of seniority of appointment, Washington sat with Marshall for 28 years, presiding over the Third Circuit (Pennsylvania and New Jersey) from 1803 to 1823. Livingston served on the Court for 15 years, riding the Second Circuit (Connecticut, New York, and Vermont) from 1808 to 1823. Story joined the Court in 1811 and spent 24 years with Marshall and on the First Circuit (Massachusetts, Maine, New Hampshire, and Rhode Island). Finally, Thompson replaced Livingston on the Court and on the Second Circuit after his death in 1823; he served with Marshall until the latter's death in 1835.

---

[60] The *Federal Cases, 1789–1880*, 30 vols plus index (St Paul, Minnesota: West Publishing Company 1894–1897) contain opinions by the following associates, Washington (540); Story (456); Thompson (77); Baldwin (48); Livingston (47); McLean (33); Paterson (18); Todd (11); William Johnson (10); Samuel Chase (9); Duvall (4); Cushing (2); Moore and Trimble (0).

[61] G Edward White's assessment of Baldwin is of 'a contentious, erratic, vehement maverick', *Marshall Court and Cultural Change,* 302. White cites a letter from Justice Story, who was invariably very generous in his appraisal of the character and ability of a colleague, to Federal District Judge Joseph Hopkinson who sat with Baldwin on circuit. Story wrote, 'I am sure he cannot be sane. And indeed the only charitable view which I can take of any of his conduct is that he is partially deranged at all times', 298. White also quotes from a letter from the Supreme Court Reporter, Richard Peters, to Hopkinson contending that the general view of Baldwin is that 'his mind is out of order', 302. Story's letter of 9 May 1833 and that of Peters dated 18 March 1838 were sourced by White from the Joseph Hopkinson Papers, Historical Society of Pennsylvania, Philadelphia.

The circuit opinions of Justice Washington between 1803 and 1827 are to be found in *Federal Cases* and in three volumes edited by Richard Peters which he compiled from the justice's manuscript notes.[62] In 1827, Elijah Paine Jr edited a volume of New York, Connecticut and Vermont circuit cases, containing a small selection of the opinions of Justice Livingston between 1810 and 1822 and those of his successor, Justice Thompson, between 1823 and 1826.[63] There is much more primary material to assist with an evaluation of Joseph Story's work in the 14 volumes of his circuit opinions edited by four law reporters with some degree of overlapping which, taken with the *Federal Cases,* provide substantial evidence for a reliable assessment of the circuit aspect of his career.[64] The reports of Story's circuit and Supreme Court opinions are complemented by the justice's many law books and, in particular, by his *Commentaries on the Constitution of the United States*. William Story's *Life and Letters of Joseph Story* and *The Miscellaneous Writings of Joseph Story* are invaluable sources of primary material on the thoughts and jurisprudence of this innovative scholar from Massachusetts.[65]

During his 28-year tenure, Justice Washington wrote 80 opinions for the Supreme Court; 540 of his circuit opinions have also survived. Justice Livingston wrote 30 Supreme Court opinions and 47 of his circuit opinions were reported. Justice Story was more prolific with 149 Supreme Court opinions and 456 reported circuit opinions. Justice Thompson delivered 57 opinions of the Court and had 77 circuit opinions reported. The reason for the high number of reported circuit opinions of Washington and Story as opposed to the other two justices is due to Washington's extensive notes (which were later transcribed) and because Story had the advantage of an efficient law reporter. The Second Circuit, unlike the New York State Supreme Court, had no official law reporter. Consequently, few circuit opinions were recorded. As Livingston and Thompson had been justices of the New York State Supreme Court, a large number of their state opinions are available. These supplement their rather meagre federal circuit court opinions and help to create a fuller picture of the jurisprudence of each justice.[66] The choice of

---

[62] Richard Peters, *Reports of Cases Argued and Determined in the Third Circuit: Comprising the Districts of Pennsylvania and New Jersey, Commencing at April Term, 1803–1827,* 3 vols (vol 1, Philadelphia: William Fry, 1819; vols 2 and 3 (Philadelphia: Philip H. Nicklin, 1827).

[63] Elijah Paine Jr, *Reports of Cases Argued and Determined in the Circuit Court of the United States for the Second Circuit: Comprising the Districts of New-York, Connecticut, and Vermont* (New York: R Donaldson, 1827).

[64] John Gallison (ed), *First Circuit Reports, 1812–1815,* 5 vols (Boston: Wells & Lilly, 1815–1817); Charles Sumner (ed), *First Circuit Reports,* 3 vols (Boston: Charles C Little & James Brown, 1836–1841); William P Mason (ed), *First Circuit Reports, 1816–1830,* 5 vols (Boston: Hilliard, Gray, Little & Wilkins, 1819–1831); WW Story, *First Circuit Reports,* 3 vols (Charles C Little & James Brown, 1842–1845).

[65] Joseph Story, *Commentaries on the Constitution of the United States,* 3 vols (Boston: Hilliard, Gray & Company, 1833); WW Story (ed), *Life and Letters of Joseph Story,* 2 vols (London: John Chapman, 1851); WW Story (ed), *The Miscellaneous Writings of Joseph Story* (Boston: Charles C Little & James Brown, 1852).

[66] For a comprehensive study of the history of law reporting see, Erwin C Surrency, 'Law Reports in the United States' (1981) 25(1) *The American Journal of Legal History* 48–66. It was not until 1817 that Congress authorised the appointment of an official law reporter for the US Supreme Court.

two justices from the same circuit is justified by the importance of New York as the leading port and commercial centre of the United States and, therefore, the source of much litigation.

Other scholars, apart from Johnson, have examined Washington's work. Having placed a selection of his major circuit opinions against a background of 'dramatic, social, cultural, and economic change', and of a new nation requiring a new legal system, Faber (2000) detects a cautious approach to Washington's jurisprudence and argues that he had a restraining effect on the more controversial approaches of Marshall and Story, which 'moderating influence enhanced the wisdom of the great constitutional decisions by restricting their reach'.[67] Stonier (1998) concludes that Washington's strength lay on circuit rather than in the Supreme Court. He does not find him to be a cautious justice. Instead, he describes his attitude to decision making as that of 'a confident authority of one who sees himself as the embodied voice of federal law'.[68] Faber and Stonier acknowledge that they could not do justice to Washington's voluminous reported circuit opinions and, therefore, confined themselves to a limited selection. This examination of all of Washington's reported circuit opinions will show whether he was the confident judge seen by Stonier or too dependent on precedent and overly concerned should his opinions fail to survive appeals.

The lack of emphasis on circuit courts and the activities of the less prominent justices is evidenced by the fact that, apart from a short essay by Dunne (1969) and terse entries in biographical dictionaries, little is known of Justice Livingston. No research has been undertaken on his circuit and Supreme Court activities. Dunne believes Livingston's significant judicial work to have been performed, not on the Supreme Court, but as a puisne judge of the New York State Supreme Court and rightly describes Livingston as 'an elusive and half glimpsed figure of his age'.[69] No detailed comparisons of his work have been published—in fact, he has been largely ignored by scholars for 45 years. Justice Thompson has suffered a similar fate; since Roper's 1963 doctoral thesis, published in 1987, there has been no scholarly attention to his Supreme Court and circuit work for over 50 years.[70]

Justice Story has not suffered the same anonymity as his two colleagues. Aside from the wealth of primary material described earlier, there is a detailed 1970 'exploratory essay' by one of his biographers, R. Kent Newmyer which deals with the neglected topic of how an examination of the circuit courts collectively and

---

[67] David A Faber, 'Bushrod Washington and the Age of Discovery in American Law' (2000) 102 *West Virginia Law Review* 735–807 at 807.

[68] James R Stonier, 'Heir Apparent: Bushrod Washington and Federal Justice in the Early Republic' in Scott Gerber (ed), *Seriatim: The Supreme Court before John Marshall* (New York: New York University Press, 1998), 322–49, 341.

[69] Gerald T Dunne, 'Brockholst Livingston' in Leon Friedman and Fred L Israel (eds), *The Justices of the United States Supreme Court, 1789–1969*, vol 1 (New York: Chelsea House Publishers, 1969), 387–403, 395.

[70] Donald M Roper, *Mr Justice Thompson and the Constitution* (New York: Garland Publishing, 1987).

individually will lead to a better understanding of the decision-making process of the Supreme Court.[71] Newmyer explains why the circuit courts deserve further study by examining Joseph Story's work on the First Circuit.[72] Although his essay touches only briefly on the nature of Story's circuit opinions, it is valuable in setting the caseload against the need for the courts to cope with current events such as the expansion of American shipping during the early years of the Napoleonic Wars and the rise in home manufacturing as a result of the embargo on trade with belligerent nations. Newmyer points to the declaration of war on Britain by the United States in 1812, leading to many questions of international, and maritime and prize law relating to the disposition of captured vessels and cargo; these were determined, in the first instance by either the federal district or circuit courts. He believes Story to have been well qualified to deal with these branches of the law simply because of his extensive practice at the Bar.[73] I consider whether his sittings in the circuit court not only consolidated, but greatly enhanced the knowledge gained as an advocate.

Newmyer considers Story's resolution of commercial disputes to be 'the framework for the regular and orderly conduct of economic affairs'.[74] Merchants respected his opinions and were better able to arrange their business affairs in the light of his pronouncements. As to his circuit opinions generally, he observes that during Story's 33 years on the circuit bench, 734 of his opinions were printed and circulated in legal journals, thereby securing his national importance.[75] This would have the practical effect of making his opinions more readily accessible to lawyers outside New England for citing on their circuits; another step on the road to consistency across the nation. There have been biographies of other of Marshall's associates which, although dated, are still very useful; they also pay little attention to the importance of circuit work.[76]

This work examines the approach of circuit justices to the questions of vested interests in land, the promotion of commerce on land and at sea, and the establishing of rights and responsibilities of merchants in respect of commercial contracts and negotiable instruments. Those circuit opinions also shed light on the vulnerability of the nation during hostilities with Britain around the time of the War of 1812; the troubled issue of slavery; and reveal how individual justices on circuit resolved politically sensitive, emotionally charged and historically

---

[71] Newmyer, 'Justice Joseph Story on Circuit', 112–35. See also Gerald T Dunne, *Justice Joseph Story and the Rise of the Supreme Court* (New York: Simon & Schuster, 1970); James McClellan, *Joseph Story and the American Constitution* (Norman: University of Oklahoma Press, 1971).

[72] Newmyer, 'Story on Circuit', 112.

[73] ibid, 116.

[74] ibid, 125.

[75] ibid 129–30.

[76] Francis P Weisenburger, *The Life of John McLean: A Politician on the United States Supreme Court* (Columbus: The Ohio University Press, 1937); John E O'Connor, *William Paterson: Lawyer and Statesman, 1745–1806* (New Brunswick, NJ: Rutgers University Press, 1979); James Haw, Francis Beirne, Rosamund Beirne and R Samuel Jett, *Stormy Patriot: The Life of Samuel Chase* (Baltimore: Maryland Historical Society, 1980).

significant questions. The opinions of both circuit and Court also reflect the tensions between Federalist and Republican over the nature of government and the powers of the federal judiciary to monitor state legislatures and courts. These placed the justices under extreme political pressure; they were acutely aware of the need to strike a delicate balance between state sovereignty and the power of federal government. This led the Supreme Court, on occasion, to deliver compromise opinions designed to avoid direct confrontation with hostile Republican opponents at a time when the Court was reeling from the restoration of circuit riding duties, threats of impeachment, and the suspension of its sittings for over a year.[77]

Against this background, the federal judiciary found it prudent to exercise caution so as not to antagonise a Republican majority in Congress. The justices had constant reminders that a substantial part of the public did not share Marshall's vision of a Supreme Court tasked with interpreting the Constitution and the intent of its framers. Republicans were incensed at the prospect of the Court overruling legislation enacted by a Republican majority in Congress. The justices, therefore, realised that every opinion of the Court which impinged upon state sovereignty would be subjected to close critical scrutiny, adding to the temptation to avoid controversy at a time of weakness.

To establish uniformity of federal law and procedure across the circuits, with only a few Supreme Court opinions and federal statutes to guide them, the justices, whose legal training had centred on *Blackstone's Commentaries on the Laws of England*, looked to the English cases and writers to solve problems upon which United States law had still to make provision. An examination of circuit opinions reveals how the justices drew from all available sources, and, to varying degrees, how they adapted English law to fit the social and economic needs of the new Republic.[78]

The book is divided into six chapters. Chapter one examines the importance of the associate justices' circuit experiences and the importance of their contribution to the rise in influence of the Supreme Court. Chapter two investigates the origins of the federal court system against fierce opposition to the concept of federal government in the Constitutional Convention and ratification debates to the establishment of the Supreme Court and the circuit and district courts by Congress.

---

[77] *Stuart v Laird*, 5 US 299 (1803) where the Court, whilst complaining bitterly in private, refused to contest the re-introduction of circuit riding by a Republican-dominated Congress and *Marbury v Madison*, 5 US 137 (1803) in which the Court, whilst declaring it had the power to judicially review an Act of Congress, said that it did not have the power to order the Jefferson administration to deliver Marbury his commission as a justice of the peace.

[78] *Blackstone's Commentaries* was first published in England between 1765 and 1769. In 1771 it was printed in the United States for the first time; an exact copy of the 4th edition published in London in 1770. In 1803, St. George Tucker's American version of *Blackstone* was published in Philadelphia by William Young Birch and Abraham Small. Its value to American lawyers lay in the fact that it explained how the United States Constitution and the Bill of Rights had altered English law in America. It also covered subjects such as freedom of expression and slavery laws. For a comprehensive essay on Tucker's *Blackstone*, his law papers and significant opinions see, Charles F Hobson, 'St George Tucker's Law Papers' (2006) 47(4) *William and Mary Review* 1245–78.

It also examines the relationship between federal and state courts and considers the business of the circuit courts against the historical and cultural background of cases generated by an expanding market economy, immigration, westward expansion, land disputes, neutrality, and embargo restrictions arising from European conflicts and the 1812 War with Britain. It explores the political divide between Federalist, Anti- Federalist and, from the early 1790s, the Democratic–Republican Party led by Thomas Jefferson and James Madison and its effect on the way in which the federal courts decided cases. It further explains the way in which the justices overcame the lack of guidance from United States statutes and Supreme Court opinions; how they sought to achieve a consistent system of law across the nation by using state opinions, English law and by exchanging circuit experiences. It examines the importance of circuit riding in the consolidation of federal authority through local federal justice and by the justices' use, in the very early days, of the politically charged grand jury address.

Chapter three focuses on specific aspects of the circuit and Supreme Court opinions of Justice Washington to discover the extent to which his jurisprudence was founded on the strict application of the doctrine of binding precedent despite a rigidity which occasionally resulted in injustice; his Federalist approach to balancing state sovereignty with the powers of a strong central government which generally came down in favour of the federal government; and the extent to which his view of his own slaves as mere items of property to be disposed of as and when he wished affected his approach to the slavery cases he tried.

The reasons for Justice Livingston's changing political alliances from Federalist to ardent Republican are examined in chapter four as an example of the fluidity of political allegiances during this period. Also considered is his contribution to the development of United States commercial law with particular reference to the responsibilities flowing from bills of exchange and promissory notes, the lifeblood of interstate and international trade. His belief, unusual for this period, in the fallibility of jury verdicts and his willingness to set aside those which did not accord with his view of the case is also worthy of investigation.

Justice Story's wish for clarity in federal law, revealed by his determined but failed efforts to import the common law into federal criminal and admiralty law, is investigated in chapter five, together with his success in importing common law into commercial cases with a diversity aspect and his codification of criminal law to bolster the inadequate federal criminal legislation then in force. Also explained is how, by repeated exposure to maritime contracts and embargo cases on circuit, he became the Court's leading admiralty expert. Last, but not least, the chapter acknowledges the great value to researchers of his voluminous correspondence illuminating the inner workings of the Marshall Court.

Chapter six explores why Justice Thompson's efforts to promote state sovereignty and affirm state legislation disappointed his nominating president, James Monroe, and how his unwillingness to strike down state legislation stemmed from a lack of separation of powers in New York State where he sat as a State Supreme Court justice and on the Council of Revision, which vetted all state bills and invariably approved them. The chapter also examines his efforts to shape federal law to protect the Cherokee Nation from Georgia's oppression and his less successful attempts to alleviate the plight of the African-American slave.

This study, whilst acknowledging the considerable contribution of the Chief Justice and the landmark opinions to the Court's success, establishes the circuit courts as the foundation of federal court authority by establishing a rapport between government and citizen and by its creation of a uniform system of federal law across the nation acceptable to the majority. The circuit court experience enhanced not only the justices' individual reputations but also their collective standing as members of the nation's highest tribunal. Further, the combined expertise, gained by presiding over the increasingly busy circuit courts, gave them the confidence and authority to transform the Supreme Court from a position of weakness upon John Marshall's appointment as Chief Justice in 1801 to an institution playing a much more effective role in government by the time of his death in 1835.

# 2

# The Federal Circuit Courts: Shaping Local and National Justice for an Emerging Republic

This chapter examines the challenges faced by the justices in their efforts to establish a federal court system, the sources from which they fashioned federal law, and their efforts to achieve uniformity of decision making across the Union. Those responsible for establishing the legal system of any new nation will, of necessity, consider foreign models and adopt such principles of law which best fit their needs. The chapter explains how the justices used federal statutes, Supreme Court opinions, state and English law to establish a system of law acceptable to the majority and to fulfil the dual judicial and political role entrusted to them by Congress. Their first task was to administer law and procedure consistently across the circuits and resolve local litigation. They were also expected to convince the nation that stability and prosperity lay in strong national government underpinned by a system of federal law.[1] Both undertakings were set against a background of widespread fears that a strong federal system of government and judiciary might lead to an oppressive regime similar to that faced by the people under British rule. This chapter examines how the justices faced determined opposition to any diminution of states' sovereignty, their shaping of United States law on circuit and the ways in which they sought to convince the public of a need for strong central government and a system of federal law.

## The Politics of Federal Law

Determined opposition to the concept of a separate federal judiciary and its probable political role was expressed at the Constitution Convention, the various

---

[1] LaCroix supports the view that the Marshall Court regarded the inferior federal courts as a crucial locus of federal power because the justices came face to face with the citizen on circuit and delivered charges to grand and petit juries in which, because of their political allegiances, they were able to 'place the interests of the Union above those of the states'. A LaCroix, 'Federalists, Federalism, and Federal Jurisdiction' (2012) 30 *Law and History Review* 205 at 210.

ratification conventions and the debates preceding the passing of the Judiciary Act of 1789 which established the federal court system. Those debates show the divisions between Federalists determined to achieve a powerful national government underpinned by a federal judiciary and Anti-Federalists who were suspicious of any body, be it political, legislative or judicial, which would diminish the rights of the states to control their own affairs.[2] Watts (1987) expresses contemporary fears by painting a picture of the Federalists as a party clinging to 'paternal traditions of elitism' which 'expressed fear of, or distain for, the self-made man.' He regards the Federalist promotion of Atlantic trade solely for growing profits for the merchants to preserve the existing social order. He paints the Republicans as 'designers and shapers of a new order' in which hard-working men might thrive economically to counter the 'decay and decline which would result from Federalist domination'.[3] The suggestion that the Federalists were concerned only to further the interests of the ruling classes is not borne out by the many circuit opinions examined in the following chapters, which reveal that whilst the justices did preserve vested interests and promote commerce, they did so for the benefit of all, not just the elite. Despite the ratification of the Constitution and the passing of the Judiciary Act 1789, party differences persisted and placed at risk the future of the federal judiciary because of the insuperable problem of striking a balance between federal powers and states' sovereignty.

To fulfil these demanding judicial and political roles, President Washington appointed to the Court experienced and leading lawyers who were strongly committed to Federalist ideals. The importance to him of the political aspect is apparent from a letter he wrote to Chief Justice John Jay in 1789 describing the judicial department as 'the keystone of our political fabric'.[4] He repeated this view when writing to the justices before they went out on circuit for the first time, requesting that they let him know how the people reacted to local federal justice and to control by central government.[5]

---

[2] At the time of ratification of the Constitution and the creation of the federal judiciary there were no political parties as such. There were two factions; the Federalists who supported a strong federal government and judiciary, ties with Britain and an economy based on trade and the Anti-Federalists who advocated states' rights, opposed close ties with Britain, and favoured an agrarian economy. The Federalist and the Democratic-Republican parties did not emerge until the 1790s. A comprehensive account of the distinctions between the factions and early political parties is contained in Linda De Pauw and Charlene Bickford (eds), *Documentary History of the First Congress of the United States of America, 1789–1791*, 22 vols (Baltimore: John Hopkins University Press, 1972–2017). For a one-volume overview of the First Congress, see Charlene Bickford and Kenneth Bowling, *Birth of the Nation: The First Federal Congress, 1789–1791* (Lanham, MD: Rowman & Littlefield, 1989).

[3] Steven Watts, *The Republic Reborn: War and the Making of Liberal America, 1790–1820* (Baltimore: John Hopkins University Press, 1987), 13.

[4] Letter, President Washington to John Jay, 5 October 1789, reproduced in Henry P Johnson, *The Correspondence and Papers of John Jay*, 4 vols, vol 3 (New York: Burt Franklin, 1890), 378.

[5] Letter, President Washington to the Justices of the Supreme Court, 3 April 1790, reproduced in M Marcus, *Documentary History of the Supreme Court of the United States*, vol 2 (New York: Columbia University Press) 21. It also appears in *The Papers of George Washington Digital Edition* (Charlottesville: University of Virginia Press, Rotunda, 2008 via the Mount Vernon Archives).

The President ensured that the associate justices came from different states, thereby establishing regional diversity.[6] The practice of appointing justices by areas was sensible because each justice would be conversant with the law and procedure of his region, gained from practice at the bar or from sitting as a judge of the state court. Although the law and practice varied from state to state, there would always be one justice on the Court familiar with the law of the state from whence the appeal or writ of error came. A geographic balance was also sensible; the states were more likely to support a justice who was both well-known and respected.

As well as selecting justices from different areas, the President ensured that the justices were men who had played a significant role in the ratification of the Constitution and were, therefore, committed to the notion of a strong national government.[7] He believed the political philosophy of a justice to be more important than his judicial experience, anticipating that the federal judiciary would interpret the Constitution in a way which would fortify the position of central government. Whilst nominating some who had never sat as judges, he chose exceptional lawyers who had achieved great success at the Bar.[8] James Wilson, one of the original associate justices and a signer of both the Declaration of Independence and the Constitution, had no judicial experience but was one of the country's leading lawyers who lectured at the College of Philadelphia (later, the University of Pennsylvania).[9] His lectures, reproduced in his *Collected Works*, demonstrate an extensive knowledge of the law.[10] Washington's nomination of Wilson and his subsequent confirmation suggests that both the President and the Senate viewed the Court as a body which would not confine itself to narrow points of law but would, when delivering an opinion, have regard not only to the relevant law but also any political aspect of the case.

Whilst the Federalist Jay Court was keen to co-operate with Congress and the Executive, separation of powers issues soon arose between the departments of government over the nature and extent of the justices' duties. In 1792 Congress

---

[6] Ron Chernow, *Washington: A Life* (London: Allen Lane, 2010), 602.
[7] Melvin I Urofsky and P Finkelman, *A March of Liberty: A Constitutional History of the United States*, vol 1, 3rd edn (New York: Oxford University Press, 2011), 167.
[8] Gordon S Wood, *Empire of Liberty: A History of the Early Republic 1789–1815* (New York: Oxford University Press, 2011) 412. For a table setting out the prior judicial experience of Supreme Court Justices see, Epstein, Segal, Spaeth and Walker, *The Supreme Court Compendium: Data Decisions and Developments*, 3rd edn (Washington DC, Congressional Quarterly Press, 2003), 324–30. The *Compendium* is a mine of information. It also contains a useful list of major decisions of the Court from the Congressional Quarterly, 1790–2002 showing the majority opinion writer and the dissenters, 86–88 (1790–1833). Circuit Justice Assignments, 1802–1867 appear at 381–82.
[9] Steve Sheppard (ed), *The History of Legal Education in the United States; Commentaries and Primary Sources*, 2 vols, vol 1 (Pasadena, California: Salem Press Inc., 1999), 15.
[10] Kermit L Hall and Mark David Hall (eds), *The Collected Works of James Wilson*, 2 vols (Indianapolis: Liberty Fund, 2007). Sadly, his later years, whilst still a justice, were marred by imprisonment for debt due to failed land speculations. He died a pauper in 1798 aged 55. His fall from grace is documented in the many letters cited in Natalie Wexler, *A More Obedient Wife: A Novel of the Early Supreme Court* (Washington DC: Kalorama Press, 2006).

passed legislation dealing with the settlement of widows, orphans and invalid pensions and assigned the duty of administering the act to the federal judiciary. The justices successfully objected that the business directed by the Act was not of a judicial nature, therefore the courts, to comply with the Act, would be acting without constitutional authority. However, because of the desperate needs of the claimants, they did subsequently deal with the matters not as judges but as commissioners.[11] Undeterred, the following year Thomas Jefferson and Alexander Hamilton sought to convene the justices to act as advisors to the Executive to answer 29 questions on the power of the United States to deal with belligerent European powers. The justices gently but firmly refused the invitation pointing out once more 'The Lines of Separation drawn by the Constitution between the three Departments of Government'.[12]

The efforts of the Marshall Court to develop, once established, a uniform cross-circuit system of federal law must be viewed against the background of continuous party political divisions between Federalists and Republicans and the attacks by extremist elements of the Republican majority in Congress which threatened the very existence of the federal judiciary. A mere 12 days after President Jefferson took office, Republican Representative William Branch Giles in his letter of congratulation asked the President to dismiss all Federalist judges including those of the Supreme Court.[13] Jefferson clearly felt that he would not have the support of Congress to remove Supreme Court justices and compromised in the Judiciary Act of 1802 by dismissing the federal circuit judges appointed by President John Adams on the eve of his departure from the White House.[14] In this way he restored the justices' circuit riding duties. Another effect of the 1802 Act was to rearrange the sitting pattern of the Court so that it could not reconvene for 18 months.[15]

---

[11] See letters, 5 April 1792, New York Circuit Court judges to Congress; 18 April 1792 from Pennsylvania Circuit Court judges to Congress; 8 June 1792 from North Carolina Circuit Court judges to Congress (*Papers of George Washington* in Mount Vernon Archives). The Third Circuit justices Wilson and Blair refused to deal with pensions even as Commissioners. See Russell Wheeler, 'Extrajudicial Activities of the Early Supreme Court' (1973) *Supreme Court Review* 135–39.

[12] Questions for the Supreme Court, 18 July 1793 and Supreme Court Justices reply of 8 August, 1793 (*Papers of George Washington* in Mount Vernon Archives). The Rhode Island Constitution of 1836 is based on the former Constitution of 1843 and the Charter granted by Charles II in 1663. Surprisingly, it states in Article X, Section 3: 'The judges of the supreme court shall give their written opinion upon any question of law whenever requested by the governor or by either house of the general assembly.' Available at: www.rilin.state.ri.us/riconstitution/Pages/Constfull.aspx.

[13] Letter, William Branch Giles to Thomas Jefferson, 16 March 1801 in Dice Robin Anderson, *William Giles: A Study in the Politics of Virginia and the Nation from 1790–1830* (Menasha, Wisconsin: Collegiate Press at George Banta Publishing Co 1914), 77.

[14] Justice Story, much later in his *Commentaries*, regarded the termination of the circuit judges' offices by the Judiciary Act 1802 as an attack on the independence of the inferior judges. Whatever the questionable circumstances of their appointments, Congress had chosen 16 new circuit judges, yet despite a constitutional tenure during good behaviour, they were dismissed without payment of salary because the appointments were 'unpopular with those then in power'. Joseph Story, *Commentaries on the Constitution of the United States* 3 vols (Boston: Hilliard, Gray & Company, 1833). 3rd edn, 2 vols, EH Bennett (ed), (Boston: Little, Brown & Company, 1858), vol 2, 476–77.

[15] There is a wealth of scholarship on the Republicans' repeated attempts to undermine the federal judiciary; Joseph Wheelan's, *Jefferson's Vendetta: The Pursuit of Aaron Burr and the Judiciary* (New York: Carroll and Graff Publishers, 2005) details Jefferson's private and public attacks on Burr and on John

The successful move to repeal the 1801 Act followed a contentious two-month debate in Congress rehearsing the arguments for and against justices' circuit riding aired on the Judiciary Bill 1801. Those against the repeal stressed the hardships if justices were obliged to combine Supreme Court sittings with circuit travel. Federalist Senator Gouverneur Morris of New York, seeking to save the Act, put it well when suggesting that a President nominating a justice 'must seek less the learning of a judge than the agility of a post boy'.[16] He pointed out how burdensome it was for men of mature years to be forced to travel huge distances on circuit and that it would discourage men of the highest ability from taking on the duty. Five days later, Republican Senator David Stone of North Carolina rose to make the equally valid point that it was essential for the justices to ride circuit in order to familiarise themselves with the laws and practice of particular states in order to guide their opinions in the Supreme Court.[17]

The Court did not sit again until 24 February 1803 when Chief Justice Marshall delivered the historic opinion of *Marbury v Madison*. Whilst criticising Jefferson's Secretary of State for refusing to deliver to William Marbury his commission from President Adams appointing him a justice of the peace, the Court refused to declare that Marbury should have his commission, holding that Congress was not empowered to pass that part of the Judiciary Act of 1789 which extended the original jurisdiction of the Court to grant a writ of *mandamus*. In effect, the Court found that that part of the Act was inconsistent with the Constitution and the Constitution must prevail. In an extremely politically sensitive case the Court satisfied the Federalists to a limited extent by declaring that Marbury should have had his commission and at the same time placated the Republicans by holding that the Court did not have jurisdiction to grant the relief. Most importantly, Marshall held that the Constitution empowered the Court to review the acts of the executive and the legislature.[18] The Court exercised a power suggested by Alexander Hamilton in *Federalist 78* some 15 years earlier when he remarked that 'where the will of the legislature declared in statutes, stands in opposition to that of the people declared in the constitution, the judges ought to be governed by the latter, rather than the former'.[19] Jefferson's biographer, Berstein (2003), rightly comments that

---

Marshall who presided over the circuit trial of Burr; Richard E Ellis, *The Jeffersonian Crisis: Courts and Politics in the Young Republic* (New York: Oxford University Press, 1971), argues that the struggle over the federal court system was generated by extremists of both parties; James F Simon's *What Kind of Nation: Thomas Jefferson, John Marshall, and the Epic Struggle to Create a United States* (New York: Simon & Schuster, 2002) charts Jefferson's determination to thwart a Federalist-dominated Court.

[16] Senator Gouverneur Morris of New York. 8 January 1802. *Annals of Congress*, 7th Congress. 1st sess, 38. Reproduced in Bruce A Ragsdale, *Debate on the Federal Judiciary: A Documentary History*, vol 1, 1787–1875 (Federal Judicial Center: History Office, 2013), 111–12.

[17] ibid, 113. 7th Congress, 1st sess, 71, 13 January 1802.

[18] *Marbury v Madison*, 5 US 137 (1 Cranch), 1803.

[19] Publius (Alexander Hamilton), *The Federalist* No 78, 28 May 1788 in Joanne B Freeman (ed), *Hamilton: Writings* (New York: Library of America, 2001), 423. The layman may be forgiven for believing that judicial review began with *Marbury*. See, however, the comprehensive review of the exercise of the power of judicial review by federal courts prior to that case by William Michael Traynor entitled, 'Judicial Review before *Marbury*' (2005) 58(2) *Stanford Law Review* 455–562.

'Chief Justice Marshall faced a seemingly no-win situation. If he issued the writ, he knew that Madison would ignore it and he had no way to make Madison obey it, for the federal courts rely on the executive to enforce their orders'. The compromise was Marshall's way out of the trap.[20]

Marshall's compromise rankled with Jefferson for the remainder of his life and he made his distaste for the federal judiciary clear in a letter the following year to Abigail Adams, the wife of former President John Adams, complaining of the partiality of the Federalist judges, and, in a clear reference to *Marbury v Madison*, expressing the view that the right claimed by the Court to review the acts of the executive and the legislature made the judiciary a despotic branch of government.[21]

Jefferson believed that one way in which he might curb what he considered the excesses of the judicial branch was by impeaching its judges. He was no stranger to the impeachment proceeding process. In 1797, justifiably aggrieved at the presentment of a grand jury against a Republican state representative on an allegation that he had breached the Sedition Act of 1798 by criticism undermining the federal government, he wrote to James Monroe suggesting that the grand jury be impeached for interfering with a citizen's freedom of speech. His petition requesting impeachment was received favourably by the Virginia House of Delegates but not acted upon.[22] Jefferson himself faced the threat of impeachment in 1781 for allegations of incompetence whilst Governor of Virginia.[23]

Impeachment reared its head once more when Jefferson sought to attack the federal judiciary by instigating proceedings to remove from office federal District Judge John Pickering of New Hampshire. Pickering was clearly unfit to remain in office due to mental illness, but the Constitution provided for removal from judicial office only in the case of treason, bribery or other high crimes and misdemeanours.[24] Nevertheless, the Republican majority in the Senate removed him from office.[25] Significantly, shortly before the Senate tried Pickering, Jefferson was instigating impeachment proceedings against Justice Samuel Chase for his intemperate bias during Alien & Sedition trials against Republicans and for his public attacks on the Maryland Republican administration. Jefferson wrote to Congressman Joseph Hopkinson who was managing the Pickering trial suggesting impeachment

---

[20] R B Bernstein, *Thomas Jefferson* (New York: Oxford University Press, 2003). Folio Society edition with emendations, 2008, 156.
[21] Letter Thomas Jefferson to Mrs Abigail Adams, 11 September 1804 in Lester Capon (ed), *The Adams-Jefferson Letters* (Chapel Hill: University of North Carolina Press, 1959), 278–80.
[22] Letter, Jefferson to Monroe, 7 September 1797 in Paul Leicester Ford, *The Works of Thomas Jefferson*, vol VIII (New York: GP Putnam's Sons, 1904), 339–40.
[23] Peter Charles Hoffer and NEH Hull, *Impeachment in America, 1635–1805* (New Haven: Yale University Press, 1984), 85–86.
[24] United States Constitution, Article II, section 4.
[25] See President Jefferson's message of 3 February 1803 to the House of Representatives placing Pickering's case before the House for consideration of impeachment in James D Richardson, *A Compilation of the Messages and Papers of the Presidents*, vol 1 (Washington DC: Bureau of National Literature and Art, 1905), 356.

proceedings against Chase but wishing not to be known as the instigator.[26] The impeachment proceedings instigated in 1804 against Chase failed as the Senate decided that his conduct did not meet the necessary 'high crimes and misdemeanour' threshold. District Judge Richard Peters was threatened that he too would be impeached, on the grounds that he had sat with Chase on the Alien and Sedition trials. Fortunately for him, the House refused to sanction his impeachment, but the possibility of proceedings caused him great anxiety.[27]

President Jefferson's desire to achieve his objectives by encouraging another to take the leading role and to keep his involvement secret was a tactic he employed on more than one occasion as another of his biographers, Jon Meacham (2012) observes of the Chase proceedings: 'It was a characteristic Jeffersonian tactic, instigating a course of action from afar.'[28] Although he publicly initiated proceedings against Pickering, he acted against him behind the scenes. He covertly pulled the strings in the impeachment proceedings of Justice Chase and secretly had the conduct of the prosecution of Aaron Burr for treason. Further, in 1803, he wrote to Governor William Harrison of Indiana Territory, that the government trading posts should encourage the more influential Indians to incur debts beyond their ability to pay so that they would be forced to cede land to settle their obligations. He said 'but this letter being unofficial and private, I may with safety give you a more extensive view of our policy respecting the Indians'. His opinion was that the Indians must either become citizens of the United States or move beyond the Mississippi. Having suggested that the Indians ought to be led into debt he concluded by reminding Harrison that he should 'perceive how sacredly it [the letter] it must be kept within [your] own breast, and especially how improper to be understood by the Indians. [for] their interests and tranquillity it is best they should see only the present age of their history'.[29] Clearly, he would not want the Indians to know the stark choice they had; either integrate which was unlikely as the vast majority of Whites would not agree or be removed thousands of miles away. Equally, he would not want them to discover his part in underhanded attempts to acquire their land. Attacks on judges threaten an independence crucial to the fair and impartial

---

[26] Henry Adams, *History of the United States of America during the Administration of Thomas Jefferson* (C Scribner's Sons, 1889), Library of America Edition edited by Earl N Habert, 1986), 402–03.

[27] Letters, District Judge Richard Peters to Senator Timothy Pickering, Pickering Papers MSS, XXVII, 46 & XXXI, 101, cited in Warren, *The Supreme Court*, vol 1, 281–82. Richard Peters was the most prominent of the federal district judges of the period. He is championed by Stephen B Presser in *Studies in the History of the United States Courts of the Third Circuit, 1790–1980* (Washington DC: Bicentennial Committee of the Judicial Conference of the United States, 1982). Because of Peters' contribution to the development of maritime jurisprudence, Presser regards him as the 'grandfather of American admiralty law' with, not surprisingly, Joseph Story as the 'father' 61, n 38.

[28] Jon Meacham, *Thomas Jefferson: The Art of Power* (New York: Random House, 2012), 375.

[29] Letter, 27 February 1803, from Thomas Jefferson to William Henry Harrison in Barbara B Oberg (ed), *The Papers of Thomas Jefferson*, vol 39 (Princeton: Princeton University Press, 2012), 589–93. For a comprehensive account of President Jefferson's policy towards the Indians, see Anthony F C Wallace, *Jefferson and the Indians: The Tragic Fate of the First Americans* (Cambridge, MA: The Belknap Press of Harvard University Press, 1999).

administration of justice. The judiciary must be open to reasonable constructive criticism but they must be free to perform their duty without political pressure, personal abuse, or threats of dismissal for failure to follow the policies and ideals of a ruling party.[30] It would appear, however, that during Jefferson's presidency, for the federal judiciary to assert its independence and claim the power to review an Act of Congress, was deemed sufficient cause to undermine federal law and remove judges from office. This was a far cry from Jefferson's view expressed in a letter to George Wythe as far back as 1776, when he wrote 'The judicial power ought to be distinct from both the legislature and executive, and independent upon both ... they [the judges] should not be dependent upon any man.' He did, however, propose impeachment for 'misbehaviour'.[31] Subsequent events would appear to indicate that he later viewed as misbehaviour any form of opposition to Executive policy.

A campaign against the Federalist judiciary was also directed at state judges. The Pennsylvania Republican party began a campaign to impeach and remove a number of Federalist state judges. In 1803, the State Senate impeached and removed from office Judge Alexander Addison on purely party political grounds just eight days before Jefferson began to pursue District Judge Pickering.[32] The following year the Pennsylvania House of Representatives impeached Chief Justice Edward Shippen and associate justices Thomas Smith and Jasper Yeates, all Federalists, for alleged high misdemeanours. All three judges were acquitted by the State Senate as moderates within the party refused to support the dismissals.[33] There were no

---

[30] Unfortunately, uninformed and offensive attacks on the judiciary are on the increase. Right-thinking members of society must be vigilant to ensure that politicians and the media do not cross the line between moderate constructive criticism and vituperative comment and should protest vigorously when they do so if justice is to survive. I would venture to suggest that the line was well and truly traversed by calling the ruling of federal judge with whom he disagreed the 'ridiculous' opinion of a 'so called judge'. (Tweet, 4 February 2017, President Donald J Trump of US District Judge James Robart). It is not a problem confined to the United States. A far worse example occurred on the other side of the Atlantic. On 3 November 2016, the Lord Chief Justice of England and Wales and two senior colleagues held that Parliament must be consulted before the British Government could trigger Article 50 of the Lisbon Treaty which would start the United Kingdom's formal process of European Union withdrawal—a ruling later upheld by the Supreme Court. The following day a national newspaper, the *Daily Mail*, published the judges' photographs on the front page under the banner headline, 'Enemies of the People'. Justice Minister and Lord Chancellor Liz Truss, whose constitutional duty is the protection of the judiciary, stated that the government intended to appeal the judgment and refused to condemn the headline. She said that whilst she believed in the independence of the judiciary, she also strongly supported a free press. Giving evidence before the House of Lords Constitution Select Committee on 1 March 2017, the Lord Chief Justice said that the *Daily Mail* article caused him to ask 'the police to give advice and protection in relation to the emotions stirred up for the first time in his judicial career'. He also complained that a number of circuit judges had been called 'enemies of the people' by litigants in person.
[31] Letter, Jefferson to Wythe, July 1776 in Paul Leicester Ford (ed), *The Works of Thomas Jefferson*, vol 2 (New York: GP Putnam's Sons, 1904), 219.
[32] Albert J Beveridge, *The Life of John Marshall* (Boston & New York: Houghton Mifflin Company, 1919), vol III, 163–65.
[33] Hoffer & Hull, *Impeachment in America*, 221–27.

further impeachments. In 1807, Jefferson announced in a letter to Senator William Giles that the device was of no use in dislodging members of the federal judiciary. The letter also reveals his orchestration of the prosecution for treason of his former Vice-President Aaron Burr in the Richmond circuit court presided over by John Marshall. Jefferson complained of Marshall's trickery and his search for loopholes in the prosecution case.[34] He was furious when the jury acquitted Burr of treason and believed that Marshall had connived in the acquittal.[35] Normally he restricted his criticisms of the judiciary to private correspondence. However, in his Seventh Annual State of the Union Message he expressed his profound disagreement with the not guilty verdict, questioning whether the acquittal was due to 'a defect in the testimony, in the law, or in the administration of the law'.[36] Here, by suggesting that the acquittal may have been caused by the 'administration of the law', he was asking the country to accept his view that Marshall connived in Burr's escape from the sentence of death. Jefferson was not the only one outraged by the jury's verdict. Republican feelings were running high and shortly after the trial large crowds gathered in Baltimore in early November 1807, hanging and burning effigies of Burr, John Marshall, Luther Martin, who was Burr's counsel, and Herman Blennerhassett, an alleged co-conspirator.[37] The acquittal clearly preyed on the President's mind because seven years later he complained to President John Adams of 'our cunning chief justice twisting Burr's neck out of the halter of treason'.[38] The fact that Burr had presided impartially over the Senate in the failed impeachment proceedings of Justice Chase will have been a factor in the President's wish to see his former Vice-President hanged.

There were no further impeachment proceedings during the remainder of his second term of office, but this undermining of the judiciary between 1801 and 1809 and threats to remove from office those judges who displeased him made the justices' duties on circuit and on the Court much more challenging. Although Jefferson had abandoned impeachment, his opposition to the federal judiciary

---

[34] Letter, Thomas Jefferson to Senator William Branch Giles, 20 April 1807 in Albert Ellery Bergh, *The Writings of Thomas Jefferson*. Available at: www.constitution.org/tj/jeff.htm 1173–76.

[35] For a penetrating analysis of the trial and its background, see R Kent Newmyer, *The Treason Trial of Aaron Burr: Law, Politics, and the Character Wars of the New Nation* (New York: Cambridge University Press, 2012). Newmyer, rather than analysing the work of scholars, focuses on contemporary accounts of the case and two stenographic transcriptions of the trial in particular. Interestingly and typical of the time, the fact that Edward Carrington, the judge's brother-in-law and close friend, ended up not only on the jury but also as its foreman was not thought problematic. ibid, 111–12. Also apparently acceptable to the judge, which he later regretted, was his attendance at a party for Burr shortly before the trial and after arraignment, 141–48.

[36] Fred L Israel, *The State of the Union Messages of the Presidents, 1790–1966*, 3 vols (New York: Chelsea House/Robert Hector Publishers, 1966), vol 1, 93.

[37] *American Citizen* (New York) of 5 December 1807, reproducing an account of the disturbances from John B Colvin's Baltimore paper, *Weekly Register of Politics and News*. Also cited in Nancy Isenberg, *Fallen Founder: The Life of Aaron Burr* (New York: Viking Penguin, 2007), 368.

[38] Letter, President Thomas Jefferson to President John Adams, 14 January 1814, in Capon, *Adams-Jefferson Letters*, 423.

remained strong long after he had left office.[39] In 1826, ten days after President Jefferson's death, Marshall complained to Story about the effect the President's attacks had on the judiciary. He wrote,

> It grieves me because his influence is still as great that many—very many will adopt his opinions however unsound they may be & however contradictory to their own reason. I cannot describe the surprise and mortification I have felt at hearing that Mr Madison has embraced them with respect to the judicial department.[40]

## The Grand Jury Charge: A Bond between Government and Citizen

At the beginning of each term, on all circuits, the presiding justice delivered a charge to the grand jury, the main purpose of which was to inform its members of the law applicable to cases they were later to try. At the same time it enabled a justice to proclaim and endorse federal government policy and many early grand jury charges had heavy political overtones. The importance of the grand jury was recognised in the Fifth Amendment to the Constitution which provides that 'no person shall be held for a capital or otherwise infamous crime, unless on a presentment or indictment of a grand jury'. The differences between the currently approved grand jury charge and those of the late eighteenth and early nineteenth centuries are striking. Federal judges today simply remind the grand jury of its function under the Fifth Amendment, stressing the jury's independence, and that it stands between the government and the person under investigation.[41] This is a far cry from the overtly political statements of the early justices. Albert J Beveridge, John Marshall's biographer, observed, in 1919, that the justices used their charges to preach on religion, morality, and partisan politics.[42] This was, as Henderson (1971) noted, merely a continuation of the practice of

---

[39] In 1810 Jefferson regarded the death of Federalist Justice William Cushing as 'a circumstance of congratulation' because it enabled President Madison to nominate a Republican justice. Letter, Jefferson to Madison, 15 October 1810 in James Morton Smith (ed), *Republic of Letters: The Correspondence between Thomas Jefferson and James Madison, 1776–1826*, 3 vols. (New York: WW Norton and Company, 1995), vol 3, 1646; There are also his attempts to interfere with the practice of the Supreme Court's single opinion by writing to Justice Johnson and President Madison to persuade justices to issue seriatim opinions. Letter, Jefferson to Johnson, 27 October 1822 in Merill D Peterson (ed), *Thomas Jefferson: Writings* (New York: Library of America, 1984), 1459–63. Letter, Jefferson to Madison, 13 June 1823 in Ford, *Jefferson: Works*, vol 12, 296.

[40] Letter, 13 July 1826, John Marshall to Joseph Story. Massachusetts Historical Society, Joseph Story Papers.

[41] Model grand jury charge approved by the Judicial Conference of the United States, March 2005. The model is merely a guide to judges and may be amended to suit circumstances.

[42] Albert J Beveridge, *The Life of John Marshall*, 4 vols, vol 3 (Boston: Houghton, Mifflin Company, 1916–1919), 30, n 1.

judges during the colonial and revolutionary periods.[43] The charge stemmed from the institution of the grand jury established in England from the time of the Constitutions of Clarendon of 1166, surviving until 1933 when it fell into disuse and was finally abolished by the Criminal Justice Act of 1948.[44]

Grand jury charges during the first decade of the federal courts were printed in local newspapers, therefore the justices' message to the jury would have a wide circulation.[45] The most comprehensive source of grand jury charges is that compiled by Krauss (2012). He has included transcriptions of every grand jury charge given before 1801 from colonial, state, and lower federal courts, having extracted them from the papers of judges, published books, pamphlets and every publicly available eighteenth-century newspaper. He observes that the charges cover 'politics, foreign and domestic policy, religion, local social and economic development, and the status of roads and schools as well as the rules of criminal procedure evidence, and substantive criminal law'.[46] He does not include the charges of Supreme Court Justices on circuit as they are contained in Marcus, *Documentary History of the Supreme Court*.

So many of the grand jury charges collected by Krauss owe more to politics than the law. It is, therefore, refreshing to read the charge of Judge George Walton to the Burke County, Georgia grand jury on 1 March 1799. Walton ticked all boxes. He was a delegate to the Continental Congress; a signer of the Declaration of Independence; wounded in the Revolutionary War; taken prisoner by the British; served Georgia as Chief Justice, Senator, and Governor and finally as a judge of the Superior Court of Justice. His charge, confined to law and procedure, included the following: 'The malignant voice of party and factions shall not be admitted within the pale of the Tribunal. The business shall proceed according to the established rule of law, independent of motives of policy, or political influence; for wretched is that country where such considerations can reach the purity of its jurisprudence.'[47]

One contrasts Judge Walton's model charge with that of Justice Samuel Chase. It is not surprising, given the widespread newspaper coverage, that the intemperate charge to a Baltimore grand jury in 1803, in which Chase fiercely denounced the Republican administration, taken with his general intemperance on the bench,

---

[43] Dwight F Henderson, *Courts for a New Nation* (Washington DC: Public Affairs Press, 1971), 40.

[44] For the origins of the grand jury, its legal and political functions, and reception in America see, Helen L Schwartz, 'Demythologizing the Historic Role of the Grand Jury' (1972) 10 *American Criminal Law Review* 701 at 703; Mark Kadish, 'Behind the Locked Doors of an American Grand Jury: Its History, Its Secrecy, and Its Process (1996) 24(1) *Florida State University Law Review* 1–77, 5–12. For a comprehensive compilation of seventeenth and eighteenth-century English grand jury charges, many with religious and political overtones see Georges Lamoine (ed), *Charges to the Grand Jury, 1689–1803* (London: Royal Historical Society, 1992), Camden Fourth Series, vol 43.

[45] Erwin C Surrency, *History of the Federal Courts* (New York: Oceana Publications, Inc, 2002), 281, n 47.

[46] Stanton D Krauss, *Gentlemen of the Grand Jury: The Surviving Grand Jury Charges from Colonial, State and Lower Federal Courts before 1801*, 2 vols (Durham, North Carolina: Carolina Academic Press, 2012), vol 1, xxv.

[47] ibid, vol 1, 216 (extracted from the *Southern Centinel & Gazette*).

resulted in the impeachment proceedings other justices were unlikely to face as their charges were mild in comparison and which despite a political element attracted little attention from Republican newspaper proprietors.[48]

On his first circuit in 1790 Chief Justice Jay set the tone by explaining to the grand jury that the new nation needed a federal system of justice to overcome many differing state laws which were for the benefit of individual states rather than the whole Union.[49] When dealing with the birth of the federal court system, in language that was moderate and persuasive, Jay stressed the importance of administering federal justice locally and accepted that putting such a system in place was not an easy undertaking.[50] He acknowledged the task of reconciling state and federal court jurisdictions as complex, but promised that every effort would be made to ensure that they would be 'auxiliary instead of hostile to each other'.[51] Jay declared the grand jury system as the best possible means of bringing offenders to justice.[52] His purpose was to forge a bond between the national government and the federal judiciary on the one hand and the grand jury (and through it the wider public) on the other hand. His concluding remarks to the grand jury are suggestive of a partnership between the citizen and the government to be overseen by the good offices of the federal judiciary. His message, in concluding his charge, was very clear. If the citizens supported the national government and its laws, the government and the federal judiciary would ensure that their rights and liberties were fully protected.[53]

Jay's charge to the grand jury in Boston that spring was in like terms. It was well received. The foreman of the grand jury praised the 'very excellent charge', and expressed the hope 'that the circuits might continue to be visited by justices of the same, learning and integrity and ability as the current incumbents'. The foreman requested and was given in due course copy of the charge for the press which ensured a much wider audience.[54] Justice James Wilson received similar praise in Philadelphia in the same term and, again, a request from the grand jury foreman for a copy of the charge for publication. It was printed in full in the *Pennsylvania Gazette* of 12 April 1790. The charge also received wide coverage in newspapers in New York, Boston, New Hampshire, and North Carolina as did the same charge by Wilson in Delaware, Virginia, Maryland, and Rhode Island between May and July 1790.[55] The Boston-based *Massachusetts Centinel* of 1 May 1790 acclaimed Wilson's 'able and masterly' delivery and his demonstration of 'the efficacy and

---

[48] The controversial extract from Chase's charge is reprinted in J Haw et al, *Stormy Patriot* (Baltimore: Maryland Historical Society), 214–15.
[49] Charge of John Jay to the Grand Jury of the Circuit Court for the District of New York on 12 April 1790, reprinted in Marcus, *Documentary History*, vol 2, 25–30.
[50] ibid, 27.
[51] ibid, 28.
[52] ibid, 29.
[53] ibid, 30.
[54] ibid, vol 2, 61.
[55] ibid, 33.

## The Grand Jury Charge: A Bond between Government and Citizen

superiour (sic) excellence of that [government] established in the United States'.[56] Wilson's charge was unusual because, although it praised the Constitution and the institutions of grand and petty juries, it did not seek to promote the virtues of either federal government or federal justice. The charge was simply a commentary on the Constitution and the relevant law.[57] He was at pains to assure the grand jury that the citizen was protected because all acts of state and federal legislatures must conform to the Articles of the Constitution which was meant to accommodate 'the dispositions, manners, and habits of those, for whom it was intended'.[58] At the suggestion of a friend, Justice Story sent to her copies of his charge to a Salem grand jury for circulation beyond Massachusetts.[59] However, he was not keen to have the first charge of the term published until he had delivered it to grand juries on the circuit towns and cities he had yet to visit.[60]

Wilson's politically neutral charge was also in stark contrast to that which the turbulent Justice Samuel Chase delivered to a Baltimore Grand Jury on 2 May 1803. He used the charge to protest the Republican-led Judiciary Act of 1802 which terminated the offices of 16 federal circuit judges. He also denounced the Maryland Assembly's decision to abolish the State General Court and its extension of suffrage based on property-owning rights to include all white males, which he declared would 'rapidly destroy all protection to property and security to personal Liberty; and our Republican Constitution will sink into a Mobocracy, the worst of all possible Governments'. He ended his charge with a personal attack on the framers of the current Maryland legislation, accusing them of 'pulling down the beautiful fabric of wisdom, and republicanism, that their fathers had erected'.[61]

Justice James Iredell's charge to a Republican grand jury, which appeared in the *Augusta Chronicle* of 17 October 1791 met with faint praise. Whilst the Georgia

---

[56] ibid, 41.

[57] ibid, vol 2, 33–45.

[58] ibid, 33. Wilson was very popular on circuit. The editor of the *Gazette of the United States* (New York) of 6 October 1792 praised Wilson's recent address as an 'elegant and pertinent charge to the grand jury' at Hartford, Connecticut, remarking upon the justices' 'humanity and compassion' for agreeing to act as Commissioners in executing pension law cases, a task which they felt they were not obliged to perform. In the same issue the editor recorded a further 'elegant' grand jury charge, on this occasion by Justice Cushing in the absence of Chief Justice Jay through illness.

[59] His friend Elizabeth Walker of West Farms, Massachusetts, when thanking Story for the documents, wrote, 'they were sent into different states for insertion in their public papers, thou mentioned'. In the same letter Mrs Walker touched upon another troubling issue when stating: 'Thy belief that slavery will become effectively suppressed in America is truly encouraging.' Letter, Elizabeth Walker to Joseph Story, 15 January 1821 in Story Papers, William L Clements Library, University of Michigan.

[60] Story's note to the grand jury dated 20 October 1812 reads: 'Gentlemen. I beg you to return my sincere thanks to the Grand Jury for the polite manner in which they have been pleased to notice my charge delivered to them yesterday. As my duties extend to three states … I am obliged to deliver one and the same charge in each state. Its publication at the present time would oblige me to prepare another charge which my present arrangements would render impracticable.' Joseph Story Papers, Library of Congress, microfilm reel 1, vol 1. For an example of a grand jury request for a copy of the charge for publication signed by all of its 18 members see ibid, Microfilm 1, vol 2. Note from Boston Grand Jury, 15 October 1819.

[61] Samuel Chase, Charge to Grand Jury, 2 May 1803. Vertical File. Maryland Historical Society cited in Haw, *Stormy Patriot*, 214–15.

jury thanked the justice for his charge on the law, the foreman launched into a comprehensive list of objections to federal government policies and a demand for a Bill of Rights guaranteeing a Republican form of government to each state.[62] Finally, to add to Iredell's discomfort, the foreman complained that the federal judiciary of the United States was too expensive to maintain.[63] The grand jury clearly resented a federal government interfering with state sovereignty. The complaint that the federal judiciary was too expensive was just another way of saying the state's judicial system was fit for purpose and could cope very well without federal intervention. Having played a major role in North Carolina's tortuous process of constitutional ratification, Iredell knew there were many opponents of the federal system of government; he was not surprised by the hostile reception. Writing to his wife about the charge, he made light of the protest by referring to 'some Presentments they made discovering some dissatisfaction at particular things, but decently expres[sed?]'.[64] "Philanthropos" writing in the *Augusta Chronicle* of 26 November 1791 was more forthcoming in his criticism of Iredell's charge, commenting that he had spent so much time extolling the virtues of the federal government that he 'forgot to instruct the grand jury on its duty to preserve order in society'.[65]

One looks to the message in the charge, the way in which it was formally accepted by the grand jury and its reception in local and national newspapers to discover whether it achieved its desired effect. Its influence depended on where the message was delivered. Thus, as has been seen by comparing reactions to the charges, in the generally Federalist North the charge was usually well received and was more likely to cement relationships between the federal government and the local people, whereas charges supporting the federal government would make little impression on local opinion in any state resenting perceived federal government interference with state sovereignty. However, after the impeachment proceedings

---

[62] Marcus, *Documentary History*, vol 2, 216–24 for Iredell's charge, and 224–25 for the grand jury's presentments.

[63] ibid, vol 2, 225.

[64] ibid, 225–26. Iredell wrote often to his wife during lengthy absences on official business. Some of the letters appear in the *Documentary History*, of which Natalie Wexler was an associate editor. During her research on the multi-volume set she collected letters passing between Justices Iredell and Wilson and their wives which were not considered relevant for the main work as they were largely of a personal and domestic nature. Fortunately, Wexler has skilfully incorporated the text of the letters into a novel on the lives of Hannah Iredell and Hannah Wilson. The importance to the researcher is the insight the letters give to the justices' life on circuit separated for long periods from family and friends.

[65] ibid, 233. Iredell met with a more sympathetic North Carolina grand jury on 2 June 1794 which thanked him for his assurances that neutrality was the prudent course to adopt in response to the 'belligerent powers' and requested a copy of the charge for publication. (*Gazette of the United States & Daily Evening Advertiser* (Philadelphia), 7 July 1794. The editor of the same newspaper on 9 April 1799 praised Iredell for having delivered to the grand jury at Trenton New Jersey 'a truly patriotic charge' in which he defended the Alien and Sedition laws which he considered to be perfectly consistent with the Constitution and concluded by remarking on the 'mild and virtuous administrations of government'. The grand jury (with only one dissenting voice) approved the charge. Both charges are good examples of the political element of the grand jury charge.

of Justice Chase, whilst the federal courts generally furthered Federalist policies the overtly political element disappeared from the grand jury charge. One is entitled to draw this inference from the absence of reporting of charges in the primary documents examined. Had there been any controversial charges, it is more than likely they would have surfaced.[66] The grand jury charge did serve a useful purpose in the Court's first decade as a party political broadcast on behalf of the federal government.

## The Circuit Court Discourse in the Constitutional Ratification and Senate Debates

Whilst awaiting a body of Supreme Court guidance any jurisprudential advances depended upon the justices determining the applicable law and procedure to resolve the many and varied disputes they faced on circuit. The need to adopt a consistent approach across the circuits was crucial to the survival of the federal justice experiment. One aspect of the search for uniformity was the justices' practice whilst on circuit of writing exchanging experiences and seeking advice from colleagues more experienced in particular branches of law. They also looked to state laws and, because of a common legal education, relied heavily on guidance from English law to supplement available United States law.

The United States Constitution gave little guidance on the nature and extent of the powers of the federal courts. Whilst the Constitution outlined the original and appellate jurisdiction of the Supreme Court, it was silent on the extent of the jurisdiction of the 'inferior' district and circuit courts, and how the federal courts would co-exist alongside state courts, leaving jurisdictional issues to Congress. Ellis (2004) believes that President Washington deliberately avoided a battle over the shape and powers of the federal courts and left it to Congress because the concept was so controversial.[67] However, an alternative view is that many items of detail were deferred for full debate in Congress after the Constitution was law. The pressing task was to have the points of principle enshrined in the Constitution ratified by nine of the thirteen states as required by Article VII as soon as possible.

The difficulties facing the framers of the Constitution in establishing the federal courts are evident from the proceedings of the Constitutional Convention at Philadelphia between May and September 1787 and best illustrated in the speeches

---

[66] In Hobson's 12-volume set of *The Papers of John Marshall I*, the only reference to the grand jury charge is to that delivered by Marshall at the trial of Aaron Burr for treason in 1807, in which he confined himself to the definition of treason and the evidence required to prove the offence. No text of the charge has been found (vol vii, 22).

[67] Joseph J Ellis, *His Excellency: George Washington* (New York: Alfred A Knopf, 2004), 200. 'A compromise by postponement' (Bickford and Bowling, *Birth of the Nation*, 45).

of George Mason and John Marshall at the Virginia Ratifying Convention in June 1788.[68] Mason believed the establishment of federal district and circuit courts would erode the rights of the state legislatures and courts to order their own affairs and posed the question, 'What is to be left to the State Courts?' He suggested that the object of establishing federal courts was 'the destruction of the legislation of the states'.[69] He argued that appeals to the Supreme Court should be limited to questions of law as to empower the Court to review the facts would undermine jury verdicts.[70] It is plain from his speech that two matters which concerned him greatly were his belief that the federal courts might re-open land purchases and enforce payments of debts to British subjects which many state courts had refused to countenance.[71] Mason's proposed amendment, which was lost, was to limit the intervention of federal judicial power to those causes of action accruing after the ratification of the Constitution.[72] In reply, Marshall assured the Committee of the Convention of the impartiality of the federal judges, going as far as to suggest that they might well be more independent than the judges of the state courts, and emphasising the need for federal courts to alleviate overcrowded state court dockets, but, most importantly, that the state courts would not lose jurisdiction of the cases they currently decided.[73] Marshall's questioning of the independence of the state judiciary resulted from the susceptibility of resident judges to local pressure due to a lack of security of tenure. This tension between the powers of federal courts and the functions of state legislatures and judicial functions, expressed at such an early stage, would dominate political and legal thinking throughout the Marshall era and beyond. Much later, in 1833, Justice Joseph Story gave his view of the reason why the state courts had not been entrusted with cases of federal cognizance. He believed that it was perceived that local or sectional interests would prevent state courts from dealing with national issues in an independent manner, particularly as some state justices might be more concerned about the effect of their opinions on their continuing in office rather than on the national interest.[74]

The Senate began to debate the Judiciary Bill in early April 1789 and the extensive political wrangling which followed delayed its signing into law by President Washington until 24 September of that year. The main hurdles delaying the bill were the fundamental questions of how much power the Constitution would

---

[68] A full record of the debate is contained in Max Farrand (ed), *Records of the Federal Convention of 1787*, 4 vols (New Haven: Yale University Press, 1937); James H Hudson (ed), *A Supplement to Max Farrand's Records of the Federal Convention of 1787* (New Haven: Yale University Press, 1987); Bernard Bailyn (ed), *The Debate on the Constitution*, 2 vols (New York: Library of America, 1993). More recent scholarship is to be found in Richard Beeman, *Plain Honest Men: The Making of the American Constitution* (New York: Random House, 2009) and Pauline Maier, *Ratification: The People Debate the Constitution, 1787–1788* (New York: Simon & Schuster, 2010).
[69] Bailyn, vol 2, 721.
[70] ibid, 723–24.
[71] ibid, 727–29.
[72] ibid, 729.
[73] ibid, 730–32.
[74] Joseph Story, *Commentaries on the Constitution*, vol III, 447–48.

transfer from the states to the nation and whether state courts should be permitted to decide on federal rights and powers, but with a right of appeal to the Supreme Court.[75] The cost of the federal judiciary was another obstacle to be overcome. Senator Paine Wingate of New Hampshire, although supporting the Bill, believed that the estimated cost of between $50,000 and $60,000 dollars per annum was far too high for the likely business which the federal courts would attract, a point also made by made by other senators. Eventually over the objections of two Anti-Federalist and four Federalist Senators the Bill passed on 17 July.[76]

## The Jurisdiction of the Federal Circuit Courts

The Judiciary Act of 1789 provided that the United States Supreme Court should consist of a chief justice and five associate justices and that it should sit in February and August of each year at the seat of government.[77] As to the inferior courts, the country was divided into thirteen districts with a district court for each district presided over by a district judge resident in the district.[78] The thirteen districts were organised into three circuits. The Eastern Circuit comprised New Hampshire, Massachusetts, Connecticut and New York. The Middle Circuit had within its boundaries New Jersey, Pennsylvania, Delaware, Maryland and Virginia, whilst the Southern Circuit consisted of South Carolina and Georgia (North Carolina was added in 1790). At this time Maine and Kentucky were part of Massachusetts and Virginia respectively. Each circuit court was to consist of two justices of the Supreme Court and the district judge of the district, any two of whom were to constitute a quorum. However, the district judge was not permitted to vote on any appeals from his own decisions.[79]

The requirement that two justices attend each sitting of the circuit court was relaxed in 1793 by Section 1 of the Judiciary Act 1793 largely due to the justices' complaints to Congress of the hardship of circuit riding and only one justice was required to attend with the district judge.[80] The Judiciary Act of 1801 reduced the number of Supreme Court justices from six to five, established six federal judicial circuits and appointed 16 new circuit judges to staff the courts, thereby relieving

---

[75] Urofsky and Finkelman, *A March of Liberty*, vol 1, 164.
[76] Bickford and Bowling, *Birth of the Nation*, Chapter VI, 'Defining the Federal Judiciary,' 45–49.
[77] An Act to Establish the Judicial Courts of the United States, Chapter XX, Section 1, 1 Stat, 73. The Court commenced sitting in New York in 1790, moving to Philadelphia the following year before finally settling in Washington DC in 1800.
[78] ibid, Sections 2 and 3.
[79] ibid, Section 4.
[80] A recent essay details the arguments of the justices, marshalled by Jay, against circuit riding on the grounds of hardship and constitutionality: Matthew Van Hook, 'Founding the Third Branch: Judicial Greatness and John Jay's Reluctance' (2015) 40(1) *Journal of Supreme Court History* 1–19.

the justices of their circuit riding duties.[81] The Republicans rightly believed that the reduction in the number of justices was a political manoeuvre designed to limit the incoming President Jefferson's ability to make appointments to the Court. The new circuits were designated as the First Circuit (New Hampshire, Massachusetts, and Rhode Island); the Second Circuit (Connecticut, New York, and Vermont); the Third Circuit (New Jersey and Pennsylvania); the Fourth Circuit (Maryland and Delaware); the Fifth Circuit (Virginia and North Carolina), and the Sixth Circuit (South Carolina and Georgia).[82]

The repeal of that part of 1801 Act creating the new circuit judges was not far off. The outgoing President John Adams had packed the bench with committed Federalists which the incoming Jefferson regarded as a blatant political manoeuvre. Kerber (1970) rehearses the debate in Congress surrounding the repeal of the 1801 Act, arguing that the issue between the parties was more than a saving of salaries of the newly appointed circuit judges; the repeal of the Act was an attempt to make 'federal justice less available—all for the benefit of local government'.[83] The Act of 1801 had created 16 new circuit judges; three for each circuit save for the Sixth Circuit which received only one; this meant that the circuit courts would sit far more often than the Supreme Court justices could, given their other duties. The abolition of the new posts resulted in fewer federal circuit sitting times, hence Kerber's reference to local government benefit (i.e. the state courts taking in more business). The Republican majority in Congress passed the Judiciary Act of 1802, abolishing the posts of the newly appointed circuit judges and re-instating the circuit riding duties of the justices whilst retaining the new circuits.[84] The Act assigned one justice to each circuit and restored the number of justices to six.[85] The Seventh Circuit was established in 1807 for Ohio, Kentucky, and Tennessee, presided over by a seventh justice, Thomas Todd. The various Judiciary Acts set out in precise terms the venues on each circuit at which the court would sit, and the day of the month each sitting was to commence. The circuit courts were to sit twice annually in each district.[86]

The criminal jurisdiction of the federal district court, which was exclusive of the state courts, was limited to crimes against United States law, 'where no other

---

[81] Judiciary Act 1801, Section 3.

[82] ibid, Sections 4 and 7.

[83] Linda K Kerber, *Federalists in Dissent: Imagery and Ideology in Jeffersonian America* (Ithaca: Cornell University Press, 1970), 156.

[84] Starr, the Clerk of the New Hampshire District Court between 1984 and 2014, deals with the precarious position of the 'midnight judges' John Lowell, Benjamin Bourne, and Jeremiah Smith appointed to the First Circuit by President Adams. He writes: 'The entire nation questioned whether these men deserved to hold their positions ... In their two days in New Hampshire they allowed seven continuances [which] may have been due to the tenuousness of their position.' They even had to find a Crier to call on the cases. James R Starr, *History of the New Hampshire Federal Courts* (Clerk's Office of the United States District Court for the District of New Hampshire, 1991), 24.

[85] Judiciary Act 1802, Section 4, 2 Stat 156. President Jefferson nominated his first justice, William Johnson in 1804.

[86] Judiciary Acts of 1789, 1801 and 1802.

punishment than whipping, not exceeding thirty stripes, a fine not exceeding one hundred dollars, or a term of imprisonment not exceeding six months is to be inflicted'. The district court also had exclusive original jurisdiction in civil cases of admiralty and maritime matters which included seizures on the high seas or navigable waters, seizures on land, and for penalties and forfeitures. All cases in the district court except admiralty and maritime matters were to be tried by a jury where issues of fact were to be resolved.[87]

The circuit court had concurrent jurisdiction with the district court in respect of criminal cases but exclusive jurisdiction in all criminal cases carrying greater punishment than that which the district judge could impose.[88] In civil cases the circuit court had concurrent jurisdiction with state courts in what were termed diversity cases, involving citizens of different states or non US citizens, or cases in which the United States was a petitioner and the amount in dispute exceeded $500. In other civil cases the jurisdictions of the circuit and district courts coincided so that litigants could choose where to commence an action. Appeals from district to circuit court in admiralty cases where the disputed amount exceeded $300 and appeals in all other cases where the claim exceeded $50 were by way of a full hearing in which the district judge had no vote but was permitted to record the reasons for his original opinion.[89] The Judiciary Act 1789 delivered the promises of the Federalists during the debates on the bill by giving the states' concurrent jurisdiction with the district and circuit courts in many cases, the state courts retaining jurisdiction on all matters arising under state civil and criminal law.[90]

## 'A Certain Uniformity of Decision in United States Law'

Congress gave little guidance to the justices as the law they should apply to resolve the disputes they encountered. The Constitution extended the judicial power 'to all cases in law and equity, arising under this Constitution, the laws of the United States, and treaties made, or which shall be made, under their authority ... and to all cases of admiralty and maritime jurisdictions'.[91] The jurisdiction of the circuit courts (i.e. the types of cases they were permitted to try) was quite straightforward. The difficulty lay in deciding what laws were to be applied to the cases. Obviously the justices would interpret existing and future treaties, but apart from defining the law of treason, the Constitution was of little help in this regard and the justices awaited legislation from the first Congress. To add to the difficulty, the Supreme Court would not produce a body of precedent for some years to come.

---

[87] Judiciary Act 1789, Section 9.
[88] ibid, Section 11.
[89] ibid, Sections 4, 21 and 22.
[90] ibid, Sections 9 and 11.
[91] United States Constitution, Article III, Section 2.

The Judiciary Act of 1789, whilst not solving the problem, did provide by Section 34 that 'the laws of the several states ... shall be regarded as rules of decision in trials at common law in the courts of the United States in cases where they apply'.[92] Congress was directing the federal courts to apply American law in the shape of state law until sufficient United States statutes and Supreme Court opinions were available for guidance.[93] As Congress was pre-occupied in the early years with essential legislation establishing government departments such as the War Office, the Treasury and a temporary Post Office, very few statutes were passed to aid the justices in the performance of their duties. The primary importance in passing revenue laws meant that a law of secondary importance such as the Crimes Act of 1790 was not enacted until 30 April 1790, one year after Congress first met.[94] Whilst the statute covered the most serious offences such as treason, piracy, murder and arson, and the more prolific crimes of larceny, forgery, perjury and bribery, it did not prohibit all federal criminal activity. Those omissions would present problems for a justice who had no burning desire to fill the vacuum using English common law principles.

The direction in section 34 of the Judiciary Act 1789 to apply state laws to disputes in the federal courts was extremely difficult to comply with because no state at that time had judges who wrote opinions or reporters to record the spoken words. Some states had no statute codes; others had codes which were incomplete. When in 1785 the states were asked to supply copies of all of their statutes to Congress and to the other states they were unable to comply. This meant that the Supreme Court justices began their circuit riding without copies of the local statutes.[95] The federal justices did have the benefit of pre-statehood reports of cases which circulated in manuscript form such as those of Josiah Quincy's Massachusetts Reports between 1761 and 1772 but which were not printed until 1865 and Ephraim Kirby's Connecticut reports commencing in 1789.[96]

---

[92] Judiciary Act 1789, Section 34.

[93] Wilfred J Ritz, edited by Wythe Holt and LH LaRue, *Rewriting the History of the Judiciary Act 1789* (Norman; University of Oklahoma Press, 1990), 148.

[94] An Act for the Punishment of Certain Crimes against the United States in Richard Peters (ed), *The Public Statutes at Large of the United States*, vol 1 (Boston: Charles C Little and James Brown, 1845), 112–19. This volume also contains the Regulations for the Collection of Duties on Tonnage and Merchandise (28) and the Act for Appropriations for the Support of Government (95), examples of essential legislation competing for the attention of Congress.

[95] Ritz, 50–51.

[96] Josiah Quincy Jr, *Reports of Cases Argued and Adjudged in the Superior Court of Judicature of the Province of Massachusetts Bay, Between 1761 and 1772* (Boston: Little, Brown, 1865). Ephraim Kirby, *Reports of Cases Adjudged in the Superior Court of the State of Connecticut, From the Year 1785 to May 1788; with Some Determinations in the Supreme Court of Errors* (Litchfield: Collier and Adams, 1789). Further, lawyers such as Thomas Jefferson, Bushrod Washington, and Edmund Trowbridge of Boston and others collected law reports. For a comprehensive record of pre-statehood statutes and law reports available to the justices see Michael Chiorazzi and M Most, *Prestatehood Legal Materials: A Fifty-State Research Guide: Including New York City and the District of Columbia*, 2 vols (New York: Haworth Information Press, 2005).

In time, the states formalized court hierarchies and established supreme courts with appellate jurisdictions whose opinions were reported, and the statutes of states' legislatures were printed, enabling federal judges to consult state laws when forming their opinions. In the meantime they had little choice but to look to English law for guidance, as the following brief overview demonstrates. A more detailed examination of how each justice found his way will appear in the following chapters.

Justice Washington was one who drew heavily on state laws. Pennsylvania law reports were certainly available by the April 1803 term in Philadelphia when he set aside an arbitration award relying on the opinions of the Chief Justice of the Pennsylvania Supreme Court and the President of Pennsylvania Court of Common Pleas.[97] An examination of all of Justice Washington's circuit opinions show him to be a judge who relied heavily on the opinions of the Pennsylvania superior courts. He expressed his confidence in state sources when writing: 'Although not bound by their decisions, they are and ought to be highly respected.'[98] He admitted being led into error in one case by relying too much on an opinion of the Pennsylvania chief justice.[99] However, the reported circuit opinions of Justice Livingston show almost no reliance on state court opinions. Indeed a feature of his opinions is the absence of citations. Many of his cases are resolved by findings of fact rather than by points of law. The absence of citations may be due to poor reporting as many of his opinions are summaries in the third person, but it may be that, like Marshall and unlike Story, he preferred, wherever possible, not to cite cases, relying on broad principles.

Justice Smith Thompson regularly relied upon state court opinions. It was to be expected that the opinions of the New York Supreme Court would loom large in his federal circuit jurisprudence as he had been an associate justice and later chief justice, serving on that court for 16 years before his appointment to the nation's highest tribunal. A good example of his reliance on state supreme court decisions is his lengthy opinion in *Vermont v The Society for the Propagation of the Gospel* (1827) in which he cited no less than 24 New York State opinions.[100] He, like Story, preferred to support his opinions with cited cases, and this was made easier by the meticulous reporting of William Johnson, New York State's first official law reporter. Unlike the reports of Thompson's federal circuit opinions, Johnson's reports were verbatim transcripts of the opinions delivered and, therefore, much more useful as precedents because the arguments and reasoning were readily apparent.

In the first circuit opinion of Justice Story reported in the *Federal Cases*, his reliance upon state opinions is apparent. In that one case turning on the

---

[97] *Hurst v Hurst*, 12 F Cas 1028, April, 1803.
[98] *Barnes et al v Billington et al*, 2 F Cas 858, April 1803.
[99] *Hylton v Brown*, 12 F Cas 1122, October, 1805.
[100] *Vermont v The Society for the Propagation of the Gospel*, 28 F Cas 1155, 1827.

liability of a common carrier, he cited three opinions of the Supreme Court of the Commonwealth of Massachusetts, two opinions from William Johnson's New York Supreme Court reports, and one opinion of the New Hampshire Superior Court of Justice.[101] Story's circuit cases between 1811 and 1835 show frequent favourable citations of state opinions. It is apparent from surviving federal circuit opinions that the views of state superior courts were important sources to the justices in those early years. They looked for guidance, not only to the superior courts of the states comprising the circuits upon which they sat but also to the state court opinions of other states as shown in the above example of Justice Story's opinion in *Citizens Bank v Nantucket Steamboat Co.*

The circuit opinions of the justices, save for Justice Livingston, show a greater dependence on English law than the assistance afforded by the state superior courts. The lawyers of the early Republic, whether attending university, the Inns of Court in London, or serving as clerks in lawyers offices, had been trained in the principles of the English common law. They had been brought up on a diet of *Blackstone's Commentaries on the Laws of England, Littleton on Coke,* and the major decisions of prominent English jurists.[102] It was, therefore, likely that the justices would lean heavily on English law in the absence of US statute and case law, despite an understandable resistance to the use of English statutes and cases to resolve American disputes, given the suffering under colonial rule before and during the Revolutionary War. A New York law of 1786 declared that the common law was in force in the state but the only English statutes to be applied were those recognised by the colony on April 9, 1775. Yet 12 years later that state prohibited the citation of any such statutes in the state courts and, to further complicate matters, in 1833, a New York court held that certain English statutes had become part of the common law and, as such, were receivable in court.[103]

In 1807 Kentucky went beyond the New York restrictions by banning outright the citation of any English cases decided after the commencement of the Revolution. The following year the chief justice of the Kentucky Court of Appeals enforced the prohibition by refusing counsel permission to read from the report of an English case decided five years earlier.[104] The fear of some states that their legal systems were in danger of being unduly influenced by their former rulers did not extend to the reception of English law in the federal court, whether district, circuit or Supreme Court. On the contrary, the federal court reports show a widespread acceptance of English law by the justices provided it did not infringe the Constitution or existing United States law. This was the case until the end of the Marshall Court era despite the great increase in Supreme Court opinions

---

[101] *Citizens Bank v Nantucket Steamboat Co,* 5 F Cas 719, 1811.
[102] For a table of the education and legal training of Supreme Court Justices see, Epstein *et al, Supreme Court Compendium,* 280–92.
[103] See Lawrence M Friedman, *A History of American Law* (New York: Simon & Schuster, 1973), 93–100 for a discussion of the tensions created by the use of English law.
[104] ibid, 98.

to guide the justices. However, the imported English law had to be relevant and adapted to the needs of many ordinary American citizens who, unlike their European counterparts, had much greater opportunities to purchase land and establish businesses in a country expanding geographically and economically.

As will appear in chapter three, Justice Washington relied heavily on English law throughout his time on circuit. In his very first sitting in Philadelphia in the April 1803 term he was very disappointed to find that there were no English authorities on the point he had to decide.[105] This is a theme which runs through his circuit opinions. He relied frequently on the decisions of Lords, Coke, Stowell, Ellenborough and—his particular favourite—Lord Mansfield. The *Federal Cases* reveal Washington's reliance on legal precedent to support his opinions, and the manner in which he searched for sources.

Justice Livingston's approach to the use of English decisions differed markedly from Washington's practice. Despite having English authorities cited to him by counsel in argument, Livingston often handed down opinions devoid of or with minimal reference to precedent. He expressed high regard for the authority of an English judge in only one of his reported opinions when he referred to Chief Baron of the Exchequer Comyn as 'an authority in himself'.[106] He followed English law or practice in only two of his reported cases. In one case he refused a continuance because the affidavit failed to give the name of the missing witness in accordance with the English practice.[107] In the other he followed decisions of Sir William Scott and Lord Mansfield on an admiralty point.[108] However, as will be observed from chapter four, there are examples of a determination to oust English law in favour of American law and his opinions disclose a certain pride in and a distinct preference for the emerging body of United States law.

Joseph Story's opinions were erudite and displayed a willingness to review the law from all possible sources and from English law in particular. He made this plain in his first term of the Massachusetts circuit court. He was delighted when he found that his own view of a case had been confirmed by a recent English case 'where the subject was very elaborately considered by Lord Denman'. In the same case he cites with approval a treatise on shipping by Lord Tenterden and a decision of Mr Justice Dampier.[109] The following year in an embargo case, Story followed

---

[105] *Dusar v Murgatroyd*, 8 F Cas 140, 1803.
[106] *Slocum et al v Hathaway*, 22 F Cas 339, 1820.
[107] *Smith v Barker*, 22 F Cas 454, Conn, September 1808.
[108] *The Grand Turk*, 10 F Cas 956, 1817. A report of a court case in the *Repertory* (Boston) of 4 February 1815 shows the regard in which Story held Sir William Scott. Mr Attorney Blake, having made a remark in the Circuit Court in some degree impeaching the soundness of an opinion of Sir William Scott, His Honour Judge Story instantly said: 'Stop, Sir, you must be extremely careful in arraigning Sir William Scott. The lawyer or the Judge should be very well satisfied of his own research and accuracy before he should question those of that learned judge ... I doubt whether a single opinion of that learned man can be found not conformable to the established principles of international law.'
[109] *Citizens Bank v Nantucket Steamboat Co*, 5 F Cas 719, 729, 1811. The case turned on the liability of the owners of a steamboat as common carriers of bank bills.

a doctrine of Lord Hale declaring that there could not be any better authority.[110] These two cases early on in Story's judicial life reveal an eagerness to rely upon the English authorities and his opinions in the *Federal Cases* show that this was so throughout his time on the First Circuit. His respect for them never diminished.

In 1825 in a circuit court case involving the court's power to order amendments at common law and by statute, Justice Thompson considered in detail the practice of English judges on amendments, English statutes from Edward III to George I and the decisions arising under them, analogous to United States statutes.[111] Again, the *Federal Cases* show that Thompson regularly relied upon English decisions through to the end of the Marshall Court in 1835 when he had to decide whether admiralty had jurisdiction in an action for salvage for the retaking on land of property captured by pirates, and called in aid Lord Hale's construction of a statute of Henry VIII.[112] It follows, therefore, that, Livingston apart, the four justices were eager to use English law to help them resolve their circuit cases.

That justices generally looked to the same sources for legal precedents meant that they were more likely to achieve consistency of decision making across the circuits. This need for consistency had been recognised before the Judiciary Act of 1789. Supreme Judicial Court Justice David Sewell wrote to the newly elected Senator for Massachusetts, Caleb Strong that 'a certain uniformity of decisions throughout the United States, whether in the federal or State Courts, is an object that may be worthy of consideration'. Sewell would soon have a more than casual interest in the concept of uniformity as he was shortly to be appointed a federal district judge for Massachusetts.[113]

Justices not only looked to state law and English law for guidance: wherever possible they followed each other's circuit opinions. Justice Washington followed a circuit opinion of Justice Story; a decision which was, not surprisingly, affirmed by the Supreme Court in an opinion delivered by Justice Story.[114] Washington again followed an opinion of Justice Story in a patent case.[115] In a case involving the circulation of banknotes, Washington followed not only one of his own circuit opinions but also an opinion from the circuit court of the District of Columbia.[116] Washington held Chief Justice Marshall in the highest regard and, in 1827, relied upon Marshall's opinion on the admissibility of evidence in the trial for treason of former Vice-President Aaron Burr, which Washington used in a counterfeiting trial on circuit.[117] He also valued the opinion of Justice Todd and followed his opinion

---

[110] *The Bolina*, 3 F Cas 811, 812, 1812.

[111] *Smith v Jackson*, 22 F Cas 576, 577–578, 1825.

[112] *Davidson v Seal-Skins*, 7 F Cas 192, 194, 1835.

[113] Letter, David Sewell to Caleb Strong, 28 March 1789 (Caleb Strong Manuscripts, Forbes Library, Northampton, Mass). Reprinted in Wythe Holt, 'To Establish Justice: Politics, the Judiciary Act of 1789, and the Invention of the Federal Courts' (1989) 6 *Duke Law Journal* 1421–1531 at 1529.

[114] *Evans v Hettick*, 8 F Cas 861, 1818. Affirmed, 7 Wheat (20 US) 453 (1822).

[115] *Treadwell et al v Bladen*, 24 F Cas 144, 1827. Story's opinion was in *Goodyear v Matthews* (Case No 5576, F Cas).

[116] *Martin v The Bank of the United States*, 16 F Cas 885, 1821.

[117] *United States v Moses*, 27 F Cas 5, 1827.

in a Kentucky banking case, expressing himself entirely satisfied and concurring entirely with Todd's view of the law.[118] Thus Washington sought consistency by following the circuit opinions of his brethren despite the fact that they were not binding upon him. However, it was not always one-way traffic. He did comment helpfully on other justice's opinions.[119]

Justice Livingston also wished for consistency of decisions across the nation and would look to the decisions of his brethren on circuit to achieve this objective. In 1810 in New York when trying an alleged breach of the embargo, he expressed his high regard for the opinions of Justice Washington writing that they 'would always receive the most respectful consideration from this court'.[120] He did, however, point out the difficulties he sometimes faced when opinions from other circuits were cited to him because of the absence of a full report which meant he was unable to discern the arguments advanced and the reasoning behind the opinion.[121] A justice was unlikely to follow the fact of a decision of another court without knowing the basis of the opinion, so the absence of accurate and available law reports hampered but did not defeat the justices' desire for uniformity of opinions. In the same year in another embargo case, this time in Connecticut, Livingston held over the amount of penalty because he wanted to learn the practice in the circuit courts of New York and Virginia where similar actions had been brought.[122] This is another example of a justice looking to the wider picture, concerned not merely to establish patterns on his own circuit, but determined to achieve, as a member of a team, nationwide uniformity of law and practice.

In *Adams v Story* (1817), Livingston acknowledged the right of each state to pass insolvency and bankruptcy laws but made the point that in a country as extensive as the United States, those laws should be uniform, so that none of the larger 'commercial' states should be without a code on the subject. He believed that Congress should determine such a uniform plan displacing state legislation. He also expressed regret that the issue had not yet received a decision of the Supreme Court which would have 'produced a uniformity of judgment, at least in the courts of the United States'.[123] Although Justice Story was a staunch supporter of consistency across circuits the *Federal Cases* reveal that he rarely cited circuit opinions other than his own.

Justice Smith Thompson was also keen to follow the circuit opinions of the other justices where appropriate. There are numerous examples of this in the *Federal Cases*. He followed Justice Story in *The Mary* (1824) and in *United States v Sturges et al* (1826). In the latter case, he made express reference to the importance

---

[118] *Bank of the United States v Northumberland Union and Columbia Bank*, 4 Peters 108, 1821.
[119] In 1825 he commented favourably on a number of opinions which Justice Smith Thompson (a new boy on the Court) had sent for his attention. Letter, 6 October 1825. Bushrod Washington to Smith Thompson in Papers of George Washington, Reel #3, Mount Vernon Archives.
[120] *The Enterprise*, 8 F Cas 732, 736, 1810.
[121] ibid, 736.
[122] *United States v Allen*, 24 F Cas 772, 1810.
[123] *Adams v Story*, 1 F Cas 141, 148, 1817.

of consistency when he wrote, 'By finding the point directly adjudicated upon in one of the courts of co-ordinate jurisdiction with this, I shall adopt it as governing the present case. It is of the highest importance that there should be uniformity of decision in the construction of statutes.'[124] Further, in 1829, when holding that the federal courts had power to make rules of practice under the Judiciary Act 1789, Thompson followed two circuit opinions—those of Justices Washington and Story.[125]

Lest it be thought that all justices were eager to follow others' opinions, Justice William Johnson was not always so co-operative. He was, on occasion, unwilling to accept even the authority of the Supreme Court. In a dissent in 1828 Johnson angrily complained when the majority held that the circuit court in a trial by jury had no power to compel a plaintiff to submit to a non-suit (i.e. to force a plaintiff to abandon his claim against the defendant). Johnson protested against 'the right of forcing upon my circuit, the practice of other circuits' pointing out that 'I can never know the practice of my own circuit until I come here to learn it'.[126] Clearly he was unhappy that a practice which he had adopted on his circuit was not one which the Court could endorse. One question which divided the justices on circuit and which did not advance consistency was whether United States law recognised a common law of crime; this will be investigated fully in chapter four.

Consistency and collegiality was also achieved by conversations between justices when together in Washington and by correspondence when apart on circuit. This exchange of information was crucial to the decision-making process. It also had a large part to play in relation to circuit business. The justices boarded in the same lodging-house in Washington, which facilitated their ability to decide cases promptly as they discussed the day's oral arguments; they often reached decisions during the evening. This collegiality engendered a spirit of friendship and co-operation which is revealed in Story's letters to Nathaniel Williams and Samuel Fay set out in the Introduction and is also shown in the correspondence between justices exchanging circuit news and seeking and receiving advice on difficult points of law.

## Conclusion

The federal judicial system had troubled beginnings. From the outset, Federalists contended with determined political opposition at the Constitutional Convention, various ratification conventions and the debates during the passage of the Judiciary Act 1879. Whilst the Act successfully negotiated the Congress, reasonable Anti-Federalist fears remained that a federal judiciary would so interpret the

---

[124] *The Mary*, 16 F Cas 938, 941: *United States v Sturges et al*, 27 F Cas 1358, 1362, 1826.
[125] *Koning v Bayard Jr et al*, 14 F Cas 843, 845.
[126] *Doe on the Demise of Elmore v Goymes*, 26 US (1 Pet), 469.

Constitution so as to strengthen the power of central government at the expense of state sovereignty.

President Washington's nomination of Supreme Court justices who were notable and experienced lawyers from different parts of the country and who had played a significant role in the ratification of the Constitution went a long way towards ensuring a positive reception of federal law regionally. Local people were more likely to accept the concept of federal justice if judges visited the main cities on circuit so that they might observe, first-hand, federal justice at work, or read of the justice's activities in the local press.

The justices had both a judicial and political function on circuit. First, they administered criminal law and tried civil claims. Second, they promoted the concept of federal government locally, attempting to forge a bond between government and citizen using the grand jury charge at the beginning of each circuit session to extol the virtues of the Constitution and the institutions it had established. The reception the charge met depended very much on where it was delivered. That political element of the charge was much in evidence during the first decade of the federal courts, but after its misuse by Justice Chase leading to his impeachment in 1804, it was used merely to direct the grand jury on the law relating to matters relevant to the cases they were to try.

The Alien & Sedition Acts of 1798, rigorously enforced by the federal judiciary, were ostensibly designed to combat revolutionary fervour arising from events in France but were also used to restrict criticism of the Federalist government. Those unpopular measures resulted in the Republican-led Virginia and Kentucky Resolutions of 1798 and 1799 asserting the right of states to disregard federal legislation which they deemed unconstitutional. This heavy-handed statutory denial of freedom of speech and of the Press was a factor in the defeat of President John Adams. The election of President Jefferson in 1801 did little to advance the popularity of the federal justices.

The justices realised how vulnerable they were when President Jefferson repealed that part of President Adams' 1801 Judiciary Act creating 16 'Federalist' circuit judges, thereby restoring their circuit riding duties. The 1802 Act also suspended sittings of the Supreme Court for over a year. Whilst the Court in 1803, in *Marbury v Madison*, asserted the power to judicially review acts of Congress, the justices generally kept a low profile, avoiding a direct confrontation with President Jefferson as was demonstrated by their meek acceptance in, *Stuart v Laird*, of the reintroduction of circuit riding. The actions of a powerful majority in Congress hampered, certainly during President Jefferson's two terms, the Court's desire to play a more active role in government.

The justices went on circuit with no specific guidance as to the approach they should adopt to achieve the uniform system of federal law and procedure essential to the stability of the emerging nation. They were left very much to their own devices. They did not start with a clean slate because many years of British rule had left their mark on the legal systems of individual states. There were few Supreme Court opinions and hardly any federal statutes to guide them so they looked to other sources to fashion American law pending a greater output of federal legislation and Supreme Court authorities. Meanwhile, they sought uniformity in the decisions of state supreme courts, each other's circuit opinions, and, in particular, the English common law. Consistency was achieved by exchanges of ideas when together in Washington and by writing to each other on circuit seeking help on unfamiliar branches of law together with exchanges of semi-annual reports of interesting cases between Justices Washington and Story. In this way the justices achieved the uniformity of law and procedure essential to the stability of the vast areas administered by the federal government.

# 3

# Bushrod Washington: The Role of Precedent and the Preservation of Vested Interests

Joseph Story's eulogy at the death of his close friend and colleague Bushrod Washington described him as 'a good old fashioned Federalist' with a 'cautious mind' who was 'distinguished for moderation.' Story added,

> He indulged not the rash desire to fashion the law to his own views ... Hence, he possessed the happy facility of yielding the just the proper weight to authority; neither, on the one hand, surrendering himself to the dictates of other judges, nor, on the other hand, overruling settled doctrines upon his own private notions of policy or justice.[1]

It was appropriate that Justice Story should touch upon the part played by legal precedent in Washington's jurisprudence because it is a doctrine apparent even from a cursory examination of his circuit and Supreme Court opinions. District Judge Joseph Hopkinson's eulogium on Washington was similarly even-handed by praising Washington as 'respectful of the authority of decided cases but equally careful and discriminating in applying them'.[2]

However, an in-depth analysis of the justice's opinions reveals a constant search for precedent to underpin his opinions and a feeling of unease when having to break new ground. Whilst recognising the sometimes over-fulsome praise of valued colleagues and friends, the eulogies are a useful starting position from which to open up the debate about the source of legal authority in the early Republic and invite an investigation to reveal this justice's part in the creation, on circuit, of a uniform body of federal law and procedure. It is interesting that Story and Hopkinson, whilst not suggesting that it dominated his jurisprudence, should both raise Washington's approach to the doctrine of precedent.

Washington's role in the shaping of American law was founded in the expertise gained whilst presiding over the United States Third Circuit between 1803 and 1829.[3] The main thrust of the inquiry involves an examination of his belief in the

---

[1] Joseph Story, Eulogy on Justice Washington, December 1829 in WW Story, *Life and Letters*, vol 2 (Boston: Litte Brown, 1851) 29–33.
[2] Joseph Hopkinson, *In Commemoration of the Hon Bushrod Washington, Late one of the Justices of the Supreme Court of the United States* (Philadelphia: TS Manning, 1830), 16.
[3] On 20 December 1798, Washington was confirmed by the Senate as an Associate Justice of the United States Supreme Court. After riding for short periods on the Southern, Middle, Eastern, and

need for uniformity which flowed from adherence to legal precedents. By far the most important factor in Washington's jurisprudence was his strict application of the doctrine of precedent.

A conservative Federalist, Washington upheld existing property rights and endeavoured to secure the nation's economic prosperity by promoting interstate and international trade. This aspect of Federalist philosophy was a significant stabilising factor in which precedent featured strongly. The quest for uniformity, the preservation of property rights and the advancement of trade becomes apparent upon an analysis of his circuit court and Supreme Court opinions. His work on circuit has been largely neglected by scholars despite the fact that the available opinions are far more numerous than his Supreme Court majority holdings and, therefore, admit a greater insight into his jurisprudence and political outlook. Two further aspects of his jurisprudence are highlighted, namely his personal and judicial approach to the issue of slavery and the way in which he dealt with the tension between central government powers and state sovereignty.

## A Federalist's Journey from Revolutionary Virginia to the Supreme Court

Bushrod Washington was born into the colonial aristocracy in Bushfield, Virginia on 5 June 1762. His father, John, was President George Washington's younger brother and his privileged position enabled him to send his son to the prestigious William and Mary College from which he graduated A.B. in 1778.[4] He also studied law at the college, attending the lectures of George Wythe, and there met John Marshall; the beginning of a lifelong friendship at the Bar and on the Supreme Court Bench.[5] That friendship was strengthened by their collaboration on the

---

Second Circuits, he went to the Third Circuit on 3 March 1803 where he remained for 26 years. His return to the Third Circuit coincided with the conferment on him of the title Doctor of Laws from the College of New Jersey at Princeton (*Trenton Federalist*, 18 April 1803). Stephen B Presser has written the excellent, *Studies in the History of United States Courts of the Third Circuit, 1790–1980* (Washington DC: Bicentennial Committee of the United States, 1982). However, other than to note Washington's assignment to the Third Circuit on 1 July 1802, the studies do not cover the period of the justice's tenure. The focus is on the District Judges and, in particular, during the early years, District Judge Richard Peters. There are comprehensive accounts of the parts played by other Supreme Court Justices on circuit in the Fries and Whiskey Rebellion trials and the Alien & Sedition prosecutions of the 1790s.

[4] He was always very close to his uncle, visiting him regularly at Mount Vernon, keeping him informed of his progress and receiving valuable advice and financial support. He adopted his uncle's family motto and coat of arms '*Exitus Acta Probat*' (The outcome justifies the deed). See the justice's bookplate in the Bushrod Washington Papers, David M Reubenstein Rare Books and Manuscript Library, Duke University, Durham, North Carolina.

[5] Many of the more affluent pre-Revolution American law students completed their legal education at the Inns of Court in London, Middle Temple being the Inn of choice for the majority. See, Stockdale and Holland, *Middle Temple Lawyers and the American Revolution* (Eagan, Minnesota: Thomson

mammoth five-volume *Life of George Washington* written by John Marshall using the President's papers held by his nephew.[6] Although Marshall wrote the biography, Washington spent a great deal of time collating the papers before sending them to his colleague.[7]

Having enlisted as a private during the Revolutionary War, Washington witnessed the surrender of General Cornwallis at Yorktown. After the war, supported financially by his uncle, he studied law in Philadelphia in the offices of James Wilson who was to be one of President Washington's first appointees to the Supreme Court. Washington began his law practice in Westmoreland County, Alexandria and later moved to Richmond specialising in chancery cases. Politically active in the Federalist cause, he was elected to the Virginia House of Delegates in 1787, supporting the adoption of the Constitution at the ratification convention the following year.

Despite stiff competition in Richmond from outstanding advocates such as John Marshall and Patrick Henry, Washington's practice grew. His own *Virginia Court of Appeals Reports* reveal that between 1792 and 1796 he had appeared as counsel in approximately one-quarter of the 149 reported cases. Having acted in several matters for his uncle, his reputation was such as to persuade Thomas Jefferson to instruct him in a chancery suit.[8] Horace Binney, a noted advocate, described Washington's practice at the Bar as 'mainly on the Chancery side with a good grounding in common law, but no experience of commercial law or

---

West, 2007), In his Foreword to the book (xv–xvi) The Honorable John G Roberts Jr, Chief Justice of the United States (himself an Honorary Bencher of Middle Temple) observes that by the time of the American Revolution, 'more than 100 American-born lawyers could call themselves Middle Templars [including] five signers of the Declaration of Independence, the president of the first Continental Congress, four of the drafters of the Articles of Confederation, and seven drafters of the Constitution'. The strong link between the Inn and America continues, evidenced by the Honorary Call to the Bench in 2016 of the then Attorney-General of the United States, Loretta Lynch. See also, Anthony Arlidge QC, *The Lawyers Who Made America* (Oxford and Portland, Oregon: Hart Publishing, 2017) for a general overview on the influence of English law throughout American legal history.

[6] There is a detailed account of the writing of the work, publication and distribution problems, the financial aspects, how the books were received by politicians and the general public in Jean Edward Smith's *John Marshall: Definer of a Nation* (New York: Henry Holt & Company Inc, 1996), 328–34. According to the *Weekly Museum* of 30 June 1804, 'Mr Philips, Bookseller, of St. Paul's Churchyard, London, has given the Hon. Bushrod Washington fifteen hundred guineas for the English copy-right of the life of his illustrious Uncle ... Seventy thousand dollars were given for the American copy-right!' The President had bequeathed to his nephew all his civil, military, and personal papers and all his books and pamphlets should his wife Martha not want them. Will, 9 July 1799 (George Washington Papers at Mount Vernon).

[7] Writing on 16 September 1801 to the courier who was to deliver to John Marshall trunks containing the Presidents papers, Washington remarked that he would 'devote this winter to arranging & compiling [the papers] so as to assist the Chief Justice and hasten the work'. Harvard Law School Library, Bushrod Washington, Small Manuscript Collection.

[8] Jefferson had an urgent problem. His neighbour below was raising a dam which would result in the drowning of Jefferson's millseat. Washington was urged to obtain an injunction 'without a moment's delay that can be avoided'. Letter, Thomas Jefferson to Bushrod Washington, 23 September 1795 in John Catanzaritu (ed), *Papers of Thomas Jefferson*, vol 28, (Princeton: Princeton University Press, 2000), 479–80.

jury trials'.⁹ He gained expertise in land disputes and his written opinion in such a claim between a father and family members delivered shortly before he went on the Bench is brief and decisive.[10]

Although his practice grew he did struggle financially from time to time. In November 1788 he wrote to his uncle that he might be sued for £1,000 as executor of his father's estate—the amount of a bond which his father had given to cover the liability of a family member whose executor, another family member, was refusing to honour.[11] Later the same month he informed his uncle that he intended to give up the plantation and focus on his law career. He explained that he could not do justice to both. A factor in the decision was the need to pay £2,000 to clear his father's debts, which meant selling slaves and personal property. His uncle agreed with that proposed course of action.[12] Further, in 1804, Washington wrote to a friend, greatly embarrassed, requesting money to repay a loan he had taken out when moving to Mount Vernon to furnish the house and buy farm machinery. His wheat crop and fishery had failed. He offered to pay interest on the loan, although he mentioned the fact that she had refused to take interest on a previous loan.[13] In 1804 his salary as an Associate Supreme Court Justice was $3,500 per annum.[14]

Justice Washington was a deeply religious man, a life-long member of the Episcopal Church of the United States, leading morning and evening prayers at Mount Vernon. Binney believed that Washington was sustained in his private life and public duties by a constant observance of his religious beliefs.[15] He had been active on behalf of his church as an advocate, successfully resisting Virginia's attempts to seize church lands.[16] He was also a vice-president and charter member of the American Bible Society, attending its meetings, and taking great interest in its work.[17] Casper (2008) believes that it was his religious beliefs which led him to become President of the American Colonisation Society in 1816, which was committed to creating African colonies of freed slaves. In 1820 Washington explained the objective of the Society as 'an instrument in the conversion of Africans to Christianity' in order to establish 'the kingdom of the Messiah in every quarter of the globe.'[18] The venture was open to the criticism that the objectives

---

[9] Horace Binney, *Bushrod Washington* (Philadelphia: C Sherman & Son, 1858), 11–12. Library of Congress (MARCXML).

[10] Mr Washington's Opinion. Richmond, 24 March 1798, Harvard Law School Library, Bushrod Washington, 1762–1829, Letters and Legal Opinion, Small Manuscript Collection.

[11] Letter, 9 November 1788, Bushrod Washington to George Washington (Mount Vernon Archives).

[12] Letter, 20 November 1788, Bushrod Washington to George Washington. Reply, 25 November 1788 (Mount Vernon Archives).

[13] Letter, 10 May 1804, Bushrod Washington to Elizabeth Willing Power (Mount Vernon Archives).

[14] Federal Judicial Center, History of the Federal Judiciary, Salaries.

[15] Binney at 27.

[16] Albert P Blaustein, and Roy M Mersky, 'Bushrod Washington' in Friedman and Israel, *The Justices of the United States Supreme Court, 1789–1969* (New York: Chelsea House Publishers, 1969), 247.

[17] Bushrod C Washington, 'The Late Mr Justice Bushrod Washington' *The Green Bag*, vol IX, No 8 (Boston, August 1897), 334.

[18] Scott E Casper, *Sarah Johnson's Mount Vernon* (New York: Hill and Wang, 2008), 13–15, citing Bushrod Washington, 'The People of Color' (1897) 11 *Niles Weekly Register*, 25 January 1817, 355–56, and Adam Hodgson, *Letters from North America* (London: Hurst, Robinson & Co, 1824), 15–17.

were impossible in view of the large numbers involved or that it was a device to rid the nation of potentially troublesome former slaves.[19]

Washington did not find his deep religious convictions incompatible with his ownership of slaves, whom he regarded as property to be disposed of as and when he thought fit. Like Justice William Johnson of South Carolina, he was born into a slave-owning family and inherited the family plantation and 42 slaves from his father in 1787.[20] When he inherited Mount Vernon from his uncle in 1802, Washington brought with him those slaves he had retained.[21] George Washington had declared that the 123 slaves he owned were to be freed upon the death of his wife Martha. However, his nephew persuaded Martha to free them immediately because of security concerns. A series of suspicious fires at Mount Vernon after George Washington's death convinced Martha and her family that the slaves were restless and they were granted freedom on 1 January 1801.[22] It is also likely that 'Gabriel's Conspiracy' in August 1800, when 26 slaves were hanged after a failed plot to take control of Richmond by force, had a bearing on the decision to free the late President's slaves.[23] In the event, many of the freed slaves remained at Mount Vernon where food, clothing, shelter, and medical care were available.[24] They would have had little choice given the unlikely prospect of successful independent living.

Contemporary attitudes towards slavery are much in evidence from the following extract from *The Times, and Hartford Advertiser* of 23 March 1824 under the heading, 'A Novel Case'.

> The House of Delegates in Virginia, on the 4th inst. had under consideration a novel and interesting case. A letter from Governor Pleasants to the House, relative to an infant born in State Penitentiary of an enslaved mother under sentence of death, had been referred to

---

[19] According to the United States Census Bureau, the 1810 census revealed that out of a total United States population of 5,660,067, there were living predominately in the Southern States 1,005,685 slaves and 167,691 'free non-whites'. Available at: http://faculty.weber.edu/kmackay/statistics_on_slavery.htm. The Sixteenth Annual Report of the American Society for Colonizing the Free People of Color of the United States was considered by the *American Monthly Review*, vol 4 (1833) at 283, which whilst observing that some members wished for better conditions for the freed slaves, suggested that others, for purely selfish reasons, desired to be rid of a troublesome population and thereby render themselves more secure as masters.

[20] Donald Morgan, 'William Johnson' in Friedman & Israel, *Justices*, 356.

[21] President Washington bequeathed Mount Vernon to his nephew because he had promised it to his father for looking after the estate during the Revolutionary War. Will dated 9 July 1799 (George Washington Papers at Mount Vernon).

[22] See www.mountvernon.org/george-washington/martha-washington/martha-washington-slavery/. According to the *Spectator* (New York) of 12 May 1804, there was a further act of arson at Mount Vernon a few days earlier which caused the judge to adjourn his circuit sitting and return home. Writing to Judge Richard Peters on 21 May 1804, Washington said 'it is obvious that it was the work of an incendiary' but he was unable to say who. He had no proof that it was one of his 'domestics' as they all exerted themselves to extinguish the blaze which caused great damage. He concluded, 'I shall not feel entirely at ease until some discovery is made.' Papers of George Washington, Reel #3. Mount Vernon Archives.

[23] See, Douglas R Egerton, *Gabriel's Rebellion: The Virginia Slave Conspiracies of 1800 and 1802* (Chapel Hill: University of North Carolina Press, 1993).

[24] David L Annis, *Bushrod Washington* (University of Notre Dame, August 1974). (PhD), 202.

the Committee for "Courts of Justice." The committee, upon due consideration, reported the following resolution. *Resolved*, as the opinion of this committee, That the Executive cause the said child to be sold, and the money arising from the sale, to be deposited, as public funds, in the treasury of the commonwealth. After the reading of the Resolution, Mr Thompson of Fairfax offered the following resolutions as substitutes, *Resolved*, that the child is free. *Resolved*, That the Executive cause the same to be bound apprentice to some humane tradesman, till it shall attain the age of 21 years. A motion by Mr O'd, to substitute the following Resolution, was determined in the affirmative. "*Resolved*, as the opinion of this Committee, that the said child is the property of Bushrod Washington, the owner of the woman at the time of her condemnation."

In 1821 Washington sold 54 of his slaves from Mount Vernon to pay for losses incurred in the running of the estate. The story of the sale appeared in the influential Baltimore newspaper *Niles Weekly Register* which criticised him for selling the slaves as if they were 'hogs or cattle' and accusing him of dividing families. Washington's reply in the *Baltimore Federal Republican* revealed the mind-set of the typical slave-owner, questioning the right of any person to criticise what he perceived as his legal and moral right to sell his property. He did not feel obliged to free his slaves just because his uncle had done so and did not free his slaves in his will.[25] Despite expressing an abhorrence of the slave trade, Washington's opinions examined later in this chapter reveal a pattern of upholding the rights of the 'owners' of those Africans already held as slaves in the United States.

## Justice Washington and the Role of Precedent in the Federal Legal System

John Marshall, having declined the vacancy on the death of Justice Wilson, the Senate confirmed the nomination of President Adams and Washington went to the United States Supreme Court on 20 December 1798.[26] At 36, he was the youngest man to be appointed to the Court until the elevation of William Johnson in 1804 and Joseph Story in 1812, both of whom were 32. Story holds the record as the

---

[25] ibid, 198–203. Washington's response was taken up by several newspapers. The full letter appears in the *New York Spectator* of 28 September 1821. One of a number of explanations given for the sale of the slaves was that he 'had good reason for anticipating the escape of all the labouring men of any value to the northern states as soon as I leave home', pointing out that 'During my last circuit, and soon after my return, three of them eloped without the pretence of a cause—one of them, a valuable cook, is at this time a fugitive in one of the northern states; the other two were retaken on their way to Pennsylvania—but I had to pay about $250 on these accounts.'

[26] He had had to wait nine years for a federal appointment. His approach to his uncle in 1789 seeking an appointment as attorney to the federal district court had been refused as the President feared charges of nepotism if he overlooked far more experienced candidates. Letter, George Washington to Bushrod Washington, 27 July 1789 (Mount Vernon Archives) and *The Papers of George Washington Digital Edition* (Charlottesville: University of Virginia Press, 2008).

youngest-ever appointee; he was two months younger than Johnson when confirmed by the Senate. Washington feared that his uncle would be unhappy with his decision to go the Supreme Court as he had wanted him to run for Congress, but the President wrote that he was 'perfectly right in accepting the appointment ...'[27] Washington thereafter confined himself to his work on circuit and on the Court but was not averse to contacting influential friends to promote legislation which the Supreme Court supported.[28]

Washington's recognition of the importance of case law is shown by his compilation of two volumes of Virginia Court of Appeal case reports in the early part of his law practice.[29] He gathered them for his own use for citing in court, not with a view to publication.[30] The most striking aspect of his jurisprudence is this search for and reliance upon precedent which is well illustrated by his circuit opinion in *United States v Bright* (1809) when he wrote,

> Miserable indeed, must be the condition of the community where the law is unsettled, and decisions on the very point are disregarded, when they come up again, directly or incidentally into discussion ... There is no standard by which the rights of property, and the most estimable privileges to which citizens are entitled, can be regulated.[31]

This observation reveals his vision of a federal legal system founded upon a strict adherence to precedent to ensure that citizens would have some idea of the prospects of success in litigation as well as knowing their rights and obligations under the law. The preservation of 'rights of property' and 'privileges' as well as the promotion of commerce loomed large in Federalist philosophy and had its origins in James Madison's *Federalist Paper No. 10* in which 'the protection of the faculties of men from which the rights of property arise is the first object of government'.[32] This preoccupation with the preservation of vested rights and the promotion of commerce is a common thread running through the opinions of all four justices.

In 1765, Blackstone, in the first volume of his *Commentaries*, spoke of 'the rule of precedent as one of general application' and 'an established rule to abide by former precedents, where the same points come again in litigation' making it clear that a judge should not act according to his own private view of a case and

---

[27] Letter, 19 October, 1798, Bushrod Washington to George Washington. Reply, 24 October 1798. *George Washington Papers*—Mount Vernon Archives.

[28] On 7 January 1817, Washington wrote to his lawyer colleague and friend Joseph Hopkinson, the Member of the US House of Representatives from Pennsylvania First District, hoping that the Judiciary Bill would come to a satisfactory conclusion reminding him that 'the Judges of the S.C. depend mainly upon your support, knowing that you approved the plan'. He then went on to ask that the Judicial Bill be pressed forward, ('the same which we read over in my room'). Harvard Law School Library, Bushrod Washington, Small Manuscript Collection.

[29] Bushrod Washington, *Reports of Cases Argued and Determined in the Court of Appeals of Virginia*, 2 vols. (Richmond: Nicholson, 1798).

[30] Charles F Hobson, 'St George Tucker's Papers' (2006) 47(4) *William and Mary Law Review* 1250–51.

[31] *United States v Bright*, 24 F Cas 1232, 1809.

[32] James Madison (Publius), *Federalist Paper No 10, 1788* in Clinton Rossiter (ed), *The Federalist Papers* (New York: Signet Classic, 2003), 73.

that precedent was essential because it secured stability in the law. He set out one exception to an otherwise inflexible rule and that was where an 'authority was contrary to reason or divine law'.[33] Alexander Hamilton was another who believed that judges should be bound by strict rules and precedents defining their duty in every case they tried. Writing in 1788 he anticipated a large volume of precedents which would require men of skill and integrity to master so many opinions. This argument gave support to the need for security of tenure for the few who would undertake such an arduous task. It would have been difficult, if not impossible for a federal justice to master a large body of authorities if his tenure was fixed for a short term, or determinable at the will of the legislature or electorate.[34]

Achieving a balance between precedent as a crucial element of stability and the injustice which might flow from the slavish adherence to a doubtful authority is a question which has troubled judges since the early days of the federal judicial system. Any prior decision which is prima facie absurd or is shown by subsequent evidence to have been based on a false premise must be reviewed. However, it is difficult to justify the re-examination of a case without a compelling reason. The difficulty lies in drawing the line. Justice Thurgood Marshall identifies the certainty which results from adherence to precedent in his dissent in *Payne v Tennessee* (1991), expressing the view that fidelity to precedent was fundamental 'to a society governed by the rule of law ... if governing standards are open to revision in every case, deciding cases becomes a mere exercise of judicial will'. He argues that if the doctrine of precedent was weakened, it would destroy the Court's power to resolve disputes between those with power and those without.[35]

Despite refusing to follow the Court's opinion in *House v Mayo*, 324 US 42 (1945) because the rule it enunciated had been frequently disregarded in the past it was Justice Kennedy, writing for the majority in *Hohn v United States*, who observed that *stare decisis* 'is the preferred course because it promotes the even-handed, predictable, and consistent development of legal principle, fosters reliance on judicial decisions and contributes to the perceived integrity of the judicial process'.[36]

Lee (1999) examines how the doctrine of precedent was applied in the Marshall Court. He finds tension between the importance of following past decisions to preserve stability and certainty in the law and the common law declaratory theory which permitted some examination of the prior decision. He concludes that the Marshall Court sought to resolve the tension by a strong presumption in favour of precedent with a limited notion of the right to correct past errors.[37] He records the

---

[33] William Blackstone, *Commentaries on the Laws of England*, First ed, vol 1 (Oxford: Clarenden Press, 1765–69), 69–70.

[34] Alexander Hamilton, Federalist Paper No 78 (The Judiciary Department) in C Rossiter, *The Federalist Papers* (New York: Signet Classics, 2003) 470.

[35] Cited in Harold J Spaeth and Jeffrey Segal, *Majority Rule or Minority Will* (Cambridge: Cambridge University Press, 1999), 6–7.

[36] *Hohn v United States*, 524 US 236, 251 (1998).

[37] Thomas R Lee, 'Stare Decisis in Historical Perspective: From the Founding Era to the Rehnquist Court' (1999) 52 *Vanderbilt Law Review* 666–86.

Chief Justice's reluctance to cite authorities even when they supported his argument, often preferring a lengthy analytical discussion of the merits before reaching a conclusion. Lee highlights Washington's deference to precedent in *Ogden v Saunders* (1827). Some eight years earlier in *Sturges v Crowninshield*, Washington had concurred in an opinion which had upheld the power of state legislatures to pass bankruptcy laws even though he believed that that power was vested exclusively in Congress. He did so because he believed that dissent weakened the authority of the Court. When the point arose again in *Ogden*, Washington felt compelled to follow *Sturges* even though his private view of the correctness of the original opinion had not altered.[38] Blaustein and Merskey (1969) when dealing with Washington's opinion in *Ogden* concluded that his respect for precedent tended to make him choose the narrower of any two interpretations.[39]

This examination of Washington's opinions supports the view that he went out of his way to seek precedent from any source, feeling vulnerable to appeal without authorities to underpin his opinions. He relied on precedent even though, on occasion, he anticipated it might result in an injustice. He acknowledged this in *Scriba v Insurance Co of North America* (1807) when declaring, 'We have nothing to do but pronounce the law without considering how it may affect the parties on either side.'[40] He took the same line in *Kirkpatrick v White et al.* (1826) holding that he had no option but to follow the rules of law and equity and refuse jurisdiction, again stressing that it was not for him to consider the consequences of his decision.[41]

His opinions also demonstrate a strict and restrictive approach to the application of statutory interpretation; all flowing from a philosophy in which caution and the preservation of the status quo outweigh the risk of an innovative solution meeting the justice of a case. Justice Story's description of Washington as a man with a 'cautious mind' who was 'distinguished for his moderation' accurately summarised his colleague's jurisprudence. Whilst deference to precedent has the obvious benefit of making future decisions more predictable, too rigid an approach to the doctrine may perpetuate injustice. Duxbury (2008) suggests that 'constant recourse to precedent might indicate that a decision maker has few or no other solutions at his disposal [or] might betray a fondness for the easy option or an unwillingness to think seriously about what is at stake'.[42] That comment fits Washington's approach to precedent rather well.

Washington displayed such a rigid approach to precedent in *Croudson & Ors v Leonard* (1808) when, relying on English authorities, he held that the sentence

---

[38] ibid at 673. *Sturges v Crowninshield*, 17 US 122, 1819. *Ogden v Saunders*, 25 US 213, 1827.
[39] Blaustein & Merskey, 256.
[40] *Scriba v Insurance Co of North America*, 21 F Cas 874, Penn, October 1807.
[41] *Kirkpatrick v White et al*, 14 F Cas 685, Penn, April 1826. For further examples of Washington's seemingly indifferent attitude to the consequences of his opinions see *Beardsley v Torry* 2 F Cas 1188, Penn, October 1822 and *New Jersey v Babcock*, 18 F Cas 82, New Jersey, April 1823.
[42] Neil Duxbury, *The Nature and Authority of Precedent* (Cambridge: Cambridge University Press, 2008), 31.

of a Barbados admiralty court condemning a vessel and cargo was conclusive evidence against the insured, proving that he had falsified his warranty of neutrality, thereby forfeiting his insurance cover. He believed that he was bound by the legal principle which upheld the decisions of all admiralty courts of competent jurisdiction, despite accepting that such a strict adherence to precedent might prove oppressive to citizens of neutral nations; he felt it was a matter for government to remedy the mischief not the judges.[43] Because it is not possible to detect a general judicial philosophy from just two Supreme Court opinions, his reported circuit court opinions have been examined to ascertain whether his strict adherence to *stare decisis* in *Ogden* and in *Croudson* were isolated examples of his practice or comprised a pattern of rigid compliance.

Washington looked to federal and state precedents to support his opinions on circuit, but those reports also reveal a significant reliance on the reported cases of the English judges, many of whom he held in the highest regard. He did, however, distinguish between English decisions pre and post the Revolution. In *Crawford et al v The William Penn* (1819) he rejected the Exchequer case of *Anton v Fisher* because 'it was decided long after our Declaration of Independence, and even after the treaty of peace; and is, therefore, not to be considered an authority in the courts of this country, so as to overrule the decision in *Ricord v Bettenham* [an English case] of 1765.'[44] Washington again voiced respect for English law in *Barnes v Billingham* (1803) commenting favourably on state supreme court and federal circuit court opinions which were 'in perfect unison with the English decisions.'[45] Lord Mansfield was a particular favourite whom he followed wherever possible. In the bail case of *Bobyshall v Oppenheimer* (1822) Washington wrote, 'I choose to adhere to the long established rule recognized and confirmed by Lord Mansfield, in preference to the modern practice of the English courts; particularly as the rule of the supreme court of this state is not pretended to be different from that stated by Lord Mansfield.'[46]

Lord Mansfield received further praise in *Ferguson v Zepp* (1827). When construing a will, Washington followed the English judge's 1775 decision in *Hogan v Jackson*, Cowp. 299 writing, 'As these expressions have received a definitive judicial interpretation, by the highest authority, more than half a century ago, it can only be necessary to look to the authority itself for their meaning.'[47] It is indicative of Washington's high regard of English law that he should deem an English judge as 'the highest authority,' despite the fact the United States Supreme Court

---

[43] *Croudson v Leonard*, 8 US 434, 1808.
[44] *Crawford et al v The William Penn*, 6 F Cas 781, New Jersey, October 1819.
[45] *Barnes et al v Billington et al*, 2 F Cas 858.
[46] For a selection of favourable references to Lord Mansfield see *Calbraith v Gracy*, 4 F Cas 1030, Penn, April 1805. *Marshall v Delaware Ins Co*, F Cas 16838, Penn, April, 1807, *Penn v Klyne et al*, 19 F Cas 166, Penn, April 1817. *Bobyshall v Oppenheimer*, 3 F Cas 785, Penn, October, 1822. *Rhoades et al v Selin et al*, 20 F Cas 631, Penn, October 1827.
[47] *Ferguson v Zepp*, 8 F Cas 1154, Penn, April 1827.

was in its thirty-ninth year and had by then handed down over a thousand opinions defining the shape of American law. Lord Mansfield was not the only English judge guiding Washington who also looked for support from the judgments and writings of Sir William Scott, Lords Ellenborough, Loughborough, Coke, and Sir William Blackstone.[48]

Washington's regard for the English authorities was not confined to case law. In *Krumbar v Burt et al* (1809) he wondered why the legislature of the United States had not taken from the English statutes the provisions regarding contingent interests in bankruptcy.[49] Further in *Hurst v Hurst* (1807), he noted that the Pennsylvania Statute of Frauds was an exact copy of the English Statute of Frauds which entitled him to examine all the English decisions on the issue.[50]

Even though English precedent was available to assist him, Washington also looked to the opinions of state superior courts to support the English authorities despite the fact that state decisions were merely of persuasive authority, observing in *Campbell et al v Claudius* (1817) that he had great respect for the opinions of the Pennsylvania Supreme Court and the Court of Common Pleas.[51] He also followed decisions of the New York Supreme Court and the Court of Chancery, particularly, James Kent, the eminent New York jurist.[52] This reliance on non-binding state opinions adds further support to the argument that Washington was anxious to explore every avenue for material which might help him arrive at a conclusion. However, where there was a conflict between state procedure and the English practice, Washington preferred the latter. Thus, in *Craig* (1803) where at an early stage of the organisation of the federal courts, the circuit courts had adopted a practice of the state courts based on the English practice, Washington held it improper to depart from the federal court practice because the state's practice had changed.[53]

Washington also used the persuasive authority of his brother circuit judges. If consistency was to be achieved in the federal justice system, the justices needed to follow opinions delivered on other circuits wherever possible. In an action for infringement of patent, Washington followed a circuit opinion of Justice Story and

---

[48] Examples of his reliance on these judges are: *Sperry v Delaware Ins Co* (Penn, October 1808) (Ocean marine insurance, Sir William Scott); *King v Delaware Ins Co* 14 F Cas 516, Penn, October 1808 (Ocean marine insurance, Lord Ellenborough); *United States v Colt*, 25 F Cas 581 Penn, April 1818 (Embargo bond, Lord Loughborough whose opinion he preferred to that of Sir William Blackstone); *Ramdulollday v Darieux*, 2 F Cas 211 Penn, April 1821 (Promissory notes, Lord Ellenborough); *Field v Joel Gibbs et al*, 1 Peters 155, New Jersey, October 1815 (Conclusiveness of judgments, Lord Coke).

[49] *Krumbaar v Burt et al*, 14 F Cas 872, Penn, October 1809.

[50] *Hurst v Hurst*, 12 F Cas 1031, Penn, April 1803.

[51] *Campbell et al v Claudius*, 4 F Cas 1161, Penn, October 1817; *Barnes et al v Billingham et al*, 2 F Cas 858, Penn, April 1803; *Hurst v Hurst*, 12 F Cas 1031, Penn, April, 1803; *Kingston v Kincaid et al* 14 F Cas 590, Penn, April 1806; *Hylton v Brown*, 12 F Cas 1123, Penn, October 1806; *Mott v Maris*, 17 F Cas 905, Penn, April 1808; *Talbot v Simpson*, 23 F Cas 644, Penn, October 1815; *Lanning v London et al* 14 F Cas 1123, Penn, October 1821; *Burton et ux v Smith*, 4 F Cas 876, Penn, October 1826.

[52] *Marshall v Delaware Ins Co*, 16 F Cas 838, Penn, April 1807; *Potts v Gilbert*, 19 F Cas 1203, Penn, April 1819; *United States v Astley et al* 24 F Cas 875, Penn, October 1819; *Ridgway v Underwood*, 20 F Cas 760, New Jersey, October 1821; *Pendleton v Evans*, 19 F Cas 140, Penn, October 1823.

[53] *Craig*, Trenton, New Jersey, April 1803 in Peters, *Reports of Third Circuit Cases, 1803–1818*, vol 1, 1.

was, not surprisingly, affirmed on appeal as Justice Story wrote for the Court.[54] He followed Story again in *Treadwell et al v Bladen* (1827), another patent case.[55] In *Martin v Bank of United States* (1821) when Washington had to rule on the practice of cutting bank notes in half to send parts by different mail, he followed an opinion of the circuit court of the District of Columbia, holding that the bank could not refuse payment if all parts were produced.[56] In the counterfeiting trial of *United States v Moses* (1827), Washington ruled that the arresting officer should not answer the defendant's request for the name of the informer as to do so would be prejudicial to the administration of justice by deterring persons from making disclosures of crime. He wrote that he was following a ruling made by Chief Justice Marshall in the Virginia circuit court during the trial for treason of former Vice-President Burr.[57] The reported cases reveal only one instance in which Washington disagreed with a colleague's circuit opinion. In *Beach v Woodhull* (1803), he refused to follow an opinion of Justice Chase cited to him on precisely the same point. In *Walter v Perrine*, Justice Chase had granted relief to a mortgagee who held a lawful mortgage on the land of a man subsequently convicted of treason, whereupon his land was sold with all proceeds claimed by the state.[58] Despite describing the New Jersey Act barring foreclosure of mortgages on land forfeited to the state as 'retrospective, and unjust in its operation' Washington concluded, 'it is not for this court to correct it or declare it a nullity. It is not repugnant to the Constitution'.[59]

His reliance on the authorities depended very much on the quality of reports of cases cited to him. He highlighted the problem of inadequate law reports in *Crawford et al v The William Penn* (1819), complaining of precedents cited to him without a full and accurate report of the case which meant that he could not understand counsels' arguments or the justice's reasoning.[60]

Despite his experience as a busy advocate, Washington's opinions do not exude the confidence of those of Justices Story, Livingston and Thompson. In *Odlin v Insurance Co of Pennsylvania* (1808), Washington set out his approach to decision making which was to seek out Supreme Court opinions, state court decisions and English cases upon which to base findings. If he had no guiding precedent he was comforted by the fact that, if he was wrong, the Supreme Court would correct his error.[61] He again publicly expressed his unease in *McFadden v The Exchange* (1811), deciding that the circuit court had jurisdiction over a vessel which had been captured by a French warship and was then in port in Philadelphia under

---

[54] *Evans v Hettick*, 8 F Cas 861, Penn, October 1818. Affirmed in 20 US 353.
[55] *Treadwell et al v Bladen*, 24 F Cas 144, Penn, October 1827. Story's circuit opinion was *Goodyear v Matthews*, Case no 5578 in F Cas.
[56] *Martin v Bank of United States*, 16 F Cas 885, Penn, October 1821.
[57] *United States v Moses*, 27 F Cas 5, Penn, October 1827.
[58] *Walter v Perrine*. Case no 17,121 in F Cas. An opinion no longer accessible.
[59] *Beach v Woodhull*, Trenton, New Jersey, April 1803 in Peters, *Reports of the Third Circuit, 1803–1818*, vols 1, 2.
[60] *Crawford et al v The William Penn*, 6 F Cas 781, New Jersey, October 1819.
[61] *Odlin v Insurance Company of Pennsylvania*, 18 F Cas 583, Penn, October 1808.

French colours. His reversal of the district judge troubled him and he wondered if his decision would bear the close scrutiny of the Supreme Court. He wrote: 'I feel cheered that the error of my judgment, if I have committed one, can and will be corrected by a superior tribunal; for surely a question of such national importance as this is, ought not, and I hope will not rest upon a decision of this court.' His call for an appeal was accepted by the parties and he was reversed in the Supreme Court.[62] Again in *Consequa v Willings* (1816) he suggested a possible correction by the Supreme Court if he was mistaken but the parties compromised the suit after Washington had handed down his opinion.[63]

These expressions of uncertainty explain Washington's constant search for support in precedent and his unease at having to decide a novel point without the comfort of a binding or persuasive authority. In *Hurst v Hurst* (1807) he was called upon to interpret a Pennsylvania statute and, bemoaning the absence of precedent to guide him, he wrote 'This being a case of first impression, and arising out of a state law, I have only to regret that it has fallen to the lot of this court to give a construction to it, before it has been considered and decided upon by the supreme court of this state.'[64] He wanted an interpretation by the Pennsylvania Supreme Court upon which to formulate his own view of the law. It is likely that Joseph Story would have been delighted to be the first to proffer an opinion on a new statute and this demonstrates their different approaches.

Washington did not always confine the authorities he followed to those in which the facts were materially the same. In the same term in *Bond v The Cora* (1807), when performing a salvage calculation in an admiralty action, he remarked, 'But although no certain rule can be established to govern every possible case, yet it is proper to refer to former decisions in cases not very dissimilar from that under consideration.' He then followed a Supreme Court decision remarking that it 'does, in all the circumstances, nearly represent the present as any I have met with'[65] His use of the phrases, 'not very dissimilar' and 'nearly represent' suggest a willingness to use a past decision which he believed, although not materially the same, was close enough to underpin his opinion. The following year in *Mott v Maris*, Washington and District Judge Peters doubted whether their construction of the law on the question of priority of payment out of a bankrupt's estate was correct, Washington wrote:

> But, as it has been adopted by the supreme court of this state, our respects for the talents of that court, and our wish that as little collision as possible should take place between the decision of the federal and state tribunals upon the same question, will induce us to adopt the same construction.[66]

---

[62] *McFadden v The Exchange*, 16 F Cas 85, Penn, October 1811.
[63] *Willings v Consequa; Consequa v Willings*, 30 F Cas 53, Penn, October 1815.
[64] *Hurst v Hurst*, 12 F Cas 1031, Penn, April 1807.
[65] *Bond v The Cora*, 3 F Cas 838, Penn, 1807. The Supreme Court precedent was *The Blairau*, 6 US 240.
[66] *Mott v Maris*, 17 F Cas 905, Penn, April 1808.

Both judges were not fully convinced but because the state supreme court had reached a decision on the point, they followed it for the sake of harmonious federal and state relationships. Nowhere in his reasons does Washington say that he believed the state opinion to be correct.

Whilst the decisions of eminent English judges were generally regarded as to be of high persuasive authority, in *Hylton v Brown* (1806) he followed a decision reached by Lord Hardwicke in *Metcalf v Hervey*, 1 Ves Sr 248, despite the fact that he did not agree with it, simply because he regarded the English decision as 'an authority binding upon us, and is too strong to be got over'.[67] At an earlier hearing in *Hylton* when deciding whether two witnesses were required to validate a will made in Pennsylvania, Washington found no precedent to guide him so District Judge Peters consulted directly and informally with two former state superior court judges to ascertain the usual practice. In *Delancy v M'Keen* (1806) Washington again looked for assistance outside the usual channels when, unable to find any 'adjudged' case, he took to asking the opinions of 'three gentlemen of the bar', not connected with the case, whether a copy of a title deed could be proved in evidence.[68] Asking former judges and members of the bar who had no involvement in the cases is a very useful way of assisting the decision-making process. However, it is an unsatisfactory practice because those outsiders were not called as expert witnesses or subjected to questioning on their views. These cases support the view that Washington generally felt the need to find some support his opinions, even from unorthodox sources, so as not to have the responsibility of interpreting a new statute or decide a novel point of law. He felt more confident following principles of law well established by others.

This view of Washington, as a justice on occasion expressing a lack of confidence, is at odds with that of Stonier (1998) who, whilst acknowledging that his Supreme Court opinions were 'modest, even diffident in tone,' argues that his circuit opinions, 'which usually take the form of his charges to the jury ... bespeak the confident authority of one who sees himself as the embodied voice of federal law'.[69] While the cases which follow support Stonier's view of Washington's rapport with juries, the opinions do not confirm the view of a justice of 'confident authority' when difficult points of law arose.

A good example supporting Stonier's assessment of Washington's diffidence on the Court is to be found in his majority opinion in *Ogden v Saunders* (1827) when he differed from Marshall on whether a state bankruptcy law passed before the execution of a contract was incorporated into the contract. Washington wrote:

> I should be disingenuous, were I to declare, from this place, that I embrace it [my conclusion] without hesitation, and without a doubt of its correctness ... it must remain for others to decide whether the guide I have chosen is a safe one or not.[70]

---

[67] *Hylton v Brown*, 12 F Cas 1129, Penn, April 1806.

[68] *Delancy v M'Keen*, 7 F Cas 371. Penn, April, 1806.

[69] Stonier, James R Jr, 'Heir Apparent: Bushrod Washington and Federal Justice in the Early Republic' in Gerber, Scott (ed) *Seriatim: The Supreme Court before John Marshall* (New York: New York University Press, 1998), 341.

[70] *Ogden v Saunders*, 25 US 213 (1827).

Washington was much more confident in his dealings with the jury. As the sole arbiters of fact, juries were just as important to the court process as the judge and a good relationship between the two was essential to the administration of justice. Washington's many comments in the reports show that he believed trial by jury to be fundamental to a free society. Its members were drawn from all walks of life; that some had experience of commercial life is apparent from Washington's charge in the bill of exchange case of *Bell et al v Davidson* (1818) when he remarked, 'This is a question of account, and the jury will not expect assistance from the court; they will examine the accounts, and form an opinion on them.'[71]

Despite fully accepting that the resolution of factual disputes lay entirely with the jury, where the law was clear and the evidence compelling, Washington occasionally charged the jury on the verdict they should return. An example is *Calhoun v Vechio* (1812) in which he said: 'This is a very plain case ... the plaintiff is therefore entitled to a verdict for the principal and interest of his account.' The jurors, as they invariably did, complied with the charge.[72] He was also not averse to expressing strong views in a criminal trial. In *United States v Morrow* (1827) the jury found the defendant not guilty after Washington observed that the counterfeit coins were such a miserable imitation of the genuine half dollar as to fool no-one.[73] In *Consequa v Willings* (1816) he explained that, contrary to the generally accepted practice, he always expressed a view on the facts if they were clear but never when they were in doubt.[74] The problem with that approach is that by reserving to himself the decision as to whether the facts were plain or doubtful, he usurped the function of the jury. That he should take such a forceful line is at odds with his mainly cautious attitude to his circuit duties. It may be that he was more forceful dealing with factual issues than difficult points of law because section 22 of the Judiciary Act 1789 and the Seventh Amendment to the Constitution prohibited, save for exceptional circumstances, a review of a finding of fact but directions on law were always open to higher scrutiny.

There are only two reported cases where Washington refused to accept the verdict of a jury. In *King v Delaware Insurance Co* (1808) he ordered a new trial because he considered the jury's verdict a finding of law which they were not competent to make.[75] He took the same course in *Willis v Bucher et al* (1818) observing that the law must be for the judge as if he wrongly interpreted the law, it would be open to the Supreme Court to look at his reasoning and correct him. In that case he expressed great satisfaction at having to refuse to accept verdicts of the jury on just two occasions in 16 years.[76]

Once the jury had returned a verdict, Washington refused to re-open the case for some perceived irregularity. In *Harrison v Rowan* (1820) he would not inquire

---

[71] *Bell et al v Davidson*, 3 F Cas 100, Penn, April 1818.
[72] *Calhoun v Vechio*, 4 F Cas 1049, Penn, April, 1812.
[73] *United States v Morrow*, 26 F Cas 1352, Penn, October 1827.
[74] *Consequa v Willings*, 6 F Cas 336, Penn, April, 1816.
[75] *King v Delaware Insurance Co*, 14 F Cas 516, Penn, October 1808.
[76] *Willis v Bucher et al* 30 F Cas 63, Penn, April 1818.

into the jury's deliberations despite affidavits from jurors complaining of undue pressure from other members of the jury. He would not tolerate the undermining of a verdict solemnly delivered in open court by delving into the secrets of the jury room.[77] One can understand this approach as there must be some finality to litigation and the fact that jurors occasionally have second thoughts ought not to be a sufficient reason for re-opening the issues. The case of *United States v Haskell et al* (1823) brings to life the hardships sometimes faced by juries. In this mutiny at sea trial the jury had been kept together deliberating for three days and without food for 24 hours because they were not allowed to separate until they reached a verdict. Washington gave instances of the proper and necessary discharge of juries such as exhaustion, tampering with a juror, drunkenness or a juror becoming insane, which on the extant reports, were problems he never faced.[78]

## Property Rights and Commercial Law on Circuit

The 520 reported circuit opinions of Washington demonstrate how he preserved existing titles to land and ownership of personal property. They also reveal his part in promoting the economic prosperity of the nation by settling substantive federal law and procedural guidance which, in turn, promoted commercial activity. He used, both on circuit and in the Court, the constitutional prohibition against 'the impairment of contracts' to preserve existing and future contractual obligations. The protection of vested rights was a crucial aspect of the Court's jurisprudence. Kutler (1971) remarks in his study of *The Charles River Bridge Case* (1837) that 'the protection of vested interests, particularly in the first three decades of the nineteenth century, was the most obvious and convenient means to secure desirable public goals'.[79] This question of vested rights went to the heart of the case of *The Trustees of Dartmouth College v Woodward* (1819). The Court held that a charter or franchise was a contract between the state and the person to whom it is granted and was within Article 1, Section 10 of the Constitution prohibiting the passing of any law impairing the obligation of contracts, thereby invalidating New Hampshire's attempt to force a private school to accept state control.[80] The preservation of extant property rights also applied to both state and federal governments, the Fifth Amendment to the Constitution prohibiting the depriving of any person of property without due process of law and the taking of private property for public use without just compensation.

---

[77] *Harrison v Rowan*, 11 F Cas 663, New Jersey, April 1820.

[78] *United States v Haskell et al*, 26 F Cas 207, Penn, October 1823.

[79] Stanley L Kutler, *Privilege and Creative Destruction: The Charles River Bridge Case* (Philadelphia: JB Lippincott Company, 1971), 67. *Charles River Bridge v Warren Bridge*, 36 US 420 (1837).

[80] *Trustees of Dartmouth College v Woodward*, 17 US 518 (1819).

The *Charles River Bridge* opinion saw a marked shift in the Court's approach to vested rights. In 1785 Massachusetts granted a charter to the plaintiffs to build the Charles River Bridge but in 1826 permitted the defendants to construct another bridge so close to that of the plaintiffs as to seriously reduce toll revenue. The plaintiffs asserted that the charter granted exclusive rights to a crossing and complained that Massachusetts had thereby broken the contracts clause of the Constitution. When the case came before the Marshall Court in 1831 Justice Story was unable to gain sufficient support for an opinion favouring the plaintiffs' case and the Court was unable to reach a decision. The case was not reargued for six years and when it came before the Taney Court in 1837, the majority found for the Warren Bridge, an opinion in which public benefit prevailed over vested rights.[81] This recognition of the right of the state to sanction competing commercial interests led to a transportation revolution with 'Ferries competing with bridges, railroads with canals; later on airplanes and trucks competed with railroads and each other.'[82]

Washington's reported opinions went beyond the confines of vested rights. They cover the following branches of law: Maritime, marine insurance, and prize law (121); Land disputes and interpretation of wills (94); Mercantile law (78); Criminal law (33); Patent infringements (23); Bankruptcy (19); Revenue Duty (11); *Habeas corpus* (6); Slavery (6); Constitutional law (3). There were 13 opinions covering diplomatic immunity, husband and wife, and the duties of trustees but too few of each to discern any patterns. The remaining opinions deal with procedural issues such as the admissibility of evidence, continuances, dismissal for want of prosecution, competency of witnesses, jurisdiction, costs, and order of speeches which show the need for a thorough grounding in procedural as well as substantive law if cases were to be concluded efficiently and expeditiously.

Many of Washington's land dispute cases arose because of the manner in which land was described in warrants. Often there were no man-made boundaries and it was difficult to identify natural borders such as mountains, rivers and streams in regions little explored, resulting in competing claims to the same land. There were five basic documents created in the transfer of title to land at this time:

1. An application for a warrant to have a survey made which was an informal document usually on a slip of paper without the applicant's signature.
2. The warrant which was a certificate authorising the survey of the land requested.

---

[81] For an account of this shift in emphasis from vested rights to public interest and the effect of the composition of the two Courts see, Kutler, at 54–73. See also, Morton J Horwitz, *The Transformation of American Law: 1780–1860* (Cambridge, MA: Harvard University Press, 1977) *Law*, Chapter 4, 109–39 in which he argues that in less than a generation and by the time of the *Charles River Bridge* case 'judges and jurists had come to agree that a policy in favour of competition was a *sine qua non* for further economic development' 139.

[82] Jonathan Hughes and Louis P Cain, *American Economic History*, 5th ed (Reading, Mass: Addison-Wesley. Longman, 1998), 138.

3. The survey conducted by a deputy surveyor usually drawn on paper with corner markers and adjoining property owners marked and with an exact acreage.
4. Return of survey which was a written document combining the warrant and completed survey and confirming that the purchase fee had been paid.
5. The patent which was the final deed conveying title to the land.[83]

Bartlett (1974) dealing with the system of land claims in Pennsylvania and southwards, identified weaknesses which gave rise to continual litigation. 'Trees and boulders marking a boundary with someone else's land were apt to disappear. Even a stream could dry up; and there was "the problem of the creeping fence," which inevitably enlarged one piece of property at the expense of another.' An example of how boundaries were particularised is found in a 1798 deed conveying land to Justice Washington:

> All that tract or parcel of land containing twenty-eight hundred acres or thereabouts called or known by the name of Hollis's Marsh in the County of Westmoreland bounded by the road to Stratford Mill and by the road from Stratford to Chantilly, by the Chantilly line and by the Potowmack River including Hollis's Marsh.[84]

Washington's task was to bring as much order and certainty into real property ownership as possible. In his first circuit court in Philadelphia he set out his approach to resolving such disputes by declaring that title to lands under the Pennsylvania Act of 3 April 1792 required occupancy and a bona fide intention immediately to reside on the land either personally or by a tenant. Carrying out improvements to the land was not conclusive and was merely evidence of an intention to settle.[85] He stressed the importance of a warrant holder using due diligence in having the land surveyed or he would lose priority over another warrant holder who, without knowledge of the earlier warrant, obtained the first survey.[86] His guidance to occupants of land was designed to ensure that titles were not defeated by failing to observe technicalities of land law.

*Milligan v Dickson* (1817) is an example of Washington's determination to uphold existing rights of ownership of land. He had to decide whether he ought to approve the practice of admitting in evidence a power of attorney which went to proof of title. He declared: 'This usage forms one of the great and essential landmarks of real property in this state; and if titles depending upon it are to be uprooted this day, I will not be the judge to commence this work of devastation.'[87] In *Huidekoper v Burrus* (1804), he preserved the ownership of land by the then

---

[83] These documents are set out in Donna Bingham Munger, *Pennsylvania Land Records: A History and Guide for Researchers* (Wilmington, Delaware: S R Scholarly Resources, 1991), 40.

[84] A document handwritten by Justice Washington dated 22 September 1803 which supplements a deed of 17 April 1798 in the Bushrod Washington Papers, David M Rubenstein Library, Duke University, Durham.

[85] *Balfour's Lessee v Meade*, 2 F Cas 543, Penn, April 1803.

[86] *Gordon v Kerr et al*, 10 F Cas 801, Penn, October 1806.

[87] *Milligan v Dickson et al*, 17 F Cas 376, Penn, April 1817.

occupiers against an argument that settlement of United States land was essential if title was to pass. He ignored, when considering persistence in settlement, the failure to enter upon the land between 1792 and 1798, because of the real danger to life during the Indian wars.[88]

Washington extended his protection of property rights even to those who had assisted Britain during the Revolutionary War when, in *Gordon v Holiday* (1805), he held that the Paris Peace Treaty of 1783 avoided all state proceedings, subsequent to the treaty, for the confiscation of enemy property. Therefore, an heir was entitled to succeed to the land owned by an alien.[89]

On occasion, land titles were challenged on the basis that the requisite formalities of transfer or registration had not been complied with. Washington refused to interfere with title in *Griffith v Tunckhouser* (1817) holding that a warrant and survey returned into the land office and accepted in Pennsylvania transferred the legal title and the regularity of the survey made by a sworn officer would be presumed unless the contrary was proved.[90] Failure to produce the original patent was not necessarily fatal to proving title. In *Willis v Bucher et al* (1818), he preserved the status quo by charging the jury that an entry in the books of the land office in Pennsylvania that the balance of the purchase price had been paid by the person 'to whom the patent had issued' was evidence that the patent had actually been issued. Surveyors were required to enter and trace the land after a warrant had been granted. However, in *Torrey v Beardsley* (1818), Washington rejected a challenge to a title where the surveyor had traced the lines of the tract of land before a warrant for the land had been granted and had applied that original survey to a later general warrant on unappropriated land without returning to the land to make a fresh survey.[91] These cases support the conclusion that the preservation of existing titles to land was high on Washington's list of priorities. His circuit opinions reveal a determination to preserve existing land titles and, by setting out clear procedural rules, to ensure that ownership of land did not fail on a technicality.

That Washington had more than a passing acquaintance with Pennsylvania land law and would be well qualified to field disputed land questions on the Supreme Court is evident from his reported circuit opinions. Despite the fact that his cases had been solely concerned with Pennsylvania and New Jersey titles, principles of land law common to other states coupled with the assistance of colleagues from other circuits would see him through if asked to write for the Court on this topic.

Whilst this examination of Washington's jurisprudence, in part, looks to the use to which circuit expertise was put on the Supreme Court, his circuit opinion in *Bleeker v Bond* (1819) highlights how knowledge gained sitting in the Supreme Court might be put to use in the circuit court. In this circuit case Washington was able to bring to bear the knowledge he had acquired as a justice who had joined

---

[88] *Huidekoper v Burrus*, 12 F Cas 840, Penn, April 1804.
[89] *Gordon v Holiday*, 10 F Cas 798, Penn, April 1805.
[90] *Griffith v Tunckhouser*, 11 F Cas 42, Penn, April 1817.
[91] *Torrey v Beardsley*, 24 F Cas 65, Penn, April 1818.

in the majority opinion in the landmark Supreme Court case of *Fletcher v Peck* (1810). The Supreme Court had ruled unconstitutional a Georgia statute which had sought to avoid fraudulent sales in 1795 by corrupt Georgia legislators to land speculators of 35 million acres of Georgia land (now the States of Alabama and Mississippi) at rock-bottom prices. Some 15 years later the land had been subdivided and ended up in many different hands, many of which were purchasers for value with no notice of the original fraudulent transfers. Attempting to unravel so many titles would have been a nightmare situation. The Supreme Court held the Georgia statute unconstitutional because it infringed Article 1, Section 10, Clause 1 of the Constitution, prohibiting any state from passing a law 'impairing the obligation of contracts', despite the fact that the original sales had patently arisen as a result of bribery.[92] This was the first time the Court struck down, as unconstitutional, a state statute. By upholding this dubious agreement, it was sending a clear message to the business community that it would uphold on this ground even their less-questionable contracts wherever possible. The Court interpreted the contracts clause of the Constitution in such a way as to promote free enterprise and stimulate the economy. Washington applied the *Fletcher ratio* to his circuit case, doing so with the confidence of a justice who had heard the issues fully argued at the highest level.

Whilst Washington protected existing proprietary rights, he did acknowledge the right of the federal and state governments to acquire private property for the general good. In *Bleeker*, he gave a glimpse of his political philosophy, and an exception to the sanctity of contracts, observing, 'It is true, that private interests must be subservient to the public necessities. This results from the nature of the social contract. Under every government ... private property may be taken for the public good, provided fair compensation be paid for it.'[93] However, he further demonstrated his commitment to the sanctity of contracts when, in *Golden v Prince* (1814), he held as unconstitutional a Pennsylvania law which authorised the discharge of a contract by payment of a smaller sum at a different time and in a different manner than originally agreed on the ground that it impaired the obligation of contracts.[94]

Washington promoted commerce by setting out firm rules governing bills of exchange, promissory notes and accommodation bills so that men of business would know precisely their rights and obligations in relation to these negotiable instruments, the lifeblood of national and international trade.[95] He protected the

---

[92] *Bleeker v Bond*, 3 F Cas 687, Penn, October 1819; *Fletcher v Peck*, 10 US 87 (1810).

[93] For examples of changing attitudes to the appropriation of private property for the public good and the right to compensation following the exercise of the power of eminent domain see Horwitz, 63–74.

[94] *Golden v Prince*, 10 F Cas 542, Penn, April 1814.

[95] *Humphreys v Blight's Assignees*, 12 F Cas 875, Penn, April 1803; *Perry et al v Crammond et al*, 19 F Cas 277, Penn, April 1804; *Corser v Craig*, 6 F Cas 601, Penn, April 1806; *Gallagher v Roberts*, 9 F Cas 1089, Penn, April 1808; *McMurtry v Jones*, 16 F Cas 312, Penn, April 1813.

rights of an enemy alien on a bill of exchange holding that, if the debtor knew that the alien had an agent in the United States, interest on the bill did not abate during the war.[96] Meticulous in ensuring that the parties to a bill of exchange abided by the original terms, he held in *Craig v Brown* (1819) that where a defendant promised to pay the amount due under the bill 'when able' and the plaintiff did not wait and sued immediately, Washington held that the creditor could not afterward resort to the promise to pay when able.

He extended his promotion of commerce by clarifying the law and procedure governing maritime contracts and ocean marine insurance. There were so many such cases in the busy port of Philadelphia that definitive statements of law and practice were needed to assist those engaged in this expanding mode of international trade, crucial to the United States economy. In *McGregor v Insurance Company of Pennsylvania* (1803), he regulated the relationship between insurer and insured by holding insurers bound by the terms of the contract and unable seek to reduce compensation on a total loss of freight by relying on an alleged local custom which was not well known in the trade and which was unreasonable.[97] He insisted, in *Delaware Insurance Company v Hogan* (1807) that the terms of a marine insurance policy could not be departed from unless fraud or mistake was clearly made out.[98]

The marine insurance issues presented to Washington were many and varied. Avoidance of a policy due to a deviation from an agreed route was a common source of dispute. In times of war, vessels were liable to capture by the enemy and it was, therefore, important to know the route and port of destination to assess the risk and fix a premium. Washington held, in *Martin v Delaware Ins Co*, (1808), that the smallest unjustified deviation from an agreed course avoided the policy.[99] Thus, in *Cruder v Pennsylvania Ins Co* (1809) he avoided a policy where the ship went off course to pick up additional hands, holding that a ship should have sufficient hands to man her at the departure port.[100] He did, however, admit of exceptions to his strict view of these cases and in *Coles et al v Marine Insurance Co* (1812) he found acceptable a deviation to effect essential repairs of storm damage or landing to obtain fresh provisions.[101] However, in another aspect of *Cruder*, a deviation to effect repairs which were required at the commencement of the voyage avoided cover.[102] That Washington was sympathetic to the difficulties facing masters of vessels in wartime was demonstrated in *Goyon v Pleasants* (1814) by his ruling that a deviation to evade British cruisers did not vitiate the policy.[103]

---

[96] *Denniston et al v Imbrie*, 7 F Cas 485, Penn, April 1818.
[97] *McGregor v Insurance Company of Pennsylvania*, 16 F Cas 129, Penn, April 1803.
[98] *Delaware Insurance Company v Hogan*, 2 Peters 4, Penn, April 1807.
[99] *Martin v Delaware Ins Co*, 16 F Cas 894, Penn, October 1808.
[100] *Cruder v Pennsylvania Ins Co*, 6 F Cas 921, Penn, October 1809.
[101] *Coles et al v Marine Insurance Co*, 6 F Cas 65, Penn, April 1812.
[102] See *Cruder*, above.
[103] *Goyon v Pleasants*, 10 F Cas 891, Penn, April 1814.

The effect of misrepresentation and the concealment of information which would affect the risk in marine insurance contracts was another topic familiar to Washington's circuit court and one which required opinions to guide the conduct of the parties. In *Kohne v Insurance Company of North America* (1804) the insured failed to disclose to the insurer that his vessel was carrying goods from Cuba to Spain despite a prohibition by the British government of a neutral vessel trading between a colony and a belligerent mother country. Washington directed the jury that the risk of capture and forfeiture had been increased and the failure to give full disclosure avoided the policy.[104] He came down heavily on fraudulent or negligent disclosure of the fate of vessels before effecting insuring. He obviously avoided the policy in cases where the insured knew the ship had already been lost and extended the bar to recovery in *Vale v Phoenix Insurance Co* (1805) where the plaintiff had reliable information which would have led him to believe the ship which had his goods on board may well have been lost at sea.[105] He sent a clear message to insured trading with a belligerent country or carrying goods which infringed the United States neutrality laws that, unless they made disclosure of those material facts, the insurers would be entitled to vitiate the policies in addition to any forfeiture for breach of embargo.[106]

Washington acknowledged the need to deviate from the agreed route to repair and re-provision vessels after damage and delays caused by abnormal weather conditions so that the ship might resume her voyage or return home. In *Ross v The Active* (1808) he held that a master was entitled to sell part of the cargo to effect essential repairs to the vessel where the owner of the ship also owned the cargo.[107] However, when a master borrowed money on the security of the ship and cargo which enabled the lender to claim the property if the loan and interest was not paid upon the ship's safe return to its home port, the lender had to satisfy the court that the loan was necessary for the continuance of the voyage.[108]

He was not the only justice to realise that international trade could not flourish unless there were sufficient seamen to man the nation's mercantile marine. He tried cases of misconduct at sea, arising from excessive punishment by the master or conduct ranging from mere insubordination to open revolt by the crew. In *United States v Smith et al* (1809), he went outside the facts of the case to explain carefully to the jury the limits of the master's authority to correct his seamen and their duty of submission to lawful orders. In that case he directed the jury that where a master used an unlawful weapon or put the seaman in danger of his life,

---

[104] *Kohne v Insurance Company of North America*, 14 F Cas 835, Penn, April 1804.
[105] *Vale v Phoenix Insurance Co* 28 F Cas 687, Penn, April 1805. See *Johnson v Phoenix Insurance Co* 13 F Cas 782, Penn, April 1806 where the plaintiff was non-suited as the evidence showed clearly that he had known the vessel to be lost.
[106] *Marshall v Union Ins Co*, 16 F Cas 849, Penn, October 1809. (Breach of neutrality laws); *Baudy et al v Union Insurance Co*, 2 F Cas 1039, Penn, October 1809), (Trading with belligerent country).
[107] *Ross v The Active*, 20 F Cas 1231, Penn, October 1808.
[108] *Walden v Chamberlain*, 28 F Cas 1353, Penn, April 1814.

the seaman was entitled to use reasonable force to protect himself.[109] On occasion, unscrupulous masters and owners attempted to avoid paying seamen their wages. Washington was keen to protect the position of the crew by insisting that no charge of desertion or absence without leave justifying loss of all or part of the remuneration would be accepted unless there was a contemporaneous entry in the ship's log recording the allegation.[110] Where in *Sims v Jackson* (1806) a seaman hired for a return voyage from Philadelphia to Batavia died in Batavia, Washington affirmed the district judge's decision to award his widow the full wages instead of the half offered by the owners. Experience and common sense prevailed in *Ketland v Lebering* (1808) to ensure that the administrators of a deceased received his wages. The owners claimed that no-one named John Lebering had served on board their vessel. Washington called for the ship's muster roll which showed a John Lebrun on board. He remarked 'We know by everyday experience that a false pronunciation of surnames is frequently given, particularly with the abridgment of them.'[111] Washington again came down on the side of the crew in *Girard v Ware et al* (1815). A United States vessel was captured by the British blockading Delaware Bay and the crew forced ashore. After a ransom was paid the ship was permitted to proceed to Philadelphia with a new crew, the old crew not being given the option to continue the voyage. Washington held that the crew were entitled to wages for the entire trip but, in a judgment of Solomon, he held that they had to contribute towards the ransom.[112] By laying down clear rules as to the conduct of the parties in maritime contracts and by protecting those who manned the vessels, Washington was again actively promoting commercial enterprises.

The above cases reveal how the circuit opinions of this committed Federalist were designed to preserve existing property rights, the obligation of contracts, and stimulate national and international trade by setting out guidelines for business relationships on land and at sea. The examination of the justice's circuit work now turns to the generality of his case load, covering not only significant circuit opinions but also those of limited jurisprudential value to ascertain the overall expertise Washington gained from the day to day resolution of the many varied legal problems he faced in Philadelphia and Trenton.

## States' Rights, the War of 1812, and Slavery

An examination of Washington's reported circuit cases reveal opinions which were useful in establishing law and procedural rules to be followed on his circuit

---

[109] *United States v Smith et al*, 27 F Cas 1247, Penn, October 1819.
[110] *The Phoebe v Dignum*, 19 F Cas 530, Penn, April 1803; *The Betsey v Duncan*, 3 F Cas 308, Penn, October 1808.
[111] *Ketland v Lebering*, 14 F Cas 433, Penn, April 1808.
[112] *Girard v Ware et al*, 10 F Cas 441, Penn, April 1815.

and possibly on other circuits where his brethren found his reasoning attractive. However, many of his opinions were of no moment other than to the parties to the dispute. There were very few cases involving constitutional issues of national significance.

Two of Washington's important constitutional cases on circuit spring to mind; one involving a state's attempt to deny by force the authority of a federal court and the other a state's determination to protect its natural resources against outsiders. He also delivered many opinions resolving competing claims to captured merchant vessels and warships before and during the 1812 War between the United States and Britain and settled the fate of vessels attempting to breach United States embargo and neutrality laws. Although he dealt with a small number of slavery cases, the opinions do permit an insight into his approach to this troubled issue but reflect the deep tensions facing the nation in its formative years.

The constitutional cases were *United States v Bright* (1809) and *Corfield v Coryell* (1823).[113] *Bright* was a case in which Washington resisted severe local pressure when holding that no state had the power to defy an order of a federal court. The dispute involved competing claims for prize money following the capture of the British sloop, *The Active*. Gideon Olmstead and other Connecticut sailors had been taken by the British during the Revolutionary War and forced to serve on the sloop. Olmstead and his mates gained control of the sloop but, while *en route* for New Jersey, it was captured by a Pennsylvanian warship. Both captors claimed the sloop as a prize of war and a jury of the Pennsylvania state admiralty court, without stating any facts, gave Olmstead a mere quarter share. Olmstead then took his case to the court of appeal in prize cases, set up by Congress under the Articles of Confederation and he was awarded the whole of the prize. The state court refused to acknowledge the award and in 1779 the three-quarter share was paid to the state treasurer. As late as 1802, Olmstead took action in the federal district court to enforce payment of the full share he had been awarded 23 years earlier. District Judge Peters found in his favour whereupon the Pennsylvania legislature, in open defiance of the federal court order, passed an act ordering the treasurer's representatives to pay the three-quarter share into the state treasury. The Supreme Court issued *mandamus* compelling Judge Peters to enforce his order. General Michael Bright and his militia, on the express orders of the governor, assembled outside the home of the treasurer's representatives with muskets and fixed bayonets and resisted the efforts of the federal marshal to enforce the district judge's order. The general and his men were subsequently indicted by a federal grand jury for resisting United States law and tried by Washington, Peters and a jury. With local sentiment running high in favour of the defendants, Washington took charge of a highly charged situation. The defendants argued that the federal court had no jurisdiction to reverse a jury verdict of a state court and that they had been acting under the direct orders of the state governor. Washington charged the

---

[113] *United States v Bright*, 24 F Cas 1232 (1809); *Corfield v Coryell*, 6 F Cas 546 (1823).

jury that the Supreme Court in *Penhallow v Doane* (1795) had established that an appellate prize court had the power to reverse a state admiralty court on findings of fact and law and that was settled and at rest.[114] He was emphatic in his charge to the jury that no state had the power to declare the judgments of the national courts null and void because the Constitution had declared United States law to be the supreme law of the land. If that were not so, government would be undermined and liberty curtailed and the threat of physical violence with potentially terrible consequences was a monstrous reaction which could never be justified.

The jury returned a special verdict which placed the responsibility on Washington's shoulders. It found that the defendants had resisted the federal marshal but had done so on the orders of the governor, leaving the court to decide whether acting on superior orders was a defence to the indictment. Washington had no hesitation in holding that the threatened use of force to resist a lawful federal court order was no legal justification as the general and his men had a paramount duty to the Union and not to the state governor. Taking the view that obedience to the governor was a mitigating factor, he imposed modest sentences which were never served, the situation having been defused by President James Madison's immediate grant of pardons. The case illustrates the tensions between state and federal authorities and how, on occasion, the circuit court tried disputes with potentially nationwide repercussions. It also demonstrates how important it was to have a Supreme Court Justice presiding who had the standing, courage, and determination to uphold the Constitution, the Union, and the authority of the federal courts against intense state pressure.

*Bright* was not the only case in which Washington vehemently condemned those resisting federal authority. In *United States v Lowry et al* (1808), three armed defendants threatened to kill a deputy federal marshal who had served on them court orders for possession of land. Sentencing each man to three months' imprisonment, Washington said, 'the courts of justice are the sanctuaries of the law; and it is through the law that that the government speaks and acts. Impair by any means ... the power of these tribunals ... and you attack the majesty of the law ... and the foundations of the republic.'[115]

His other major constitutional opinion arose much later in his tenure and is probably the most important case he tried on circuit. *Corfield v Coryell* (1823) turned on the constitutionality of an 1820 Act of Assembly of the State of New Jersey prohibiting non-residents of the state from gathering oysters in New Jersey waters from May to December. He gave his opinion after much thought as the legal issues were argued in the October 1823 term and the opinion was not handed down for six months. The case was important for two reasons. First, Washington had to decide whether the prohibition contravened Article VI, Section 2 of the Constitution which conferred on the citizens of each state 'all the privileges and

---

[114] *Penhallow v Doane*, 3 Dall (3 US) 54 (1795).
[115] *United States v Lowry et al*, 26 F Cas 1008, Penn, April 1808.

immunities of citizens in the several states'. Second, and because the vessel seized and condemned had been hired out with its coastal licence to a citizen of Pennsylvania, it was argued that a state prohibition usurped the power bestowed upon Congress by virtue of Article 1, Section 8 of the Constitution 'to regulate commerce ... among the several states.' These constitutional challenges gave Washington the opportunity to expound his view of the purpose, meaning and effect of the freedoms guaranteed by the Constitution.

The most important privileges and immunities enumerated by Washington were:

> Protection by the government; the enjoyment of life and liberty, with the right to acquire property of every kind, and to pursue and obtain happiness and safety; subject to such restraints as the government may justly prescribe for the general good of the whole; the right of a citizen to pass through or reside in any other state for the purpose of trade, agriculture, professional pursuits or otherwise; to claim the benefit of the writ of habeas corpus; to institute and maintain actions of any kind in the courts of the state; hold and dispose of property, either real or personal; and an exemption from higher taxes or impositions than are paid by other citizen of the state.[116]

The list is not exhaustive, but includes the crucial freedoms, echoing the rights to, 'Life, Liberty, and the Pursuit of Happiness' enshrined in the Declaration of Independence. This early attempt at defining the 'privileges and immunities' clause, unusually for a circuit court opinion, was extensively cited by the Supreme Court in the 1873 *Slaughterhouse Cases* when considering the meaning of the 'privileges and immunities' clause of the 1808 Fourteenth Amendment.[117]

In *Corfield*, Washington stressed the importance of engendering mutual friendship and intercourse among the citizens of the different states of the Union but in the event held that the state law was not unconstitutional because the oyster beds were the common property of the citizens of New Jersey whose legislature had the power to regulate the use of such a natural resource. Washington disposed of the privileges and immunities argument by similar reasoning, holding that any fishery or oyster bed was as much the property of the individual who owned it as was any dry land he owned. Therefore, it was lawful for the state legislature to pass laws protecting such ownership against others whether they were fellow citizens or outsiders. A state legislature can never be compelled to extend to citizens of other states the rights which belong exclusively to its own citizens. To have held otherwise would have undermined the right of a state to control assets owned in common by its citizens. This case was one of the few occasions when Washington in a circuit opinion threw his normal caution to the wind and expressed himself forcefully on an issue of supreme national importance.

*Bright* and *Corfield* demonstrate how important the federal circuit courts were not only to the development of American law but also to the resolution of

---

[116] *Corfield v Coryell*, 6 F Cas 551–552, Penn, April 1823.
[117] *Slaughterhouse Cases*, 86 US 36 (1873).

potentially dangerous tensions between both the federal government and a state and significant competing claims between states. A state prepared to use violence to defy an order of the United States Supreme Court and attempts by outsiders to use the natural resources of a sovereign state were issues which required determination by a judge who had Supreme Court status and not by a local district judge upon whom the pressures would have been far greater. These two cases and the 1812 War cases which follow show the wisdom of Congress in sending justices out on circuit anticipating that not all of their functions would have purely local significance.

The bulk of Washington's circuit work comprised maritime law, prize cases and marine insurance of which there are 121 reported opinions. Prize cases alone account for 24 of the maritime cases.[118] During the war between the United States and Britain from 1812 to 1815, 1,634 British vessels were taken as prizes by Americans, 1,500 of which were sent with prize crews to American ports but it is estimated that half were recaptured *en route* by British privateers.[119] Much of Washington's maritime work arose as a result of the Embargo Act of 22 December 1807 passed by Congress as a counter measure to repeated violations of United States neutrality by Britain and France who were seizing American vessels and impressing crews. The Act prohibited any ship leaving a United States port for a foreign port. In fact the embargo hit the United States harder than it did the European powers and American manufacturers and farmers suffered great hardship because of the total ban on imports and exports. Ships were idle and seamen out of work. Because of widespread opposition, on 1 March 1809, the Embargo Act was replaced by a Non-Intercourse Act which confined the ban to trade with Britain and France. Section 2 of the 1807 Act required all masters or owners of vessels to give a bond with sureties to a local collector for double the value of the ship and cargo guaranteeing that she was bound for another American port. Pennsylvanian and New Jersey merchants, ship owners, and masters devised ways of evading the embargo despite heavy penalties. Unsuccessful attempts resulted in appearances before Justice Washington, fighting to avoid the forfeiture of vessel and cargo.

Washington saw through desperately spurious excuses quite easily. In *United States v The Paul Sherman* (1815), the master of a vessel took on board cargo at a port where trade was prohibited. He then sailed into a US port ostensibly to land men saved from a wreck. Washington, in rejecting, the master's story observed, 'The illegality of the transaction is attempted to be concealed by a drapery too thin to impose on the most credulous mind.'[120] He did, however, examine each case

---

[118] The Marshall Court dealt with a total of 111 prize court cases indicating how widespread these cases were as only a small proportion went to the Court. See James Brown Scott, *Prize Cases Decided in the United States Supreme Court, 1789–1918, Including Also Cases on the Instant Side in which Questions of Prize Law were Involved*, vol 1 (Oxford: Clarendon Press, 1923).

[119] *Niles Weekly Register*, 12August 1815, cited in Donald A Petrie, *The Prize Game: Lawful Looting on the High Seas in the Days of Fighting Sail* (Annapolis: Naval Institute Press, 1999), 165.

[120] *United States v The Paul Sherman*, 27 F Cas 467, New Jersey, April 1815.

scrupulously. Thus, in *Parker v United States* (1806) he reversed the district court's condemnation of a vessel for breach of embargo when he reasoned that forfeiture could not be claimed after the vessel had arrived within the jurisdiction of a foreign power and he refused forfeiture in *United States v Dixey et al* (1811) when he was satisfied that a vessel bound from Philadelphia to New Orleans struck the Bahama Bank and was obliged to put into Havana for essential repairs.[121] Further, in *United States v Morgan et al* (1811) he held an embargo bond void because it was more onerous than the Act.[122]

Washington's opinions are invariably expressed in measured and moderate language. However, in one prize case, he expressed his anger when he perceived an injustice which he felt unable to remedy. In *Armroyd et al v Williams et al* (1811) a French admiralty court condemned as a prize an American vessel on the ground that she was in violation of the Milan Decree by which Napoleon prohibited all trade with Britain. Washington upheld the forfeiture but with the utmost reluctance, complaining that the regular order of things had been disturbed by the 'violence and rapine of the belligerents' [Britain and France]. He wrote, 'we sicken with disgust in giving the appellees the benefit of a general principle of law which complies submission to so daring an assault on our neutral rights'. Despite his anger at the action of the French court, he felt constrained to reach his holding because it was a competent court of the law of nations and its decisions, however unpopular, were binding. His view was that it was for the courts to follow the law of nations and for the government to protect its citizens.[123] That opinion was affirmed by the Supreme Court. Chief Justice Marshall, writing for the Court, also believed the French decree to be subversive of the law of nations but not one which the Court could examine.[124] The attitude of Washington and the Court, through Marshall, is indicative of a new nation which, notwithstanding the unreasonable and unjust actions of powerful European countries, was not prepared to be known as a republic unwilling to subscribe to international law doctrines, however distasteful the circumstances.

Despite their maritime differences, France, Britain and the United States were as one in their desire to stamp out the slave trade. The Act of 22 March 1794 prohibited any citizen or resident of the United States from equipping vessels within the United States to carry on the trade or traffic in slaves to any foreign country. There are only six reported slavery opinions delivered by Washington on circuit, three of which give an insight into his approach to the issues. In *Tryphenia v Harrison* (1806), he dealt with an allegation of breach of the 1794 Act. Two French women were aboard a brig with their two slaves for whom they had paid passage from St Thomas to Havana. The district court found the brig to be in breach of the Act

---

[121] *Parker v United States*, 18 F Cas 1179, Penn, October 1809; *United States v Dixey et al*, 25 F Cas 871, Penn, April 1811.
[122] *United States v Morgan et al*, 26 F Cas 1315, Penn, April 1811.
[123] *Armroyd et al v Williams et al*, 1 F Cas 1132, Penn, April 1811.
[124] *Williams et al v Armroyd et al* 7 Cranch (11 US) 423.

but Washington reversed the district judge, holding that the slaves were not carried for sale but as attendants. Notwithstanding his condemnation of the slave trade as 'this inhuman and unjustifiable traffic', he then distinguished between those free Africans then being transported into slavery and those already in bondage. He wrote, 'why should congress prohibit the carrying of persons, already slaves in one of the West Indian Islands, to be sold in another? The situation of these unfortunate persons cannot be rendered worse by this change of situation and masters'.[125] This view of African slaves as personal property to be disposed of at will was to be echoed when justifying the sale of his own slaves in 1821.

There are two of Washington's reported cases in which slaves achieved freedom. In *Butler v Hopper* (1806), Washington held that a former Member of Congress from South Carolina who lived, attended by his slave, both in South Carolina and Pennsylvania, had breached the Pennsylvania Act of 1780 which prohibited the holding of a negro in the state unless registered under the Act. The Act provided exemptions for the domestic slave of a member of Congress or of a person passing through or sojourning in the state without becoming a resident. Washington charged the jury that the 'owner' could not claim either exemption because he had been out of Congress for two years and was a resident of Pennsylvania as he lived in each state for half of the year. The slave was declared a free man.[126] Similarly in *Ex parte Simmons* (1823), another slave who resided with his master in Philadelphia for a period in excess of six months, with no attempt to return him to the plantation in Charleston until his application to the court, was held by the jury, on Washington's charge, to be free under the provisions of the same Act.[127] The two opinions in favour of freedom resulted from clear breaches of statutory provisions and are examples of the justices' very limited success in the area of domestic slavery.

The resolution of maritime disputes or slavery cases was not achieved by Washington alone. For a greater part of the time, he sat with a district judge and a jury. It was very much a team effort. District Judge Peters who sat with Washington in Philadelphia from 1792 to 1828 described their working relationship when dealing with an application for a new trial in *Lessee of Lanning v London* (1822). Washington was minded to grant a new trial. Peters was not, remarking, 'I have a great reluctance at all times, and seldom have I had occasion to differ with the presiding judge, but in this case I was so well satisfied with his charge to the jury, and still so remain, that I cannot join in with the opinion that a new trial be granted.'[128] Usually when both judges disagreed, the Supreme Court would resolve the issue upon a certificate of division of opinion. However, this device was not available on an application for a new trial and unless both judges consented the application failed.

---

[125] *Tryphenia v Harrison*, 24 F Cas 252, Penn, October 1806.
[126] *Butler v Hopper*, 4 F Cas 904, Penn, October 1806.
[127] *Ex Parte Simmons*, 27 F Cas 151, Penn, October 1823.
[128] *Lessee of Lanning v London*, 4 Peters 332, Penn 1822.

Washington's expertise in specific areas of law was gained from his practice at the Bar and from his work on circuit.[129] What remains to be examined is the extent to which this expertise was put to use in the Supreme Court majority opinions he was assigned to write and any shifts in jurisprudential attitude from circuit court to Supreme Court. His Supreme Court opinions are sparse when compared with his circuit output. Unlike the 520 surviving reported circuit opinions which comprise only a fraction of Washington's opinions, every Supreme Court opinion he delivered was recorded in the *United States Reports*. The first 27 volumes show that, during his 31 years on the Court, Washington wrote, when compared with John Marshall and Joseph Story, a modest 80 opinions. Eight were handed down *seriatim*, two were dissents, two concurred with the majority and the remainder were written as the opinion of a unanimous Court or on behalf of the majority. His opinions covered the following topics: 23 maritime, prize and marine insurances cases; 11 land disputes; ten cases with a contract and mercantile background; nine constitutional law cases; six wills or intestacy disputes; five criminal cases; two infringement of patents; and one slavery case. The remaining opinions settled procedural issues such as the admissibility of evidence, whether an action was statute barred or how many counsel were permitted to argue on each side of the case.

Washington's two dissents were delivered with great reluctance. He believed dissenting opinions weakened the authority of the Court as shown by his urging Justice Story not to dissent in what he described as 'ordinary cases' because it 'was of no benefit to the public'.[130] In *Mason v Haile* (1827) he announced his custom of never dissenting when he disagreed with the majority unless he was considering important constitutional issues.[131] This public admission was made at the end of his tenure. If he had publicly confessed to this practice much earlier it would have provided President Jefferson with much-needed ammunition with which to attack Marshall's departure from the *seriatim* opinions of his predecessors. The problem with this approach is the difficulty in defining 'ordinary cases'. There are so many cases which do not raise 'important constitutional issues' but which are sufficiently important to merit a dissenting view. It is clear that his reluctance to dissent arose solely from his wish that the Court present a united front to the nation.

In *Mason*, he was unable to accept the majority view that the states had the right to regulate or abolish imprisonment for debt retrospectively as it altered the contractual position of debtor and creditor and, therefore, infringed the contracts clause of the Constitution. In dissenting, Washington demonstrated the rigid adherence to the sanctity of existing contracts he had adopted in his circuit opinions. His only other dissent occurred in *Lambert's Lessee v Payne* (1805) when

---

[129] Washington's expertise in land law cases is apparent from a reading of his two-volume set of Virginia Court of Appeals reports.

[130] Letter, Joseph Story to Henry Wheaton [court reporter], 8 April 1818 in WW Story, *Life and Letters*, vol 1, 304–05.

[131] *Mason v Haile*, 25 US (12 Wheat) 370 (1827).

abandoning his usual strict interpretation of words used in legal documents, he sought to look with indulgence at technical words used by a testator unused to legal phrases, but his was the lone voice.[132] It is easy to understand his dissent in *Mason* which was a case with constitutional implications. However his dissent in *Lambert's Lessee* is difficult to comprehend as it affected only the immediate parties and was contrary to his custom expressed in *Mason*.

Washington concurred in the landmark case of *Dartmouth College v Woodward* (1819). The New Hampshire legislature enacted laws upheld by the New Hampshire Superior Court placing appointments to the college board in the hands of the state governor, effectively nationalising a private institution in the early days of a nation dedicated to free enterprise. The college had been established by a Crown Charter in 1769. Controversially, John Marshall held the charter to be a private contract between the college and the Crown. It followed, therefore, that the legislation was unconstitutional, contravening the prohibition on a state passing laws impairing the obligation of contracts. Marshall cited no authorities to support his view that the charter was a contract, in typical fashion boldly declaring that, 'it can require no argument to prove the circumstances of this case constitute a contract'. Washington, troubled that such an assertion had been made devoid of any supporting precedent, took the unusual step of filing a concurrence which cited United States and English decisions supporting Marshall's view. Justice Story took a wide entrepreneurial approach, seeking to bring all corporations and charters within the protection of the contracts clause, whereas Washington believed that it should cover only institutions such as the college.[133] This case illustrates Washington's commitment to promoting commerce through the contracts clause but confirms the 'moderation' described by Story in his eulogy by severely limiting the category of institutions entitled to protection under Article 1, section 10.

That commitment to contractual obligations resurfaced in the constitutional case of *Green v Biddle* (1823), when Washington, delivering the majority opinion, refused an application for a rehearing. Virginia had, by compact, surrendered to the United States land which later became the state of Kentucky but restricted Kentucky's right to interfere with any titles already granted by Virginia. Washington held, as Justice Story had on the original hearing, that Kentucky's legislation restricting the titles granted by Virginia was an infringement of the obligation of contract.[134]

Washington wrote for the Court on slavery on just one occasion when, in 1824, it rejected the argument that the Acts of 1794, 1810, and 1818 to suppress the slave trade were limited to a prohibition against bringing into bondage persons who were free in their own country. The district court of Alabama had confiscated a vessel and cargo, which included slaves, for contravening the Acts by transporting,

---

[132] *Lambert's Lessee v Payne*, 7 US (3 Cranch) 97 (1805).
[133] *Dartmouth College v Woodward*, 17 US (4 Wheat) 659 (1819).
[134] *Green v Biddle*, 21 US (8 Wheat) 1 (1823).

on an American vessel, slaves from one slave holding country to another. Washington affirmed the district judge but, following his circuit court opinions and his view of slaves as mere 'property', he wrote for the majority that those existing slaves on board who were passengers 'to be delivered to their owners or to those to whom they had been consigned' should be returned to their owners.[135]

Save for Washington's opinion in *Ogden v Saunders* (1827) his contribution to bankruptcy and insolvency law on the Court was small. In that case, the Court pondered whether the federal government had exclusive powers in bankruptcies. Congress had been authorised by the Constitution to establish uniform bankruptcy laws throughout the Union but had not exercised the power. Washington, for the majority, held a New York bankruptcy law to be within the Constitution on the narrow ground that it had been enacted before the contract had been entered into and would have been in the parties' contemplation and, therefore, did not impair the contract. Washington expressed his respect for 'the wisdom, the integrity, and the patriotism of the legislative body' and declared that he would always presume that legislation complied with the Constitution unless the contrary was proved 'beyond all reasonable doubt'.[136] This was an admission further supporting an unwillingness to look at existing laws with a critical eye.

One of Washington's few patent cases, *Evans v Jordan* (1815), sheds light on Marshall's opinion assignment practice. Marshall did not sit because it was an appeal from his circuit opinion and Washington was the senior associate whose view clearly coincided with the majority. During the course of his opinion he revealed that he had dealt with the same point on his circuit. His seniority, coupled with knowledge of the specific point of law, made him the ideal candidate for the task. It is difficult to imagine a failure to mention his familiarity with the topic before being asked to write the opinion.[137]

Because civil disputes formed the major part of the Court's work, there were few criminal cases to be assigned by the Chief Justice. Washington authored only five. One is relevant because it highlights a way in which the circuit court shaped American law. In *United States v Kelly* (1826), Washington merely stated that the Court was considering a division of opinion from the judges of the Pennsylvania circuit court. In his circuit opinion, however, he made it clear to counsel that he and the district judge had reluctantly given a definition of the crime of revolt because other judges had done so on circuit. He believed it was for Congress to define the offence, so he invented a division of opinion to have the law clarified by the Court. In the event, he gave the opinion of the Court and, no doubt emboldened by his brethren, had no hesitation in declaring it competent to define the offence.[138]

---

[135] *The Merino*, 22 US 391 (1824).
[136] *Ogden v Saunders*, 25 US (12 Wheat) 213 (1827).
[137] *Evans v Jordan*, 3 US (9 Cranch) 199 (1815).
[138] *United States v Kelly*, 26 F Cas 700, Penn, October 1825; *United States v Kelly*, 24 US 417 (1826).

# Conclusion

Washington was an extremely cautious justice, almost entirely dependent on the doctrine of precedent for guidance as to what his opinion should be; unhappy when he was faced with a novel point of law and overly concerned about the view the Supreme Court would take if his rulings were taken on appeal. That his defining jurisprudence was the need for certainty and uniformity of federal law is supported by his opinion in *United States v Bright* of the 'miserable' condition facing any community disregarding precedent. He felt constrained by legal principles in *Croudson & Ors v Leonard* even though he accepted injustice would arise, taking the view that a judge should not usurp the function of government by remedying injustices in the law. He was firmly of the view that a judge was duty bound to follow the law and not consider the effect on the parties as he did in *Scriba v Insurance Company of North America* and in *Kirkpatrick v White et al*. His refusal to investigate alleged irregularities in jury deliberations and his obvious pride in declaring that he disagreed with his juries only twice in 16 years are further examples of an inflexible approach to the administration of justice (*King v Delaware; Willis v Bucher; Harrison v Rowan; United States v Haskell et al*).

In *Ogden v Saunders*, Washington felt compelled to follow the earlier decision of *Sturges v Crowninshield*, in which he had concurred, despite believing it to have been wrongly decided. This approach, for the sake of unanimity, was also evident in his advice to Story not to dissent because it weakened the Court's authority and also by his remark in *Mason v Haile* that he never disagreed with the majority unless it was a constitutional issue. It is further supported by only two dissents in 30 years; once in *Mason* and the other in *Lambert's Lessee v Payne* which was not even a constitutional matter.

In his search for support, Washington and the other justices looked for guidance to the small number of federal statutes and Supreme Court decisions; to state laws and, in particular, to the decisions of the English courts and the textbooks of the English jurists. Washington was more reliant than his colleagues on the decisions of English judges and Lord Mansfield, in particular, whom he regarded as the highest authority (*Ferguson v Zepp; Bobyshall v Oppenheimer* and *Barnes v Billingham*). His reliance on English law and practice was such that, in *Craig*, where state law conflicted with English law, he preferred the latter. Washington readily adopted the opinions of other circuit courts even though of only persuasive authority (*Treadwell et al. v Bladen; Martin v Bank of United States, and United States v Moses*). On occasion, he was so keen to find cases to guide him that he looked at decisions based on facts which were not materially the same as those under consideration, as he did in *Bond v The Cora*. His uncertainty was apparent in *Mott v Maris* where he followed a state court decision about which he had doubts. In *Hylton v Brown*, unable to find any direct authority, the court approached informally two retired judges for advice. Further, in *Delancy v M'Keen*, Washington sought the advice of counsel unconnected with the case. These cases show the lengths to which he went to form an opinion.

His public expressions of doubt as to the correctness of his opinions in cases such as *Odlin v Insurance Company of Pennsylvania*; *McFadden v The Exchange* and *Consequa v Willings* give the impression of a judge constantly looking over his shoulder to the Supreme Court and are in stark contrast to his robust indications to juries on factual issues which were not open to appeal and to his firm handling of the politically explosive cases of *Bright* and *Corfield*.

Criticisms of Washington's narrow interpretation of statutes, his rigid dependence on the doctrine of precedent, his uncertainty and his lack of concern about the consequences to the parties of his opinions should be balanced against the undoubted benefits of stability which precedent brought to his circuit court. This meant that industrious counsel, willing to research the authorities, would have been well placed to advise their clients on the reasonable prospects of success of their litigation.

Due to his extensive grounding at the Bar and on the circuit bench, Washington approached his maritime opinions for the Court with more confidence as those cases generally depended on findings of fact rather than difficult points of law. He, alone, had to decide whether to accept or reject excuses for breaches of embargo or revenue laws. He was quick to see through spurious defences (*United States v The Paul Sherman*) but willing to refuse forfeiture where the explanation appeared reasonable (*Parker v United States*; *United States v Dixey et al*; *United States v Morgan et al*). Overall, his enforcement of the embargo laws was more even-handed than the approach of his brother Story.

Washington's protection of vested rights was demonstrated in *Milligan v Dickson* when he refused to overturn many titles to land on a point of evidence and in *Gordon v Holiday* he safeguarded from confiscation the title of an heir to an enemy alien. Generally his approach to land disputes was pragmatic; he waived minor irregularities whenever he could in order to preserve the status quo (*Griffith v Tunckhouser*; *Huidekoper v Burrus*; *Willis v Bucher et al*; *Torrey v Beardsley*). His conservative Federalism was also evident in his promotion of commerce by the rules he laid down governing bills of exchange and promissory notes (*Craig v Brown*; *Humphreys v Blight's Assignees*; *Perry et al v Crammond et al*; *McMurtry v Jones*) and by his clarification of the law and procedure governing maritime contracts and marine insurance (*McGregor v Insurance Company of Pennsylvania*; *Delaware Insurance Company v Hogan*; *Vale v Phoenix Insurance Co*).

*Corfield v Coryell* and *United States v Bright* were the two most significant circuit opinions Washington wrote. Not only do they reveal momentous constitutional issues facing the Union, they show why it was prudent to have Supreme Court justices ride circuit to deal with such politically sensitive matters. The opinions are also notable because they present the normally diffident Washington in a new light. In *Corfield*, his restricting to its citizens the right to harvest the state's natural resources and his willingness to break new ground by an interpretation of the privileges and immunities clause of the Constitution reveal a justice determined to preserve property rights. In *Bright*, by vehemently condemning a state's use of force to defy an order of a federal district judge, he made it plain that federal law was supreme and would be enforced.

Washington's view of his slaves as mere items of personal property was evident in his approach to the one reported circuit opinion on slavery he wrote when in *Tryphenia v Harrison*, he was unable to see the harm to a slave, uprooted to another master on a different Caribbean island. It is fair to observe that he strictly enforced the prohibition placed on the international slave by the Act of 1794 and declared slaves free for clear registration and residence breaches of the Pennsylvania 1780. Otherwise he had no impact on the plight of those already held to slavery within the United States.

In short, Washington's jurisprudence is well illustrated by his many surviving circuit opinions. His approach was dominated by precedent which provided the stability and uniformity he sought, despite occasional injustices. His opinions, whilst sometimes expressing uncertainty, reveal the importance to him of the supremacy of the national government and federal justice and the need for unanimity on the Supreme Court. They also disclose a resolve to preserve existing property rights and to seek economic prosperity by shaping contract law to promote inter-state and international trade. That he was very well respected is revealed by the eulogies in national and local newspapers. The editor of *The Spectator* (New York) of 12 January 1829, when bemoaning the inevitability of 'One by one the men of other days are thus passing away from the scene of their conflicts and triumphs,' concluded quaintly that 'It is for us to tale care that pigmies do not succeed them in their high places.'

There can be no doubt but his was a life spent unstintingly in the service of others. The law dominated his existence and despite ill health he continued to discharge his duty on circuit virtually to the day he died on 26 November, 1829. Six days before his death and despite his failing health, the judge was keen to discuss the Virginia Convention, Virginia University, the unsettled state of the country's politics and how important it was for the Supreme Court to retain its independence and act as a corrective to legislative bodies. The judge felt that 'although all of the decisions [of the Court] had not yet been made, there were enough to establish principles, and to define the boundaries of state rights, and those of the general government'. He revealed that 'it had always been a maxim of the Court to presume that the legislature meant well, that therefore on indifferent points their pretensions were admitted but when the pretensions were such that the operations of the general government could be cramped by them, they were quashed'.[139]

---

[139] These quotes are contained in an undated Journal of Law but were clearly published shortly after Washington's death. The informant is said to be an unnamed friend with a family connection who visited the judge six days before he died. The sentiments said to have been expressed by the judge coincide with the jurisprudence contained in this chapter. Extract from a *Journal of Law*, in Harvard Law School Library, Bushrod Washington, 1798–1823, Letters and Legal Opinion in Small Manuscripts Collection, Hollis No 002229211.

# 4

# Henry Brockholst Livingston: Consolidating Mercantile Law

Despite holding office as a justice of the New York State Supreme Court for five years and as a United States Supreme Court Justice for 16 years, Brockholst Livingston is one of the lesser-known associate justices of the Marshall Court and has been largely ignored by scholars. There has been no book-length biography and so little has been written about his life and cases that the only way to discern his jurisprudence is by an examination of his state, federal Second Circuit and Supreme Court opinions. This will reveal his role in the resolution of the political and economic issues of the period and show how he developed the law to meet such challenges. Special attention is paid to his time as presiding justice of the Second Circuit and to those opinions he delivered which helped to shape the commercial law of the United States between 1802 and 1823.

The source of all references to Livingston in biographical dictionaries is a 12-page sketch written by Gerald T Dunne in 1969 with four additional pages setting out the text of one New York and one Supreme Court opinion.[1] Dunne had earlier edited and commented upon ten letters passing between Livingston and Justice Story between 1812 and 1822 which touched upon circuit and Supreme Court business.[2] Unfortunately, the Livingston Papers in the New York State Library have nothing to say about his life in the law.[3] That is the extent of the scholarship on this Supreme Court Justice. No-one has taken up Dunne's call, 46 years ago, for a biography of a man who had close connections with the 'Revolution, the evolution of the first political parties, the emergence of an authentically American *corpus* of commercial law, and the institutional development of the Supreme Court under a Federalist Chief Justice with Democratic-Republican

---

[1] Gerald T Dunne, 'Brockholst Livingston' in L Friedman and F Israel, *The Justices of the United States Supreme Court, 1789–1969, vol 1* (New York: Chelsea House Publishers, 1969) 387–403. There is no manuscript collection of Livingston's papers. All of his surviving documents are spread across the collections of others. See, Peter A Wonders, *Directory of Manuscript Collections Related to Federal Judges, 1789–1997* (Washington DC: Federal Judicial Center, 1998) 122.

[2] Gerald T Dunne, 'The Story-Livingston Correspondence' (1966) 10 *The American Journal of Legal History* 224–36.

[3] The papers cover property transactions and personal accounts. There is a letter from Livingston to Governor Clinton dated 31 July 1807 recommending an acquaintance for a public position and a letter of 30 January 1821 confirming himself as a subscriber to the Law Register of the United States. That is the extent of the collection.

associates.'[4] G Edward White's description in 1988 of Livingston as 'the third of the "silent" Justices of the Marshall Court's cohesive years', may explain the reluctance of scholars to study him.[5] Whilst Livingston was not amongst the first rank of the Marshall Court justices, to describe him as 'silent' thereby placing him with Justices Todd and Duvall does him a disservice. This examination of all of his reported opinions from three jurisdictions begins a response to Dunne's suggestion for further research and demonstrates not merely a supportive acquiescent role on the Court but an active participation in the shaping of the substantive and procedural constituents of United States business law.

## The Early Years: Political Allegiances: From Federalist to Republican

Livingston was born in New York City on 25 November 1757 into one of the most distinguished New York families, his father having been Governor of New Jersey during the Revolution. Livingston was graduated BA from the College of New Jersey (now Princeton University) in 1774, with fellow student, James Madison, later to become the fourth president of the United States. His plan to study law was interrupted by service in the Continental Army. Having attained the rank of Lieutenant-Colonel at just 21 years of age, he served as an aide to General Benedict Arnold and witnessed the surrender of General John Burgoyne in 1777. Coming from such a privileged background it was only to be expected that he would support Federalist ideals.

Between 1779 and 1782, while serving as private secretary to his brother-in-law, John Jay, his adherence to the Federalist cause came under intense pressure because of the extreme personal animosity between the two men. Livingston, who had an explosive temper, was frequently insolent towards his brother-in-law and often made disparaging remarks about Congress to foreigners.[6] This does not appear to be as a result of disillusionment with Federalist policies but more due to his extreme dislike of his brother-in-law. Jay, a leading Federalist was then United States Minister to Spain and later, in 1789, the first Chief Justice of the

---

[4] Dunne, 'Brockholst Livingston' at 397.
[5] G Edward White, *A History of the Supreme Court of the United States, vols III–IV: The Marshall Court and Cultural Change, 1815–1835* (New York: Cambridge University Press, 2010), 327. First published by Macmillan Publishing Company in 1988.
[6] Whilst in Spain, Livingston's sister Sarah (John Jay's wife) wrote to their father of her 'discontent & disgust' at her brother's 'insolent' treatment of her husband and his bad behaviour generally, and of his disparaging remarks about the Congress to foreign visitors. In her letter she refers to 'my brother's temper I always knew to be irritable to an unhappy excess'. Letter, Sara Jay to William Livingston, Madrid, 24 June 1781 in Landa M Freeman, Louise V North and Janet M Wedge, (eds) *Selected Letters of John Jay and Sarah Livingston Jay* (Jefferson, North Carolina: MacFarland and Company Inc, Publishers, 2005), 107–08.

United States Supreme Court. He had been sent abroad in 1779 to obtain recognition and economic aid for the United States and when, in 1782, Jay left for France to negotiate the treaty which ended the Revolutionary War, Livingston returned home. On the voyage from Spain, Livingston's vessel was intercepted and he was captured by the British. Upon reaching New York he was held there for a time as a prisoner of war but was set free upon giving his parole to a British General, Sir Guy Carlton, a decision which required a letter of explanation to President Washington.[7]

In 1796 a ship Livingston part-owned was captured by the British and burnt.[8] The seizure by the British in 1804 of another vessel in which Livingston had a substantial financial interest and her subsequent condemnation by a British Admiralty court caused him great inconvenience and an anxious wait of nine years before he recovered his losses after suing his insurers.[9] His own capture and that of two of his ships would have soured his attitude towards Britain.

Upon his release Livingston began reading law in Albany under Peter Yates. Yates was an anti-Federalist delegate to the Continental Congress who spoke against ratification of the Constitution, and who was later appointed a state judge of the Western District of New York. While there is no evidence to suggest that Yates sought to bring Livingston within the Republican fold, he would have been exposed to his master's extreme political views. Livingston was admitted to the Bar in 1783, practising in New York until his appointment to the New York Supreme Court in 1802. He had an extensive practice at the Bar and in one murder case was co-counsel with Alexander Hamilton, later Secretary of the Treasury, and Aaron Burr whose main claim to fame, apart from killing Hamilton in a duel in 1804, was his appointment as Vice-President of the United States and subsequent trial for treason.[10]

That Livingston had also been involved in at least two duels and had actually killed his opponent in a contest in New York in 1798 was not seen as a bar to his political or legal ambitions. The editor of the *Vermont Gazette* strongly criticised the resolution of political differences in this manner, writing,

> It is certainly a matter of regret, that genteel murder is so frequently heard of in civil society; that party dissention so often exceeds the bounds of prudence, and that brutal

---

[7] Friedman and Israel, vol 1 at 388.

[8] *The Weekly Museum* (New York) reported it thus, 'We understand that the *Diana* East Indiaman, lately captured by the British, and burnt at Martinico, belonged wholly to Messrs Le Roy and Banyard, John Vanderbelt, Brockholst Livingston, Philip Livingston, and Charles Clarkson, of this city. These gentlemen are all natural born Americans.'

[9] *Livingston & Gilchrist v Maryland Insurance Co.* 11 US (7 Cranch), 506 (1813). A jury found against Livingston in the Maryland Circuit Court but the Supreme Court, which Livingston had just joined and recused himself, ordered a new trial on the ground of the justice's misdirection.

[10] Burr and Hamilton had been bitter enemies for over a decade before the fatal duel, Burr's biographer, Isenberg (2007) argues that Burr was the object of Hamilton's relentless political and personal attacks in an attempt to destroy him by lies and slanderous letters to persons of influence. Conversely, Chernow (2004) in *Alexander Hamilton,* justifies his subject's efforts to undermine Burr, writing that 'Hamilton was a man of such deep, unalterable principles that Burr was bound to strike him as devoid of any moral compass.' Nancy Isenberg, *Fallen Founder: The Life of Aaron Burr* (New York: Viking Penguin, 2007) 107, 119–21; Ron Chernow, *Alexander Hamilton* (New York: The Penguin Press, 2004), 421–22.

force or assassinating skills so frequently robs the child of its father, or blasts the fairest hopes of worthy families. Addresses to the President, approving of his [Livingston's] conduct are still presented from various quarters, and from very respectable bodies.[11]

Livingston's proficiency in law, his powerful family connections and his ties to the wealthy of the City brought him success despite his lack of self-control. His relationship with John Jay further deteriorated when, in 1785, Jay sued and obtained judgment against Livingston for repayment of a loan and, during the course of the proceedings, accused him of insulting and libelling him whilst serving as his private secretary in Spain. The rift never healed.[12] Livingston served as a Federalist on the New York Assembly between 1786 and 1789 and his political and professional prospects were enhanced when, on 5 July 1789, he delivered the first Independence Day oration in St. Paul's Church, New York to an audience which included President Washington and members of Congress.

Jay, having served three years as Chief Justice of the United States Supreme Court and tired of riding circuit, ran for the governorship of New York State in 1792. It was a bitter campaign and he was narrowly defeated. Livingston and others had successfully argued that crucial and potentially decisive votes cast for Jay in Otsego County should not be counted because they had been delivered by a sheriff whose commission had expired. This led Livingston's sister (Jay's wife) to complain that she felt that he had disgraced the family name by his opposition to his brother-in-law.[13] It is clear that within a few short years Livingston would have a political party, led by Jefferson and Madison, to further his ambitions and to support in his vendetta against Jay.

Jay was elected governor in 1795 and was re-elected in 1798 despite Livingston's open and vocal support for opponents in both elections. One of the principal features of the generally unpopular 10-year treaty Jay negotiated with Britain in 1794 was the strengthening of trade between the two countries. Although passed by the Senate and ratified by President Washington, the treaty was denounced by Anti-Federalists in every state, fearing that close links with monarchic Britain would undermine republicanism. They favoured France in the European wars and Jefferson's hatred of Britain was such that he hoped that the French would invade England to establish liberty and republicanism throughout the island.[14] Livingston echoed Jefferson's sentiments by roundly condemning the treaty during Jay's 1795 election campaign, support which was noted by the future President and rewarded in 1807.[15]

---

[11] *Vermont Gazette,* 18 May 1798. Many years later an account of the duel appeared in a West coast newspaper from a 'correspondent' glorifying Livingston's action but making the absurd claim that he 'never passed an hour without remorse. It preyed upon him until his own heart ceased to beat; for he was a strictly religious man' (*San Francisco Bulletin,* 15 October 1874, taken from *The New York Evening Post*).
[12] Walter Stahr, *John Jay* (New York: Hambledon & Continuum, 2005), 231.
[13] Freeman, *Selected Letters*. Letter, Sarah Jay to John Jay, 10 June 1792, 211.
[14] Henry Augustine Washington, *Writings of Thomas Jefferson,* vol IV (New York: Derby & Jackson, 1859) 118.
[15] Timothy L Hall, 'Henry Brockholst Livingston' in *Supreme Court Justices: A Biographical Dictionary* (New York: Facts on File Inc., 2001), 56.

Livingston's political prevarications were not unusual. Justices William Johnson, Story and Thompson were disappointments to the Republican presidents who had nominated them because of their failure to uphold state sovereignty vigorously and by generally falling in line with the Federalist agenda of the Marshall Court. These changes in political allegiance cast light on the political fluidity of the period when earlier expectations of how the Constitution would be interpreted had yet to be met, whereas Samuel Chase's conversion to Federalism from fierce opposition to the Constitution because it infringed state sovereignty was due in large measure to his wish for federal judicial office.[16]

A good illustration of swings in political affiliations is that of the fourth president, James Madison. His drafting of the Constitution and the Bill of Rights, coupled with his crucial role in the Virginia Ratification Debate placed him as a committed Federalist supporting the notion of a strong national government with authority over the states.[17] The first clear evidence of political change is his opposition to an all-powerful central authority contained in an essay he wrote in 1792 labelling members of his former party as the 'anti-Republican party' and as 'stupid, suspicious, licentious' and 'accomplices of atheism and anarchy'.[18]

The Alien and Sedition Acts of 1798, passed in the aftermath of the French Revolution and war with France were designed to strengthen national security but were misused by the Adams administration and the federal courts to prosecute Republicans who ventured to criticize the president or members of his government.[19] Madison countered the misuse of those acts with an anonymous drafting in December 1798 of the *Virginia Resolution against the Alien and Sedition Acts* declaring them to be unconstitutional and asserting the right of states to 'interpose for arresting the progress of the evil'.[20] Having been elected president in 1807 Madison moderated his extreme views and attempted to strike a balance between the power of central government and respect for the powers of the states.[21] Whilst Madison is an extreme example, it does reveal how political views

---

[16] James Haw and Ors, *Stormy Patriot: The Life of Samuel Chase* (Baltimore: Maryland Historical Society, 1980), 174–75. Stephen B Presser, *Studies in the History of the United States Courts of the Third Circuit* (Washington DC: The Bicentennial Committee of the Judicial Conference of the United States, 1982), 37–8.

[17] Jack N Rakove (ed), *Madison: Writings* (New York: Library of America, 1999). Involvement in; Framing and Ratifying the Constitution, 357–58; Federalist Papers Nos 41–46; 226–72; Virginia Ratifying Debate (Judicial Power), 393–400; Constitutional Amendments (Bill of Rights), 437–52.

[18] ibid, 'Who are the Best Keepers of the People's Liberties?' 532–34.

[19] Section 2 of an Act for the Punishment of Certain Crimes Against the United States, approved 14 July 1798 in Richard Peters (ed), *The Public Statutes at Large of the United States of America*, vol 1 (Boston: Little & Brown, 1845), 596–97.

[20] *Virginia Resolution* approved by the Virginia House of Delegates 21 December 1798 in Rakove, *Madison: Writings*, 589–91. Jefferson went further in his draft of the *Kentucky Resolution* by actually threatening nullification and suggesting that legislation deemed by the states to be unconstitutional 'might drive these states into revolution and blood'. This was how he acted even while Vice-President under John Adams. See Merill D Peterson, *Jefferson: Writings* (New York: Library of America, 1984), 453–54.

[21] First Inaugural Address in Rakove, *Madison: Writings*, 681.

can change when new responsibilities are assumed, whether it be the presidency or high judicial office. It explains why justices after appointment might be more concerned with the stability of government underpinned by a viable judicial system rather than fulfilling party expectations. The fact that, by virtue of Article III, Section 1 of the Constitution, the justices held office during good behaviour gave them the independence to act in a manner they believed beneficial to the nation, unlike many state judges whose tenure depended upon the pleasure of the legislature, party backers, and the electorate.

Livingston's ability as a lawyer aside, a seat on the state Supreme Court seemed likely through family connections; Edward Livingston was mayor of New York and three Livingston in-laws, Thomas Tillotson, Morgan Lewis and Smith Thompson were, respectively, Secretary of State of New York, Chief Justice and Associate Justice of the New York Supreme Court. In the event his elevation was due to Republican and not Federalist patronage. Following his support of Republican candidates and opposition to John Jay, Livingston helped carry New York for Thomas Jefferson during the presidential elections of 1800 and he spoke publicly for Jefferson and against President John Adams. Jay's son, Peter, remarked that Livingston, as voting took place, 'made speeches to the mob, though he himself was one of the candidates'.[22] It would appear that the transition from Federalist to Republican was complete.

## Commercial Law for New York State

In 1802 Livingston joined family members Morgan Lewis and Smith Thompson on the bench of the New York Supreme Court, an appointment which had a mixed reception depending on the politics of the reporting newspaper.[23] He had the good fortune to have as a colleague on that bench, James Kent, one of the finest legal minds of his generation, which will have greatly enhanced the experience. The New York Supreme Court consisted of a Chief Justice and four associates which, when all justices sat, enabled the handing down of a majority opinion. The law reports reveal that on occasions because a justice was absent through illness or a recently appointed justice had not heard the arguments of counsel or had been counsel in the case, no opinion could be delivered because the court was evenly

---

[22] Letter, Peter A Jay to John Jay, 3 May 1800 in Stahr, *John Jay* at 360.
[23] *The Republican Watch Tower* (New York) of 16 January 1802 declared: 'We are authorised to state, and we do so with much pleasure, that Mr Brockholst Livingston, whose talents and probity are universally admired; and Mr Smith Thompson, a gentleman learned in the law, and of brilliant parts, are appointed by the hon. the council of appointments of this state, judges of our supreme court.' The editor of the Federalist *Salem Gazette* did not join in the universal admiration. He wrote for the edition of 22 January, 'BROCKHOLST LIVINGSTON, who not long since shot a fellow citizen dead in a duel, has by the democratic government of New York been recently appointed a Judge of the Supreme Court in that State.'

divided. In *Jackson v Horton* (1805) the problem of an equally divided court was overcome by counsel turning the dispute into a special verdict for determination by the Court for the Correction of Errors, much in the same way as a disagreement between federal circuit and district judge was placed before the United States Supreme Court on a certificate of division of opinion.[24]

A very dubious method of resolving the embarrassment of an equally divided court occurred in *Jackson v Munson* (1806), a case involving land forfeited for adhering to the enemy. The case is extraordinary for a blatant breach of the protocol that a justice who had appeared for a party in the court below should play no part in the appeal. The reports of George Caines and William Johnson contain numerous examples of recusals for this specific reason. Despite the convention, Justice Spencer, who had appeared earlier as counsel for the defendant, broke the deadlock by holding in favour of his former clients, deciding that they were entitled to compensation for improvements to land. He may well have come to the correct decision but justice was not seen to be done. He regretted delivering an opinion remarking that he did so 'reluctantly'. His unwillingness would have been of little consolation to the losing party.[25]

The law reports of Caines and Johnson give the names of the justices who gave the opinion of the court, those who concurred and those who dissented and reveal that a greater number of the opinions were delivered *per curiam* (by the court) without naming any justice. For example, between May and October 1811 of a total of 304 opinions handed down only 19 were attributable to specific justices. Justice Livingston wrote 149 opinions whilst on the New York Supreme Court and, when considered with the 47 reported cases from the Second Circuit between 1808 and 1822 and the 38 majority opinions, six concurrences, and eight dissents he delivered in the United States Supreme Court, they provide a reasonable insight into his jurisprudence. An examination of the significant output from his time on the state court reveals his own vision for the development of the law, his attitude towards jury verdicts and the dynamics of decision making in New York at the beginning of the nineteenth century as well as his grounding in all aspects of commercial law.

The New York Supreme Court judges were kept extremely busy. Not only did they hear appeals, like the United States Supreme Court justices, they were obliged to ride circuit throughout New York State trying, generally with a jury, civil and criminal cases at first instance. The judges also sat on the New York Court for the Trial of Impeachments and Correction of Errors which heard appeals from the state supreme court and the chancery court. There was no separation of powers within the Court for the Correction of Errors which was predominantly a political body, comprising the Lieutenant Governor, members of the New York Senate, the Chancellor and the justices of the state supreme court.

---

[24] *Jackson v Horton*, Caines' Reports, vol 3, 202, August 1805.
[25] *Jackson v Munson*, Johnson's Reports, vol 1, 283, May 1806.

This hierarchy made it possible for a judge to try a case on circuit, sit on the appeal or writ of error to the state supreme court and, finally, be permitted to explain his reasoning to the Court of Correction of Errors but not have a say in the final outcome.[26] An examination of the state court opinions reveals numerous instances where judges not only sat on appeals from cases they tried at first instance, but also gave the opinion of the state supreme court affirming their original ruling. This, as in the United States Supreme Court, was considered perfectly acceptable; the only time a judge refrained from delivering an opinion was when he had a financial interest in the outcome, was related to one of the parties to the suit, or had been counsel in the case at first instance.

Article 25 of the New York Constitution of 1777 provided for the continued use by state courts of British statute and case law which had been adopted by the colony prior to 19 April 1776, subject to any amendments by the state legislature. It follows, therefore, that the New York State Supreme Court reports are dominated by constant favourable references to the decisions of British judges and writers. The reports reveal that Hale, Blackstone, Lords Mansfield, Holt, Ellenborough and Kenyon, were generally held in high regard by Livingston and Thompson.[27] This was to be expected given that the legal education of lawyers of this period was based on Hale's *Pleas of the Crown* and Blackstone's *Commentaries on the Laws of England*. Livingston was willing to follow post-1776 British authorities remarking in the marine insurance embargo case of *Penny v New York Insurance Company* (1805) that he was willing to adopt the English rule despite it being post Revolution and not on the grounds of authority but merely because it was the most reasonable approach to the problem.[28] He did not always follow English decisions. In *Leroy v Lewis* (1803), Livingston pointedly announced that he had not founded his judgment on a British decision but on a former decision of the state supreme court.[29]

When dealing with admiralty and marine insurance cases he was quick to protect insurance companies by examining carefully potentially fraudulent claims, such as the subsequent insuring of a vessel lost at sea or spurious explanations for route deviations. Thus in *Watson v Delafield* (1804) he sent out a clear warning that a partner who knew that a vessel had been lost was under a strict duty to inform the other partner of the crucial fact to prevent him from arranging ineffective insurance.[30] His expertise in marine insurance was gained by dealing with

---

[26] New York Constitution 1777, Article 33.

[27] The law reports of the New York Supreme Court and the Court for the Correction of Errors upon which this aspect of the research is based comprise: George Caines, 3 vols, May 1803–November 1805, 3rd ed revised by William G. Banks (New York: Banks and Bros. Law Publishers, 1883–1885); William Johnson, 3 vols, 1799–1803 and 20 vols, 1806–1823. These two law reporters cover the periods on the state court by Justice Livingston, 1802–1806 and Justice Thompson, 1802–1818.

[28] *Penny v New York Insurance Company*, Caines' Reports, vol III, August 1805, 157.

[29] *Leroy v Lewis*, May 1803, Caines' Reports, 175.

[30] *Watson v Delafield*, November 1804, Caines' Reports, vol II, 224. See also *Livingston v Delafield*, Caines' Reports, vol III, 53 which turned on the question of whether the insured knew that the vessel had already perished.

issues such as the seaworthiness of a vessel at the beginning of a voyage; whether a mere intention to deviate from an agreed route avoided the policy; who was to pay for seamen's wages and provisions after capture by the enemy; and the duty to insure a vessel against the need for repairs on voyage. The list is not exhaustive as the reports reveal all manner of maritime issues. What is clear is that he was well prepared to deal confidently with admiralty matters on the Marshall Court.

Livingston's state opinions on commercial law underpinned the status of partnership which he believed to be crucial to the development of trade and industry, being aware of the need to protect one partner against the fraud or incompetence of another. In *Green v Beals* (1804) he held that one partner could not execute a bond without the express authority of the other as this would permit him to dissipate the partnership assets, declaring that it would otherwise render partnerships more dangerous than they were already and might even discourage them altogether.[31] He continued this theme in *Casey v Brush* (1805) by refusing to allow a claim by one partner against another in respect of a 'joint transaction' when the other had not expressly consented to the venture.[32] The protection thus afforded by the court would allay the fears of and reassure the competent and careful member of a partnership.

Trade and the maintenance of government revenue required a substantial body of federal officials to supervise all aspects of commercial life from seizing goods shipped in breach of embargo or non-intercourse laws or the avoidance of customs duties to the inspection of foodstuffs to ensure they were fit for human consumption. In *Henderson v Brown* (1803) a revenue collector was sued personally for trespass when he levied execution on a theatre which was wrongly described as a dwelling-house in a list he had been given. Thompson held the collector liable, but Livingston favoured the majority view that a government official should not be held liable for the mistakes of his superiors and be put in a position where he looked to his employers for ex gratia recoupment.[33] He confirmed his belief that public officials acting in good faith should be protected in *Seaman v Patten* (1805) when observing that the court would protect from liability government employees who acted mistakenly but honestly in the performance of their duties. In that case an inspector wrongly condemned a quantity of beef. Livingston directed the jury that the inspector should not be held liable unless he acted with malice as it 'seems cruel not to protect them when they act with integrity'.[34] Thus, a trader who had suffered loss due to the incompetence of an honest official had no redress.

Justices, whether on state or federal courts, generally tried cases with a jury and the verdict, if disputed, fell for review before the state supreme court and later the United States Supreme Court. The jury system was the cornerstone of the United States justice system and, as far as criminal trials were concerned, that

---

[31] *Green v Beals*, Caines' Reports, vol II, November 1804, 255.
[32] *Casey v Brush*, Caines' Reports, vol II, February 1805, 295.
[33] *Henderson v Brown*, May 1803, Caines' Reports, vol I, 94.
[34] *Seamen v Patten*, Caines' Reports, vol II, February 1805, 314.

crucial protection of the citizen was enshrined in Article III, Section 2 of the Constitution. Most judges considered the verdict of a jury, in civil and criminal cases, as sacrosanct and were reluctant to inquire into the jury's deliberations, not welcoming evidence of misconduct. Justice Washington, as has been noted earlier, announced that in 16 years sitting on circuit in Pennsylvania a jury had reached a verdict contrary to the opinion of the court on only two occasions.[35] Furthermore, Washington in *Harrison v Rowan* refused to look into affidavit evidence from jurors complaining that they had been pressured by other jurors to reach a verdict. Washington would not interfere with a verdict solemnly delivered in court.[36]

Judges burdened with heavy dockets would not wish to re-open cases, some of which had been determined after lengthy argument and consideration. Livingston, however, did not believe that juries were infallible and was prepared to hear of irregularities in their deliberations, and, in obvious cases, would set aside the verdict and order a new trial. Thus, in *Smith v Chetham* (1805), he delivered the court's opinion setting aside a jury's verdict of damages in a libel action condemning it as a verdict based on 'chance or lot' and not one based on 'reflection'. In that case a constable supervising a jury in retirement reported that the jury could not agree on an appropriate award of damages so each juror put forward his figure and the aggregate was divided by 12. Livingston's concern was that litigants were entitled to a verdict based on the evidence and if they could not rely on jurors doing their duty, they might resort to more intemperate means of obtaining redress. In the course of his opinion Livingston took the opportunity of rehearsing the many instances, both in the United States and England, where verdicts had been set aside because of jury misbehaviour including the case of *Mellish v Arnold* in which the jury decided whether $200 or $300 was appropriate by tossing up a cross and a pile.[37]

In the same month Livingston, for the court, set aside another jury verdict in the land dispute of *Brandt v Ogden*, describing it as palpably wrong and against the weight of the evidence. The jury had disregarded the evidence of four wholly independent witnesses and had preferred the evidence of a single witness who had an interest in the outcome of the proceedings.[38] In *Smith v Chetham*, when referring to judges' unwillingness to question surprising jury verdicts, Livingston wondered 'why judges are so tender of the jury'.[39] The use of this phrase indicated that he recognised that jurors were not above human frailty and he was not was prepared to treat all jury verdicts as inviolable. It may also reveal a lack of faith in the jury system from one whose wealthy background gave him a sense of superiority and the confidence to question the ability of ordinary citizens to properly evaluate evidence and put aside prejudices. His readiness to overturn jury verdicts sets him apart from his brethren.

---

[35] *Willis v Bucher* 30 F Cas 63, Penn, April 1818.
[36] *Harrison v Rowan*, 11 F Cas 663, New Jersey, April 1820.
[37] *Smith v Chetham*, Caines' Reports, vol III, May 1805 p 58; *Mellish v Arnold*, Bumb 51.
[38] *Brandt v Ogden*, Caines' Reports, vol III, 10, May 1805.
[39] *Smith v Chetham* at 60.

When considering the range of cases which form the basis of Livingston's experience on the New York Supreme Court between 1802 and 1806, it is important to look beyond the 149 opinions he handed down because in five years he sat on over 1,000 cases covering virtually every conceivable point of law. He will have participated in the many *per curiam* opinions and listened to the arguments in and heard and contributed to the opinions delivered by fellow justices. In Livingston's final year on the court, opinions were delivered on 252 cases.[40] It follows that Livingston's expertise extended far beyond the points of law involved in his own opinions and his New York apprenticeship well prepared for him the challenge of the Marshall Supreme Court. Justice Livingston came to the Court in February 1807, bringing with him his experience as an advocate and five years as a puisne and appellate associate justice of the New York court and considerable experience in commercial and admiralty law.[41]

## A Republican on a Federalist Supreme Court

President Jefferson determined to fill any vacancies on the Supreme Court with committed Republicans in an effort to balance its political composition and to ensure that the Court did not rival the legislature and the executive in power and influence. Although Jefferson considered Livingston as a possible replacement for Justice Alfred Moore in 1804, he nominated the more experienced William Johnson of South Carolina. When a vacancy arose in 1807 upon the death of Justice William Paterson, Jefferson had no hesitation in naming Livingston who had demonstrated, by his political activity in New York, that he was a man dedicated to the Republican cause. Upon appointment, Livingston went on the Second Circuit which meant that in addition to his sittings in Washington on the Supreme Court, his previous New York state circuit travels were extended to include Connecticut and Vermont. As did other circuit justices, Livingston suffered the physical hardship associated with travelling circuit. Apart from the discomfort of travelling many miles on very poor roads, he was on one occasion severely injured. He wrote to Justice Story in 1813 that he was suffering violent persistent headaches arising from a stage coach accident.[42]

Livingston's federal circuit opinions will have run into many hundreds but only a very small number have survived to the *Federal Cases,* in turn extracted from the reports of Elijah Paine Jnr published in 1827.[43] Paine's reports contain only one

---

[40] William Johnson, *Reports,* vol 1.
[41] According to the *True American* (Trenton) of 17 June 1805 Livingston had 'declined the nomination of District Judge offered by the President'. He was clearly waiting for higher honours.
[42] Letter, Livingston to Story, 23 April, 1813 in Dunne, 'Story-Livingston Correspondence' 226.
[43] Elijah Paine Jnr, Reports of Cases Argued and *Determined in the Circuit Court of the United States for the Second Circuit: Comprising the Districts of New York, Connecticut and Vermont,* vol 1 (New York: R Donaldson, 1827).

case from the April 1813 term at Connecticut despite the fact that the lists were long. This was revealed in letter written by Livingston to Joseph Story at the end of that term in which he wrote, 'I have had a very busy term in Connecticut & have no doubt laid the foundation for some trouble for yourself and my other brethren at Washington'.[44] Also only four Vermont cases were reported through the whole of Livingston's tenure, strongly suggesting the absence of a law reporter in that district. The remaining reported cases are almost equally divided between New York and Connecticut. This lack of reporting of federal cases in the early years contrasts sharply with the abundance of law reports emanating from the New York Supreme Court who had appointed George Caines as its law reporter in 1804. He was the first official law reporter in the United States.[45] The United States Supreme Court did not appoint an official law reporter, Henry Wheaton, until 1817.[46] Despite the paucity of Livingston's reported federal circuit opinions, there are a sufficient number, when taken with his state court opinions, to discern patterns of court business as the reported cases appear to have been written up at random covering most branches of law and including cases both significant and ordinary.[47]

President Jefferson had hoped that the appointment to the Court of Republican William Johnson in 1804, followed two years later by the anti-Federalist Livingston would go some way to curb what he saw as the excesses of a Federalist-dominated Court. Whilst Justice Johnson pleased Jefferson by delivering dissents and separate concurrences, he had the temerity to censure an executive order of the President in an 1808 embargo case in the circuit court at Charleston. This incurred the wrath of the President and his Attorney General, Caesar A Rodney. Jefferson distributed widely to the press the Attorney General's opinion undermining Johnson's decision. Rodney wrote to Jefferson complaining that Johnson had 'enlisted fairly under the banner of the Judiciary, and stands forth the champion of all the *high church* doctrines on the Bench'. He referred to what he perceived as a Federalist

---

[44] See Dunne, 226.

[45] Caines produced three volumes of law reports covering decisions from May 1803 to November 1805. He was succeeded by William Johnson who between 1806 and 1822 edited 20 volumes of New York Supreme Court reports. Available at: www.courts.state.ny.us/reporter/History/page_24.htm. James Kent believed that Caines was incompetent and appointed Johnson who proved to be an excellent law reporter (see John H Langbein, 'Chancellor Kent and the History of Legal Literature' 93(3) *Columbia Law Review* 547–94 at 575, 578–79).

[46] Erwin C Surrency, 'Law Reports in the United States' (1981) 25(1) *American Journal of Legal History* 48–66 at 56.

[47] For an overview of law reporting in the Early Republic see, Alan V Briceland, 'Ephraim Kirby: Pioneer of American Law Reporting, 1789' (1972) 16(4) *American Journal of Legal History* 297–319; Erwin C Surrency, 'Law Reports in the United States' (1981) XXV *American Journal of Legal History* 48–66. Surrency notes that certain states such as Connecticut and Alabama, in the early nineteenth-century required judges to reduce their opinions to writing and to so do in Pennsylvania at the request of either party. (55); Daniel R Coquillette, 'First Flower—The Early American Law Reports and the Extraordinary Josiah Quincy Jr (1744–775)' (1996) 30 *Suffolk University Law Review* 1–34. Quincy's reports covered the cases in the Massachusetts Superior Court of Judicature between 1761 and 1772 and, as Coquillette observes, predate Kirby's reports and make Quincy the first American law reporter. The importance of his excellent early law reports is that they were there to advance the development of United States law.

stance taken by Johnson in that case as a 'disease' and further protested that 'you can scarcely elevate a man to a seat in a Court of Justice before he catches the leprosy of the bench'. Rodney wished to know whether the President wished him to use the press to further undermine Johnson.[48] This typical reaction of President Jefferson and his Attorney General reveals not only the political pressures faced by justices on circuit but also the complete failure of certain lawyer politicians to fully understand or accept the concept of an independent judiciary.

The President suffered further disappointment when Livingston deserted the Republican cause, reverting to the Federalist principles of his youth. It is reasonable to argue that Livingston's hatred of the arch-Federalist John Jay and support of any person who opposed him gave the impression that he had espoused a new political philosophy when, in fact, the protection of existing property rights, the promotion of commercial activity, and the need for a strong federal government were Federalist ideals he never abandoned.

Jefferson's nomination having been confirmed by the Senate on 13 December 1806, Livingston went from the highest court in the state to the nation's highest tribunal, taking his seat on the Court in the February 1807 term. He brought with him a confidence flowing from him time as a New York State trial and appeal court judge. It was a self-assurance readily apparent to Story who, whilst still an advocate, saw him in action in Washington just one year later. Even though Story was generally fulsome in his praise of all others, Livingstone made a particularly deep impression on him. Story, having spent a day observing the Court in action, wrote to a friend in 1808, describing the new justice and future colleague, as 'a very able and independent judge. He evidently thinks with great solidarity and seizes on the strong points of argument. He is luminous, decisive, earnest and impressive on the bench'.[49] Livingston's experience on the state supreme court was clearly much in evidence. He was not the diffident new boy.

Livingston's opinions have a refreshing lack of prolixity and an absence of convoluted language. Unlike many of his colleagues, he kept his opinions short and the content clear. His use of language is what one might expect of a much later age. A good way of illustrating his crisp and clear style is by contrasting his approach to an issue upon which there has been no definitive legal precedent with Justice Washington's much lengthier plaintive discourse. In the New York circuit court bankruptcy case of *Adams v Story*, Livingston wrote: 'After all that has been said, the court considers this question as one of considerable difficulty and regrets that it has not yet received a decision at Washington, which would produce uniformity of judgment; at least in the courts of the United States.'[50] In the Pennsylvanian

---

[48] The Charleston circuit case was *Ex parte Gilchrist*, Federal Cases no 5420; Letter of Attorney General Rodney to President Jefferson, 31 October 1808 Jefferson Papers MSS cited in Charles Warren, *The Supreme Court in United States History*, vol 1 (Boston: Little Brown, and Company, 1926), 336–37.

[49] Letter, Joseph Story to Samuel PP Fay, 25 February 1808, in William W Story, *Life and Letters of Joseph Story*, vol 1 (London: John Chapman, 1851), 167.

[50] *Adams v Story*, 1 F Cas 141, New York, April 1817.

circuit case of *Odlin v Insurance Co of Pennsylvania* (1808) Justice Washington, when faced with the absence of legal authority wrote,

> It is admitted that this precise case has never received a judicial decision in any courts of Great Britain or the United State, although it has been frequently glanced at by the judges; from whom, however, nothing beyond hints of their opinions can be collected. We are sensible of the difficulty of the question, as well as its importance to the parties, in this and other similar cases; we derive consolation, however, from reflecting that our opinion, if wrong, is subject to revision elsewhere.[51]

The difference in style, language, and brevity is marked. Washington is more representative of judicial opinion writing of the time, although the impression he gave of a lack of confidence, expressed on more than one occasion, is not.[52]

Livingston's opinions were further enhanced by humour which was shown at its best in his dissent in the New York Supreme Court case of *Pierson v Post* (1805), a decision which retains a place in the textbooks of American law students today. The case involved a dispute over the ownership of a fox pursued by one man and slain by another who came in at the end of the chase. Thompson, Livingston's brother-in-law and the justice who was to replace him on the United States Supreme Court, gave the Court's opinion in favour of the man who killed and carried away the fox. Livingston began his dissent by observing that the case ought to 'have been submitted to the arbitration of sportsmen, without poring over Justinian, Fleta, Bracton, Pufendorf, Locke, Barbeyrac, or Blackstone, all of whom had been cited.' As to the character of the fox, he continued, 'Both parties have regarded him, as does the law of nations, as a pirate. His depredations on farmers ... have not been forgotten ... Hence ... our decision should have in view the greatest possible encouragement to the destruction of an animal so cunning and ruthless in his career.'[53] He was more able to express humour in a case of little moment pursued by men with money to spend and time on their hands.

Livingston spent his entire tenure of the circuit court sitting in New York City; New-Haven and Hartford in Connecticut; and Burlington, Rutland and Windsor in Vermont. He was fortunate in having the same district judge sitting with and supporting him in each seat throughout; Elijah Paine in Vermont and Pierpont Edwards in Connecticut. District Judge William P Van Ness sat with Livingston for 13 years in New York.[54] The district judges who were obliged by Congress to

---

[51] *Odlin v Insurance Co of Pennsylvania*, 18 F Cas 583, Penn, October 1808.
[52] *McFaden v The Exchange*, 16 F Cas 85, Penn, October 1811. 'I feel cheered that the error of my judgment, if I have committed one, will be corrected by a superior tribunal'; *Consequa v Willings*, 30 F Cas 55, Penn, October 1816. 'I shall not be afraid of adding another precedent, leaving it to the Supreme Court, where I perceive this cause is likely to go, to correct this court, if I am wrong.'
[53] *Pierson v Post*, 3 Gai R 175 (1805).
[54] The names of and dates of service of the district judges and the court venues are taken from Edwin C Surrency, *Federal District Court Judges and the History of Their Courts*. This is a privately printed essay entitled, 'History of the Federal Courts Pamphlet #1, 1996 which in turn is based on a combination of the following essays; 1. (1963) 28 *Missouri Law Review* 214 and 2. (1966) 40 *Federal Research Division* 139.

be local residents would make the circuit judge aware of local trade customs and specific problems.

Constitutional cases were rare on circuit; there are only two reported decisions touching upon the constitutionality of state laws. In *Fisher v Harnden* (1812), a New York grand jury found an indictment against Fisher, a British subject, that he had adhered to the enemies of the state and in October 1783 judgment was signed forfeiting all of his real and personal estate. Fisher died in 1798 leaving his heirs, also British subjects, in possession of his land. However, by the Treaty of Peace between the United States and Great Britain signed on 3 September 1783 any confiscation proceedings after the signing of the act were void. Livingston charged the jury that the adoption of the treaty by the United States operated as a repeal of state law and the judgment was void and the jury found for Fisher's heirs.[55] The opinion illustrates a shift in Livingston's political ideology in that, despite his background as a state judge and politician, he did not seek to promote state sovereignty and acknowledged the supremacy of federal law over state legislation unless it violated the federal Constitution.

Livingston took the opposite view in his other constitutional case, *Adams v Story* (1817). This was by far the most important opinion Livingston wrote whilst on circuit and the only case in which he expressly regretted the absence of Supreme Court precedent.[56] In that case Livingston upheld the right of New York State to pass an insolvency law which discharged debtors from liability in respect of debts contracted either before or after the passing of the Act, and which purported to bind out of state creditors. In so doing, by emphasising the differences between bankruptcy and insolvency, he rejected arguments that the state law was in effect a bankruptcy measure contravening the right of Congress to 'establish a ... uniform law on the subject of bankruptcies throughout the United States'.[57] He also refused to accept the proposition that the state insolvency law was an unconstitutional impairment of the obligation of contract.[58] He used his opinion as a means of exploring the historical context justifying the granting of relief to debtors from the time of the first colonists from Britain until its universal adoption by every state of the Union. He felt very strongly about the issue believing that if there was no relief from debt and imprisonment for debt, the debtor would sink under the burden and make no effort to begin anew and contribute to the general good. This opinion was music to the ears of Republicans as Livingston was asserting the right of a state to legislate without federal government interference unless it was in clear violation of the federal Constitution.

However this particular Republican tendency was short lived. His feeling was not sufficiently strong to compel him to dissent when the same issue was dealt

---

[55] *Fisher v Harnden*, 9 F Cas 129, New York, April 1812.
[56] *Adams v Story*.
[57] Article 1, Section 8 of the Constitution of the United States.
[58] Article 1, Section 10 of the Constitution of the United States.

with by the Court in *Sturges v Crowninshield* two years later. Chief Justice Marshall, writing for a unanimous Court, held that a state law expressed to grant relief to a debtor in respect of debts accruing before the passing of the law was an impairment of the obligation of contract and therefore unconstitutional.[59] He was less forthcoming as to whether the sole power of passing bankruptcy laws resided in the states or in Congress. Prefacing his remarks with the phrase, 'Without entering further into the delicate inquiry', Marshall limited himself to holding that until Congress passed uniform bankruptcy laws, the states were not forbidden to pass a bankruptcy law provided it did not infringe the Constitution. He did not think it necessary to rule on whether the law in question related to bankruptcy or insolvency.

The 'delicate' nature of the inquiry was revived in *Ogden v Saunders* (1827), which, whilst it occurred after Livingston's death, is examined because it reveals the judicial compromises in *Sturges*. When Justice Johnson delivered the Court's opinion in *Ogden* he felt the need to explain how the justices had reached a decision in the earlier case. He wrote that the Court in *Sturges* was 'greatly divided in its views of the doctrine, and the judgment partook as much as a compromise as of a legal adjudication. The minority thought it better to yield something than risk the whole'.[60] The minority he referred to were those justices, of which he was one, and Livingston another, because of the views he expressed in *Adams v Story*, who supported the right of states to pass bankruptcy laws, having so held on circuit The compromise was the willingness of Johnson and Livingston to join in the holding of impairment of contract in return for the remaining justices agreeing that the states had the power to pass bankruptcy laws, at least until Congress exercised that power. The case shows that, rather than acting as Jefferson had hoped, as a thorn in the side of a Federalist-dominated Court, Livingston was prepared to acquiesce in the general view, despite his own feelings, in an effort to strive for that unity which would enhance the authority of the Court in the eyes of the nation.

Bankruptcy was a persistent and troublesome topic because of the need to satisfy creditors and at the same time to give debtors a fresh start, many of whom had been imprisoned in degrading conditions for failing to meet their financial obligations. Due to the efforts of men such as Justice Story, American federal bankruptcy law was placed on a statutory footing by the short-lived Bankruptcy Act of 1841, which enabled almost 40,000 insolvent debtors to return to commercial life.[61]

---

[59] *Sturges v Crowninshield*, 17 US (4 Wheat) 122 (1819).
[60] 25 US (1827), 272–73.
[61] For a comprehensive account of bankruptcy during this period see Edward J Balleisen, *Navigating Failures: Bankruptcy and Commercial Society in Antebellum America* (Chapel Hill: University of North Carolina Press, 2001) and 'Bankruptcy and the Entrepreneurial Ethos in Antebellum American Law' (2004) 8 *Australian Journal of Legal History* 61–82. See also Bruce H Mann, *Republic of Debtors: Bankruptcy in the Age of American Independence* (Cambridge, MA: Harvard University Press, 2002).

There is a pattern to the six reported criminal cases which Livingston tried on circuit which reveal a strict interpretation of the criminal law in favour of defendants who faced the death penalty. In 13 years, Livingston presided over many criminal cases, the details of which have not survived because of the lack of a law reporter. One must always exercise caution before reaching conclusions on such a very small sample. We know, however, that the six surviving reports of criminal cases, taken with some other circuit opinions, reveal a jurisprudence founded, wherever possible, on a compassionate view of men and their failings.[62]

Livingston also demonstrated a sympathetic approach in two revenue cases with a commercial law aspect. He reversed forfeiture orders made by district judges, accepting in one case that shippers had entered goods in the New York customs house at less than the correct quantity because they had been packed in haste in France due to a real danger of pillage by advancing Prussian troops.[63] In the other case, he took the view that a valuation of imported goods based on the cost of raw material, labour and shipping as opposed to the likely sale price was a sufficient estimate to avoid forfeiture for breach of customs law.[64] Lest it be thought that Livingston was naive, the manner of his rejection of some of the more bizarre explanations of masters for route deviations in maritime embargo cases shows him to be an astute observer of human nature.

There were 14 maritime cases in the 48 reported circuit opinions. By far the most revealing is *United States v The James Wells* (1808) in which Livingston was not disposed to accept a master's explanation for breaching the embargo by arriving in the West Indies instead of Georgia because of the condition of his vessel. Livingston found that the cargo had been chosen for the West Indian market and that holes had been bored into the ships bottom to support the route deviation. The case is noteworthy not only for Livingston's robust attitude to this class of case, but also for his comments on the difficulties facing judges who, under the Embargo Acts, tried cases without a jury. Despite a willingness on occasion to set aside jury verdicts, he found the responsibility of having to decide law and fact a burden but stressed the importance of ensuring that laws were not broken with impunity. He set out the difficulty facing a judge alone construing penal statutes and of the temptation of one who might not have the firmness to enforce a statute and who mitigated the severity of it instead of bearing down hard.[65] He was not timid in enforcing breaches of sailing licences even if it meant the forfeiture of vessel and cargo.

---

[62] See *United States v Hoxie*, 26 F Cas 397, Vermont, October 1808; *United States v Bass*, 24 F Cas 1028, New York 1819; *United States v Smith*, 18 US (5 Wheat) 153, 164–83 (1820); *United States v Porter*, 27 F Cas 598, Connecticut 1818; *United States v Phelps*, 27 F Cas 526, Connecticut 1810; *United States v Skinner et al*, 27 F Cas 1123, New York 1818.
[63] *United States v Nine Packages of Linen*, 27 F Cas 154, New York, April 1818.
[64] *Ninety-five Bales of Paper v United States*, 18 F Cas 266, New York, April 1820.
[65] *United States v The James Wells*, 26 F Cas 585, Conn, September 1808.

In *The Active* (1809), Livingston had no hesitation in forfeiting a vessel for breach of commercial fishing licences; the vessel had been passed for cod fishing and had been found carrying other goods.[66] The following year, in *The Elizabeth*, he affirmed the district judge's forfeiture order in respect of a vessel licensed only to sail on the Hudson River and which had been found in Long Island Sound, 110 miles from New York, carrying goods for which no manifest had ever been delivered. He refused to hold that the embargo laws, which had a vast impact on commercial life, were unconstitutional, observing that he would never come to that conclusion, unless, 'it were scarcely possible for any two men to differ in sentiment on the subject'.[67]

Of the 14 reported maritime opinions, two were simple breaches of licences to trade; in those cases, Livingston affirmed forfeiture orders. However, in nine embargo opinions, Livingston affirmed the district judge in two but reversed forfeiture orders in the remaining seven. Those reversals and the five directed acquittals in criminal cases, albeit a very small sample, are indicative of a justice unwilling to inflict penalties unless the law was precisely stated and its breach clearly established.

There is only one reported case on the question of the circuit court's jurisdiction and the commerce clause of the Constitution. *Livingston v Van Ingen* (1811)[68] was noteworthy because it involved a dispute over the exclusive right to navigate passenger steamboats on the Hudson River granted by United States patent. It was a case which had constitutional and commercial implications and in which, eventually, free enterprise won the day. The complainants, wishing to preserve a monopoly, sought from Livingston an injunction preventing the defendants from either using their steamboat or constructing another. Livingston disposed of the case on the basis that the circuit court had no jurisdiction to try the case, failing to recuse himself despite that the fact that the person who held the monopoly was his brother.[69] Eventually, the dispute came before the Supreme Court after Justice Livingston's death entitled, *Gibbons v Ogden* (1824) when Chief Justice Marshall, for the Court, held that the steamboat monopoly granted to Ogden was unconstitutional, basing the decision on the commerce clause of the Constitution which vested in Congress the exclusive power to regulate commerce among the states. Commerce embraced navigation on lakes, rivers and oceans and, therefore, included steamboat traffic. Marshall did not seek to exclude state control of commerce, acknowledging that a state had the exclusive right to regulate all commerce which occurred entirely within her borders and did not affect other states.[70] The decision was a blow to those who sought to monopolise commercial transport and an encouragement to those supporters of open competition.

---

[66] *The Active*, 1 F Cas 69, Conn, April 1809.
[67] *The Elizabeth*, 8 F Cas 468, New York, April 1810.
[68] *Livingston v Van Ingen*, 15 F Cas 697, New York, April 1811.
[69] G Edward White, *The Marshall Court and Cultural Change*, at 569.
[70] *Gibbons v Ogden*, 22 US (9 Wheat) 1 (1824).

# Maritime and Commercial Law for the United States

The opinions Livingston delivered on circuit and for the Supreme Court made him the leading exponent of commercial law before Joseph Story's arrival on the scene in 1811. After Story's appointment the reported cases reveal that both justices were heavily involved in formulating business law and procedure to promote economic prosperity. Livingston's Second Circuit cases show a preponderance of maritime cases followed closely by opinions resolving commercial disputes; a continuation of the type of case he had faced regularly in the state court. The reported commercial cases range from the time for completion of a contract to the persons entitled to sue upon a contract. In *Smith v Barker* (1809) he held that a contract to build a ship within about a month was not fulfilled by completing it in six months so as to authorise the enforcement of a note made payable upon fulfilment of the contract.[71] Livingston refused to permit the United States to sue upon a contract to which it was not a party even though it had an interest in the property which the subject matter of the action, observing that the United States, in a contract case, had no privilege or rights beyond those of the individual citizen.[72]

The bulk of Livingstone's commercial work centred on the liability of parties in respect of bills of exchange, the lifeblood of commerce during this period. They enabled the drawer of the bill to order the drawee to pay money to a third party (the payee); when the drawee was willing to undertake the payment he was said to have accepted the bill. The usefulness of the bill was in its negotiability; the third party was permitted to endorse it to a fourth party, who could further endorse. The last endorsee was the holder in due course who was in a very favourable position with a right of action on the bill against the original drawer and intermediate endorsers regardless of any disputes arising between those others. Bills were a useful means of payment for long-distance trade, particularly between merchants and brokers in the United States and Great Britain and because of their negotiability they were often sold to pay debts. On occasion, disputes around these bills became difficult to resolve because of the number of parties involved.

It was crucial that merchants who took a bill or note in good faith should be protected if commerce was to prosper. Livingston laid down clear rules of law and procedure which enabled businessmen to know how the federal court would deal with disputed contracts. In *Codwise et al v Gleason et al* (1808), when safeguarding the position of an indorsee, he wrote 'Gleason & Cowles gave the weight of their names to the world and must be responsible to every man who trusts the note relying on their credit.'[73] Thus, Livingston was emphasising the obligations of indorsees of notes. In *Cobb v Haydock* (1810) he also protected the indorsee of

---

[71] *Smith v Barker*, 22 F Cas 454, Conn, April 1809.
[72] *United States v Parmele*, 27 F Cas 415, Conn, April 1810.
[73] *Codwise et al v Gleason et al* 5 F Cas 1167, Conn, April 1808.

a note who had obtained judgment against one of two joint makers of a promissory note. He refused to allow a set off against the judgment debt of a sum owed to him personally by the drawee, of which the indorsee had had no notice. Livingston gave indorsees further comfort in *Childs v Corp* (1810) a case in which the defendant sold a bill of exchange, taking the plaintiff's note in payment and retaining the bill as collateral security. The bill of exchange was subsequently protested (ie there was a refusal to pay it) and the drawers became bankrupt. The defendant refused to return the bill to the plaintiff and took no steps to pursue any dividends in the bankruptcy. Livingston held that the defendant was liable to make good the plaintiff's loss.[74]

Livingston's view that bills and notes, as binding contracts, were so essential to commercial life that in *United States v Barker* (1816) he refused to declare illegal a bill drawn by a citizen of the United States on a citizen of Great Britain whilst the two countries were at war. Furthermore, he held that a delay of three months in presenting for acceptance the bill drawn in New York on Liverpool was not excessive in view of the state of war. He observed that during the Revolutionary War, 'scarcely a ship sailed from the United States ... for any port of Europe that was not almost loaded with bills of exchange on British houses'.[75] These reported opinions reveal, in Livingston's holdings on bills and notes, a determination to inspire confidence in the business world that the court would ensure that obligations would be enforced.

Again, acknowledging the paucity of circuit court opinions, the 49 cases examined reveal, as one would expect, in busy commercial centres, a variety of cases but with a preponderance of commercial disputes and maritime cases which would enable Livingston to approach confidently if invited to write for the Court on those issues. Chief Justice Marshall was well aware of Livingston's particular expertise because, of the 36 majority opinions he wrote for the Court, he was chosen to author 21 maritime and 14 commercial law cases which shows, as far as this associate justice is concerned, that experience in particular branches of law was an important factor in the Chief Justice's opinion assignment practice. The very first opinion he wrote for the Court was, appropriately, a maritime case in which he affirmed the forfeiture of the cargo of a vessel which had had imported goods from Cuba to Maryland in breach of a licence confining her to United States coastal waters.[76]

Livingston wrote ten reported opinions for the Court relating to forfeiture or detention of vessels for breaches of embargo and, in a shift away from the pattern established in his circuit court opinions, he affirmed each and every forfeiture or penalty imposed by the court below. He made it plain that he rejected the

---

[74] *Childs v Corp*, 5 Cas 622, Vermont, October 1810.
[75] *United States v Barker*, 24 F Cas 987, September 1816.
[76] *Keene v United States*, 9 US (5 Cranch) 304 (1809). Livingston held that the appropriate venue for a trial was the court of the district in which the goods were seized, regardless of the district where the forfeiture accrued.

excuses advanced for the various breaches. Many of these cases offered very similar questionable explanations. In *The Brig Struggle* (1815), Livingston rejected the master's excuse that he was prevented from reaching Charleston because of storms and was obliged to sail to the West Indies to save lives. He commented on the many cases of 'fictitious distress' offered to the courts for violations of the embargo and observed that the Court would look 'with considerable jealousy and caution on evidence which is so perpetually recurring'. He went as far as to hold that those who raise the defence of an Act of God must establish it so as to leave no reasonable doubt, thereby reversing the burden of proof in respect of an allegation of breach of a penal statute.[77]

Livingston's critical approach to such claims was justified. There was a flood of embargo breach cases before both circuit courts and the Supreme Court. Ship owners and masters were becoming desperate and willing to risk losing vessels and cargoes. As Wood rightly observes of New England, 'ships were lying idle in the harbors and thousands of sailors, dock workers, and others employed in mercantile activities were out of work'.[78] In fact, the embargo was doing far more economic damage to the United States than it was to any European power.

The *vis major* embargo defences were not rejected on the ground of public policy. Each case was investigated fully before such a severe penalty was affirmed. The defence had to have been shown to be spurious. Livingston's opinion in *The New York* (1818) demonstrated an extensive knowledge of maritime practices when examining the master's explanation and highlighting the deficiencies in his story and which caused him to conclude that 'he has made out as weak a case of necessity as was ever offered to a court in the many instances of this kind which occurred during the existence of this restrictive system'.[79]

Public policy considerations did apply in *Otis v Watkins* (1815) in which Livingston, for the majority, held that a port collector who detained a vessel under the Embargo Act 1808, pending instructions from the President, need not show that his opinion was correct, nor that he used reasonable care and diligence in ascertaining the facts. It was sufficient if he honestly entertained his opinion and did not act out of malice. Livingston said, in effect, that if it were otherwise, no public official would act for fear of the consequences. Chief Justice Marshall, in one of his rare dissents, argued that despite the absence of a requirement in the statute to take reasonable care in the collection of the information for transmission to the President, there should be such a duty on the collector.[80] This would

---

[77] *The Brig Struggle*, 13 US (9 Cranch) 71 (1815).

[78] Gordon S Wood, *Empire of Liberty: A History of the Early Republic* (New York: Oxford University Press, 2009), 655.

[79] *The New York*, 16 US (3 Wheat) 59 (1818). For further examples of Livingston's hard line approach to breaches of the embargo legislation and illegal captures see *The Aeolus*, 16 US 392 (1818); *The Rugen: Buhring, Claimant*, 14 US 62 (1816); *The Estrella*, 17 US (4 Wheat) 298 (1819); *The Santa Maria*, 20 US (7 Wheat) 490 (1822).

[80] *Otis v Watkins*, 13 US (9 Cranch) 339 (1815).

seem to be the preferable approach to the issue as it is difficult to understand how the collector could hold an honest opinion if he took no care in collecting and transmitting the evidence.

Public policy featured again, this time in contract law in *Lee v Munroe & Thornton* (1813) when Livingston, for the Court, held that the United States was not bound by the declarations of its agent founded on a mistake of fact unless the declaration was within the scope of his authority and he was empowered to make it. Livingston put it bluntly when he declared that it was better that an individual should occasionally suffer than the United States should lose liens on valuable and large tracts of land.[81]

In *Dugan v The United States* (1818) Livingston again rejected the argument that the United States should not be permitted to sue in its own name stating that the action should be in the name of the agent who conducted the business on behalf of the government department. He questioned why the United States should be denied a right which was secured to every citizen.[82] However, he preferred other creditors' claims to those of the United States in *United States v Bryan & Woodcock* (1815). The United States had attempted to achieve priority of payment out of a bankrupt's estate who had been surety for a customs collector. Livingston held that debt was incurred before the act of Congress bestowing priority came into force even though the accounts were not settled until after the act's passage.[83] An even-handed approach was demonstrated in *United States v Giles* (1815) when Livingston rejected the claim of the United States on a bond against the surety of a marshal who had collected monies under an execution on goods and had failed to account to the Comptroller of the Treasury. The marshal had collected the monies before the surety had executed the bond even though the money was still in the marshal's hands.

Livingston wrote only one slavery opinion for the Court when he rejected a defence of entering port as a necessity in *The Joseph Segunda* (1820) and forfeited the vessel because it had been used for the purpose of selling slaves and had entered the Mississippi in breach of an act of Congress prohibiting the importation of slaves into the United States after 1 January 1808. He made his feelings clear on the issue when affirming the forfeiture order, referring to 'this inhuman traffic' and 'this unrighteous commerce,' observing that at that time slaves were being sold at New Orleans for $1,000 each.[84]

The maritime case of *Hudson & Smith v Guestier* (1810) is noteworthy not for the point of law decided, but for the fact that the Chief Justice, after Livingston had handed down the opinion of the Court, referred to the Court's earlier opinion in the same case in his dissent. He observed that 'he supposed [it] had been

---

[81] *Lee v Munroe & Thornton*, 11 US (7 Cranch) 366 (1813).
[82] *Dugan v United States*, 16 US 172 (1818).
[83] *United States v Bryan & Woodcock*, 13 US (9 Cranch) 374 (1815).
[84] *The Joseph Segunda*, 18 US (5 Wheat) 338 (1820).

concurred in by four judges, But in this he was mistaken. The opinion was concurred in by one judge'.[85] A fundamental mistake which makes one wonder how formal the justices' deliberations were at the conclusion of evidence and arguments. One would have expected the Chief Justice as chairman of the post-case discussions to note carefully those justices who concurred in the opinion to be delivered.

The bulk of Livingston's opinions for the Supreme Court in commercial matters related to negotiable instrument disputes in which, in order to assure those taking bills of exchange and promissory notes, he generally favoured the creditor. Such an approach recognised the negotiable instrument as the cornerstone of trade payments and made merchants confident that the Court would ensure that solemn obligations were enforced. Thus in *Riggs v Lindsay* (1813), where the defendants ordered the plaintiff to purchase salt for them and to draw on them for the amount he expended, Livingston held that they were bound to accept and pay his bills.[86] However, he did hold in *Young v Grundy*, in the same year, that where a payee failed to perform his part of the contract upon which the promissory note was given and a new agreement was reached between the parties in substitution for the old, the original failure could not be investigated. Any subsequent indorsee of the note could not be affected by any dispute between the original parties.[87] Where the bill or note had passed through a number of hands, Livingston ensured that there was no collusion between the parties to an action. Thus, in *Marshall v Beverley*, he refused to grant an injunction on judgments already obtained until all the parties involved had filed answers setting out their cases. He was not satisfied by the agreed assertions of just two parties.[88]

Whilst we do not know how co-operative Livingston was in conferences, the number of dissents he wrote indicates that he was not the expected Republican thorn in the side of a Federalist Chief Justice. He was willing to hide his personal views to enable the Court to speak with one voice as he did in *Sturges v Crowninshield*. His letters to Justice Story thanking him and praising him for his draft opinion in *Trustees of Dartmouth College v Woodward* (1817) indicates a spirit of cooperation borne not just from friendship but also from shared fundamental values.[89] Although ostensibly members of different political parties, the Supreme Court justices came from the same affluent background and wished to see the economy flourish and property rights protected. Therefore, they had a mutual interest in furthering trade and preserving existing rights to real and personal property, whatever the political label attached to them on appointment.

---

[85] *Hudson & Smith v Guestier*, 10 US (6 Cranch) 281 (1810).
[86] *Riggs v Lindsay*, 11 US (7 Cranch) 500 (1813).
[87] *Young v Grundy*, 11 US (7 Cranch) 548 (1813).
[88] *Marshall v Beverley*, 18 US (5 Wheat) 313 (1820).
[89] Letter, Livingston to Story, 27 January 1819 in Dunne, 'Story-Livingston Correspondence,' at 231–32.

# Conclusion

Justice Livingston's circuit opinions and his majority opinions for the Court support the view that expertise gained on circuit was a crucial factor in the development of federal law on the Supreme Court and also key to the Court's opinion-assignment practice. Livingston differs from Washington in that, although he adhered to the doctrine of precedent, the English authorities, for personal reasons discussed earlier in this chapter, did not hold the same magic for him. His remark in *Penny v New York Insurance Company* that he followed the English rule as it was a reasonable approach and not because he regarded it as an authority and his pointed comment in *Leroy v Lewis* that he preferred a state court decision to a British authority suggests that, wherever possible, he would look first to federal and local laws.

Constitutional matters rarely featured at circuit level. Livingston presided over two such cases which are notable not only for the important issues in dispute but also for revealing the tensions facing a justice appointed by a Republican president, torn between state sympathies and a professional role that supported federal power. Livingston's acknowledgment of the supremacy of federal law over New York legislation in *Fisher v Harnden* and his holding the contrary, in *Adams v Story*, that a New York insolvency law did not impair the obligation of contract clause of the Constitution reveal a willingness to decide each case on its merits without a pre-conceived partisan approach.

The opinions examined here establish Livingston's specialties on circuit and, before that, on the New York Supreme Court, as maritime and commercial law. Of a total 48 surviving circuit court opinions, 14 covered maritime disputes and ten resolved commercial issues in which he had acquired special circuit expertise. Of the many legal points in the remaining categories, Livingston was never invited to write opinions on crime, constitutional law, international law, real property, public lands or patents as he had not demonstrated any circuit skills in those branches of the law. He was invited to write only on those cases involving disciplines with which he was completely familiar and John Marshall knew the value of circuit expertise, where it lay and how best to use it on the Court. He would have appreciated that by giving maritime and commercial cases to Livingston, other justices would respect the opinions he wrote and any waverers might be persuaded to the majority view.

Although as a state justice and a Supreme Court justice sitting on the Court and on circuit, Livingston had to deal with a wide spectrum of legal issues, those opinions he delivered in all three jurisdictions mark him as a leading authority on commercial law. His opinions began the process of ensuring that men of commerce understood their contractual obligations and specifically their responsibilities in relation to negotiable instruments, even in respect of bills drawn on a citizen of Britain during wartime (*Codwise et al v Gleason et al*; *Childs v Corp*; *United States v Barker*). His state court opinions in *Watson v Delafield*; *Green v Beals* and *Casey v Brush* clarified the rights and obligations of members of partnerships, which he believed to be integral to the development of trade and industry. His overall object was to provide a legal and procedural framework regulating the conduct of commerce and promoting trade at home and abroad. Story, himself no mean commercial lawyer, wrote, in the eulogy he delivered in 1823 upon Livingston's death, that the justice's 'genius and taste had directed his principal attention to the maritime and commercial law; and his extensive experience gave to his judgments in that branch of jurisprudence a particular value which was enhanced by the gravity and beauty of his judicial elegance'.[90]

Unlike Thompson, Livingston was eager to protect from personal liability public officials acting in good faith in the performance of their duties. However, when jurors performed their public function, Livingston was quick to reverse verdicts with which he disagreed. In *Smith v Cheetham* he wondered why judges regarded jury verdicts as sacrosanct. He was very willing to investigate alleged irregularities and set aside verdicts which were against the weight of the evidence as in *Mellish v Arnold* and *Brandt v Ogden*. However, his willingness to overturn jury verdicts and order new trials is at odds with his sentiments in *United States v James Wells* where he stressed the burden on judges trying alleged breaches of penal statutes without a jury which might result in the forfeiture of a vessel and her cargo. He appeared to want the protection of a jury when serious consequences flow from an adverse finding but not in the run of the mill case.

In the busy port of New York, Livingston presided over many allegations of breaches of embargo laws, sailing licences, and revenue laws. Like Story, he was generally unsympathetic to the dubious excuses advanced by ship-owners and masters for route deviations, failure to report on entering harbour or avoiding the correct import duty (*Ninety-Five Bales of Paper v United States*; *United States v James Wells*; *The Active*; and *The Elizabeth*). However, his reversal of seven forfeiture orders shows him to be a justice who was more accepting of defence explanations than Story (*United States v Nine Packages of Linen*).

Ultimately, Livingston's most significant contribution to United States law was through his commercial and maritime opinions. His writings for the Court on negotiable instruments in cases such as *Riggs v Lindsay*; *Young v Grundy*; *Lennox v Prout*; and *Marshall v Beverley* consolidated business law. His clear formulation of contractual rights and obligations gave the business community the confidence to trade and accept bills of exchange and promissory notes knowing that the federal courts would deal promptly and consistently with any breaches. Justice Livingston died in Washington on 18 March 1823, aged 66 years leaving behind a respectable jurisprudential legacy.[91]

---

[90] Preface to the *United States Reports* (8 Wheat) 1823.

[91] Rumour and poor communication were apparent when the *Spectator* (New York) announced his death in its issue of 4 March. The *Vermont Gazette* of 18 March 'contradicted' the death notice and indicated that the latest reports from Washington indicated 'his health was improving'.

# 5

# Joseph Story: Admiralty Expertise and the Importation of Common Law

Justice Story's significant impact on the development of United States law during his 24-year tenure of the Marshall Supreme Court is apparent from the reports of cases he tried as presiding judge of the United States First Circuit Court for Massachusetts, Maine, New Hampshire and Rhode Island. His circuit and Supreme Court opinions reveal his role as a justice who, whilst a master of most branches of law, was the Marshall Court's leading exponent of admiralty law. The opinions also reveal his efforts to make United States law more readily accessible and easily understood by importing common law principles into admiralty, criminal and commercial law and by a codification of federal criminal law. They also show that he brought to the judicial function a more professional approach based on a meticulous approach to research, attention to detail and streamlining of procedure by discouraging prolix speeches and over-lengthy written pleadings; all of which led to a more efficient dispatch of business. His prolific correspondence is extremely valuable because it aids an understanding of his thoughts on how a uniform system of federal law and procedure was achieved.

Joseph Story was born on 18 September 1779 at Marblehead, Massachusetts into a very large and deeply religious middle-class family of English stock. His father was a physician who had participated in the Boston Tea Party and served as a surgeon during the Revolutionary War.

Dr Story had seven children by his first wife who died in 1777 and eleven by his second wife of which Joseph was the eldest. Due to the size of the family and its limited means, Joseph Story's early existence was frugal so he did not have the privileged upbringing enjoyed by many of his brethren on the Marshall Court.

He graduated from Harvard College in 1798, second in his class to the great Unitarian theologian William Ellery Channing. In the space of just over three months, largely by self-tuition, he had managed to achieve not only the stringent college entrance standard but also the requirement that he be examined in all of the subjects in which the freshman class had a six month's head start. His considerable efforts to master the subjects to gain entrance to Harvard and his love of Latin and Greek grammar are recorded in an autobiography he wrote for his son in 1831.[1] That love of language shines through his correspondence, text books and many of his circuit and Supreme Court opinions.

---

[1] WW Story, *Life and Letters of Joseph Story*, vol 1 (London: John Chapman, 1851) 38–41.

112  Joseph Story: Admiralty and Common Law

Even at such an early age, Story was demonstrating the determination and industry which was to characterise his entire professional life and which was to lead to the accolade of the most learned jurist of his age. This extraordinary driving force was evident throughout his time at the Bar, on the Bench and in academic life. As a justice when at home 'resting' from his labours on circuit or in Washington, he would rise at seven and, apart from short breaks for meals and for his lectures at Harvard, he would work in his library until the light failed.[2]

After Harvard, Story began to read law with Congressman Samuel Sewall of Marblehead who was later to become Chief Justice of the Massachusetts Supreme Judicial Court. Although Harvard was established in 1636, it did not have a law school until 1817. Clerking for a local lawyer was the only means of training open to a law student in New England.[3] Unfortunately, Sewall was away for half of the year on political business and Story, once more, was left to his own devices, studying up to 14 hours a day. He was unhappy with this haphazard method of legal education, finding reading *Coke on Littleton* a useless, obsolete exercise. His initial failure to unlock its secrets brought him to tears but he persevered and 'began to see daylight'.[4] Sewall's library contained *Blackstone's Commentaries on*

---

[2] ibid, vol 2, 103–04.

[3] Arthur E Sutherland, *The Law at Harvard: A History of Men and Ideas, 1817–1967* (Cambridge, MA: Harvard University Press, 1967) 59. This was the common method of training lawyers in the early nineteenth century. University training in law was extremely rare. 'Law was learned mostly by clerking as an apprentice in a lawyer's office. The apprentice read text books and case reports and entered notes on his reading in an alphabetised notebook called a 'commonplace book.' See, John H Langbein, 'Blackstone, Litchfield and Yale' in Anthony T Kronman, *History of Yale Law School: The Tercentennial Lectures* (New Haven: Yale University Press, 2004) 19. For a comprehensive account of legal training during this period, see, Steve Sheppard (ed), *The History of Legal Education in the United States: Commentaries and Primary Sources*, vol 1 (Pasadena: Salem Press, Third Printing in 2010 by Lawbook Exchange of the 1999 ed.). Sheppard charts the legal education of John Adams, John Marshall and Joseph Story and confirms that the bulk of students' studies comprised, 'solitude, reading and copying from English law books' (9) and the decline in popularity of *Coke on Littleton* and the rise in popularity of *Blackstone's Commentaries* (11–12). Thomas Jefferson had no time for Blackstone who had opposed American Independence. He had been brought up on *Coke on Littleton* which he later recommended to all law students. See Frank L Dewey, *Thomas Jefferson, Lawyer* (Charlottesville: University of Virginia Press, 1986), 10–11. Writing in 1812, Jefferson praised 'those who have drawn their stores from the rich mines of Coke Littleton' whilst wishing to 'uncanonise Blackstone whose book, altho' the most the most elegant & best digested of our law catalogue, has been perverted more than all others to the degeneracy of legal science'. Letter, Thomas Jefferson to Judge John Tyler, 17 June 1812 in J. Jefferson Looney (ed), *The Papers of Thomas Jefferson*, Retirement Series, vol 5 (Princeton: Princeton University Press, 2008), 134–37. The most easily digestible edition of *Blackstone's Commentaries* is the four-volume edition published by Oxford University Press in 2016. It is in modern format and traces the evolution of English Law through the first nine editions. Each volume is edited by a leading authority on the subject matter. Story wrote an article in 1817 entitled 'Course of Legal Study' for the *North American Review*. It is reproduced in WW Story (ed), *The Miscellaneous Writings of Joseph Story* (Boston: Charles C. Little & James Brown, 1852) 66–92. The article traces the history of legal education and concludes by commending instruction in law school before training in an attorney's office.

[4] WW Story, *Miscellaneous Writings*, 19–20. Unfortunately for Story and other fellow sufferers, Thomas Coventry's *Readable Edition of Coke on Littleton* was not published in London by Saunders & Benning until 1830. According to Coventry, the problem with previous editions was the inclusion of the quotations from early scholars which were 'a matter of curiosity rather than use'. The 1830 edition omitted all 'incongruous' notes and comments and 'added a few references to modern leading decisions and statutes' (Preface, iv–vi).

the Laws of England which Story was advised to read first. He devoured all four volumes regarding them as the 'most elegant of commentaries' but bemoaned the fact that there were only five or six volumes of American reports available, which meant that a student was unable to apply the learning of the common law to his own country or distinguish what had been adopted in the United States.[5] Story's grounding in *Blackstone* and, therefore, in English common law and the decisions of the justices of the Queen's Bench and Chancery Courts constituted the basis of his judicial philosophy, adapted in such a way to meet the challenges facing the Early Republic.[6] In this regard he was following Sewall's advice that he 'need not fear. That when you have the law of England as a system of political, moral and economical rules, you will find no difficulty in ascertaining the variations which our situation & difference of manners and general policy have required'.[7]

When Sewall went to the Bench in January 1801, Story continued his apprenticeship with Samuel Putnam of Salem who also attained high judicial office. His change of master was much more rewarding, as he was permitted to apply the knowledge gained from law books to the particular problems facing Putnam's clients. However, he did not remain there for long as he was admitted to the Essex Bar in 1801 and set up as a sole practitioner in the port of Salem. He began his practice at a time when virtually all the offices of importance in the Commonwealth of Massachusetts were occupied by Federalists.[8] This presented a real problem for Story who had inherited the Democratic Republican political outlook of his father.[9] Thomas Jefferson had been sworn in as President in March 1801 after a bitter contest with President John Adams and those lawyers, including Story, who made no secret of their Republican ideals were ostracised. Story wrote in his *Autobiography* 'For some time I felt the coldness and estrangement ... being left 'solitary at the bar'.[10] His Federalist colleagues were clearly finding the idea of a Republican government difficult to accept.

---

[5] WW Story, vol 1, 70–74.

[6] Much later, in 1841, on a visit to America, Lord Morpeth met Story, by then enjoying a high international reputation. His Lordship was pleased by Story's high regard for the judgments of the English judges, Lords, Mansfield, Hardwicke & Stowell and records Story as saying, 'Sir ... on the prairies of Illinois this day Lord Mansfield administers the law of commerce'. Lord Morpeth gives an insight into Story's boundless energy and enthusiasm for the law when writing, 'I must admit one thing, when he was in the room few others could get in a word; but it was impossible to resent this, for he talked evidently not to bear down others, but because he could not help it.' The Rt. Hon. The Earl of Carlisle (Lord Morpeth), *Travels in America* (New York: GP Putnam, 1851), 11.

[7] Letter, Samuel Sewall to Joseph Story, 12 February 1799 in Story Papers, William L Clements Library, University of Michigan. In that letter, Sewall also commended to Story an examination of 'the theory & general doctrines and the origins of the Municipal law and descending from generals to particulars, to discover afterwards the partial applications & limits of the system'. Although Sewall was away on Congressional business a good deal of the time, he answered Story's requests for suggested reading with a comprehensive list of authors and reports. See, in the same collection, letter from Sewall to Story, 3 April 1800.

[8] WW Story, vol 1, 95–6.

[9] 'My father was a Republican ... and I naturally imbibed the same opinions.' In WW Story. *Miscellaneous Writings of Joseph Story*, 20.

[10] WW Story, *Life and Letters*, 97.

Despite the political climate, within two years, Story had built up a thriving practice. In 1804 he began writing the first of many legal tomes, his well-received *Selection of Pleadings in Civil Actions*.[11] The secret of Story's success is best illustrated by the case of *Rust v Low*, 6. Massachusetts Reports, 90. Eminent counsel opposing Story believed that a note made by Lord Hale to Fitzherbert's *Natura Brevium* would win him the case. Story had other ideas as he had translated from the Latin approximately 30 cases from the *English Yearbooks* showing that Lord Hale had misunderstood the passage in Fitzherbert.[12] This approach was typical of Story's meticulous preparation as advocate and judge. Presser (1990) contrasts the approach to legal issues of Story with that of his Chief Justice and writes: 'Joseph Story is the thinking man's John Marshall. Story supplied the citations [and] erudite opinions ... while Marshall garnered virtually all the glory with a little law encased in some deft and ringing phrases.'[13] No doubt due to his industry and painstaking approach, Story quickly built up an extensive practice within Massachusetts with occasional forays into New Hampshire. Within five years of his admission as counsel he was opposing the leaders of the Bars of New England and had begun the mammoth task of digesting all the reported state and Supreme Court opinions on Insurance, Admiralty and Prize law.[14]

Many of the Marshall Court justices combined law and politics and Story was no exception.[15] He was elected to the Massachusetts legislature in 1805 and served on many committees. Although a Republican and supporter of the policies of President Jefferson, Story was an unusual member of that party because of his admiration for President Washington's vision of a strong national government instead of a loose confederation of states. Thus, he was that rare animal, a politician of independent mind who, whatever the official party line, voted according to his view of the merits of the issues, remarking that a 'Virginian Republican ... was very different from a Massachusetts Republican' and that Virginia's anti-federalist policy met with little support in his home state.[16] It is difficult to see how Story could possibly support resolutions which purported to grant to the states the power and duty to declare unconstitutional Acts of Congress which they believed were not authorised by the Constitution.[17] It is clear that by 1815, if not before, he was fully committed to the notion of a federal government with all-embracing powers.

---

[11] ibid, 112.

[12] ibid, 117–18. Story's ingenious argument was adopted by Chief Justice Parsons as if he had researched the point himself, giving Story no credit for his considerable efforts.

[13] Stephen B Presser, Foreword (vii) to 1990 second printing of James McClellan, *Joseph Story and the American Constitution*, (Norman: University of Oklahoma Press, 1971).

[14] WW Story, *Life and Letters*, vol 1, 119–24.

[15] Marshall and Smith Thompson had been, respectively, Secretary of State and Secretary of the Navy. Washington had been a member of the Virginia House of Representatives and Livingston spent three years as a member of the New York Assembly.

[16] WW Story, *Life and Letters*, vol 1, 128.

[17] Kentucky Resolutions 1798 and 1799; Virginia Resolution 1798.

This appears in a letter he wrote to a friend that year giving a powerful indication of his general approach to disputes between the federal government and the States.

> Let us extend the national authority over the whole of the power given by the Constitution. Let us have great military and naval schools; an adequate regular army; the broad foundations laid of a permanent navy; a national bank; a national system of bankruptcy; a great navigation act; a general survey of our ports and appointments port-wardens and pilots; Judicial Courts which shall embrace the whole constitutional powers; national notaries; public and national justices of the peace, for the commercial and national concerns of the United States. By such enlarged and liberal institutions, the Government of the United States will be endeared to the people and the factions of the great States will be rendered harmless. Let us prevent the possibility of a division, by creating great national institutions which shall bind us in in an indissoluble chain.[18]

Story displayed his independence by the unpopular but crucial role he played in 1806 to establish the salaries of the Federalist judges of the Supreme Judicial Court in Massachusetts on a permanent basis.[19] The judges had been granted $500 per annum on their own petition but limited to one year. Story, as chairman of the relevant committee, saw through a measure which gave the Chief Justice $2,500 and the other judges $2,400. In this way he bolstered the independence of the judges by a salary made constitutionally permanent. Three years later he engineered further increases. His actions brought him into conflict with his own party because all of the judges were Federalists whom the Republicans wished to starve out of office. That he was roundly denounced for his actions in the Republican Press was only to be expected.[20] Despite his critics he was elected to the Massachusetts House of Representatives in 1805 where he remained until December 1808 when he represented Essex County in Congress, replacing Jacob Crowninshield who had died on the floor of the House.[21] Story spent only a month in Washington. He went home to resume his law practice and did not seek re-election. He was appointed Attorney for Essex County in 1807.[22]

He brought upon himself even greater censure because of his eventual opposition to President Jefferson's embargo policy. The Embargo Act of 1807 and the subsequent Non-Intercourse Acts, brought about by the seizure of American ships and impressment of seamen by the Royal Navy, prohibited American ships from engaging in foreign trade during the Napoleonic Wars. The objective of the

---

[18] Letter, Joseph Story to Hon Nathaniel Williams, 22 February 1815 in WW Story, *Life & Letters*, vol 1, 253–54.
[19] ibid, 130–35.
[20] ibid.
[21] In his issue of 31 May 1808, the editor of *The Repertory* (Boston) whilst writing, 'We do not pretend that Mr Story is to be considered a decided federalist', welcomed him as a replacement for Crowninshield, praising his independence and willingness 'to break the bonds of party connection ... for the publick [sic] good'.
[22] *The Sun* (Pittsfield, Mass.), 31 October 1807.

legislation was to cause economic hardship to the belligerents.[23] It almost wrecked the United States economy because of the lack of international markets for cotton, tobacco and wheat products. In all major ports ships were idle, merchants were facing bankruptcy and many thousands of seaman were struggling to survive. Story originally supported the Act's objectives on the basis that it was preferable to war.[24] However, the disastrous effect of the embargo forced him to reconsider his support and during his extremely short time in Congress, he argued for its repeal, thereby incurring the displeasure of former President Jefferson and the Republican Party.[25] The embargo, he declared 'prostrated the whole commerce of America and produced a degree of distress in the New England States greater than that which followed the (Revolutionary) War'.[26] He described the legislation as a 'miserable and mischievous failure' and 'almost a crime'.[27] In 1809, 1,300 men were imprisoned for debt in New York simply because their business had been destroyed by the embargo.[28] The editorial of *The Repertory* (Boston) of 6 January 1809 contained a report that a total of 625 vessels were in four Massachusetts ports, 'the principal part of which are totally dismantled, having been deprived of their usual channels of trade by those "unrighteous edicts" called embargo laws'.

Hickey (1981) deals with the effect of trade restrictions during the War of 1812 noting the attempts to avoid embargo laws using inland waterways from Canada and 'some merchants outfitted privateers and made dummy captures of goods purchased by their agents in Montreal'.[29] Despite the damage to the American economy as a result of the international trade restrictions imposed by the

---

[23] The 1807 Act was passed to strengthen the Non-Importation Act 1806 which had banned the importation from Britain of many goods including those of which the chief ingredients comprised leather, silk, hemp, flax, tin and brass. The earlier Act had no effect on the British economy and it was deemed necessary, short of war with Britain, to pass the 1807 Act which was much more far reaching but which was repealed as a failure in 1809. 1805 Act (Ninth Congress, Session 1, Chapter 29). 1807 Act (Tenth Congress, Session 1, Chapters, 3, 4 & 5).

[24] Story, *Life and Letters*, 136–39.

[25] ibid, 171–72.

[26] ibid, 183–84. See Thorp, Lanter and Wolford, 'Democratic-Republican Reaction in Massachusetts to the Embargo Act 1807' (1942) 15(1) *The New England Quarterly* 35–61 for the reaction of politicians, merchants and farmers to the catastrophic effects of embargo. SE Morison in his *Maritime History of Massachusetts* (Boston: Houghton Mifflin Company, 1921) notes that Massachusetts was hardest hit of all states because her registered tonnage was 37 per cent of the total of the United States and twice as much as New York (188). He also records that 'mechanics and master mariners had to resort to soup kitchens in the seaport towns, or exhaust their savings, or emigrate to Canada in search of work' (191). See also, John D Forbes, 'European Wars and Boston Trade, 1783–1815' (1938) 11(4) *The New England Quarterly* 709–30.

[27] ibid, WW Story, *Life and Letters*, 185.

[28] Douglass C North, *The Economic Growth of the United States, 1790–1860* (New York: WW Norton & Company Inc, 1966, 55. Originally published in New Jersey: Prentice-Hall Inc, 1961). North cites John B McMaster, *History of the People of the United States from the Revolution to the Civil War*, 8 vols (New York: Appleton-Century Crofts, Inc, vol 3), 462–63.

[29] Donald R Hickey, 'American Trade Restrictions during the War of 1812' (1981) 68(3) *The Journal of American History* 517–38 at 534. Hickey concludes that the trade restrictions had little effect on Britain, but reduced American trade and deprived the government of much-needed revenue (538).

Non-Intercourse and Embargo legislation between 1806 and the end of the 1812 War with Britain, the prohibitions had one beneficial, if unintended, effect which was a marked surge in home manufacturing to compensate for lost imports. However, after the war, British imports once more began to flood into the United States; in order to protect emerging American businesses, Congress felt it necessary to impose tariffs on imports of iron, woollens and cotton goods.[30]

Story's opposition to the Act caused former President Jefferson to attempt to persuade President Madison not to nominate him to the United States Supreme Court on the death of Justice William Cushing. Writing to President Madison in 1810, President Jefferson's deep dislike of the federal judiciary was apparent when he regarded the death of Cushing as a 'circumstance of congratulation', describing Story as 'a pseudo-Republican' who had deserted the republicans on the embargo measure, and was 'unquestionably a tory ... and too young'.[31] Story's defence of the Massachusetts judiciary and his stance against the embargo in the face of his party's hostility showed him to be a man whose political independence was a likely obstacle to his attaining high political office but which better suited him to the judicial role. There was no love lost between Jefferson and Story. In 1822 Story wrote 'Mr Jefferson stands at the head of the enemies of the Judiciary and I doubt not will leave behind him numerous progeny bred in the same school'.[32] Story, a deeply religious man, took issue privately and publicly with a letter written by Jefferson in 1824 which received wide publicity and in which he asserted that Christianity was no part of the common law.[33]

Throughout his career there is tension between his membership of a party which advocated the right of states to govern themselves and his overriding belief in the need for strong national government. His belief in an independent judiciary to monitor the activities of the other departments of the national government, state courts and legislatures was a view which flew in the face of Republican policy. Justices William Johnson, Livingston, Todd, Duvall and Smith Thompson also grappled with the dilemma, having been nominated to the Supreme Court by

---

[30] Michael Lind, *Land of Promise: An Economic History of the United States* (New York: Harper Collins Publishers, 2012) 43.

[31] Letter, Thomas Jefferson to James Madison, 15 October 1810 in James Morton Smith, *Republic of Letters: The Correspondence between Thomas Jefferson and James Madison*, 3 vols (New York: WW Norton and Company, 1995, vol 3) 1646. The 'pseudo-Republican' epithet was contained in a letter President Jefferson wrote to General Dearborn on 16 July 1810 contained in Story, *Life and Letters*, vol 1, 186. In his reply to Jefferson on 19 October 1810, Madison merely said that Story's name had not yet been brought forward. There was a difficulty in filling the vacancy as more obvious candidates had refused the nomination and he had to nominate a New Englander (ibid, 1648).

[32] Letter, Story to Hon Jeremiah Mason, 10 January 1822 in WW Story, *Life and Letters*, vol 1, 411.

[33] Letter, Thomas Jefferson to John Cartwright, 5 June 1824, *Founders Online*, National Archives. Available at: http://founders.archives.gov/documents/Jefferson/98-01-02-4313. (Early Access Document from the Papers of Thomas Jefferson: Retirement Series. See, Letter, Story to Professor Everett, 15 September 1824 in WW Story, *Life and Letters*, vol 1, 429-30. Story forcefully countered Jefferson's arguments, 'notwithstanding the specious objections of one of our distinguished statesmen,' in his inaugural address as Dane Professor of Law at Harvard University on 25 August 1829 and in *The American Jurist*, vol 9, 1833. See, WW Story, *Life and Letters*, vol 1, 431 and Newmyer, *Joseph Story*, 244.

Republican Presidents whom they disappointed by acquiescing in the establishment of federal laws binding on every state of the Union.

Story added to his extensive political and law practice commitments with the publication of three major, well-received law books: he edited and heavily annotated *Chitty on Bills of Exchange and Promissory Notes* (1809); *Abbott on Shipping* (1810) with extensive notes and references to American decisions and statutes; and in 1811 he produced an annotated edition of *Laws on Assumpsit*.[34] This in-depth research gave him an understanding of how the law had developed and been applied in other jurisdictions, enabling him to extract those principles of law best suited to the United States.

Within ten years, Story had built up an enviable law practice based on a knowledge of law and procedure which was second to none. His most notable triumph at the Bar, which gained him nationwide publicity, was his successful representation of New England investors in the 1810 Supreme Court case of *Fletcher v Peck*. They had bought 'Yazoo' lands originally sold by corrupt members of the Georgia legislature at knock-down prices in return for bribes paid to virtually every member of the governing body.[35]

Story's general reputation took him to the shortlist of New Englanders to replace Justice Cushing on the Court and to preside over the United States First Circuit. He was not the automatic choice: three other prominent lawyers were approached and declined the nomination. He was the most prominent New Englander willing to take it.[36] As a New England Republican, he did not exhibit the fervour of Virginia Republicans, such as Thomas Jefferson, who resented the federal government's encroachment upon state sovereignty and believed the Federalist-dominated Supreme Court to be an agency of national government control. On 18 November 1811, the Senate confirmed President Madison's nomination and Story, resigning his post as Speaker of the Massachusetts House of Representatives, joined the Court. He served for 33 years until his death on circuit in 1845. As McClellan (1971) rightly observes, Story's rise from obscurity to the Supreme Court in less than ten years can only be regarded as phenomenal.[37]

Although at 32 years of age, the youngest ever Supreme Court Justice with no judicial experience, his enthusiasm and reputation was such that in his first session of the Court, he delivered the Court's opinion in two cases. During his 24 years on the Marshall Court he delivered 195 majority opinions. It is perhaps unfair to contrast Story's contribution with that of Justice Duvall, a most inactive justice, who joined the Court on the same day but delivered only 16 opinions in the

---

[34] WW Story, *Life and Letters*, vol 1, 204.
[35] *Fletcher v Peck*, 6 Cranch, 87 (1810). For an in depth discussion of this gigantic fraud see, C. Peter Magrath, *Yazoo: The Case of Fletcher v Peck*, (New York: WW Norton & Company Inc., 1966).
[36] For an account of the prolonged search for a replacement for Cushing see, Hiller B Zobel, 'Pillar of the Political Fabric: Federal Courts in Massachusetts, 1789–1815' (1989) 74 *Massachusetts Law Review* 197–205 at 204.
[37] McClellan, 41.

same period. Story's workload should be set against that of the next most prolific opinion writer Justice William Johnson, who handed down 108 opinions between 1804 and 1834. These comparisons are important because they support the argument that Marshall's efforts to strengthen the power base of the Court would have been far more difficult without Story at his side.

Story did not come to the Court not as a stranger, having met most of the justices socially during his trips to Washington both in connection with his law practice and as a short-lived member of Congress. Writing to his Harvard friend Probate Judge Samuel Fay in 1808, Story, as ever, was extremely complimentary of the justices, describing Washington as 'a profound lawyer' … and whose 'written opinions are composed with ability'. Livingston was, 'a very able and independent judge … decisive, earnest and impressive on the bench'. He was clearly captivated by John Marshall's ability and personality, noting his genius, good temper and extreme patience. He wrote 'I love his laugh, it is too happy for an intriguer'.[38] These early observations are an indication that Story would fit in easily with other members of the Court. His expressed political views made it likely that he would share the Court's vision of a strong national government supported by the federal judiciary.

There is a wealth of primary evidence available upon which to evaluate Story's contribution to United States law. The foundation of this study is the examination of his circuit opinions in *Federal Cases* and other reports and his Supreme Court output within *United States Reports*. William W Story's *Miscellaneous Writings of Joseph Story* is an invaluable collection of his father's thoughts and correspondence to complement his father's *Life and Letters*. Joseph Story's monumental *Commentaries on the Constitution of the United States* is the most learned and influential treatise of the era.[39] The *American Monthly Review* of 1833 enthused over the *Commentaries* declaring that,

> Allusions are often made to the points of reference between Mr Justice Blackstone, Vinerian Professor of Law at Oxford and Mr Justice Story, Professor of Law at Cambridge. [Story's] work now before us, is, to our Constitution, all that Blackstone's Commentaries were to the English Constitution.[40]

---

[38] Letter, Story to Samuel Fay, 25 February 1808. Story ended the letter. 'As ever, the fretful MATTHEW BRAMBLE (A character from Tobias Smollett's 1771 novel, *The Expeditions of Humphrey Clinker*).

[39] Joseph Story, *Commentaries on the Constitution of the United States*, 3 vols. (Boston: Hilliard, Gray & Company, 1833); WW Story, *Miscellaneous Writings*; Charles Sumner (ed.), *Reports of Cases Argued and Determined in the Court of the United States for the First District*, 3 vols (Boston: Charles C. Little & James Brown, 1836–1847); WW Story, *Reports of Cases Argued and Determined in the Circuit Court of the United States for the First Circuit*, 3 vols (Boston: Charles C. Little & James Brown, 1842–1847); John Gallison, *Reports of Cases in the Circuit Court of the United States for the First Circuit*, (Boston: Wells & Lilly, 1815 & 1817); William P Mason, *Reports of Circuit Cases in the Circuit Court of the United States for the First Circuit*, 5 vols (Boston: Wells & Lilly, 1819–1831).

[40] *American Monthly Review*, vol 4, 1833, 500–13, 500.

Story ensured that the *Commentaries* reached the widest possible readership by producing in the same year a one-volume abridged version of the work specifically for the 'use of Colleges and High Schools'. In the preface he wrote,

> I indulge in the hope, that even in this reduced form the reasoning in favour of every clause in the constitution will appear satisfactory and conclusive; and that the youth of my country will learn to venerate and admire it as the only solid foundation, on which to rest out national union, prosperity and glory.[41]

The following year he further revised the *Commentaries* to make it more readily understood by students of the higher classes in the common schools, naming it a *Constitutional Class Book*.[42] Finally, in 1840, he produced a further one-volume version designed for the general public entitled, *A Familiar Exposition of the Constitution*.[43] Story wrote anonymous essays for the *Encyclopaedia Americana* between 1829 and 1833 on the Constitution, common law, prize law, the Congress, the Law of Nations and legislation and codes. He wrote in plain English to ensure that his message was widely received.[44]

Chief Justice Marshall has rightly received considerable scholarly attention but, save for Justice Story, his associate justices have been largely ignored. There have been very fine published biographies of Justices MacLean (1937); Johnson (1954); Paterson (1979); and Chase (1980) and two informative doctoral theses on Justice Smith Thompson (1963) and Bushrod Washington (1974). These focus on the justices' Supreme Court opinions and have little to say about their circuit court opinions and the importance of those 'inferior' courts in the formation of United States law.[45]

Justice Story has fared much better than his fellow associates. Gerald T Dunne's 1970 biography of Story, prompted by Justice Frankfurter, James McClellan's 1971 *Joseph Story and the American Constitution* and R Kent Newmyer's 1985 account of his life and contribution to the Court are all fine biographies focusing on the

---

[41] Joseph Story, *Commentaries, Abridged by the Author*, 1 vol (Boston: Hilliard, Gray and Company, 1833).

[42] Joseph Story, *A Constitutional Class Book; Being a Brief Exposition of the Constitution of the United States* (Boston: Hilliard, Gray & Co, 1834).

[43] Joseph Story, *A Familiar Exposition of the Constitution* (Boston: March, Capen, Lyon & Webb, 1840).

[44] These essays have been sourced, collected and edited by Valerie L Horowitz in *The Unsigned Essays of Supreme Court Justice Joseph Story: Early American Views of Law* (Clark, New Jersey: Talbot Publishing/Lawbook Exchange, 2006).

[45] Francis P Weisenburger, *The Life of John MacLean: A Politician on the United States Supreme Court* (Columbus: Ohio State University Press, 1937); Donald G Morgan, *Justice William Johnson: The First Dissenter* (Columbia: University of South Carolina Press, 1954); John E O'Connor, *William Paterson: Lawyer and Statesman, 1745–1806* (New Brunswick: Rutgers University Press, 1979); James Haw, Francis F Beirne, Rosamund R Beirne and R Samuel Jett, *Stormy Patriot: The Life of Samuel Chase* (Baltimore: Maryland Historical Society, 1980); Donald Malcolm Roper, *Mr Justice Thompson and the Constitution* (New York: Garland Publishing Inc, 1987. (A 1963 doctoral thesis published as submitted); David Leslie Annis, *Mr Justice Bushrod Washington, Supreme Court Justice on the Marshall Court*. (An unpublished thesis submitted to Notre Dame University in August 1974).

justice's Supreme Court work.[46] There is also a useful pen sketch of Story by G Edward White (1988) who describes him as 'unquestionably the busiest and most productive judge of Marshall's tenure ... and quite possibly the most active in the entire history of the Court'.[47] White outlines Story's contribution to the Court in his 2012 *Law in American History* but nothing new emerges because of the earlier works by Dunne and Newmyer, the extensive material in his own *The Marshall Court and Cultural Change, 1815–1835* (1988) and the wide remit of his new book.[48]

A more recent analytical examination of Story is that of Finkelman (1994) who looks with a critical eye at just one of Story's opinions: the Fugitive Slave Act case of *Prigg v Pennsylvania* (1842), discussed later in this chapter in an overview of Story's slavery opinions.[49] Baker (2014) has contributed the most recent insight into Story's opinion in *Prigg*.[50] Collections of Story's letters to Justice Livingston and to John Marshall are also available.[51] However, apart from Newmyer's essay on Story on circuit, the main emphasis of scholars has been on Story's Supreme Court opinions and academic achievements. This study offers an in-depth analysis of his circuit opinions to understand how his local experiences shaped his judicial philosophy.

# A Modernising Influence on Law and Procedure on the First Circuit

Scholars naturally focus on Story's Supreme Court opinions because their impact was much more widely felt than his circuit opinions. However, it is important to examine those local decisions to see how he established a body of circuit law and

---

[46] Gerald T Dunne, *Justice Joseph Story and the Rise of the Supreme Court* (New York: Simon & Schuster, 1970); James McClellan, *Joseph Story and the American Constitution*. (Norman: University of Oklahoma Press, 1971). McClelland is particularly good on Story's love of literature and poetry (5–11; 15–17). See also Newmyer's, 'Justice Joseph Story on Circuit and a Neglected Phase in American Legal History' (1970) 14(2) *The American Journal of Legal History* 112–35.

[47] G Edward White, *The Marshall Court and Cultural Change, 1815–1835* (New York: Cambridge University Press, 2010), 355. (First published in 1988, Macmillan Publishing Company). White contributes a very valuable account of Story's mastery of prize, admiralty and marine insurance law. (904–22).

[48] G Edward White, *Law in American History*, vol 1 (New York: Oxford University Press, 2012).

[49] Paul Finkelman, 'Story Telling on the Supreme Court: Prigg v Pennsylvania and Justice Joseph Story's Judicial Nationalism' (1994) *The Supreme Court Review* 247–94.

[50] H Robert Baker, 'A Better Story in *Prigg v Pennsylvania*' (2014) 39(2) *Journal of Supreme Court History* 169–89.

[51] Gerald T Dunne, 'The Story Livingston Correspondence (1812–1822),' (1966) 10(3) *American Journal of Legal History* 224–36. Charles Warren, 'The Story-Marshall Correspondence (1819–1831)' (1941) 21(1) *William and Mary Quarterly*, Second Series, 1–26. See also Howell J Heaney, 'The Letters of Joseph Story (1779–1845) in the Hampton L Carson Collection of the Free Library of Philadelphia' (1958) 2(1) *The American Journal of Legal History* 68–86.

procedure to resolve what he believed to be the most important and satisfying function he exercised as a justice. In 1840 he wrote: 'If my fame shall happen to go down to posterity, my character as a judge will be more fully & accurately seen in the opinions of the circuit court than in the Supreme Court.'[52] He was more able to express his views in circuit court without the need to accommodate the opinions of his brethren on the Court (evidenced by Story's complaint that he had withdrawn a dissent because Justice Washington thought that 'dissenting opinions on ordinary occasions weakens the authority of the Court and is of no public benefit').[53]

Story sat on circuit in the main centres of Boston, Massachusetts; Portland, Maine; Portsmouth, New Hampshire; and Providence, Rhode Island. He rode circuit each May and October. Depending on the amount of work awaiting him, each circuit might take two months to complete; he would travel each year approximately 4,000 miles along poor roads often in very trying conditions. He also sat on the Court in Washington which could take up to a further two months of his time; in all, he sat for about half of the year. His journey home from Washington to Salem was very arduous—it took him 12 days to cover the 500 miles.[54] He was, however, more fortunate than Justice Todd who was obliged to travel considerably further through Kentucky, Ohio and Tennessee on the Seventh Circuit.

The search for patterns of jurisprudence in Story's circuit cases has involved an examination of the 458 of his opinions, between 1811 and 1835 which have survived to the *Federal Cases*. Although Story covered all branches of law on circuit, he spent by far the greater part of his time on admiralty matters upon which he became the acknowledged expert of his age: 169 of his opinions flow from prize cases, general admiralty disputes and marine insurance cases, 101 of which arose between 1812 and 1813 due to attempts by ship-owners and masters to evade embargo and non-intercourse acts. According to his son, Story's docket was overloaded with such cases when he first came on circuit due to the inability of his predecessor, Justice Cushing, to attend to business because of illness. Story dealt with the backlog by removing 130 cases from the docket with one opinion. He held that no appeal lay from the district court to the circuit court except in civil maritime and admiralty cases and that any jury verdict in the district court could come up to the circuit court only upon a point of law or a writ of error. There was no entitlement to a second jury trial.[55] This no-nonsense attitude was typical of

---

[52] Letter, Story to District Judge Joseph Hopkinson, 16 February1840, extracted from the Hopkinson papers by Newmyer in *Joseph Story*, 318. Zobel regards Story as 'this country's first modern nisi prius judge', Zobel, 'Pillar of the Political Fabric,' 205.

[53] Letter, Justice Story to Court reporter Henry Wheaton, 8 April 1818. WW Story, *Life and Letters*, vol 1, 303–04.

[54] Letter, Story to his wife, 12 March 1812. ibid. 219. Story wrote that he anticipated that the New England roads would be very bad and although anxious to reach home, he might have to rest on his journey.

[55] ibid, 221. The opinion was *United States v Wonson*, 28 F Cas 745, Mass, May 1812.

his approach to circuit work, streamlining practice and procedure for the efficient dispatch of business. This opinion was never considered by the Supreme Court, the report of the case indicating that the district attorney was satisfied with this peremptory clearance of the docket, as must have been the parties and the lawyers involved in the affected litigation because the opinion was not challenged.[56]

Story was unhappy with the long-accepted tradition of excessively lengthy pleadings and legal argument because it stood in the way of a reasonably manageable docket. After his first Supreme Court sitting in February 1812, he complained to a friend of lists crowded with overloaded documents and a brief of 230 pages with legal arguments lasting five days.[57] His determination to simplify the court process was illustrated by his circuit opinion in *Harding et al v Wheaton et al* (1821) when he complained of the length and prolixity of the pleadings which could easily have been reduced by half and threatened in future to send such cases to the master before trial to be corrected at the expense of the parties.[58] His modernising influence was not confined to his circuit court. He adopted the same robust attitude to procedure in his Supreme Court opinions. In *The Pizarro* (1817) he expressed surprise at the irregularities in the procedure in the district court when prize law practice should have been clear.[59] He made his displeasure known in *Carver v Jackson* at the practice of bringing up the whole of the judge's charge to the jury when only alleged mistakes in law should be highlighted.[60]

Story's wish to streamline procedure was a necessary prerequisite to bringing disputes to the earliest possible conclusion and is apparent from his opinions

---

[56] Story had experience of a no-nonsense approach to reducing a long list of outstanding cases having appeared before Theophilus Parsons, the Chief Justice of the Supreme Court of Massachusetts between 1806 and 1813. See, WW Story, *Life and Letters*, vol 2, 495–503. Parsons, in order to get through the docket, often refused to allow counsel to argue the case. His general practice was to default or non-suit if the parties were not ready for trial. Story's attitude to reducing lists was modest by comparison. As to Parsons' highly questionable practice see, Justin Winsor (ed), *The Memorial History of Boston Including Suffolk County, Massachusetts, 1630–1880*, vol 4 (Boston: James R Osgood and Company, 1881), 594.

[57] Letter Joseph Story to Samuel Fay, 24 February 1812. WW Story, *Life and Letters*, vol 1, 216.

[58] *Harding et al v Wheaton et al* 11 F Cas 491. Rhode Island, November 1821. The editor of the *Providence Gazette* (in an item carried in the *Salem Gazette* of 19 November 1824) complained that 'Within a few years the business of the US Court in this District has greatly increased. This has its rise in the delay incident in causes in our State Courts, a subject of very general complaint, for which there seems to be no remedy.' He noted that in order to obtain a speedy remedy in the federal circuit court, some litigants were becoming temporary residents of another state to achieve jurisdiction. This may well have been a purely local problem due to a lack of sufficient able state judges to match the speed and efficiency of Justice Story. The very same complaint was made by the editor of *The Providence Microcosm* (carried in the *Salem Gazette* of 21 November 1826) He wrote, 'Is it not humiliating that we should be dependent on the United States Government, for a Court to decide our causes? And is it not striking at the root of the sovereignty and independence of the state? Let our Legislature consider this matter and it cannot fail to stimulate them to a reform of our judicial process.' What he was acknowledging was the superiority of the federal court not just in terms of the speedy dispatch of litigation but also the quality of the decision making.

[59] *The Pizarro*, 15 US (2 Wheat) 227 (1817).

[60] *Carver v Jackson*, 29 US (4 Pet) 1 (1830).

in the circuit cases of *Hatch v Ellis* (1812),[61] *Green v Watkins* (1821),[62] *Mandeville v Riggs* (1829),[63] and *Gammell v Skinner* (1814).[64] In *Hatch v Ellis* a party died between verdict and judgment. Story did not order a rehearing, taking the practical and sensible course of holding that, provided the judgment was entered within two terms of the verdict the deceased was to be treated as though he was still alive. The verdict did not lapse and the litigation was brought to a speedier conclusion. He took a similar view in *Green v Watkins* (1821) when holding for the Court that the death of a plaintiff in error before the writ was determined did not cause a dismissal or abatement of the suit. If the deceased's personal representatives did not volunteer, the Court had the power to compel them to join in and pursue the writ of error to a conclusion. Again writing for the Court, Story, in *Mandeville v Riggs* (1829) sent out a message that the federal courts were not to be overburdened by a multiplicity of cases arising from the same cause of action. To achieve this objective he held that all interested parties who were known and within the jurisdiction and the personal representatives of those who had died must be made parties to the action to ensure that all claims were dealt with in one fell swoop. In *Gammell v Skinner* (1814) he insisted that parties answer interrogatories to narrow the issues, thereby saving time and expense at the trial and easing the task of the judge trying the case. These important procedural opinions were crucial in discouraging prolix pleadings and argument and streamlining outmoded practices and procedures; all designed to ensure cheaper and speedier federal justice.

In his very first full circuit sitting Story also complained about government legislative language which he found 'loose and inartificial', giving judges little guidance on the intention of Congress or the state legislature.[65] In another case in the same term he explained that his approach to imprecise penal statutes was to refuse to punish defendants by giving effect to doubtful passages.[66] He reinforced this practice the following term in New Hampshire when in the embargo case of *United States v Mann* (1812) he declared, 'I will not be the first judge sitting in this seat to strain a proviso against a citizen.'[67] These cases show that from his earliest sittings, Story's mastery of law and procedure gained from his practice at the Bar gave him the confidence to exert firm authority over litigants, sending messages to Congress and state legislatures that he was not prepared to remedy deficiencies in drafting at the expense of citizens. Unless the meaning of a statute was plain it

---

[61] *Hatch v Ellis*, 11 F Cas 806, Mass, May 1812.
[62] *Green v Watkins*, 19 US (6 Wheat) 260 (1821).
[63] *Mandeville v Riggs*, 27 US (2 Pet) 482 (1829).
[64] *Gammell v Skinner*, 9 F Cas 1142, Mass, May 1814.
[65] *The Argo*, 1 F Cas 1100, Mass, May 1812. According to the *Federal Cases* Story had actually sat on circuit in Boston during the October 1811 term. There is only one reported case from that term dealing with the liability of a carrier of banknotes (*Citizen's Bank v Nantucket Steamboat Co* 5 F Cas 719, Mass, October 1811). He must have tried the case in November because his nomination the Court by President Madison was not confirmed by the Senate until 18 November 1811.
[66] *The Falmouth*, 8 F Cas 981, Mass, May 1812.
[67] *United States v Mann*, 26 F Cas 1153, New Hampshire, October 1812.

would be construed in favour of a defendant facing a possible penalty such as the loss of a vessel and cargo. He was not out to punish the draftsman. His wish was to protect the citizen.

## Admiralty and the Enforcement of Embargo Laws

During Story's first full term in Boston in May 1812, 21 of the 28 reported opinions he handed down determined allegations of breaches of the Embargo Act including trading with a foreign nation, sailings without first obtaining clearance, failing to enter into the required bond and breaches of coastal fishing licences.[68] Despite his opposition to embargo as a politician, he treated established contraventions seriously; his opinions reflected his refusal to accept many of the excuses advanced for breaches. Hearing the same unconvincing excuses so often, he became rather cynical in his approach to them.[69]

His opinions show that excuses for breaches were many and varied; a severe storm had blown the vessel off course into a United States port; the ship's owners were citizens of a neutral country; the cargo had not been taken on in England; the goods had been transhipped into the vessel on her homeward voyage. Story treated these explanations with the utmost suspicion and, after a rigorous investigation, more often than not rejected them, making or confirming a forfeiture order made by the district judge. He was determined to get to the bottom of each excuse, insisting on a survey of the vessel when severe storm damage was raised. He considered whether the cargo was more readily saleable in the United States than in the supposed original destination, always insisting on an examination of the ship's manifest and log to see whether they had been tampered with. In *The Sally* (1813), an allegation of trading with the enemy, he declared that he regarded the

---

[68] The earlier Non-Intercourse & Embargo Acts expired at the beginning of the 1812 War with Britain. Story's embargo opinions were founded originally on breaches of the 1807 Act and later on the replacement legislation. The Trading with the Enemy Act 1812 was virtually a repeat of the 1807 Embargo Act (Statutes at Large, 12 Congress, Statute 1, 778). The draconian Embargo Act 1813 prohibited all United States vessels from leaving American ports and imposed a complete ban on the importation of most goods from Britain and her colonies. Foreign ships were not permitted to trade in American ports unless three-quarters of the crew were citizens of the country of the vessel's flag. The ransoming of ships was outlawed (Statutes at Large, 13 Congress, Statute 1, 88).

[69] Between 1812 and 1814 privateers commissioned by the president captured an estimated 2,000 vessels. 150 such commissions were granted in Massachusetts alone and Story's home town of Salem sent out 43 privateers, which during the war with Britain, accounted for 300 prizes of which 130 were condemned by the district and circuit courts. These figures are taken from Capt Michael H Rustein, *The Privateering Stroke: Salem Privateers and the War of 1812* (Salem: Create Space Independent Publishing Platform, 2012). See also the Act of 27 January 1813, which set out the procedure for applying for Letters of Marque and the rules under which privateers were to operate. Richard Peters (ed), *The Public Statutes at Large of the United States of America*, vol 2 (Boston: Charles C Little and James Brown, 1850). 759–64.

ship's papers as crucial evidence in forfeiture proceedings and would draw adverse inferences if they were withheld from the authorities and the court.[70] He went so far as to find grounds for forfeiture in *The St Lawrence* (1813) simply because the ship had sailed from a foreign port and her papers had been suppressed.[71]

In *The Short Staple* (1812) he treated an alleged breach as an offence of strict liability, placing the burden of proving that a route deviation was necessary on the master and owners of the vessel. In that case he ordered forfeiture of the vessel and foreign cargo because he regarded its capture by a privateer and subsequent entry into port as collusive, remarking that he often found it necessary to 'resist the influence of human declarations and to rely on the concurrence of probable circumstances'.[72] In *The Argo* (1812) he held that a deviation from course which breached the embargo was justified only if it was to avoid jeopardy to life or property.[73] This reversal of the burden of proof meant that in *Ten Hogsheads of Rum* (1812) the claimants were unable to prove that the rum on board ship was not of British origin and Story made a forfeiture order to the United States.[74]

This harsh approach was one which reflected his strong nationalism, a stance which during the 1812 War would be fully supported across the political spectrum. In *United States v Webber* (1813) he reversed the district judge's refusal to impose a penalty of $1,000 on a master who failed to make a report to the collector of customs within 24 hours of his vessel arriving in port. The master alleged that he had entered the port out of necessity. Story recounted his experience of similar cases when as counsel for ship-owners against the United States, he had felt embarrassed that a narrow interpretation of the statute made it easy for commanders to excuse a failure to report arrival at a port by claiming entry by necessity. He held that it did not matter whether the entry was voluntary or of necessity and hoped that vigorous examination of defences to breaches of the embargo laws would prevent a flood of spurious excuses.[75] He was a poacher turned gamekeeper.

Story even found a breach and affirmed forfeiture in a case in which notice of the embargo had not reached the master of the vessel on the basis that everyone is presumed to know the law. He held that the embargo statute took effect from the time of its passage and, despite recognising the hardship which would follow, he reluctantly affirmed the district judge's opinion.[76] Story again applied strict liability in *Cross v United States* (1812), upholding a penalty of double value of the vessel and cargo for breach of embargo even though the owner was unaware that the voyage contravened the President's proclamation prohibiting such an importation which Story believed to be 'universally known'. The ship entered Boston

---

[70] *The Sally*, 21 F Cas 243, Mass, 1813.
[71] *The St Lawrence*, 21 F Cas 180, New Hampshire, October 1813.
[72] *The Short Staple*, 22 F Cas 23, Mass, May 1812.
[73] *The Argo*, 1 F Cas 1100, Mass, May 1812.
[74] *Ten Hogsheads of Rum*, 16 F Cas 932, Mass, October 1812.
[75] *The Boston*, 3 F Cas 925, Mass, October 1812.
[76] *The Ann*, 1 F Cas 926, Mass, May 1812.

harbour having taken on board a cargo of wine from the Cape of Good Hope. However, whilst he felt bound by the strict letter of the law, he did say that 'he would leave to others, upon whom a more agreeable duty devolves, to apply the proper mitigation or remission of forfeiture'.[77]

It was his duty as a judge to enforce the statute despite the extreme hardship the ban on international trade had both on the United States and his part of the country. Story explained his approach to embargo cases in *The George* (1814). He cited favourably Sir William Scott's view of the judicial function from the English admiralty case of *The Rosalie and Betty*, (2 C. Rob Adm. 343), that 'a judge should start out with no prejudice against a party and suppose every case to be a true unless fraud is proved, but he should not shut his eyes to what was happening in the world'. Story had in mind the close proximity of the ports of Maine to British land in Canada and the great temptation to engage in illicit trade. He condemned the increasing number of collusive captures between American traders and British officers or American privateers which he described as 'very unwelcome guests to the court', pointing to the records of the district and circuit courts to show how extensive the prohibited trade was.[78]

Twice the Supreme Court believed Story had been too quick to reject explanations and hold vessels and cargo forfeit to the United States. In *The Short Staple* (1812) the Court reversed him on the ground that whilst the master's explanation raised strong suspicions it was not so incredible as to justify forfeiture. Story was upset, believing the master to have hoodwinked the Court; he dissented from the opinion, insisting that a forfeiture order was justified and noting that he had the support of one of his brethren.

Story's other embargo reversal came in *The Bothnea, The Janstoff* (1814). He found a breach on the basis of a collusive capture by an American privateer of two vessels, both sailing under false Swedish papers. Each ship had one American citizen on board who were permitted to remain after the entire crew of each vessel was removed. There was no doubt but that there was a breach of embargo. The only question was whether the capture was collusive. Story had no hesitation in finding that it was. Both vessels, in sight of each other, were met by the privateer shortly after leaving Halifax, Nova Scotia. Neither made any attempt to escape. The captain of the Bothnea stated that he yielded, believing the one gun privateer to be a British cruiser.[79] The Supreme Court disagreed, holding that all of the circumstances were equally consistent with guilt or innocence. However, an inference might reasonably be drawn from the reversal by Court's use of phrases such as 'spirit of adventure' and 'talent for enterprise' by the crew of the privateer, suggesting a strong political desire to encourage privateers to harry the enemy and illegal traders and reap the rewards of their important role.[80]

---

[77] *Cross v United States*, 6 F Cas 892, Mass, May 1812.
[78] *The George*, 10 F Cas 196, Mass, October 1814.
[79] *The Bothnea. The Janstoff*, 3 F Cas 962, Mass, May 1814.
[80] *The Bothnea* 15 US 169 (1817).

Years later, Story felt vindicated by his hardline approach when, in *Robinson v Hook* (1826), he read secret papers thrown overboard from a vessel hovering off the coast of Maine during embargo to effect collusive captures of ships leaving ports in the British provinces in Canada laden with British-manufactured goods. The 'captured' vessels were to be taken into United States ports to be forfeited to the captors, thereby getting highly desirable goods into the United States. The papers revealed how many Boston merchants had been involved in such widespread breaches of the embargo. Despite the documents having been passed to the government, it would appear from Story's expressions of surprise in 1826 that the authorities had not passed to the justices the evidence of this large-scale conspiracy. In *Robinson v Hook*, Story was dealing with a very stale dispute over shares of a much earlier forfeiture in which information from the secret documents was raised. The case gave him an opportunity to criticize 'the lenient administration of prize law during this period' and 'especially in lending an indulgent ear to the claims of our own citizens'. He was reproaching those other judges on circuit and on the Court for too readily accepting dubious explanations for breaches. His remark that 'the justice of those sentences of condemnation, which admitted of most controversy, have in an unexpected manner, been confirmed by facts recently brought to light' was a vindication of his hardline approach to embargo breaches.[81] It would have been a relief to him to know that his intense scrutiny of embargo defences had been justified.

Not all of Story's admiralty opinions flow from breaches of embargo. He frequently imposed forfeiture orders and/or financial penalties when masters attempted to land goods without notifying the port authorities to evade import duties or by deliberately misstating the value of goods or their nature to pay a reduced sum. Any obstruction of a customs officer was dealt with severely.[82] The federal government insisted upon all ship-owners posting a bond, often with sureties, for the due payment of customs duties on all imports.[83] Story handed down 30 opinions relating to breach of import duty regulations, reflecting the importance of the judicial function in ensuring the collection of much needed revenue and penalties in default for the struggling economy at a time of severely restricted maritime trade.

Another aspect of Boston maritime circuit work was the trials of criminal offences by seamen whilst on board ship which accounted for 22 more opinions,

---

[81] *Robinson v Hook*, 20 F Cas 1017, Maine, October 1826.

[82] Examples are: *The Industry*, 13 F Cas 35, Mass, May 1812 (forfeiture for unloading without a permit); *United States v Sears et al*, 27 F Cas 1006 October 1812 (resisting an inspector of customs boarding to ascertain whether a breach had occurred); *United States v Sixteen Packages*, 27 F Cas 1111, Mass, October 1819 (forfeiture because goods invoiced below cost price to avoid duties); *United States v Mantor*, 26 F Cas 1157 October 1820 (breaking the locks placed on a vessel by customs inspector); *The Alligator*, 1 F Cas 527, Mass, 1812 (sailing without giving the required bond).

[83] Examples: *The Bolina*, 3 F Cas 811, Mass, 1812 (forfeiture for failing to give a bond); *Hunt v United States*, 12 F Cas 948, Mass, May 1812 (liability of surety for principal's failure to honour the required bond).

ranging from theft to the capital offences of murder and piracy. With a jury, Story tried two allegations of piracy, six of murder on the high seas and ten indictments of seamen endeavouring to make a revolt at sea and/or confining the master of a vessel. Often the issue was not just whether an offence had been committed, but whether the court had jurisdiction to try the case. In *United States v Ross* (1813), Story held that the circuit court had jurisdiction to try a murder on board ship within half a mile of a foreign shore and assumed jurisdiction in *United States v Smith et al* (1816) in an endeavouring to revolt allegation, holding that a vessel within three miles of the shore was on the high seas.[84] Just two years later in *United States v Hamilton*, he held that a vessel did not have to be on the high seas to found an indictment for endeavouring to make a revolt.[85] These cases show a determination on Story's part to extend the circuit court's admiralty jurisdiction as widely as possible. By section 12 of the Crimes Act 1790 any person convicted of confining the master of a ship or endeavouring to make a revolt faced up to three years imprisonment and a fine of $1,000.[86]

Whilst Story was not averse to passing severe sentences, he was vigilant to ensure that a defendant received a fair trial. Thus, in *United States v Barker et al* (1829), he charged the jury that a simple refusal by one or more seamen to perform their duties was not the combination envisaged in section 10 and, where in *United States v Ashton* (1835) the independent evidence confirmed that the crew had compelled the master to return to port because the ship was unseaworthy, Story was content with the district attorney's decision not to proceed to trial.[87]

Story's oversight of mariners extended to his protection of their right to wages and medical treatment, holding that to lose pay, any disobedience must either have been habitual or a heinous act.[88] In *Harden v Gordon et al* (1823) he held that where a seaman had to be taken ashore because of illness, the cost of food, nursing and lodgings were a charge on the ship. In *The George* (1832), he extended the same protection to the master of a vessel.[89] His motives were not solely altruistic as he remarked in *Harden* that the protection of seamen served commerce and the defence of the nation by encouraging seamen to engage in perilous voyages at low wages.[90]

As well as ensuring that the cost of caring for seamen taken ashore due to illness was provided for, Story discouraged masters who rid themselves of difficult crew

---

[84] *United States v Ross*, 27 F Cas 572, Mass, October 1813; *United States v Smith et al.*, 27 F Cas 1166 (1816).
[85] *United States v Hamilton*, 26 F Cas 93, Mass, October 1818.
[86] Peters, *Public Statutes at Large*, vol 1 (1845) 115.
[87] *United States v Barker et al* 24 F Cas 985, Mass, October 1829; *United States v Ashton*, 24 F Cas 873, Mass, May 1835.
[88] See: *Spurr v Pearson*, 22 F Cas 1011, Mass, October 1816: *The Mentor*, 17 F Cas 15, Mass, October 1825. If the claim for forfeiture of wages was based on desertion, Story insisted that it had to be entered in the ship's log on the very day of the desertion for the claim to succeed; if the desertion had been condoned, wages were to be paid thereafter (*Cloutman v Tunison*, 5 F Cas 1091, Mass, May 1833).
[89] *The George*, 10 F Cas 205, Mass, May 1832.
[90] *Harden v Gordon et al*, 11 F Cas 480, Maine, October 1823.

members in foreign parts. In *Orne v Townsend* (1827), he declared that the court 'would look with a vigilant eye for discharges of seamen in foreign ports without paying to the U.S. consul the three month's pay in addition to wages accruing in accordance with the Act of 1825'.[91] He defined a master's duty towards his crew members in *United States v Ruggles* (1828) after the captain had forced a seaman into a jail in a foreign port for conduct which could have been dealt with quite easily on board ship: 'It is the duty of the master to watch over them with parental authority ... and he has no right to delegate his authority ... to gaolers and turn-keys in a foreign country.'[92] In *United States v Freeman* (1827), which involved a master charged with murder and convicted of manslaughter for brutally beating a seaman and sending him aloft in high winds from where he fell to his death in the sea, Story rejected an outrageous defence submission that seamen as a class should never be believed even on oath.[93]

His desire to ensure a fully manned merchant fleet went hand-in-hand with a wish to see that rescuers of stricken ships were reasonably compensated for placing themselves in harm's way. This is apparent from his favourable citation of a remark of the English admiralty judge Lord Stowell, who said that the remuneration in salvage cases was based 'not merely on the exact quantum of service performed ... but to the general interests of navigation and commerce of the country, which are greatly protected by exertions of this kind.'[94] These cases show how Story tempered the harsh realities of life at sea by affording sailors protection under the law and at the same time promoting maritime trade.

Story's admiralty expertise extended to marine insurance, salvage law and the authority of a master to create a lien on a vessel for repairs necessary to complete a voyage. Of Story's 169 admiralty opinions contained in *Federal Cases Reports*, 22 relate to marine insurance disputes. He held policies void for misrepresentations which materially affected the risk. Thus failure to disclose that the cargo was not all American owned was a breach of warranty and sailing on a date other than that agreed was fatal to cover.[95] Most disputes which materially affected the risk concerned the seaworthiness of the vessel at the time of sailing and deviations from route not due to life- or property-threatening emergencies.[96] The evidential burdens he set out in *Tidmarsh v Washington Fire & Marine Insurance Co Inc* (1827) were useful both to lawyers and their clients. He held that the assured must establish seaworthiness; the insurer had the burden of proving a misrepresentation which materially affected the risk to avoid the policy.[97]

---

[91] *Orne v Townsend*, 18 F Cas 825, Mass, October 1827.
[92] *United States v Ruggles*, 27 F Cas 912, Rhode Island, November 1828.
[93] *United States v Freeman*, 25 F Cas 1208, Mass, October 1827. The case excited a great deal of attention and was fully reported in the *Providence Patriot & Columbian Pheonix* of 11 March 1827, having been reproduced from the *Boston Traveler*.
[94] *The Emulous*, 8 F Cas 704, Mass, October 1832.
[95] *Bayard et al v Massachusetts Fire & Marine Ins Co*, 2 F Cas 1065, Mass, October 1826; *Baxter v New England Ins Co Inc*, 2 F Cas 1058, Mass, October 1822.
[96] *Glidden v Manufacturers' Ins Co*, 10 F Cas 476, Mass, October 1832.
[97] *Tidmarsh v Washington Fire & Marine Ins Co*, 23 F Cas 1197, Mass, October 1827.

By far the most significant of Story's marine insurance opinions was that of *Delovio v Boit et al* (1815).[98] Story reversed the district judge's holding that the district court had no jurisdiction to try a marine insurance dispute as it did not fall within the admiralty jurisdiction entrusted to the federal courts by the Constitution. This was a problem identified by Snell (2007) as arising from the Framers of the Constitution baldly stating that the federal courts were to have jurisdiction in admiralty and maritime matters without defining what this meant or specifying which federal courts had been given jurisdiction. Further, the First Congress in the *Judicature Act 1789* granted the state courts concurrent jurisdiction in maritime matters without setting any limits on that jurisdiction or identifying the source of applicable substantive law.[99]

If the District Judge's opinion in *Delovio* had stood it would have severely reduced the business and, therefore, the influence of the federal courts. Story had earlier held that his court had jurisdiction over marine insurance cases and was determined to reinforce that view in *Delovio*.[100] Writing to the court reporter, Henry Wheaton, in 1815, he described the current state of knowledge of admiralty jurisdiction, law and practice as 'a most shameful ignorance and it occasions considerable embarrassment in practice'. He said that he intended to write 'a very elaborate opinion upon the whole of the admiralty jurisdiction' reviewing 'all the common law decisions on this subject ... and all original rights before and since the statutes of Richard II'.[101] The opinion exceeded 70 pages, citing not only common law decisions and statutes but also all relevant jurists ancient and modern. It is an exposition based on scholarship and investigation which the reports reveal to be unique during this period even among Supreme Court justices and evidences a modern in-depth research-based approach to opinion writing. He concluded the opinion by wondering, 'how far a superior tribunal may deem it fit to entertain the principles', hoping that the parties would take the point on jurisdiction to the Supreme Court but they did not. A district judge was prohibited from taking part in an appeal from his own decision, so the device of a certificate of division

---

[98] *Delovio v Boit et al* 7 F Cas 418, Mass, October 1815.

[99] Steven L Snell, *Courts of Admiralty and the Common Law: Origins of the American Experiment in Concurrent Jurisdiction* (New York: Oxford University Press, 2007), 3–4. Snell charts the origin of American admiralty jurisdiction from Roman law through the English High Court of Admiralty. He pays particular attention to the importance of judges applying substantive maritime law and procedure uniformly in both state and federal courts. Story did, from time to time, look for precedents in the opinions of the Court of Appeals in Cases of Capture which had been set up by Congress to exercise jurisdiction over captured enemy vessels and cargo. This court operated until the jurisdiction was transferred to the United States Supreme Court and the lower federal courts upon the Ratification of the Constitution. The Continental Congress had in 1775 recommended that the colonies set up prize courts to deal with enemy captures. *Continental Congress Journal and Records* from 25 November 1775, 371–75. See also, Henry J Bourguignon, *The First Federal Court: The Federal Appellate Prize Court of the American Revolution, 1775–1787* (Philadelphia: American Philosophical Society, 1977).

[100] *The Jerusalem*, 13 F Cas 564, Mass, May 1815. The case was decided primarily on competing claims for a lien on a vessel for repairs, but it also had a marine insurance aspect.

[101] Letter, Joseph Story to Henry Wheaton, 5 September 1815 in WW Story, *Life and Letters*, vol 1, 267.

was unavailable. The parties did not even return to the district judge to conclude the matter. The jurisdictional issue did not reach the Supreme Court until 1870 in *Insurance Co v Dunham*, when Justice Joseph Bradley, for the Court, followed *Delovio*, holding that marine insurance contracts were within the admiralty jurisdiction. He praised Story's 'learned and exhaustive opinion', declaring that, despite doubts expressed by other judges as to the jurisdiction, the Court was convinced that Story's view was correct.[102]

The research material required to produce the opinion in *Delovio* was not easily obtainable due to the difficulty in sourcing law reports, statutes and text books, particularly those from abroad. Story's determination to equip practitioners with the tools to remedy their 'shameful ignorance' of admiralty law and practice is revealed in his letter to Henry Wheaton asking him to persuade a bookseller to publish many of the standard admiralty works. As an accomplished classicist he needed no translations of the original works. He asked Wheaton to try to obtain a copy of the works of Sir Leoline Jenkins, an English Admiralty judge and author of the Statute of Frauds 1677 for which he was prepared to pay $50.[103] Story had earlier paid a considerable sum for a copy of the Dutch jurist Bynkershoek only to find a third of the text was missing.[104] His determined efforts to make available the important admiralty texts not just for himself but also for the benefit of all practitioners marked him as the foremost scholar and educator of this branch of the law in the United States. He never lost that thirst for knowledge and avidly sought law reports and textbooks making him unique amongst judges of his time.

A footnote to *Delovio* appears in a letter written by Story to Nathaniel Williams in December 1815 in which he describes the opinion as 'the most elaborate I have ever composed' and having 'devoted all of my leisure time for more than a month to the subject'. After expressing regret that the Supreme Court would not be asked to pronounce upon his opinion, he intimated that the merchants and underwriters of Boston were very happy with his holding as the merchants were 'not fond of juries'.[105] If the federal courts had jurisdiction, the disputes were only tried by a judge, as opposed to judge and jury in the state courts. Clearly men of commerce preferred the more measured approach of a Supreme Court justice or district judge to the less predictable verdict of a jury.

Whilst Boston merchants had reservations about juries, Story was a staunch supporter of the institution, refusing to interfere with a verdict because of an innocent separation of the jury after retirement and refusing to upset an award of damages

---

[102] *Insurance Co v Dunham*, 78 US (11 Wall) 1, 77.
[103] Letter, Story to Wheaton, 15 September 1815 in WW Story, *Life and Letters*, vol 1, 266–69.
[104] ibid. vol 1, 228.
[105] Letter, Joseph Story to Hon Nathaniel Williams, 3 December 1815, WW Story, *Life and Letters*, vol 1, 269–70. H Zobel, 'Pillars of the Political Fabric: Federal Courts in Massachusetts, 1789–1815' (1989) 74 *Massachusetts Law Review* 197–205 at 205 citing Dunne, *Justice Joseph Story*, 129–30 suggests that Story developed the practice of prewriting opinions, devoid of facts, for use in future cases on the topic and gives *DeLovio v Boit* as an example because such a lengthy and complicated opinion requiring enormous research was produced only six days after legal arguments.

even though he thought the amount high.[106] He believed trial by jury in criminal matters to be 'the most sacred constitutional right of every person accused of a crime'. However, he was careful to emphasise that the jury's verdict must be based not only on the facts it found, but also accord with the judge's directions on law, explaining to the jury that if it decided the law there would be no consistency and in case of error, the defendant would have no redress.[107] He held the grand jury in the same high esteem, remarking in *United States v Coolidge* (1815) that 'it was the great inquest between the government and the citizen', expressing the hope that the 'institution be preserved in its purity and that no citizen be tried, unless he has been regularly accused by the proper tribunal'.[108]

The remaining 289 of Story's reported circuit opinions covered most aspects of jurisprudence. The major categories were commercial disputes, including contracts, negotiable instruments, banking, partnerships and insolvency (72); land (45); criminal law (39); practice, procedure and evidence (21); wills (16); and patents (14). These opinions were of importance to the parties but, unlike his admiralty holdings, many were not precedents, rules to be applied or of particular interest outside the First Circuit.

Although few in number, Story's opinions on the slave trade and slavery in general were the subject of national interest. He had always opposed slavery publicly and, although there are only five of his reported circuit opinions prior to 1835, they reflect his views on this troubling social evil. In *Fales et al v Mayberry* (1815), Story held that no action could be maintained between parties engaged in the slave trade, describing it as 'a most odious and horrible traffic contrary to the plainest principles of natural justice'.[109] It was a theme he revisited in subsequent cases ordering the forfeiture of the vessel, two-year prison terms and fines of $2,000 on persons involved for the offences of causing vessels to sail from the United States to be employed in the slave trade generally or for the purpose of procuring negroes from Africa.[110] In *The Alexander* (1823), he forfeited a vessel patently employed in the slave trade even though no slaves had been taken on board.[111]

Story denounced what he described as 'that most detestable traffic the slave trade' in a powerful charge to the grand jury at Boston in the October term of 1819.[112] He did not apologise for a lengthy speech, charting the history of the slave trade and the efforts of men such as William Wilberforce to end it. He let the

---

[106] *Burrill v Phillips*, 4 F Cas 832, Rhode Island, November 1812 (separation); *Thurston v Martin*, 23 F Cas 1189, Rhode Island, June 1830.
[107] *United States v Battiste*, 24 F Cas 1042, Mass, October 1835.
[108] *United States v Coolidge*, 25 F Cas 622, Mass, May 1815.
[109] *Fales et al v Mayberry*, 8 F Cas 970, Rhode Island, November 1815.
[110] *United States v Smith*, 27 F Cas 1167, Mass, October 1820; *United States v La Coste* 26 F Cas 826, Mass, October 1820.
[111] *The Alexander*, 1 F Cas 362, Mass, May 1823.
[112] WW Story, *Life and Letters*, vol 1, 335–48. The full text of a like charge to grand jury at Portland, Maine on 8 May 1820 is in WW Story, *Miscellaneous Writings*, 127–47. The part of the charge condemning the slave trade commences at 136.

people of Boston know of the horrors involved by explaining how 'Husbands are stolen from their wives, children from their parents and bosom friends from each other'. He described how the slaves were shackled on the ocean journey in spaces not much larger than a coffin and that about half perished within two years of captivity. His observations were based on his examination of debates in the British Parliament and from a study of first-hand accounts of those engaged in the trade or eye witnesses to its operation. That in-depth research is further evidence of a fully committed professional.

His attacks on the slave trade were not confined to circuit opinions and charges to the grand jury. He made his stand at public meetings. In 1819, at the only political meeting he attended whilst a judge in Salem he spoke in support of a resolution calling on Congress to ban slavery in all of the territories of the United States and against the proposed legislation to permit Missouri to join the Union as a 'slave state.'[113] A combination of Story's opposition to the 'Missouri Compromise' and his charge to the grand jury in Portsmouth, New Hampshire in May 1820 in which he condemned 'The existence of slavery under any shape [as] so repugnant to the natural rights of man and the dictates of justice, that it seems difficult to find for it any adequate justification', occasioned a furious response from the editor of the *St Louis Enquirer*. He accused Story of 'going beyond the line of his duty [as a judge] and that by suggesting that slavery contradicted the declaration that all men were born free and equal and went against the Christian religion, Story was 'inciting the negroes to insurrection' and 'acting as viceregent [sic] of the Deity to denounce the punishments of eternity against those who hold the negroes in bondage'.[114]

One of Story's circuit slavery opinions had international dimensions. In *The United States v La Jeune Eugenie* (1822), he affirmed the district judge's forfeiture of a captured French ship fitted out for the slave trade. Story emphasised his duty not to bow to executive and foreign pressure but to 'extinguish a trade abhorrent to the great principles of Christian morality, mercy and humanity'. However and despite his positive assertion of judicial independence, he did later accede to a request made by President Madison, through the district attorney, that he permit the French authorities to dispose of the matter on the basis that that their attitude towards the slave trade was that of the United States.[115]

Story's moral and humanitarian attitude towards the slave trade and all other aspects of his work arose from his Unitarian beliefs. He was a deeply religious man, evident from his reference to 'Christian morality, mercy and humanity' in *La Jeune Eugenie*. Religious belief became an issue in the Rhode Island circuit court case of *Wakefield v Ross* (1827), when Story declared: 'Persons who do not believe in the existence of God, or of a future state, or have no religious views are not entitled to be sworn in as witnesses and that a person with no such belief feared no religious

---

[113] WW Story, *Life and Letters*, vol 1, 359–61.
[114] *St Louis Enquirer* (St Louis, Missouri), 16 August 1820.
[115] WW Story, *Life and Letters*, vol 1, 348–58.

sanction if he lied on oath.' One of the rejected witnesses was a Universalist who believed in the 'restoration of all things'.[116] Story was fiercely attacked on his ruling in the December 1827 edition of the *Universalist Magazine* published in Boston. The editor complained bitterly that the ruling meant that Universalists were being denied their 'civil liberties' and exhorted the 'brethren to awake from their dreams of security ... and be up and doing'. As late as 1908, nine states, including seven of the original colonies, still excluded the testimony of 'non-believers'.[117]

Story drew on all available sources to craft his opinions. Having been trained in English law, his opinions regularly cited the decisions of Sir William Blackstone, Sir William Scott and Lords Mansfield, Hardwicke, Thurlow and Eldon. His remarks in an opinion on the practice of trying defendants together and jury selection in *United States v White et al*, reveal his high regard for the English judges: 'Mr Justice Blackstone in his *Commentaries* (4 Bl. Comm. 353) with his usual perspicacity and accuracy states the reasons on which the right of peremptory challenge is founded.' He then went on to consider all of the English authorities before stating, 'it remains now to examine the American cases', demonstrating his preference to look first at English law.[118]

*White* is noteworthy in two other respects. First, Story's admission in his opinion that he 'had made inquiries of among those learned minds in our own state whose situations would lead them to a thorough knowledge of the practice', is consistent

---

[116] *Wakefield v Ross*, 28 F Cas 1346, Rhode Island, November 1827. For the law and procedure on religious belief and entitlement to take the oath, see 'The Competency of Witnesses', *American Law Register*, November 1859, paras 5–9 and the cases cited in the footnotes.

[117] Paul W Kaufman, 'Disbelieving Non-Believers: Atheism, Competence and Credibility in the Turn of the Century' (2003) 15(2) *Yale Journal of Law and the Humanities* 416. The Judiciary Act 1789 gave the federal courts the power to impose and administer all necessary oaths or affirmations (s 17) and, in the taking of depositions, that the deponent be 'carefully examined, cautioned and sworn or affirmed to testify the whole truth' (s 30). Further, Article II, Section 1 of the Constitution gave the President the option of taking the oath of office or affirming and the Fourth Amendment insisted upon an oath or affirmation to support the issue of a warrant. Therefore, by the time of *Wakefield v Ross* it was possible for witnesses to affirm in federal court. The report is silent on the question of affirmations. In Rhode Island state courts a witness was not permitted to affirm. It would seem that Story was using local rules of evidence because state-to-state variation was permissible in all federal court rules. There was not much consistency as the practice varied between federal and state jurisdictions and from state to state. William Cranch, Chief Justice of the District of Columbia Circuit Court from 1806–55, in the 1807 case of *Rutherford v Moore* in which a witness who had declared his disbelief in a future state of rewards and punishments, doubted whether it did not go rather to credit than to the competency of the witness (F Cas 12174 C.C.D.C 1807). Yet in *United States v Lee* (1834) he refused to hear a witness who did not believe in a future state of existence and said that Nature was God (F Cas 15586 C.C.D.C 1834). In 1843 the Illinois Circuit Court held competent a witness who believed that bad conduct would be punished by God in this life. (*United States v Kennedy et al*, F Cas 15524 III 1843). The current version of the Arkansas Constitution of 1874 provides that: 'No person who denies the existence of a God shall hold any office in the civil departments of the state nor be competent as a witness in any court' (Article 19, Section 1). The provision clearly offends the United States Constitution and has never been implemented in modern times. For a comprehensive account of the treatment of atheists generally, see Mark Douglas McGarvie, *Law and Religion in American History: Public Values and Private Conscience* (New York: Cambridge University Press, 2016).

[118] *United States v White*, 28 F Cas 580, Mass, October 1826.

with the approach of Justice Washington who was prepared to acknowledge that he sought advice from advocates unconnected with the case. Second, judges sometimes 'divided' on an issue whereupon the point went for resolution by the Supreme Court. This is what happened in *White*. Despite the fact that Story and the district judge agreed that that the Defendants should tried together as they would each still have the right to challenge 20 jurors, they feigned disagreement so that, the Court would render a definitive opinion on a problem which arose regularly on circuit. By using this device to choose the issues for final resolution, the judges were shaping law to achieve consistency.

When called upon to interpret state legislation Justice Story looked, in the first instance, for guidance from the opinions of the state justices; a practice confirmed when he later delivered the Supreme Court's opinion in *Bell v Morrison* (1828) in which he preferred the practice in Kentucky of a five-year limitation period for actions instead of the generally accepted six years provided by English law. He wrote that he would follow the local law whose rules of interpretation must be presumed to be founded on a more just and accurate view of their local jurisprudence.[119] The case demonstrates the building of a body of law, based not on theoretical principles but founded on proven regional custom and practice reflecting the needs of the local business and property owning community.

Story's attitude towards the use of English law and to the practical consequences of federal courts opinions is further illustrated by his remarks for the Court in *Van Ness v Pacard* (1829) which dealt with the right of a tenant at the conclusion of a lease to remove buildings he had erected on the land. After considering the English authorities and holding that a tenant could not remove a dwelling-house but could remove a building erected for trade purposes, such as a bakery, he questioned whether tenants would be willing to erect buildings if they could not later be removed and suggested that the law might be changed to permit tenants to remove all buildings.[120]

Unusually for such an innovative judge, in *United States v Slade* (1820) he expressed relief at not having to give the first construction of a state statute when he could turn to state decisions for guidance. He believed the following of state decisions to be a matter of 'public policy and public interest', to achieve consistency and certainty in litigation so that citizens did not have to contend with conflicting opinions of federal and state judges.[121] That, wherever possible, he followed the decisions of state courts and upheld the constitutionality of state legislation, demonstrated he was not merely an agent of a federal government ever determined to ride roughshod over states' rights. He had a desire to forge a partnership between federal and state courts. This enhanced his popularity in New England. He was adept at sending out such messages in his circuit opinions.

[119] *Bell v Morrison*, 26 US (1 Pet), 351 (1828).
[120] *Van Ness v Pacard*, 27 US (2 Pet) 137 (1829).
[121] *United States v Slade*, 27 F Cas 1125, Mass, May 1820.

There was a world of difference between sitting on circuit with a district judge and a jury where his view of a case was generally decisive and sitting in Washington where strongly held opinions were on occasion compromised for the sake of unity. He was somewhat apprehensive of his new role but quickly settled into the business of the Court and found himself very much at ease.[122] In letters to his friends, he gave a rare insight into the decision-making process of the Court. Writing to Harvard colleague and probate judge, Samuel Fay, soon after his first sitting on the Court, he referred to the 'frank intimacy of his brethren' and reported that the 'familiar conferences at our lodgings often come to a very quick and, I trust, accurate opinion in a few hours'.[123] The following week, Story assured his wife that the lodging house accommodation was very agreeable and was made so by the companionship of the other justices. 'Perfect harmony' was how he described their relationship.[124] This bonding borne out of a common philosophy and by communal living was essential to the solidary of the Marshall Court and was the foundation of the single opinion of the Court. That the justices were a band of brothers made it much easier to find the middle ground and speak with one voice.

In his 23 years on the Marshall Court, Justice Story delivered 183 opinions of the Court. Aside from Chief Justice Marshall who took the lion's share with 537 of 1,236 opinions, no other justice matched Story's contribution. Justice Johnson was the nearest with 112 majority opinions in 29 years. Justice Duvall contributed a mere 16 opinions and Justice Todd only 12 in 18 years. These figures show Story was the dominant Marshall Court associate justice by his learning, enthusiasm and capacity for hard work.[125] There was no honeymoon period. Story delivered two majority opinions in his first year, seven during 1813 and ten in 1814. No other associate justice experienced such a flying start.

His Supreme Court opinions comprised 57 admiralty matters, 48 land disputes and 28 commercial cases including contract and negotiable instruments, which were his main areas of expertise in the circuit court. Putting his admiralty contribution into perspective one looks to the *United States Reports* which contain 252 admiralty opinions of the Marshall Court. Chief Justice Marshall reserved to himself 90, so Story's 57 opinions over 24 years constituted 35 per cent of the balance. Justice Johnson, over 29 years, delivered 35 opinions. Livingston achieved 18 over 16 years and Washington handed down 17 in 29 years. That Justice Thompson delivered only five admiralty opinions in 20 years is explained by the fact that the 1812 War and embargo cases were fading memories at the time of his appointment in 1823.

---

[122] Letter, Joseph Story to Nathaniel Williams, 16 February 1812; WW Story, *Life and Letters*, vol 1, 213–15.
[123] Letter, Joseph Story to Samuel PP Fay, 24 February 1812. ibid, 215–16.
[124] Letter, Joseph Story to Mrs Sarah W Story, 5 March 1812. ibid, 217.
[125] The figures have been calculated from a count of the opinions in the *United States Reports* between 1801 and 1835.

Story maintained his hardline approach to embargo cases in his writing for the Court. He was resolute in enforcing breaches of embargo and penalising the evasion of custom duties. In ten such cases it was thought appropriate that he should write the unanimous or majority opinion affirming his own finding in the circuit court. His strict approach to admiralty practice surfaced in the forfeiture proceedings concerning *The Pizarro* (1817) when he complained about the district court's failure to follow proper procedure, believing that the lapse enabled the crew to concoct a defence. He felt that the ship's papers should have been produced in court and the crew asked individually to answer specific questions concerning the voyage and that they should not be allowed to give evidence after conferring with counsel.[126]

Marshall decided which associate would write the Court's opinion. The *United States Reports* show a marked disparity in the allocation of opinion writing, indicating assignments on the basis of subject expertise and a willingness to write. Story was assigned so many admiralty opinions because his colleagues and the Chief Justice in particular, were aware that maritime cases constituted the bulk of his work on circuit as advocate and judge. They were happy for him to take the lead because of his renown in the field. Letters passing between Story and Marshall confirm the extent to which the Chief Justice relied upon him in maritime cases and support the suggestion that Story would have had a hand in some of the 90 admiralty opinions delivered by Marshall and in opinions on other branches of the law.[127] The letter Story wrote to Samuel Fay in April 1814 reveals the extent to which he contributed to the Court's opinion delivered by another justice. Story described a heavy list and a prize law case which he did not identify, writing 'I worked very hard and my brethren were so kind as to place confidence in my researches'. He continued, '*Juniores ad Labores*' but did not complete the quotation which ends, '*Seniores ad honores*'; a complaint that the juniors did all the hard work and the seniors took the credit.[128] If his research had resulted in his being assigned the opinion, he would not have complained.

## Consistency Through the Sharing of Expertise

That the justices were eager to help each other when apart on circuit duties is evident from their correspondence. Marshall's letter to Story in July 1819 sought guidance on the authority of the master of a vessel to hypothecate her in a state other than that of her home port. He had earlier asked Washington the same question.[129] Marshall thanked Story for his assistance in another case and

---

[126] *The Pizarro*, 15 US 227 (1817).
[127] For examples see, Marshall to Story, 13 July 1819 in *Papers of John Marshall*, vol 8, 352: Marshall to Story, 15 June 1821, *PJM*, vol 9, 167: Marshall to Story, 18 September 1821, *PJM*, vol 9, 183.
[128] Letter, Joseph Story to Samuel Fay, 24 April 1814 in WW Story, *Life and Letters*, vol 1, 261.
[129] Letter, John Marshall to Bushrod Washington, *The Papers of John Marshall*, vol 8, 31 May 1819, 315.

informed him that he would decide next term the case of the *United States v The Schooner Little Charles* in accordance with Story's reasoning which he thought was 'perfectly sound and were this even questionable, the practice of the courts ought to be uniform'. Marshall also confirmed that preparation of the Court's opinion in 'the militia case' had been committed to Story and 'could not be in better hands', but said that he would prepare an outline opinion himself and was confident that they would not differ.[130] In the event, Justice Washington delivered the Court's opinion; Story and one other justice, unnamed, but probably Marshall, joined in the dissent.[131] On the rare occasions when Marshall and Story disagreed each would draft an opinion.[132]

John Marshall was eager and pleased to receive help from his colleagues on topics with which he was unfamiliar or in troubling cases likely to attract great public interest (such as the trial on circuit in 1807 of former Vice-President Aaron Burr for treason).[133] Marshall's plea to Cushing in that case was not an isolated request for assistance. There are numerous examples of such requests, usually addressed to Washington and Story on unfamiliar topics, mainly on admiralty points but also on debt, forfeiture and insolvency, revealing his wish for consistency across the circuits.[134] Marshall continued to seek advice from Washington and Story and after Washington's death in November 1829 his surviving letters reveal Story as his sole source of guidance. Not surprisingly, the energetic Story was at the centre of these exchanges between Marshall, Washington and later, Thompson, Philip Barbour and John McLean.[135]

The following correspondence reveals Marshall's requests for help from Story on an insolvency problem (1821); debt and forfeiture (1821); marine salvage and piracy (1823) a commercial case (1827) and admiralty (1831).[136] When the two

---

[130] The militia case was *Houston v Moore*, 18 US 1 (1820).

[131] It was usual for law reports to identify the justices who dissented. In this case Story merely wrote that he had 'the concurrence of one of my brethren'. Marshall was likely to be the other dissentient in view of the letter of 31 May 1819 (n. 109).

[132] Letter, John Marshall to Joseph Story, 24 November 1823: 'In the Pennsylvania case I have come with very considerable doubt to a conclusion different to yours & therefore hope you will prepare your opinion.' Massachusetts Historical Society, Joseph Story Papers.

[133] Letter, John Marshall to William Cushing, 29 June 1807, *Papers of John Marshall*, vol 7, 60–62.

[134] Letter, John Marshall to Bushrod Washington, 25 May 1813, *Papers of John Marshall*, vol 7, 390: Letter, John Marshall to Bushrod Washington, 31 May 1819, *Papers of John Marshall*, vol 8, 315: Letter, John Marshall to Joseph Story, 13 July 1819, *Papers of John Marshall*, vol 8, 352. These are examples of ten such requests for help which have survived to the *Papers of John Marshall*.

[135] Justice Barbour requested Story's opinion on the effect of a *nolle prosequi* in an action for breach of covenant (Letter, Barbour to Story, 10 February 1837 in Story Papers, Library of Congress, Reel 4, vol 5). In the same collection are letters to Story from Justice John McLean containing general discussion of cases. (12 September 1837 (Reel, 4, vol 5); 5 May 1838 noting an opinion of Justice McKinley on a bill of exchange case in the circuit court in Louisiana (Reel 4, vol 6); 8 August 1838 and 14 March 1843 (Reel 4, vol 6).

[136] Letter, 15 June 1821, (insolvency), ibid, vol 9, p 167; Letter, 18 September 1821 (debt and forfeiture), ibid, vol 9, 183; Letter, 9 December 1823, (salvage and piracy), ibid, vol 9, 353; Letter, 11 December 1827 (commercial case), ibid, vol 11, 60 and Letter, 23 May 1831 (admiralty), ibid, vol 12, 67.

friends were together in Washington, Story would be happy to assist the Chief Justice in any way possible. He always replied promptly to Marshall's written requests with heavily researched opinions.[137] Writing to Story in November 1823, Marshall wished to know whether it was possible to have a mixed jury of citizens and non-citizens in a criminal case, having been informed by counsel that Justice Thompson had allowed such an application on circuit in New York. The letter also reveals Marshall's intention to discuss the point with the judges the following February to ensure a consistent approach across the circuits.[138] It should not be thought that Marshall was the only justice seeking help with difficult circuit cases; he also gave advice to Justice Washington in a bankruptcy case in 1814.[139]

Marshall believed that one way to achieve this consistency was to maintain a dialogue between justices during their time in Washington and whilst on circuit, which is why he relied so heavily on Story's expertise and willingness to deal with all requests for assistance. In 1831 Marshall wrote that, 'without your vigorous and powerful co-operation I should be in despair and, I think the ship must be given up'.[140] Marshall's successor, Roger Taney, also valued Story's great experience, industry and huge contribution to the work of the Court.[141]

Marshall's despair towards the end of his tenure stemmed from the realisation that the days of the virtually guaranteed single opinion of the Court had passed and dissents were far more prevalent. He believed that if the justices lodged together in Washington, collegiality would aid unanimity, which is why he appointed Story as unofficial mess secretary to arrange the justices' accommodation.[142] When Marshall learned that Mrs Story was to lodge with the justices in Washington in 1826, he wrote that, 'she must be forewarned that she is not to monopolise you, but to surrender you to us to bear that large portion of our burthens which belong to you'.[143] This is a tribute to Story's commitment and contribution to the Court. Much later, Justice John Mclean was unhappy at the loss of collegiality when writing to Story, 'It is doubtful whether no more than 3 or 4 of the judges will board together next term.'[144]

Story and Washington furthered uniformity by exchanging what G Edward White (1988) describes as semi-annual reports of new and interesting cases they had decided on their respective circuits. A fine example of this ongoing discussion

---

[137] Letter, Joseph Story to John Marshall, 26 July 1819, in *Papers of John Marshall*, vol 8, 365–70.
[138] Letter, John Marshall to Joseph Story, 24 November 1823 in CF Hobson *et al* (eds), The Papers of John Marshall, 1775–1835, 12 vols (Chapel Hill, NC, University of North Carolina Press, 2006), 346.
[139] Letter, John Marshall to Bushrod Washington, 19 April 1814, *Papers of John Marshall*, vol 8, 34–5.
[140] Letter, Marshall to Story, 10 November 1831 in Hobson, *Papers of John Marshall*, vol 12, 124.
[141] Taney 'greatly regretted Story's absence (through illness) during the discussion of pending cases'. Letter, Taney to Story, 18 March 1843 in Story Papers, Library of Congress, Reel 4, vol 6.
[142] The following letters from Marshall to Story and vice-versa are on the question of lodgings and are contained, ibid, Hobson vol 12, 3 May 1831, 62; 29 May 1831, 68; 26 June 1831, 93; 10 November 1831, 124; and 16 November 1831, 309.
[143] Letter, Marshall to Story, 30 December 1827 in Hobson, ibid, vol 11, 64.
[144] Letter, John McLean to Joseph Story, 30 September 1843 in Story Papers, Library of Congress, Reel 4, vol 7.

## Consistency Through the Sharing of Expertise

is the lengthy account of circuit cases tried by Washington which he sent to Story in 1823. It is remarkably detailed considering he was writing from Mount Vernon and had left his notebook in Philadelphia.[145] These were not isolated instances. In 1825, Washington submitted a further report to Story confining himself to 'cases decided which may be considered as containing important principles'. He later included in his report cases which he believed established points of practice which should be used to achieve uniformity in the circuit courts, pointing out the importance of having such decisions published. It is not surprising that he sent Story a report of *Corfield v Coryell*, without doubt his most significant circuit opinion. He concluded his report by declaring that, 'I shall be impatient to receive a report of the cases decided on your circuit' and significantly to widen the exchanges by reminding Story not to forget 'our compact with Justice Thompson'.[146]

In December 1826, Story promised Washington an abstract of all the cases he had dealt with on circuit that term; whilst thanking Washington for the opinions he had sent, Story noted that they had adopted the same practice in similar cases on a jurisdictional point.[147] The importance to Story of uniformity is evident from *Martin v Hunter's Lessee* (1816) when, denying the right of state courts to interpret the Constitution, he wrote that it was not because of bias, but a question of preserving the uniformity of federal law.[148] Too many different interpretations would cause much confusion. These letters reveal the importance the justices placed on a uniform system of federal law.

The 'compact' referred to by Washington is established by letters which Thompson wrote to Story about cases he had encountered on circuit. In July 1825, he thanked Story for his letter 'containing a note of your decisions' and saying

---

[145] Letter, Bushrod Washington to Joseph Story, 22 December 1823 in Joseph Story Papers, William L Clements Library, University of Michigan. Washington did not confine himself to the law and facts of each case. He expressed his irritation at the length of one equity action in which arguments had 'consumed almost a fortnight of our last term. I hope to make a final decree in April and never again to be plagued with it unless an appeal should be taken'.

[146] Letter, Bushrod Washington to Joseph Story, 8 June 1828 in Story Papers, William L Clements Library. See also letter, Washington to Story, 14 December 1825 in the same collection in which Washington expresses pleasure on learning that Story's opinions which Washington had received over the past three years were to be published in the next volume of *Mason's Reports*. Again in the same collection is a further letter from Washington to Story dated 21 December 1825 containing many opinions and referring to an issue which has gone to the Supreme Court describing it as, 'one with some nice points which cost me a great deal of thought'. The Joseph Story Papers at the Library of Congress contain the following letters from Washington to Story detailing recent cases facing Washington on circuit and/or seeking assistance from Story: Microfilm reel 1, vol 2, 25 November 1824; reel 2, vol 3, 21 May 1827; reel 2, vol 3, 12 June 1827; reel 2, vol 3, 28 September 1827 and 20 November 1827; reel 2, vol 4, 26 November 1828. The same collection in reel 2, vol 3 contains a letter dated 27 July 1827 from Smith Thompson to Story asking if he had ever had to deal with whether a state court had the power to refer a case to circuit court.

[147] Letter, Joseph Story to Bushrod Washington, 9 December 1826, cited in Howell J Heany, (1958) 2(1) *American Journal of Legal History* 75. The Joseph Story Papers in the Massachusetts Historical Society Collection include many exchanges of circuit opinion between Washington and Story. For examples see letters, 19 June 1827, 4 July 1827 and 13 August 1829.

[148] *Martin v Hunter's Lessee*, 14 US 304 (1816).

that he would comment on them after giving them 'a more attentive examination'. He, in turn, requested Story's advice on questions he had yet to resolve and reported on six cases he had decided on his last circuit 'in which questions of any importance arise'. He canvassed Story's opinion on some of his rulings which were on new points 'and may perhaps be questionable'.[149] That Story did respond is apparent; in October that year Thompson apologised for 'not being sufficiently explicit to be understood'. Setting out the procedural point more clearly, he recalled an opinion of 'the late Justice Livingston' but wanted Story's opinion as he wished to 'proceed on solid ground' before following him. The letter was not confined to matters of law. Thompson believed that the Supreme Court Justices should be given travelling expenses in line with members of Congress. He had received a favourable response from the Chairman of the Senate Judiciary Committee and suggested that Story approach Mr Webster, the Chairman of the House Judiciary Committee.[150]

These exchanges of information and the answering of calls for help were crucial to the justices' aim of uniformity. By working together on circuit, as well as in Washington, and by using law from a variety of sources and following, wherever possible, the circuit opinions of their colleagues, they strove to achieve a consistent approach to the resolution of civil and criminal proceedings. It was important that citizens, whether they were farmers, manufacturers, inventors, landowners, ship-owners or corporate bodies, could order their business and domestic affairs in such a way as to feel reasonably confident that they would receive the same protection under federal law in every state of the Union. There was little point in establishing national courts whose law and procedure differed from circuit to circuit. If the system was to work, it was the task of the justices to assure the people and, crucially, the business community, that no matter where they lived, worked or travelled, the federal courts would endeavour to implement the law in a uniform manner across the nation.

The workload of the Court was increasing and despite the spirit of cooperation between some justices, Story hinted at a certain lack of commitment when writing to Harvard Law Professor Ashmun in 1832, that 'the Charlestown Bridge case had not yet been decided because some of the judges had not prepared their opinions when they met to discuss the case'.[151] The Chief Justice also found it difficult to cope with an ever-expanding docket, writing to Story in 1829 that he had not been able to give two great cases the consideration they deserved and he hoped that Story had been able to give them his attention and asked that he put his thoughts on paper.[152] Story was in a league of his own when it came to the effort he put into

---

[149] Letter, Smith Thompson to Joseph Story, 7 July 1825 in Joseph Story Papers, William L Clements Library, University of Michigan.

[150] Letter, Smith Thompson to Joseph Story, 24 October 1825 in Story Papers, William L Clements Library.

[151] Letter, Joseph Story to Professor Ashmun, 1 March 1832, in WW Story, *Life and Letters*, vol 2, 91.

[152] Letter, John Marshall to Joseph Story, 13 July 1829, in Hobson, *Marshall Papers*, vol 11, 262.

his work on circuit and on the Court and all while editing and writing formidable works of legal jurisprudence and teaching law at Harvard University.

## The Supremacy of Federal Law

Circuit opinions permitted Story little impact on constitutional law. He remedied that in his opinion in *Mills v Duryee* (1813) holding that, if a judgment was conclusive in one American state, it must be recognised and enforced in other states under the 'full faith and credit' clause of Article 4, section 1 of the Constitution.[153] He delivered his most influential constitutional opinion three years later in *Martin v Hunter's Lessee*. As well as asserting the power of the Court over federal departments and state legislatures and tribunals, this evidenced the marked political and philosophical change from the mild Republican tendencies of his early years to the ardent supporter of a strong national government and federal judiciary.[154]

In *Martin*, the Virginia Court of Appeals refused to accept the decision of the Supreme Court in a land dispute delivered in the February 1813 term, on the ground that section 25 of the Judiciary Act 1789 giving the Supreme Court the power to review the decisions of state tribunals infringed the Constitution. Story resolved this stand-off on a matter of great constitutional consequence in a very firm manner when the case returned on a writ of error. He held that the Supreme Court had appellate jurisdiction over state court decisions which purported to interpret federal law. He argued that federal power was given by the people, not by the states and pointed to Article III, Section 2, Clause 2 of the Constitution which expressly provided for the Supreme Court to have appellate jurisdiction on law and fact in all cases mentioned in the section where it has no original jurisdiction. He addressed the mischief which would arise if state tribunals were permitted to interpret federal law, treaties and even the Constitution without the appellate oversight of the Supreme Court. Judges of equal learning and integrity in the various states might well reach different conclusions, throwing federal law into total confusion. The emphasis on the people, not the states, as the source of authority for the Constitution is key to the philosophy of Marshall and Story and enabled the Court to interpret the intent of the Founding Fathers in such a way as to provide for a strong national government, while guaranteeing its citizens' property and commercial rights.

The Court's declaration in *Marbury v Madison* (1803) that the *Judiciary Act 1789* was unconstitutional because Congress was not permitted by the Constitution to extend the Court's original jurisdiction was a crucial step in

---

[153] *Mills v Duryee*, 11 U.S (7 Cranch) 481 (1813).
[154] 14 US 304 (1 Wheat) (1816).

Marshall's quest to strengthen the Court's authority.[155] Story's recognition, in *Martin*, that the Constitution gave the Court an appellate supervisory role of state courts further enhanced the Court's status giving it the confidence to extend its sphere of influence in three constitutional cases decided in a three-week period in early 1819.[156]

In *Sturges v Crowninshield*, the Court held that a New York law which purported to apply a bankruptcy law retroactively violated Article 1, Section 10 of the Constitution because it impaired the 'Obligation of Contracts'. Impairment of the obligation of contracts raised its head once more eight days later in the *Dartmouth College* case. Yet again, the Court struck down a state statute, Marshall holding, controversially, that a charter granted to the college by the British Crown in 1769 constituted a contract. This meant that an attempt by New Hampshire's legislature to gain control of the college by altering its status from a private to a public institution violated the contracts clause. Story delivered a powerful concurrence and using the example of a bank or insurance company, expressed great concern at the prospect of a legislature attempting to replace the directors appointed by the stockholders with people who had no connection with the company. His holding and Marshall's opinion, would have reassured the commercial community that the Court supported free enterprise and would protect the interests of business corporations from federal or state interference. The letter which Story received from Justice Livingston during the Court's consideration of *Dartmouth* reveals the high regard in which he was held. Story, as a matter of courtesy, had forwarded to Livingston a copy of his draft opinion in the case. It was returned with fulsome praise and the comment that it was all he had expected of Story and the wish that it would be accepted by the Court without alteration. In the event, Livingston did concur for the reasons stated by Marshall, Washington and Story.[157]

The Court further enhanced its reputation and sphere of influence two weeks later in *McCulloch v Maryland*, when it held that Congress had the power to establish a national bank and that Maryland's purported tax on the bank because it was not chartered by the Maryland legislature was prohibited by the Constitution.[158] Maryland's action was a direct challenge to the federal government's right to impose its authority upon a state and the Court determined, by reference to the Constitution, to define the extent of the powers of Congress and to demonstrate

---

[155] *Marbury v Madison*, 5 US 137 (1803).
[156] *Sturges v Crowninshield*, 17 US (4 Wheat) 122 (opinion delivered 17 Feb 1819); *Trustees of Dartmouth College v Woodward*, 17 US (4 Wheat) 518 (opinion delivered 25 February 1819); *McCulloch v Maryland*, 17 US (4 Wheat) 316 (opinion delivered 10 March 1819). The time taken between the conclusion of arguments and the handing down of opinions in these great constitutional cases varies considerably. *Sturges*—eight days; *McCulloch*—three days and *Dartmouth College*, which clearly caused the justices some heart-searching, took 50 weeks to resolve. For a very helpful list of dates of arguments and delivery of opinions of Supreme Court cases between 1791 and 1882, see Ann Ashmore, Library of Supreme Court of United States, August 2006.
[157] Letter, Livingston to Story, 24 January 1819 in WW Story, *Life and Letters*, vol 1, 323–24.
[158] *McCulloch v Maryland*, 17 US 316.

that states' rights were subordinate to the powers of the national legislature. Although the Constitution did not expressly grant to Congress the power to establish the Bank of the United States or any bank, writing for a unanimous Court, the Chief Justice held that such a power was to be inferred from Article 1, Section 8, Clauses 1 and 18 of the Constitution. Clause 1 gave Congress the power 'to ... provide for the general welfare of the United States' and, by Clause 18, Congress received the authority to make all laws 'necessary and proper' for carrying into effect powers earlier enumerated in the section which included the powers to coin money, collect taxes, borrow money and regulate commerce between the states. The establishment of a national bank, whilst it itself not 'necessary and proper,' was essential if Congress was to exercise those fiscal responsibilities entrusted to the national legislature by the Constitution. The establishment of the national bank was, therefore, a procedural step to implement the powers granted to Congress. Having concluded that the establishment of the bank was within the Constitution it was a small step for Marshall to hold that Maryland's attempt to tax the bank was unconstitutional as the United States law establishing the bank was, by virtue of Article 6 of the Constitution, the supreme law of the land, binding upon the legislatures and tribunals of every state.[159] By upholding the legitimacy of a central bank, the Court sought to promote economic prosperity and consolidated its power to regulate inter-state commerce.

Justice Story did not deliver a separate opinion in *McCulloch* but his pleasure at the unanimous opinion of the Court is apparent from the letter he wrote to the Hon Stephen White three days before the opinion was handed down. His comments are particularly revealing because they mark a change in attitude from a judge on circuit attempting to strike a fine balance between states' rights and firm national government to one whose nationalistic views had hardened. After describing the closing arguments of William Pinkney, counsel for the bank, as the greatest speech he had ever heard, he concluded, 'All the cobwebs of sophistry and metaphysics about states' rights and state sovereignty, he brushed away with a mighty besom.' His delight at Pinkney's demolition of the state's arguments and his wish that the speech be made public to attract universal admiration is a compelling confirmation of Story's political transformation.[160]

Thus, in the space of three weeks, the Supreme Court had established not only the supremacy of the federal government over claims of state sovereignty but also its position as the sole interpreter of the language and meaning of the Constitution by construing it in such a way as to strengthen the union and send a message to the more vociferous states' rights activists of its determination to uphold all

---

[159] For an in-depth analysis of *McCulloch v Maryland*, see, Mark R Killenbeck, *M'Culloch v Maryland: Securing a Nation* (Lawrence: University Press of Kansas, 2006). See also Gerald Gunther (ed), *John Marshall's Defense of McCulloch v Maryland* (Stanford: Stanford University Press, 1969) in which he analyses Marshall's responses to the heated newspaper attacks made upon him by the Republican Judge Spencer Roane of the Virginia Court of Appeals.
[160] Letter, Story to White, 3 March 1819, in WW Story, *Life & Letters*, vol 1, 324–25.

federal laws and institutions authorised by a Constitution, ratified not by the states but by the citizens of the United States.

Story had a further opportunity to reveal his federal stance in *Green v Biddle* (1823). Virginia had entered into a compact to cede to the United States the land which subsequently became the state of Kentucky with a condition that existing land grants would be recognised. He held that Kentucky statutes restricting those grants were constitutional infringements of the compact which was protected by the 'full faith and credit' clause of Article 4, Section 1 of the Constitution. Kentucky was granted a rehearing at which Justice Washington confirmed Story's view.[161]

The *United States Reports* reveal an aspect of the Marshall Court opinion assignment practice. There are 11 reported opinions delivered by Story in which he affirms the opinion reached by a circuit court over which he presided. Eight related to admiralty business, two were on customs duties and one involved criminal law.[162] It may well have been convenient to an overburdened Court to assign the opinion to a justice already well versed in the facts and arguments despite offending the concept that justice must be seen to be done. It would have been very disconcerting to a litigant who has lost his vessel and its cargo to find that in a court comprising seven justices, the very justice against whose opinion a challenge had been launched was affirming his own view of the law. However, the reports show that it was common practice among all justices. It was a problem bound to arise from time to time in a system in which justices sat to determine appeals from their own circuit opinions and a situation which would never have arisen if the Judiciary Act of 1801, setting up a separate tier of circuit judges, not been repealed. One can understand President Jefferson's desire abolish the 'midnight' judge appointments of his predecessor. Had there been locally based circuit judges, the nation would have been deprived of the authority and expertise of Supreme Court justices on circuit; uniformity of federal law and practice across the circuits would also have been much more difficult to achieve. This greatly beneficial consequence of the retention of circuit riding was never in the contemplation of those who repealed the 1801 Act.

One way in which Story affirmed his circuit opinion was revealed in the admiralty forfeiture case of *The Julia* (1814). He delivered a short opinion which, in effect, exhibited his circuit opinion. He said that the circuit opinion had been shown to his brethren, a majority of whom had agreed with his affirmation of the district judge's confiscation finding. He approached *The Ship Octavia* in a similar manner, justifying the affirmation by extensive references to his circuit opinion.

---

[161] *Green v Biddle*, 21 US (8 Wheat) 1 (1823).

[162] The admiralty opinions are: *The Julia*, 12 US (8 Cranch), 181 (1814); *The Sally*, 12 US (8 Cranch), 382 (1814); *The St Lawrence*, 13 US (9 Cranch), 120 (1815); *The Ann*, 13 US (9 Cranch), 289 (1815); *The Ship Octavia, (Nicholls et al, claimants)*, 14 US 20 (1819); *The Caledonian*, 17 US (4 Wheat.), 100 (1819); *The Langdon Cheves*, 17 US (4 Wheat), 103 (1819); *The Experiment*, 21 US (8 Wheat), 261 (1823). The customs cases were *Arnold v United States*, 13 US (9 Cranch), 104 (1815) and *United States v Rice*, 17 US (4 Wheat), 246, (1819) which does not appear in *Federal Cases*. The criminal opinion was *United States v Marchant & Colson*, 25 US (12 Wheat) 489 (1827).

He was, however, willing to author opinions reversing his earlier pronouncements. Thus, in the land dispute case of *Ricard v Williams* (1822) he reversed his circuit opinion and he took the same course in respect of his pro forma affirmation of the district judge's condemnation in the customs duty case of *Two Hundred Chests of Tea* on the ground that the Court accepted that the description of the goods given by the owners was correct.[163]

Away from constitutional matters, Story shaped commercial law by stressing the importance of negotiable instruments in promoting trade in *Mandeville v Welch* (1820), holding that bills of exchange and promissory notes were distinguishable from all other forms of contract because they were prima facie evidence of valuable consideration between the original parties and against third parties.[164] He was also active politically, drawing up a memorandum to Congress in June 1820 on behalf of the merchants of Salem protesting its intention to discontinue credits on revenue bonds, abolish drawbacks and impose other restrictions on commerce, controls which, in his view, would 'injure, if not eventually destroy some of the most important branches of the commerce and navigation of the United States'. The memorandum was lengthy, well-reasoned and displayed a detailed, practical and theoretical understanding of business economics. It was well received by Salem men of commerce.[165]

Few criminal opinions were assigned to Story, despite his keen interest in criminal law. One is worthy of note because it confirmed his stance on circuit on the imprecise wording of statutes. In *United States v Smith* (1820), a capital offence of piracy, the Court held the Act which simply described the offence as a crime, 'as defined by the law of nations' was insufficiently particularised to support an indictment. Story wrote that it was the duty of the legislature to set out an offence in terms which would be understood immediately by the citizen. Yet again, he was unwilling to fill in defects in a penal statute, particularly one which invoked the death penalty.[166]

## The Protection of Minority Groups

Another aspect of Story's contribution to American law reflects a humanitarian approach to the plight of the Native American, in particular the Cherokee Nation. As the southern state courts and legislatures refused to recognise their basic rights, the only hope of redress for the disadvantaged lay with the federal courts.[167] Story's

---

[163] *Ricard v Williams*, 20 US 59 (1822). *Two Hundred Chests of Tea*, 22 US 430 (1822).
[164] *Mandeville v Welch*, 18 US (5 Wheat) 277 (1820).
[165] Memorial to Congress, in WW Story, *Life and Letters*, vol 1, 371–76.
[166] *United States v Smith*, 18 US (5 Wheat), 277 (1820).
[167] The negative attitude of the southern states' courts towards the Cherokee, Creek & Choctaw Nations, is fully explored in Tim Alan Garrison, *The Legal Ideology of Removal: The Southern Judiciary and the Sovereignty of Native American Nations* (Athens: University of Georgia Press, 2002). See also, Timothy S Heubner, *The Southern Judicial Tradition: State Judges and Sectional Distinctiveness,*

protection of Native Americans got off to a poor start in *Johnson v M'Intosh* (1823) when he silently acquiesced in the unanimous opinion delivered by Marshall that the Indian tribes did not own the land on which they lived. They were mere tenants at the will of the United States, to whom the land, formerly owned by the Crown by right of discovery, had passed upon independence.[168]

Story sought to made amends in *Cherokee Nation v Georgia* (1831) when the Cherokees sought to invoke the original jurisdiction of the Court by way of an injunction to prevent Georgia from exerting repressive laws over them. The majority held the Cherokee Nation not to be a foreign state but merely a 'domestic dependent nation' so the Court had no jurisdiction under Article III of the Constitution. Justice Thompson, in his dissenting opinion, joined in by Story, declared the Cherokees a foreign state within Article III and that an injunction was necessary to prevent further breaches of Cherokee treaties by Georgia.[169] Story, writing to Richard Peters at the conclusion of the case, expressed his feelings on the plight of the Cherokees when he 'rejoiced that Mr Justice Thompson has done what I requested, that is, stated my concurrence with him. I am more than satisfied we are right'.[170]

In *Worcester v Georgia* (1832), Story was a member of the Court which held unlawful Georgia's imprisonment of a United States citizen, a missionary who had entered Cherokee lands without obtaining a licence from the state. The Court declared unconstitutional Georgia's imposition of such a requirement, holding that the United States had the sole right of dealing with the Indian Nations. Although not accepting the Cherokees as the owners of the land, the Court sent a clear message to Georgia that a state had no right to harass them. Unfortunately, it was a pyrrhic victory as Georgia continued to force the Cherokees off their land and President Andrew Jackson pointedly refused to intervene.[171]

Story's letters reveal feelings which would be difficult to express in a formal opinion but which provide an insight into his support for the majority opinion in *Worcester*, Justice Baldwin being the sole dissentient. Before John Marshall delivered the opinion, Story wrote to his wife that he had been impressed by the two Cherokee chiefs he had met in Philadelphia but feared for the destruction of their race. He felt 'as an American, disgraced by our gross violation of the public faith towards them'.[172] Writing to Professor George Ticknor after the opinion had been delivered, Story correctly predicted that Georgia, 'full of anger and violence, would continue to harass the Cherokees and that the President would not interfere'.

---

*1790–1890* (Athens: University of Georgia Press, 1999). Heubner examines the opinions and correspondence of six chief justices from Virginia, Texas, Alabama, Tennessee, North Carolina and Georgia to discern their attitudes towards questions including federalism and race.

[168] *Johnson v M'Intosh*, 21 US 543 (1823).
[169] *Cherokee Nation v Georgia*, 30 US 1 (1831).
[170] Letter, Joseph Story to Richard Peters, 24 June 1831, in WW Story, *Life and Letters*, vol 2, 46.
[171] *Worcester v Georgia*, 31 US (6 Pet) 515 (1832).
[172] Letter, Joseph Story to Mrs Joseph Story, 13 January 1832, in WW Story, *Life and Letters*, vol 2, 79.

## The Protection of Minority Groups 149

He continued 'The Court has done its duty, Let the nation do theirs.'[173] The letters are noteworthy in two respects. Apart from revealing Story's compassion for the Cherokees and his disgust at the nation's treatment of them, it also shows his realisation, that despite the rise in influence of the Court by the 1830s, its orders were completely ineffective when faced with an intransigent state unwilling to acknowledge them and a President, content to see them ignored.[174]

Story's sympathy for subjugated classes of society is evidenced by his efforts to stamp out the international slave trade. His circuit opinions demonstrated a determination to enforce stringently the 1807 Slave Trade Act prohibiting such traffic but he had little opportunity, writing for the Marshall Court, to expound his views. In *The Plattsburgh* (1825), he ordered the forfeiture of a vessel for slave trade breaches where the original voyage began in the United States, holding that the Court had jurisdiction whether or not the vessel was owned by citizens or foreigners.[175] His views on the slave trade were restated and received world-wide attention in the Supreme Court opinion he wrote for the Court in *The Amistad*, an important case considered by the Supreme Court at that time.[176] Although decided in 1841, six years after the death of John Marshall, no analysis of Story's moral and judicial attitudes towards the kidnapping and transportation of Africans would be complete without a consideration of this landmark opinion. He held that those able bodied, of the 36 African men and boys and three girls, who had risen up, killed the master and taken over the vessel, were exercising their right to freedom. The Court accepted them to be native-born free Africans who had been unlawfully kidnapped and forcibly transported aboard a vessel engaged in the 'heinous' slave trade and discharged them from custody, free to return to their homeland. They were not property to be returned to Spain.

Although Story rigorously enforced the 1807 Act, he was unable to help those African slaves already in the United States. The Constitution, whilst not expressly

---

[173] Letter, Joseph Story to Professor Ticknor, 8 March 1832. ibid, 83.

[174] Writing to Brigadier-General John Coffee on 7 April 1832, President Jackson said, 'The decision of the Supreme Court has fell still born and they find they cannot coerce Georgia to yield to its mandate and I believe Ridge [a Cherokee Leader] has expressed despair and it is better for them to treat with us for their intire [sic] removal ... if a collision was to take place between them and the Georgians, the arm of the government is not sufficiently strong to preserve them from destruction.' (John Spencer Bassett, *Correspondence of Andrew Jackson*, vol IV (Washington DC: Carnegie Institute of Washington, 1926), 430. Meacham poses the possibility of the President threatening Georgia with a federal invasion force but discounts that course because Jackson favoured removal and he had his hands full dealing with South Carolina's drift towards nullification (Meacham, *American Lion*, 203–05). Remini, the leading Jackson scholar, has some sympathy with his dilemma. Whilst he acknowledges the central role played by Jackson in the passing of the Indian Removal Act which led to the huge loss of Cherokee lives on the Trail of Tears, he is certain they would have been exterminated had they remained in Georgia (Robert V Remini *Andrew Jackson and His Indian Wars* (New York: Viking Penguin, 2001), 255–71. However callous Jackson's silence and refusal to intervene appears, there can be no doubt but that Georgia, with the support of the legislature and the courts, particularly as gold had been found, would continue to take Cherokee lands by force.

[175] *The Plattsburgh*, 23 US (10 Wheat) 133 (1825).

[176] *The Amistad*, 40 US 518 (1841).

using the word slave, in Article IV, Section 1, Clause 3, permitted the recapture of 'any person held to service or labour in one state' who had escaped to another. In *Prigg v Pennsylvania* (1842), Story, writing the majority opinion, upheld the Fugitive Slave Act 1793 and overturned the conviction of a man who had forcibly removed a woman and her children from Pennsylvania and returned them to her 'owner' in Maryland. The removal contravened the 1826 Pennsylvania Personal Liberty Law, which provided for a judicial investigation before removal. Story held the Fugitive Slave Act constitutional because it was within Article IV. The Court struck down the Pennsylvania statute purporting to aid fugitives on the basis it ran contrary to the Constitution and federal law.[177] He laid great emphasis on the belief that the Southern States would not have joined the Union had that clause been omitted from the Constitution. The holding was a victory of federal law over state law because of the finding that only the federal authorities had the power to administer the Act, but this was small comfort to the woman and her children returned to slavery in Maryland. Story's strict adherence to the Constitution prevailed over his religious and humanitarian beliefs that slavery was an evil institution. Hoffer, Hoffer and Hull (2016) state the position realistically: 'Even those northern federal judges who found slavery repellent had to concede its legality where it existed in the United States.'[178]

Story's academic achievements were of great importance because they underpinned his judicial contribution. Appointed the Dane Professor of Law in 1829, he strengthened the Harvard Law School and successfully promoted academic training for lawyers, replacing the 'hit and miss' apprenticeship in a lawyer's office. He introduced his students to the study of law through textbooks, lectures and moots and brought to life dry topics by relating his experiences both on circuit and on the Court.[179] Story's academic output would have been prodigious for a man focused wholly on scholarship. His industry was even more remarkable considering his commitment to the Court and the First Circuit. Between 1809 and 1845 he edited or wrote 13 works covering many branches of law. At the time of his death in 1845, he had begun to write *Commentaries on Admiralty* and *Commentaries on the Law of Nations* and an autobiography.[180] Story's most significant academic contribution to United States law was his three-volume *Commentaries on the Constitution of the United States* (1833). Justice Oliver Wendell Holmes speaking to

---

[177] *Prigg v Pennsylvania*, 41 US 539 (1842).

[178] Peter Charles Hoffer, William James Hoffer & NEH Hull, *The Federal Courts: An Essential History* (New York: Oxford University Press, 2016), 103.

[179] For a full account of Story's academic achievements at Harvard see, Sutherland, *The Law at Harvard*, 92–139.

[180] *Chitty on Bills of Exchange & Promissory Notes* (1809); *Abbott on Shipping* (1810); *Laws of Assumpsit* (1811); *Commentaries on the Constitution*, 3 vols (1833); *Commentaries on the Law of Bailments* (1834); *Commentaries on Conflict of Laws* (1834); *Discourse on Past History, Present State & Future Prospects of Law* (1835); *Commentaries on Equity Jurisprudence* (1836); *Commentaries on Equity Pleadings* 1838); *Commentaries on Agency and Maritime Jurisprudence* (1839) and *Commentaries on Promissory Notes* (1845).

the Harvard Law School Association in 1886 was fully justified, when referring to 'Story's epoch making *Commentaries*', in asserting that 'he has done more than any other English speaking man in this century to make the law luminous and more easy to understand'.[181]

## Importing Common Law into the Federal Legal System

Story wished for a common law which could be modified to meet the needs of the United States. In *Van Ness v Pacard* (1829) he remarked that: 'The common law of England is not to be taken in all respects to be that of America. Our ancestors brought with them its general principles and claimed it as their birth-right, but they ... adopted only that portion applicable to their situation ... The country was a wilderness and the universal policy was to procure its cultivation and improvement.'[182] He was referring to the need for stability, the accommodation of an increasing population and economic growth. He made it clear in a letter to Supreme Court reporter Henry Wheaton in 1825 that his wish to codify United States law was not because of a visionary desire to establish new law, but to make existing laws more accessible and understandable to the general public and to avoid the 'labours and exhausting researches of the profession'.[183]

He did more than any other justice to promote English common law as the basis of United States jurisprudence, arguing that 'the whole structure of our jurisprudence stands upon the original foundations of the common law'.[184] He began, on circuit, by using the common law to remedy criminal conduct not then covered by United States statutes, disagreeing with Justice Samuel Chase who, in *United States v Worrall* (1798), when dealing with an alleged bribery of a revenue commissioner, had held there was no federal common law of crime. Chase insisted that before an act became a crime, it was for Congress to define the offence, fix a penalty and give jurisdiction to a court to deal with the matter.[185] Chase's circuit view was not followed by other justices, but prevailed in the Supreme Court 14 years later in *United States v Hudson and Goodwin*, an allegation of libel. The Defendants, in a Connecticut newspaper, accused the President and Congress of secretly voting for a payment of $2 million to Napoleon Bonaparte to facilitate a treaty with Spain.[186] That neither the Attorney General nor defence counsel argued the point made the

---

[181] Oliver Wendell Holmes, *Collected Legal Papers* (New York: Peter Smith, 1952), 41–2.
[182] *Van Ness v Pacard*, 27 US (2 Pet) 137 (1829).
[183] Letter, Story to Wheaton, 1 October 1825 in Henry Wheaton Papers, Pierpoint Morgan Library, cited in, James McClelland, *Joseph Story and the American Constitution* (Norman: University of Oklahoma Press, 1971), 93.
[184] Joseph Story, *Commentaries*, vol 1, 140.
[185] *United States v Worrall*, 2 Dallas 384 (1798).
[186] *United States v Hudson and Goodwin*, 7 Cranch 32 (1812).

decision to deny a common law jurisdiction in crime that much easier. The reasoning in Justice Johnson's extremely short opinion of the Court was essentially his declaration that the question had 'long been settled by public opinion', when he restated the earlier tests of Justice Chase.[187] The decision was not unanimous and, as there were no written dissents, it is not possible to identify those justices who refused to join the majority. Preyer (1986) believes the dissentients to have been Justices Washington and Story. She includes Story because, within three months of the *Hudson* decision, he was pressing the government to authorise federal courts to use the common law to deal with public crimes not covered by statute.[188]

Unable to achieve a political solution, Story used the circuit court as a public platform to express his dissatisfaction with *Hudson*. In *United States v Clark* (1813), when unable to deal with an allegation of perjury as a common law offence, Story remarked that he had never been able to satisfy himself as to the accuracy of *Hudson and Goodwin*.[189] In the same term as *Clark*, Story attempted to draw a distinction between common law offences in the admiralty jurisdiction as opposed to the general criminal law, holding that the forcible taking of a prize was an offence contrary to common law in admiralty. The district judge disagreed, so the matter came before the Supreme Court on a certificate of division of opinion. Story lost the day. Justices Livingston and Washington were prepared to join him in reviewing *Hudson and Goodwin* but, once more, the Attorney General refused to argue the case and Justice Johnson, delivering the Court's opinion, again had an easy task to reject the existence of common law jurisdiction in admiralty.[190] Undeterred, Story changed tack and endeavoured to achieve consistency in federal criminal law by drafting a criminal code which later became the Crimes Act 1825.[191] This remedied the deficiencies of the Crimes Act of 1790 which made no provision for federal offences such as rape, burglary, arson and many other serious crimes. It should be noted, however, that any deficiencies in federal criminal laws had a limited effect on the general administration of justice as the vast majority of criminal offences were dealt with under state laws.

His efforts to gain recognition of a common law jurisdiction in crime and admiralty having failed, Story turned his attention to commercial law and, in particular, to the federal courts' jurisdiction in diversity cases where the parties were from different states. In *Swift v Tyson* (1842), writing for the Court, Story held that whilst

---

[187] ibid, 32.

[188] Kathryn Preyer, 'Jurisdiction to Punish: Federal Authority, Federalism and the Common Law of Crimes in the Early Republic' (1986) IV *Law and History Review* 223–65 reproduced in Bilder, Marcus and Newmyer (eds), *Blackstone in America: Selected Essays of Kathryn Preyer* (New York: Cambridge University Press, 2009), 212–13.

[189] *United States v Clark*, 25 F Cas 441, Mass, October 1813.

[190] *United States v Coolidge*, 14 US 415 (1816).

[191] In January 1837, Story led a commission which recommended the codification of limited aspects of the common law of Massachusetts and, particular, the law 'as to the definition, trial and punishment of crimes and the incidents thereto'. The report is reproduced in WW Story, *Miscellaneous Writings*, 698–734 at 715.

the federal courts were obliged to apply state statutory laws they could ignore state common law as the state courts' decisions were merely evidence of what the law was. In the absence of an applicable state statute, the federal courts were entitled to formulate and apply rules of federal common law.[192] Story regarded a body of federal common law as essential to a uniform system of business law across the nation. Despite the fact that the decision was generally regarded as a diminution of state sovereignty, *Swift v Tyson* stood for almost 100 years until overruled by *Erie Railroad Co v Tompkins* (1938).[193] Unsuccessful in importing English common law into United States criminal and admiralty law, Story persevered and achieved his objective with federal commercial law.

# Conclusion

The many circuit and Supreme Court opinions of Justice Story reveal him as a justice who contributed to United States jurisprudence on many fronts, the most important of which was his development of admiralty law both on circuit and in the Court. His circuit opinions reveal that he had more experience of admiralty cases than any other justice. That he wrote far more admiralty opinions for the Court than any other justice supports the view that he was the acknowledged expert. A comparison of his circuit and Supreme Court opinions show him to have had a consistently hardline approach to breaches, despite his opposition to embargo as a New England politician and as an advocate who defended many a ship's master in forfeiture proceeding; a change of tack necessitated by his judicial role.

Story led the way in the strict enforcement of the embargo prohibition and set the standard for other justices to follow. In *The Boston* he called for a vigorous examination of defences to breaches of embargo laws to prevent a flood of what he considered to be spurious excuses and, as he declared in *The George*, the increasing number of collusive captures of vessels. He felt that other justices were too ready to accept dubious excuses and said so in *Robinson v Hook* when the widespread nature of the breaches was revealed in captured documents. He declared allegations of embargo breaches offences of strict liability. In *The Short Staple*, he reversed the burden of proof by holding that the owner or master of the vessel must show that the route deviation was necessary. He did the same in *Ten Hogsheads of Rum*. This robust disposal of cases led to two reversals by the Court, in *The Short Staple* and *The Bothnea, The Jahnstoff*. The Court held in both cases that Story had been too quick to condemn. Story dissented in the

---

[192] *Swift v Tyson*, 41 US 1 (1842).
[193] *Erie Railroad Co v Tompkins*, 304 US 64. For the reluctance of state court judges to follow *Swift v Tyson* see Horwitz, 245–52.

*Short Staple*, feeling strongly that the master had hoodwinked the Court. Despite Story's personal feelings, these cases show that, as a justice sworn to uphold the law, he was duty bound to enforce the embargo laws. That he did so with vigour and encouraged other justices to do likewise reflected the great animosity felt by the nation towards Britain's invasion of American soil during the War of 1812. The fact that the harmful economic effects of the embargo were more keenly felt by America than Britain mattered not. The Courts were there to enforce the will of the people through the edicts of Congress.

Story's admiralty contribution extended beyond the embargo cases. In *Harden v Gordon et al; The George; Orne v Townsend;* and *United States v Ruggles*, he tempered the harsh realities of life at sea by laying down rules which protected the wages and working conditions of masters and seamen and, at the same time, went some way towards ensuring that merchant ships were adequately manned. He clarified the law and evidential burdens in marine insurance cases on such misrepresentations as to seaworthiness, sailing dates and route deviations which were material to the risk and avoided the policy (*Tidmarsh v Washington Fire & Marine Insurance Co, Inc; Bayard v Massachusetts Fire & Marine Insurance Co Inc; Glidden v Manufacturers' Insurance Co*). The importance of Story's most notable marine insurance opinion, *Delovio v Boit et al*, which held that the federal courts had jurisdiction under the Constitution over marine insurance cases, is demonstrated by the fact that it was followed by the Court in *Insurance Company v Dunham* some 55 years later.

The extent to which the United States or individual states had adopted English common law was very much an issue during the formative years of the federal courts: Story was at the forefront of that debate. He believed the common law to be the fundamental basis of federal law, but that it should be modified in such a way as to meet the particular needs of the American people. His efforts to import common law into the criminal jurisdiction foundered with the Court's decision in *United States v Hudson & Goodwin*; his further attempt to deal with perjury at common law failed in *United States v Clark*. He did, however, achieve success in clarifying the criminal law when his draft code became The Crimes Act 1825. Story was again reversed by the Court when his attempt to import common law into admiralty law failed in *United States v Coolidge*, but his perseverance paid off in *Swift v Tyson* when he established that, in diversity cases, the federal courts were entitled to apply rules of federal common law. *Swift v Tyson* stood for almost 100 years. His objective in promoting the common law, as it was with his codification of the law, was to give United States law a more certain foundation so that its citizens and their legal representatives could have a better understanding of their rights and obligations.

Story's opinions and correspondence are valuable insights into the inner workings of the Marshall Court and the justices' resolve to achieve the necessary uniformity of federal law and procedure to ensure a smooth transition from colony to republic. The letters from Marshall to Story reveal how the justices assisted each other with issues they encountered on circuit; the exchange of semi-annual

## Conclusion 155

reports between Story and Washington of interesting cases on their respective circuits indicates the importance to the justices of consistency in decision making throughout the federal jurisdiction. *Martin v Hunter's Lessee* is a good example of Story's desire for uniformity. His denial of the right of state courts to interpret the Constitution was solely to avoid the confusion of opinions which might vary from state to state. Story's letters to his friends reveal how keenly the justices felt the need to present an authoritative face to the nation with the single opinion of the Court; how the pleasant collegiality of the justices' lodging house facilitated unanimity; and how, despite the view of some scholars that most associates contributed little, there was full discussion before decisions were reached.

Joseph Story was by far the most effective associate justice and the scholarly leader of the Marshall Court and, as Presser (1990) rightly contends, 'our most intellectually gifted Supreme Court Justice'.[194] His was the greatest contribution of any associate to the Court and to the shaping of United States law. His development of the admiralty jurisdiction, his codification of criminal law, the establishment of common law as the basis of federal commercial law in disparity cases, his academic output and his willingness to assist other justices to achieve uniformity mark him as a judge whose influence on the law played a large part in the stability of the Early Republic. That great judge New York Chancellor James Kent positioned Story at the forefront of United States legal history when he said 'for learning, industry and talent, he is the most extraordinary jurist of the age'.[195] Kent was well qualified to evaluate Story's place in legal history as his own *Commentaries on American Law* along with Story *Commentaries* and Virginian St. George Tucker's *'American Blackstone'* had the most significant effect on the direction of United States law in its formative years.[196] In praising Story's 'epoch making *Commentaries*' and regarding him as the foremost legal scholar of the age, Oliver Wendell Holmes had had an opportunity to compare Story's greater volume of scholarship with the work of Kent having edited the 1873 edition of the latter's *Commentaries*.[197]

Kent and Story were great friends and regularly corresponded on matters of law and procedure.[198] Once when Kent entered Story's circuit court, Story was giving

---

[194] Stephen B Presser's Foreword (ix) to the 1990 second printing of McClellan, *Joseph Story*.

[195] Letter, 31 July 1841, Chancellor Kent to the Editor of the *Louisiana Law Journal* cited in WW Story, *Life and Letters*, vol 2, 648. The admiration in which Kent held Story's scholarship is well expressed in letters he wrote to him, which appear in vol 2 of WW Story, *Life and Letters*; 19 June 1833, 134–35; 15 May 1834 179–80; 10 October 1836; 18 April 1837, 237.

[196] For Tucker's huge contribution to United States law see, Charles F Hobson's 3 vol set of *St George Tucker's Law Reports and Selected Papers* (Chapel Hill: University of North Carolina Press, 2013).

[197] Holmes, *Collected Legal Papers*, 41–2; James Kent, *Commentaries on American Law*, 4 vols (New York: O Halstead, 1826–1830).

[198] The Joseph Story Papers in the Massachusetts Historical Society Collection contain many letters between the two which reveal the high regard each had for the other's jurisprudence, one example of which is the letter of 30 June 1823 which Kent wrote thanking Story for sending him a copy of his opinion in the *Argonaut*. He stated it was 'a masterly view of the law of abandonment & of the numerous important Principles which belong to that head of Insurance'. Kent, who was about to retire, promised to pay Story a visit.

his opinion. As soon as he saw Kent, he left the bench to greet his friend introducing him to all counsel in court. District Judge Davis also left the bench and sat with Kent whilst Story concluded his opinion.[199] When Story died in 1845, Kent wrote that, 'He had done more by his writings and speeches to diffuse my official and professional character … than any living man' calling him a 'genius'.[200]

Story's reputation was not confined to the United States. It was just as high in Britain. In 1883, Lord Chief Justice Coleridge made a speech to the New York State Bar Association, at the time of the retirement of former Confederate Secretary of War, Judah Philip Benjamin QC who was forced to flee the United States upon the fall of the Confederacy and practised in England. Coleridge regarded Story as a legal icon, remarking, 'It is delightful that we familiarly quote your great men, Kent, Story, Parsons, Duer, Philips and Greenleaf—so you on your side are familiar not only with our old great men with Sir William Blackstone and with Lord Hale and with Lord Coke but with our modern men, with Lindley, with Pollock and with Benjamin, the common honour of both Bars of England and America.'[201] The Lord Chief Justice rightly placed Story among the legendary figures of United States law. He also received the finest accolade from one of the great English historians, William S Holdsworth who, when praising the American historian John Chipman Gray, in particular his book on Perpetuities, wrote, 'I think it would be true to say that, with the possible exception of Judge Story, no book has been so frequently cited as an authority in an English court as Gray's *Perpetuities*'.[202]

---

[199] Letter, 4 July 1836, Chancellor Kent to William Kent (son) in William Kent (great-grandson), *Memoirs and Papers of James Kent, LLD, Late Chancellor of the State of New York, Author of "Commentaries on American Law,"* Etc. (Boston: Little, Brown & Company, 1898), 266.

[200] ibid, 267–68. Letter, 17 September 1845, Chancellor Kent to Mrs Story.

[201] Ernest Hartley Coleridge, *Life and Correspondence of John Duke, Lord Coleridge, Lord Chief Justice of England* (New York: D Appleton & Co., 1904), 327.

[202] William S Holdsworth, *The Historians of Anglo-American Law* (New York: Columbia University Press, 1928), 107. Lawbook Exchange facsimile reprint, 2014. Sir William Holdsworth was well qualified to assess Story's place in legal history having been Professor of Law at Cambridge University, Vinerian Professor of English Law at Oxford University and having to his credit the 17-volume, *History of English Law*.

# 6

## Justice Smith Thompson: Promoting Commerce, State Sovereignty and the Protection of the Cherokee Nation

Justice Smith Thompson is another associate justice of the Marshall Court whose jurisprudence has been largely ignored by scholars, despite his service as a state and federal judge for 36 years. All past examinations of his career have emphasised his political aspirations; his ambition to be President of the United States and New York State Governor. This study looks beyond his efforts to achieve high political office to evaluate his jurisprudence by an examination of his state and federal opinions and to establish the extent to which those opinions contributed to the shaping of United States law between 1802 and 1835. Whilst his opinions disclose a considerable expertise in commercial law based on a desire to encourage trade and free enterprise, the chapter focuses on the two most important aspects of his judicial writing. First, before he went to the US Supreme Court, his efforts to promote the right of states to govern their own affairs without excessive federal government interference and second, whilst on the Court, his attempts to interpret and influence federal law in such a way as to protect the perilous position of the Native American and African slave.

There is no recent scholarship on Thompson and no analysis of his work as a Supreme Court justice sitting on circuit. Dunne's 17-page outline, in Friedman & Israel, was written over 40 years ago and Roper's excellent biography, although published in 1987, was a PhD thesis submitted in 1963.

Roper's thesis focuses on Thompson's political aspirations, his time on the New York Supreme Court and his contribution to the opinions of the Marshall Court. He did not examine Thompson's opinions on circuit in New York, Connecticut and Vermont.[1] White wrote an 11-page portrait of Thompson which emphasised his political aspirations but that was over 25 years ago.[2] It follows, therefore, that

---

[1] Donald Malcolm Roper, *Mr Justice Thompson and the Constitution* (New York: Garland Publishing, 1987). A dissertation submitted in partial fulfilment of the requirements for the degree of Doctor of Philosophy, Indiana University, Bloomington, July 1963.

[2] G. Edward White, *History of the Supreme Court of the United States, vols. III–IV, The Marshall Court and Cultural Change, 1815–1835* (New York: Cambridge University Press, 2010), originally published by Macmillan, 1988), 307–18. Eight of the eleven pages detail Thompson's efforts to achieve political office.

this evaluation is the first in-depth examination of both Justice Thompson's state and federal circuit opinions which allows us to understand the development of his jurisprudence in each jurisdiction.

Other scholars agree with White that Thompson was a man desperately seeking high political office. They base their views on the fact that, notwithstanding having received an offer of a seat on the Supreme Court, he sought support as a presidential candidate and, whilst a serving Supreme Court justice, he stood unsuccessfully against Martin van Buren for the governorship of New York in 1828. Clearly Thompson's involvement in New York politics and his time as Secretary of the Navy gave him a taste for political power. Dunne described Thompson as 'one of the most politically active and ambitious Justices ever to sit on the Supreme Court';[3] a view echoed by Hall (2001) in a four-page sketch, highly critical of Thompson, painting him as 'a man of insatiable political appetites'.[4] When emphasis is placed by scholars on Thompson's political aspirations there is a real risk that his jurisprudence is neglected. His political manoeuvring has no bearing on his performance as a justice which is why this chapter focuses on his state and federal jurisprudence.

In the scholarship there is only passing mention of Thompson's work as a judge. Hall regards Thompson as a justice of only modest ability whose tenure was 'a mostly unremarkable service'.[5] Dunne's evaluation of Thompson is not as harsh, but he has difficulty in deciding whether he was a real man of stature.[6] Whilst nowhere near as active as Marshall and Story, Thompson, like Livingston, was far removed from the near silent acquiescence of Justices Todd and Duvall. An examination of his state and federal opinions reveals a significant contribution to the shaping of American law in the fields of contract law and states' rights. He was also a justice prepared to speak out in support of causes he held dear, which defied the convention of unanimity and put him in dissent, particularly by his support for the Cherokee Nation in its fight for relief from Georgia's oppression.

Both Dunne and Hall address the impact of Thompson's presence on the deliberations of a Court largely composed of justices holding Federalist views. Dunne describes Thompson as 'a frontrunner ... leading the reaction against Chief Justice Marshall's ideas on the pre-emptive nature of centralist federalism'; pre-emptive in the sense of a tactical interpretation of the Constitution to consolidate the power of national government.[7] Hall rightly points out that Thompson's presence on the Court in *Ogden v Saunders* (1827) placed Marshall in dissent.[8] He goes further

---

[3] Gerald T Dunne, 'Smith Thompson,' in L Friedman and Fred E Israel, *The Justices of the United States Supreme Court, 1789–1969*, vol 1 (New York: Chelsea House Publishers, 1969) 475.

[4] Timothy L. Hall, 'Smith Thompson', *Supreme Court Justices: A Biographical Dictionary* (New York: Facts on File Inc., 2001) 70–3.

[5] Hall, 'Smith Thompson' 70.

[6] Dunne, 'Smith Thompson' 490.

[7] ibid, 475.

[8] *Ogden v Saunders*, 25 US (12 Wheat) 213 (1827). Thompson joined Washington, Johnson & Trimble in holding that a New York insolvency law, which relieved debtors of their obligations in

by asserting that Thompson's presence on the Court 'spelled ... the gradual eclipse of John Marshall's momentous influence over the course of American law'.[9] However, Thompson's recorded dissents only offer mild criticism of Marshall's federalist centralism. He dissented in only one in 80 cases on the Marshall Court as opposed to one in ten on the New York Supreme Court.[10] He was not as active in opposition as his colleague Justice William Johnson who between 1824 and 1833 wrote 15 dissents out of a total of 444 cases, a ratio of approximately one in 30 cases.[11] Abraham (1974) observes that, although Thompson occasionally stood up to Marshall toward the end of the Chief Justice's tenure, like most others, he generally fell under Marshall's influence despite their political differences.[12] I regard the main reason for Thompson falling into line with his brethren as being due not just to Marshall's charm but more to an acceptance of the need for unanimity.

## State Supreme Court: Statutory Interpretation and New York 'Hard Law'

By the time he was nominated by President James Monroe in 1823 to fill the vacancy on the United States Supreme Court created by the death of Justice Livingston, Thompson had long held high political and legal office, having been elected to the New York State Legislature in 1800 and the following year serving as a delegate to the New York Constitutional Convention.[13] In 1802 he was appointed to the New York Supreme Court where he served as an associate justice for 12 years until he was named as Chief Justice, resigning in 1818 to take up the duties of Secretary of the Navy in President Monroe's cabinet.[14] In order to

---

respect of debts created after the passing of the law, did not violate the prohibition in the Constitution of any law impairing the obligation of contracts. Story and Duvall joined in Marshall's dissent.

[9] Hall, 73.

[10] The proportions of Supreme Court dissents are calculated by joining the data in Donald M Roper, *Mr Justice Thompson and the Constitution* (New York: Garland Publishing Inc, 1987), 110 with the chart of Donald Morgan, *Justice William Johnson: The First Dissenter* (Columbia: University of South Carolina Press, 1954), 189 and counting the number of Supreme Court cases between 1824 and 1835 which results in seven dissents from 551 cases.

[11] Calculated from the number of cases in the United States Reports and a combination of the dissents set out in the charts of Roper and Morgan set out above.

[12] Henry J Abraham, *Justices, Presidents and Senators* (Lanham: Maryland: Rowman & Littlefield Publishers, Inc., 1999), 69. First edition, 1974.

[13] There were other candidates rumoured to be in the running to succeed Livingston including New York Chancellor James Kent who in 1823 reached the early mandatory retirement age of 60 for that office. Letter, Paul Sutherland to Smith Thompson, 10 March 1823 in Smith Thompson Papers, Manuscript Department, Library, New York Historical Society.

[14] His appointment to the New York Supreme Court was well received by one newspaper editor who proudly proclaimed, 'We believe the appointment of these two gentlemen [Livingston & Thompson] has produced general satisfaction. Our Supreme Court is now composed of his Honor Morgan Lewis,

supress the slave trade, he was prepared to allow the Royal Navy the right to search American ships, provided American offenders were tried in federal courts under constitutional guarantees.[15] Whilst Thompson has largely been ignored by legal scholars, his contribution as Secretary was recognised by the US Navy. In 1822 the USS Shark raised the first American flag over what is now Key West, Florida claiming the territory for the United States and calling it Thompson's Island.[16] Further, in 1919, the USS Smith Thompson was named in his honour to mark the 100th anniversary of his appointment as Navy Secretary.[17]

Thompson achieved high judicial office because, ability apart, he was very well connected. He was born in Dutchess County, New York in 1768. His father was a prosperous farmer who had been an anti-federalist delegate to the New York ratification convention of 1788. Thompson graduated from Princeton in 1788 and read law in the local office of James Kent with whom he would later spend many years on the New York Supreme Court. He could have had no better grounding in law and procedure and it is likely that the importance of full and accurate note taking was impressed upon him at an early stage as his notes of evidence of cases he later tried are meticulous.[18] In 1792 he went into partnership with Kent and Gilbert Livingston, a member of the very politically powerful New York family, whose Republican leanings dominated state politics for many years. His integration into the family was complete when, in 1794, he married Gilbert's daughter Sarah, cousin of Brockholst Livingston whom Thompson was to replace on the Marshall Court.[19]

As with Justice Washington, precedent loomed large in Thompson's jurisprudence. In *Jackson v Sill* (1814), Thompson remarked that it was preferable to follow established legal principles even though it might mean injustice in particular

---

Chief Justice; the Hon James Kent, Jacob Radcliffe, Brockholst Livingston and Smith Thompson, Associate Justices. We do not think it arrogance to add, that in point of talents and respectability, they form a tribunal not inferior to any state court in the union.' *The Spectator* (New York) 27 January 1802 (extracted from *The Albany Centinel*).

[15] Dunne, 'Smith Thompson' in Friedman & Israel, *Justices*, vol 1, 479.

[16] See www.history.navy.mil/today-in-history/march-25.html. One of Thompson's many duties as Navy Secretary was to deal with recommendations for promotions of naval officers. Andrew Jackson wrote to Thompson on 1 May 1819 and another on 11 August 1820 requesting the advancement of officers whom he considered had showed merit. Thompson was not slow in seeking favours from Jackson. On 11 March 1821 he wrote congratulating Jackson on his appointment as Governor of Florida and requested his patronage for his son Gilbert who intended to practise law in Florida and requesting for him 'some public employment under Government which will be greatly remembered by your sincere friend'. The three letters are within the Library of Congress, Andrew Jackson Papers, Series 1. General Correspondence 1775–1874.

[17] Available at: www.navsource.org/archives/05/212.htm.

[18] Some notes of evidence have survived and are contained within the Smith Thompson Papers, Library of Congress, MMC 2168. Fine examples are the unreported cases of *United States v Tillotson* (1823); *United States v Charles Stephens* (1827) and *Edwards v Percival & Paulding* (1827). The same collection houses Thompson's notes of arguments and his 'general impressions' on the merits of the writ error in the case of *Finlay v King's Lessee*, 28 US 346 (1830) in which Chief Justice Marshall delivered the opinion of the Court.

[19] Dunne, 'Smith Thompson', 475–76.

cases. He was against bending legal principles to suit a particular case.[20] Thus, on occasion, consistency triumphed over justice. He was also reluctant to hold as unconstitutional any New York state laws. Apart from a general inclination to preserve the status quo and uphold states' rights, Thompson was unwilling to strike down state legislation. This was because he had sat on the New York Council of Revision whose task, between 1777 until its abolition in 1821, was to review all bills before they became law. The Council had the power to return the bill to the legislature with written objections for reconsideration. On extremely rare occasions, bills were passed despite objections provided there was a two-thirds majority of the Senate and the Assembly. Between 1800 and 1821 of 70 bills vetoed by the Council, only seven became law despite Council objections. During his time on the Council, Thompson raised objections to only four bills.[21] It was, therefore, likely that a justice who had played a large part in the passage of legislation would be reluctant to declare that law unconstitutional. This failure to separate the functions of the state legislature and the judiciary was perfectly acceptable to judge and politician alike.

During the passage of the Eerie Canal Bill by the New York Senate in 1817, Thompson, then Chief Justice, spoke against the proposed legislation because he felt it gave commissioners rights and powers over private property without adequate safeguards. Chancellor Kent believed that the cost was too great to be borne by the state alone and required the wealth of the United States. The bill was keenly debated and passed only when Kent, who had opposed the War of 1812, changed his mind and supported the bill after a member suggested that the money should be used to prepare for yet another war with Britain. That the Chief Justice, the Chancellor and Judges Jonas Platt and Joseph Yates took part in this historic decision reveals the dual judicial and political role of the New York State Bench.[22]

Thompson went further in his support of legislation by examining the background to state legislative acts when, in *People v Utica Insurance* (1818), he declared that the Court must look to the intention of the framers of the statute when its words were obscure or doubtful. Surprisingly, he took the view that even where the wording of the legislation was clear it should be ignored if it conflicted with the makers' intention. He declared that the intention of the legislature 'ought to be followed ... in the construction of a statute, although such construction seems contrary to the letter of the statute'.[23] Justice Spencer, in disagreeing with Thompson, handed down an approach to statutory interpretation which would have had more appeal to lawyers advising clients on the import of legislation. He

---

[20] *Jackson, ex dem Van Vechten et al v Sill et al*, 11 Johnson's Reports, 201, 220 (1814).
[21] This data has been extracted from tables in Alfred Billings Street, *The Council of Revision of the State of New York: Its History, a History of the Courts with which its Members were Connected, Biographical Sketches of its Members, and Its Vetoes* (Albany: William Gould, 1859).
[22] William Kent, Memoirs and Letters of James Kent LLD, Late Chancellor of the State of New York (Boston: Little, Brown & Company, 1898), 168–70.
[23] *The People v The Utica Insurance Co*, 15 Johnson's Reports, 380–81 (1818).

asserted that 'Courts of law cannot consider the motives which may have influenced the legislature, or their intentions, any further than they are manifested by the statute itself.'[24] Thompson's attitude to statutory interpretation in *Utica* owed more to politics than the law.

Where the wording of a statute coincided with legislative intent, Thompson interpreted the legislation strictly. This he did in *Tillman v Lansing* (1809) when construing an act of 1801 allowing debtors the liberty of the jail. This device avoided keeping the debtor in a cell and permitted him the freedom of the jail walls so that he could conduct some business in an attempt to repay his debts. A kindly sheriff permitted the debtor to attend church each Sunday outside the jail walls. Thompson ruled against the sheriff in an action against him by creditors for permitting the debtor to 'escape' because the debtor's voluntary return after each service was not permitted by the statute.[25] Roper uses *Tillman* as an example of what he described as 'New York Supreme Court … hard law'.[26] By this he means handing down justice in a manner in which the strict letter of the law was paramount to the apparent justice of the case. The state reports reveal several opinions supporting this analysis. Thus, in Thompson's first reported state opinion, *Henderson v Brown* (1803), he held personally liable a revenue collector who had levied execution on goods in a theatre which was mistakenly designated as a dwelling-house on a list provided by his superiors. Fortunately for the collector, Justice Livingston, writing for the majority, held that he should not be held responsible for the mistakes of his superiors.[27] Undeterred, Thompson tried again. This time in *Walker v Swartout* (1815), Thompson held an army quarter-master general personally liable for work done for the army by boatmen simply because he had said, 'My word is sufficient. I will pay you when the work is done.' Happily for the officer, the majority of the court disagreed, preferring the view taken by Chief Justice Marshall in *Hodgson v Dexter* that, when a public officer acted in the line of his duty and by legal authority, his contracts were public and not personal.[28] Marshall had observed in *Hodgson* that no prudent man would consent to become a public agent if he was to be held personally liable on a public contract.[29]

Thompson managed to carry the court with him in *Gill v Brown* (1815), holding an army quartermaster personally liable for the cost of hiring a schooner solely for government use simply because he did not make it clear that he was merely an agent of the federal government.[30] Thompson's unwillingness to protect public officials even when they acted in good faith was further demonstrated by his opinion for the state supreme court in *Imlay v Sands* (1804) where a collector seized the

---

[24] ibid, 394.
[25] *Tillman v Lansing*, 4 Johnson's Reports 45 (1809).
[26] Roper, 50.
[27] *Henderson v Brown*, Caines' Reports, vol 1, 92, May 1803.
[28] *Walker v Swartout*, Johnson's Reports, vol 12, 445, October 1815.
[29] *Hodgson v Dexter*, 5 US 345, 363 (1803).
[30] *Gill v Brown*, Johnson's Reports, vol 12, p 386, October 1815.

plaintiff's brig and cargo for an alleged breach of the non-intercourse laws. The seizure was confirmed by the state district judge, only later to be reversed by the circuit judge. Thompson acknowledged that the officer's actions were bona fide and according to his best judgment and it appeared that he should be protected from personal liability, but held that the Court was bound to 'pronounce the law as we find it and leave cases of hardship to legislative provision'.[31] This restrictive approach was inconsistent with his general attitude towards encouraging commerce. An appreciable amount of business was carried on between the citizen and officials on behalf of local and national governments which required officials to focus on the terms of the contract and not to worry about personal liability.

Thompson's 'hard' case law was of little help to purchasers of goods which were not up to standard unless there was fraud or an express warranty as to fitness. An extreme case of *caveat emptor* was that of *Seixas v Woods* (1804) in which the plaintiff bought wood described in an advertisement as braziletto. He was supplied with the considerably less valuable peacham wood. Justices Thompson and Kent, with Chief Justice Lewis dissenting, reversed the jury's verdict in favour of the plaintiff, holding that in the absence of fraud or an express warranty, the plaintiff failed. It is difficult to understand why the court did not consider the advertisement or the bill of parcels accompanying the wood describing it as braziletto as an express warranty. In effect, the Court placed on purchasers the burden of examining the goods before finalising the contract.[32] This meant that the purchaser was at risk of receiving inferior quality goods when it was often impracticable to examine the merchandise because of the distances involved in travelling to inspect. It also was contrary to the general trend of the courts to promote commercial activity by ensuring that purchasers actually received the goods for which they had contracted. In this respect the decision lagged behind economic change and purported to impose face-to-face contractual relationships when often inspection was not possible because merchants were trading very much at arm's length and deals had to be effected quickly or be lost whilst, for example, a New York buyer was spending time arranging an agent to inspect the sellers goods in New Orleans. A purchaser who bought braziletto should not have been obliged to accept some other inferior product.

Despite the occasional unfathomable opinion, Thompson believed that that the court should promote commercial life by ensuring that merchants knew clearly the basis on which contractual rights would be protected. His general approach was that all contracts were to be construed according to the law of the place where the contract was made and any contract which offended common law or violated the policy or spirit of a statute would be void *ab initio*.[33] In his first reported first-instance state opinion, *Carpenter v Butterfield* (1802), he held that it was not

---

[31] *Imlay v Sands*, Caines' Reports, vol 1, p 572, February 1804.
[32] *Seixas v Woods*, 2 Caines' Reports, 48, New York, 1804.
[33] *Smith v Smith*, 2 Johnson's Reports, 241 (1807).

permissible, after the plaintiff had sued the defendant for debt, for the defendant to purchase a promissory note from a third party payable by the plaintiff to set it off against the plaintiff's claim. Thompson took the view that to allow such a ploy 'would embarrass the circulation of this species of paper' as it would make it unsafe for a creditor to sue if he had paper outstanding against him.[34] Furthermore, in *Mumford v M'Pherson* (1806), he held inadmissible a parol warranty that a vessel was copper bottomed where the written contract was silent on the issue. He considered it unsafe to allow a contract to rest partly in writing and partly in parol. His reasoning was clear. The parties must ensure that all material terms were reduced to writing, otherwise the outcome of any action on the contract would be difficult to predict.[35] The promissory note case of *Tittle v Beebee* (1811) is typical of his opinions protecting the rights of honest men of business when he observed, 'It has been repeatedly ruled in this court, that we will recognize and protect the rights of an assignee of a chose in action (e.g. the right to enforce payment of a debt).'[36] Bills of exchange and promissory notes were crucial to the smooth running of commercial life and the court had to ensure, if confidence was to remain in these documents, that the holder would have his rights enforced in due course.

Crucial to any system of justice, whether state or federal, was the speedy resolution of disputes; all too often, justice delayed was justice denied. Thompson was aware of the need to simplify legal principles to achieve that object. He demonstrated this in the marine insurance case of *Stevens v Columbian Insurance Company* (1805) when he had to decide whether on the total loss of a vessel the gross or net amount of freight was recoverable. He held for what he considered to be the straightforward gross amount which was 'equal, simple, and easily ascertained'. The net amount, on the other hand, would lead to much litigation and uncertainty as to the deductions to be made such as wages and provisions had the vessel arrived safely in port.[37]

His wish for certainty in the developing law and, wherever possible, the preservation of existing rights to property was illustrated by the admiralty case of *Grant & Swift v M'Lachlin* (1809). In that case a vessel illegally captured by the French was taken to a Spanish port and left to rot. The Defendants paid $50 for her at auction, and having spent $2,000 on repairs sailed her back to New York where the original owners reclaimed her. Thompson had no hesitation in holding that the sale by the Spanish authorities to the Defendants must be recognised if derivative titles were to be safeguarded.[38]

The juries in state cases, just as in federal circuit courts, were the cornerstone of the developing legal system; their verdicts were supported by justices wherever possible. This is shown by Thompson's refusal of a new trial in the marine

---

[34] *Carpenter v Butterfield*, Johnson's Reports, 1799–1803, vol 3, 145, July 1802.
[35] *Mumford v M'Pherson*, Johnson's Reports, 1806–1823, vol 1, 417, August 1806.
[36] *Tuttle v Beebee*, Johnson's Reports, 1806–1823, vol 8, 154, May 1811.
[37] *Stevens v Columbian Insurance Company*, Caines' Reports, vol 3, 46, May 1805.
[38] *Grant & Swift v M'Lachlin*, Johnson's Reports, 1806–1823, 39, February 1809.

insurance case of *Barnewell v Church* (1803) when he observed to counsel: 'These points were decided by a respectable jury of merchants.' The remark also gives an insight into the quality of juries, at least in commercial cases.[39] However, Thompson, like Livingston, was prepared to reverse a jury's verdict when he believed it was plainly wrong. Thus in *McConnell v Hampton* (1815) he ordered a new trial in a case where a jury had awarded $9,000 damages to a private citizen who had been wrongfully arrested and detained for five days by an army officer who threatened to court martial and hang him as a spy. Thompson thought that the jury's passions were so inflamed as to mislead their judgments on the amount of damages.[40] Whereas, in *Borden v Fitch* (1818) a jury had awarded $5,000 to the plaintiff when the defendant had enticed his daughter away by falsely representing that his wife had died and he was unmarried. Thompson thought the award was high but refused to intervene.[41] Two apparently conflicting approaches may be explained by the aggravating features of each case. In *McConnell* it was accepted that the officer had acted under the honest, although mistaken, opinion that he had the right to try the plaintiff on a charge for treason, whereas, in *Borden*, the Defendant had 'debauched' the plaintiff's daughter by falsely representing that his former wife was dead. In *McConnell*, Thompson underlined his support of the jury system by stressing that applications to set aside jury awards should be looked at with caution and declaring that he would do so only where the damages were outrageous or manifestly exceeded the injury sustained. Overturning a jury's award of damages is a difficult area because it involves a judge usurping the function of a jury to order a new trial. The perennial problem is where the line is to be drawn. Justice Van Ness, by his dissent, did not feel the jury in *McConnell* had awarded a manifestly excessive sum.

Throughout the whole period of Thompson's 16-year tenure, the state court looked for guidance to past state Supreme Court authorities which, of course, were readily retrieved because of the excellent system of law reporting in place in New York. It also relied heavily on English authorities; there are very few opinions reported in Caines and Johnson without favourable references to Lords Mansfield, Holt, Ellenborough, Kenyon and Sir William Blackstone. Blackstone is cited so often as his four-volume *Commentaries on the Laws of England*, first published in 1764, quickly became required reading for every colonial lawyer as was the American edition, which included United States cases, first published by St. George Tucker in 1803.[42] Tucker's version was based on his lectures at the College of William and Mary where John Marshall and Bushrod Washington had attended to hear the law lectures of George Wythe. The frequent references to Blackstone in New York State Supreme Court reports and the United States

---

[39] *Barnewell v Church*, Caines' Reports, vol 1, 230, August 1803.
[40] *McConnell v Hampton*, Johnson's Reports, vol 12, 235, May 1815.
[41] *Borden v Fitch*, Johnson's Reports, vol 15, 139, January 1818.
[42] St George Tucker, *Blackstone's Commentaries: With Reference to The Constitution and Laws of the Federal Government of the United States and of the Commonwealth of Virginia* (Philadelphia: William Young Birch, and Abraham Small, 1803). Lawbook Exchange reprint, 2011.

Supreme Court reports support the contention of MacGill and Newmyer that his *Commentaries* did more to shape American early legal education and thought than any other single work.[43]

Novel points or conflicting opinions that required resolution arose for which Blackstone and others had no answer. The court had to make the first ruling in *Foot v Tracy* (1806) where it had to decide whether, in a libel action, the defendant could give general evidence of the plaintiff's character. Thompson observed that counsel had been 'unable to furnish us with much aid from the decided cases and our practice on circuit has not been uniform. We are left, therefore, pretty much at large to establish such a rule as will be most just'.[44]

His judicial experience at the date of his appointment to the United States Supreme Court was far greater than that of Justice Livingston. Although Thompson delivered only 250 opinions during his 16 years in New York he will have heard the arguments and the court's opinions in almost 4,500 hearings during that period, as opposed to Justice Livingston's 1,000 cases in four years. Whilst Livingston's judicial experience upon appointment to the Court may properly be described as extensive, Thompson as both Associate and Chief Justice had had a far more extensive grounding as a judge than any justice who sat on the Marshall Court. He was, therefore, admirably qualified to take his place on the nation's highest court.

His tenure as an Associate and later Chief Justice in New York was characterized by a determination to preserve vested rights and to promote commerce by formulating principles of contract law and practice and to assure merchants that rights and obligations arising under bills of exchange and promissory notes would be enforced by the court. His rigid adherence to precedent, which he accepted might occasionally result in injustice and his willingness to find officials personally liable when acting for state and national government give the impression of an unsympathetic tribunal, very much at odds with his later efforts on the Supreme Court to protect vulnerable minorities. There is a tension apparent between his function as a judge and as a politician demonstrated by a refusal to strike down state legislation and an insistence on looking beyond the clear wording of an Act to seek the political intent of its framers.

## Contractual Obligations on the Second Circuit and on the Court

Of Thompson's 77 federal circuit opinions reported in Elijah Paine's casebook and included in the *Federal Cases*, 55 are dated before 1835. As Thompson sat

---

[43] Hugh C MacGill and R Kent Newmyer, 'Legal Education and Legal Thought, 1790–1920' in Michael Grossberg and Christopher Tomlins, *The Cambridge History of Law in America*. Vol II (New York: Cambridge University Press, 2008), 40.

[44] *Foot v Tracy*, Johnson, vol 1, 46, February, 1806.

until 1843, it is not possible to confirm that the remaining undated opinions were delivered during the life of the Marshall Court. Where it was not possible to discern from the body of the opinion an approximate date, the opinion has been disregarded. Consequently, there are only 55 reported cases which definitely fall within the period under review; this means that only an outline of Thompson's circuit jurisprudence is presented. However, we are fortunate to have available the reports of his considerable contract law experience on the New York Supreme Court, which show no appreciable shift in approach from state to federal circuit court. Thompson continued to promote trade and was yet another justice who realised the need to protect the position of vulnerable seamen. His no-nonsense approach to the resolution of disputes and his firm handling of jury problems are evident from his circuit opinions.

Land disputes, commercial law and maritime cases account for most of Thompson's reported federal circuit opinions. His commercial law opinions cover the fields of contract, partnership, bankruptcy and bills of exchange. Thompson's enthusiasm to promote trade and encourage business enterprise in the state court was echoed in his federal circuit court opinions. Thus, in *Six Hundred and Fifty-One Chests of Tea v United States* (1826), he reversed the district judge's forfeiture order upon a breach of payment of the correct amount of customs duties, ruling that forfeiture was appropriate only where there had been fraud, misconduct or negligence. He believed that care should be taken not to shackle trade or check the industry and enterprise of the merchant by penalising him for genuine mistakes.[45] His opinion in *United States v Hatch* (1824), advanced the protection of seamen by ordering the forfeiture of a bond given by the master of a vessel because he had left his crew behind after a foreign voyage. Thompson praised the legislation which required such a bond and which was designed to guard against seaman being abandoned abroad. His observed that 'our national strength depended upon it'.[46]

Thompson's protection of seamen extended to ensuring that they were remunerated for their efforts and were not at the mercy of unscrupulous masters or owners. In *The Elizabeth v Rickers et al* (1831), he held that the punishment of seamen by the master after an absence without leave, and continuing them in his employ, was a waiver of any claim to forfeiture of wages.[47] Although in the previous year in *The Cadmus v Matthews et al*, Thompson had held against the seamen for deserting the ship for trivial reasons, he believed that the Court should watch over and protect their rights because they were, 'generally ignorant and improvident and, probably very often signing the ship's articles without knowing what they contain'.[48]

Thompson displayed a pragmatic approach to the preservation of long-standing titles to land. In *Barker v Jackson* (1826), a New York Act of 1797 which appointed commissioners to settle land disputes had been sanctioned by state courts for

---

[45] *Six Hundred and Fifty-One Chests of Tea v United States*, 27 F Cas 253, New York, April 1826.
[46] *United States v Hatch*, 26 F Cas 220, New York, April 1824.
[47] *The Elizabeth v Rickers et al*, 8 F Cas 470, New York, December 1831.
[48] *The Cadmus v Matthews et al*, F Cas 977, New York, December 1830.

30 years, yet the district judge held the act unconstitutional. In the report of the appeal to the circuit court no reasons are given for the district judge's holding which, if undisturbed, would have resulted in the overturning of a large number of titles held by soldiers for military service. Thompson overruled the district judge and his holding is a further demonstration of a common-sense approach based very much on the reality of the situation and the preservation of the status quo. It was the solution of a politician. Had he held otherwise it would have thrown into confusion many titles to military bounty-land.[49]

In *Albee v May* (1834) Thompson encouraged tenants to take care of the land by holding constitutional a state act of 1820 permitting the recovery of the value of improvements. He took the view that an *ex post facto* law was unconstitutional only if it was penal or criminal in nature.[50] He also believed in attempting to achieve, wherever possible, the intention of a title deed, as in *Jackson v Sprague* (1825), where the boundaries described in a deed were inconsistent with each other. Thompson did not avoid the document. He resolved the case by accepting those boundaries which best served the prevailing intention set out in the deed. In other words, he was a judge who sought solutions rather than taking technical points which defeated the parties' wishes.[51]

His opinions on procedural points reveal a confident and very practical approach to the disposal of court business, particularly when discharging juries who were unable to agree. He was not one for keeping a jury out for long periods if there was no possibility of agreement. In *United States v Perez* (1823), an allegation of piracy, Thompson discharged the jury against the wishes of the district judge when the jury had retired for only four hours. He rejected the argument that juries should be discharged only for reasons of exhaustion, intoxication or mental illness and the Court affirmed his view on a certificate of division of opinion.[52] Similarly, in *Cochrane v Swartout* (1834), he discharged a jury after only three hours when they could not agree on whether coke was coal and therefore liable to duty.[53] In *Brewster v Gelston* (1825), an action by an informer to recover part of forfeited goods, the jury returned a verdict which Thompson set aside and ordered a new trial. He made it plain that where a verdict was so obviously and palpably against the evidence, the judge had a duty not to permit it to stand.[54] This was a confirmation of his view on the state supreme court of the fallibility of some juries.

Thompson's practical approach was again shown by his opinion in *Griswold v Hill* (1825). Under the common law the death of a party abated the suit. However, adopting the English chancery practice, Thompson overcame the

---

[49] *Barker v Jackson*, 2 F Cas 811, New York, October 1826.
[50] *Albee v May*, 1 F Cas 134, Vermont, May 1834.
[51] *Jackson v Sprague*, 13 F Cas 253, New York, September 1825.
[52] *United States v Perez*, 27 F Cas 504, New York, September 1823.
[53] *Cochrane v Swartout*, 5 F Cas 1144, New York, 31 October, 1834.
[54] *Brewster v Gelston*, 4 F Cas 82, New York, April 1825.

problem by predating the judgment to the day before the defendant's death.[55] He was a judge who liked to get to the heart of a case and disliked unnecessarily lengthy pleadings. In *United States v Williams* (1826), when reversing the district judge and ordering a new trial, he complained that the records coming from the Northern District Court of New York were 'vexatiously voluminous and ... an abuse of pleading' and he requested the district court to reduce the number of pleas in each appeal.[56] This common sense problem-solving approach, which eschewed technicalities and sought solutions, was an ideal model for the efficient despatch of federal court business.

There is just one available reported circuit opinion of Justice Thompson which reveals the importance to him of achieving cross-circuit consistency. In *United States v Sturges et al* (1826), Thompson held that the Secretary of State's discharge from imprisonment of a person indebted to the United States did not discharge him or his sureties from their obligations to pay the outstanding debt. In reaching this conclusion, Thompson followed a circuit opinion of Justice Story which was directly on the point and observed that it was crucial that there should be uniformity of decisions in the construction of statutes. He noted that Justice Story's opinion had not been reviewed by the Supreme Court and stated that if the instant case was appealed, there would be an opinion binding upon all United States circuit and district courts.[57] Thompson's observation reveals not only his view of the importance to the citizen and his lawyer of being able to make a reasonably accurate prediction of an action's success, but also the esteem in which he held Justice Story's opinions.

On the New York Supreme Court, Thompson was one of five justices. By the time of his first sitting on the United States Supreme Court in Washington in 1824, he was one of seven.[58] However, he was no ordinary newcomer. His expertise and confidence were high after 16 years as a judge of New York State. He was well qualified to contribute to the discussions and his voice would be listened to with respect. His four years as New York chief justice and his political experience taught him the necessary man-management skills and the benefits of group harmony.[59]

During his years on the Marshall Court, Thompson delivered 59 opinions of the Court. He sat for eight years after Marshall's death, contributing a number of significant opinions whilst a member of the Taney Supreme Court. The majority of Thompson's opinions of the Court mirrored his earlier judicial experience of commercial law and land disputes. There are 13 commercial and ten land dispute

---

[55] *Griswold v Hill*, 11 F Cas 60, New York, September 1825.
[56] *United States v Williams*, 28 F Cas 608, New York, April 1826.
[57] *United States v Sturges*, 27 F Cas 1358, New York, April 1826. Justice Story's circuit opinion was in the case of *Hunt v United States*, 12 F Cas 948, Massachusetts, May 1812.
[58] The Judiciary Act of 1789 set the number of justices at six. The short-lived Judiciary Act of 1801 reduced the number to five and the Act of 1807 increased the bench to seven justices.
[59] Following his appointment to the United States Supreme Court, Yale College conferred upon him the degree of Doctor of Laws. *Boston Weekly Messenger*, 16 September 1824.

opinions reported. The commercial cases included negotiable instruments, partnership and general contract disputes. Thompson applied his favoured maxim of *caveat emptor* in *The Monte Allegro* (1824) holding that neither the owner nor the marshal selling tobacco under a forced sale were liable for the inferior quality of the tobacco, as the owner had no control over the sale and the marshal had no authority to warrant the goods. It was for the buyer to inspect and satisfy himself on quality before the purchase.[60]

As to negotiable instruments, the transition to full negotiability of a promissory note from the concept of taking of it subject to all the claims and defences of previous holders was a long drawn-out process. Horwitz (1977) notes that by 1800 only five states had adopted the negotiability principle, observing that New York had done so in 1794.[61] This meant that Thompson was well versed in this new form of currency. He had developed a particular expertise in this aspect of the law and authored nine opinions setting out clear procedures for merchants to follow. In *Renner v The Bank of Columbia* (1824), Thompson upheld the banks' practice to demand payment of a note discounted by it up to the fourth day after the time specified in the original note.[62] Banks often purchased the amount due under a promissory note at a discounted rate. Although he received a lesser sum, the merchant was saved a longer wait for the full amount and improved his cash flow. Further, in *Bank of Columbia v Lawrence* (1828), Thompson set out rules of service of notices of non-payment of notes as 'it was important for the safety of holders of commercial paper'. In that case, the Court reversed the circuit court and held that leaving the notice at the post office in Georgetown close to the defendant's home was good service.[63] In *Boyce & Henry v Edwards* (1830), Thompson held that there must be clear evidence that a bill had been accepted. Further guidance was given in *Bank of Alexandria v Swann*, 34 US 33 (1835) when Thompson held that notice of dishonour should be given with reasonable diligence and a small difference in the description of the amount owed, particularly when there was only one note subsisting between the parties was not fatal to the claim.[64] In this way Thompson simplified an emerging system of credits so that traders knew their rights and obligations.

Although an analysis of Thompson's opinions are useful in ascertaining his views on state power and the promotion of commerce, they also give an insight into how circuit experience was put to use in the full Court. *United States v Morris* (1825) is a case in point. Thompson wrote the majority opinion absolving a marshal from liability who had levied execution but had handed the proceeds to the debtor. He had done so because the Secretary of the Treasury had exercised

---

[60] *The Monte Allegro*, 22 US (9 Wheat) 616 (1824). See the same principle applied at state level in the 'braziletto wood' case of *Seixas v Woods*, 2 Caines' Reports, 48.
[61] Horwitz, 215 and n 11.
[62] *Renner v Bank of Columbia*, 22 US 581 (1824).
[63] *Bank of Columbia v Lawrence*, 26 US (1 Pet) 578 (1828).
[64] *Bank of Alexandria v Swann*, 34 US 33 (1831).

his power to remit a forfeiture or penalty under the revenue laws at any time after judgment and before monies were handed over to the collector. As the remission was in time, the marshal's actions were justified. The case is noteworthy, not because of the Court's opinion, but because of remarks made by Justice Johnson during his concurring opinion. He observed that he had considered this problem repeatedly on his circuit and he had reached a view more than 12 years before. Such remarks were rarely expressed when actually delivering an opinion but it is likely that in conference after argument or during the course of counsel's submissions, a justice would volunteer how he had dealt with the issue on circuit more than once in the past, thereby giving the court the undoubted benefit of circuit court expertise.

## 'What is to be Left to the States?'

Perhaps the most difficult question which the courts had to determine from the beginning of the federal justice system was the legal and political relationship between the federal government and the several states, a point made forcefully by George Mason during the debate at the Virginia Ratifying Convention of 1788. Whilst the Supreme Court consisted of justices allied to the Federalist cause, the Court was united in its construction of the Constitution in favour of federal government supremacy. However, justices such as Johnson and Thompson, nominated by Republican presidents, argued, wherever possible, for the right of states to regulate their own affairs. Their dissents on this issue opened up healthy public debates essential to the democratic process.

Dunne classifies Thompson's state court jurisprudence as 'a states' rights mercantilism tempered with a humanitarian overlay'. Thompson acknowledged the right of the federal government to exercise the powers granted to it by the Constitution but he argued that those powers, wherever possible, were to be exercised concurrently by the states, particularly in relation to commerce. The issue faced by Thompson and other justices was where to draw the line between state and federal regulation. Article 1, Section 8 of the Constitution empowered the federal government to control many matters including interstate commerce, laying and collecting certain taxes, coining money and protecting the rights of authors to their writings. Obvious difficulties relating to state control presented themselves in those cases in which a party had complied with the requirements of state law but had failed to follow the procedures laid down by federal law. An example of such a problem is to be found in Thompson's dissent in the intellectual property dispute between law reporters in *Wheaton v Peters* (1834). Henry Wheaton had reported and published 25 volumes of Supreme Court opinions which he had annotated and included the arguments of counsel. His successor Richard Peters, heavily abridged Wheaton's reports reducing them to six volumes which had a disastrous effect on sales. Wheaton lost his copyright action essentially because of his failure to protect his work by complying with the provisions of federal copyright statutes. Justice John McLean, for the Court, held that there was no federal copyright common law. Thompson failed to carry the Court with his argument that a state was entitled to protect the intellectual rights of its citizens even though federal statutory protection was in place and that Wheaton should succeed because he had complied with Pennsylvania copyright law.[65] This is a further example of Thompson's failure to persuade his colleagues that the states had the right to regulate their own affairs, despite the fact that, by this time, the Chief Justice was the only remaining Federalist on the Court. All six associates had been nominated by presidents for their commitment to Republican values, the most important of which was the states' power of self- government.[66] It is plain that, Johnson and Thompson apart, the Republican principles held by the justices faced a twofold challenge upon appointment to the Court. First, the pressure to present a united front to the nation and second, dealing with the Federalist centralisation of the Marshall Court with its emphasis on the supremacy of federal government and federal law in the preservation of vested property rights and the promotion of commerce. Dunne's reference to Thompson's 'humanitarian overlay' is more difficult to discern because, whilst Thompson attempted to mould the law to favour the interests of African slaves and the Cherokee Nation, his hardline approach to precedent on occasion disregarded the hardship to deserving litigants, sacrificing justice in individual cases for a more certain decision-making process.

As an example of 'states' rights mercantilism', Dunne cites Thompson's opinion in *Livingston v Van Ingen* (1812) for the New York Court for the Correction of Errors in which he held that the state's grant of a steamboat monopoly on New York waters did not infringe the power entrusted to Congress to regulate commerce.[67] In that case Thompson was outspoken in his support of state power observing that he viewed New York as 'an independent sovereignty not having surrendered any of its constitutional powers to the United States'. He believed that courts should declare legislative acts unconstitutional with 'great caution and circumspection' because those laws had been approved by the Council of Revision which included members of the judiciary.[68] Twelve years after *Livingston v Van Ingen*, the United States Supreme Court, in *Gibbons v Ogden*, handed down another 'free enterprise' opinion designed to boost the economy, holding that such a monopoly contravened the Constitution. Thompson was denied the opportunity to dissent as the opinion came shortly before he took his seat on the Court.[69]

---

[65] *Wheaton v Peters*, 33 US (8 Pet) 591, 668 (1834).
[66] Justices Johnson, Todd and Duvall had been nominated by President Jefferson; Story by President James Madison, Thompson by President James Monroe and McLean by President Andrew Jackson. See *The Supreme Court of the United States: Its Beginnings & Its Justices, 1790–1991* (Commission of the Bicentennial of the United States, 1992).
[67] *Livingston v Van Ingen*, 9 Johns Report 507 (1812).
[68] ibid, 562–63.
[69] *Gibbons v Ogden*, 22 US (9 Wheat) 1 (1824).

He was not always so strident over state sovereignty. He concurred with Chief Justice Kent in denying a writ of *habeas corpus* to a father who wished his young son's discharge from the army. Thompson accepted that the state court had no right to intervene, although he thought that there might be cases in which it would be the duty of the state court to act, but gave no indication of the circumstances which might provoke intervention. He did concede, however, that questions of jurisdiction between federal and state courts were 'generally nice and delicate subjects', thereby highlighting the tension between federal and state jurisdictions.[70]

As a United States Supreme Court justice, Thompson's attitude towards jurisdictional disputes between federal and state courts was influenced by his political and judicial connection with New York over many years and his states' rights stance. This is demonstrated by his reported circuit opinion in *The Robert Fulton* (1826). The plaintiffs obtained an order in state court for the attachment of a vessel for non-payment of a bill for work done and materials supplied. The owners subsequently attempted to invoke the jurisdiction of the federal court. Thompson held that, as there were concurrent jurisdictions, the tribunal which first exercised jurisdiction should retain the claim.[71] There was no suggestion that the issue should be re-opened by a 'superior' court. He was content that the state court was well able to deal with the matter. In *Ward v Arrendo* (1825), Thompson laid down strict conditions before a case could be transferred to federal circuit court. One defendant could not compel a co-defendant to transfer against his will; if a transfer was granted and the parties failed to enter appearances in circuit court, the case would be remanded to state court.[72] Therefore, the transition from state to federal justice, in the early years, had no effect on his preference, wherever possible, for the state courts to have jurisdiction.

Three cases in 1827 demonstrated Justice Thompson's determination to fight for state sovereignty. In *Ogden v Saunders*, Thompson's vote was vital as the Court divided 4-3. He supported the majority view that a New York State insolvency statute, which protected the property of debtors in respect of contracts subsequent to the statute did not contravene the contracts clause of the Constitution. The majority accepted that any legislation attempting to affect existing contracts would fall foul of 'impairment of contracts' clause but in respect of future contracts the parties were presumed to know the law. Thompson was not averse to a federal insolvency law, but saw no reason why the states should not play a concurrent role in dealing with debtors within a state who were incapable of meeting their obligations.[73]

In *Brown v Maryland*, Thompson dissented from the majority holding that an act of a state legislature requiring all importers of foreign goods whilst still in the

---

[70] *In the Matter of Jeremiah Ferguson, a Soldier in the United States Army*, Johnson, vol 9, 241 (August 1812).
[71] *The Robert Fulton*, 20 F Cas 869, New York, April 1826.
[72] *Ward v Arrendo*, 29 F Cas 167, New York, April 1825.
[73] *Ogden v Saunders*, 25 US (12 Wheat) 213 (1827).

original packaging to pay for a licence or suffer penalties in default was unconstitutional. He observed that at the founding of the Union, the states had a sovereign power to tax imports and that the Constitution had not extinguished that right.[74] He was alone in that view. His opening remarks reveal the general desire of the Court to present a united front to the world. That a justice regretted dissenting was a sentiment generally expressed. However, Thompson went further by admitting that had this not been a case of constitutional importance, he would have refrained from dissent even though he did not accept the majority view. Thompson concluded his support of state sovereignty for 1827 in the case of *Mason v Haile*, an action for breach of a bond securing a debtor's detention in prison. Thompson, for the Court, held that there was no liability under the bond as the Rhode Island legislature had accepted the debtor's petition that he be discharged from prison. State legislatures had the power to abolish imprisonment for debt. There was, therefore, no unlawful escape and no liability under the bond. Justice Washington dissented because he had consistently set his face against state legislation which purported to interfere with contracts retrospectively.[75]

When Thompson arrived on the Court, the Chief Justice had begun to delegate more opinions to his associate justices but, despite the considerable expertise Thompson brought to the Court, the opinions assigned to him were of no great moment and of little constitutional importance.[76] Thompson went on to write more significant opinions under Chief Justice Roger Taney but, whilst on the Marshall Court, his dissents were more noteworthy than his majority opinions and concurrences. His dissent in *Cherokee Nation v Georgia*, below, was the most significant.

If there was an expectation of a serious clash between Thompson's state power philosophy and the centralism of the Marshall Court, it was not apparent in the early years. Indeed, in his first year on the Court in *Osborn v Bank of the United States* (1824) he agreed with the majority view that a state had no power to tax the Bank of the United States and that any attempt to enforce payment of the tax would be met with a federal injunction. Thompson did not always align himself with local legislation when conflicts arose between state and federal law and in *Bank of United States v Halstead* (1825), a shift in his attitude is evident. A Kentucky law of 1821 prohibited the sale of property taken under execution for less than three-quarters of its appraised value. The marshal refused to sell the land because he was offered only $5 per acre instead of $26. Thompson authored the Court's opinion which held that the Kentucky law could not bind a sale following the execution of a judgment of a federal court. He argued that an officer of the

---

[74] *Brown v Maryland*, 25 US (12 Wheat) 419 (1827).
[75] *Mason v Haile*, 25 US (12 Wheat) 370 (1827).
[76] In 1824 Thompson's first full year on the Court, Marshall delivered only 15 of the 41 opinions, whereas in 1809 he had taken the lion's share by handing down 32 of 46 opinions. As time went on, Marshall handed down fewer opinions: in 1830, the chief justice delivered less than half of the Court's opinions, 25 out of 56. These figures are taken from the *United States Reports*.

United States could not be governed by state law as he acts under the authority of the federal government.[77] His opinion has in it an element of pragmatism as he expressed the fear that disparate state laws would frustrate orders for sale issuing out of federal courts. He adroitly avoided the issue of whether the Kentucky law was unconstitutional by basing the opinion on the fact that the state law did not expressly cover marshals or federal court executions.[78]

## The Cherokee Nation and the African-American Slave

Whilst Thompson was sympathetic to the plight of the Native Americans, he was unable to further their cause in *Jackson v Porter* (1825). The case concerned the ownership of land which had been purchased from an Indian tribe. Thompson held that, as the Indian tribes had only a right of occupancy of the land, a purchase from them did not confer title.[79] He was obliged to follow the Court's ruling in *Johnson v M'Intosh* (1823), a case decided before his appointment.[80] However, he gave his view on Indian titles in a notable dissent, joined in by Justice Story, in *Cherokee Nation v Georgia* (1831). The majority held that the Court had no jurisdiction to grant an injunction prohibiting Georgia from passing laws which deprived the Cherokee Nation of the right of self-government because it was not a foreign state as defined by the Constitution but was merely a domestic-dependent nation.[81] That ruling meant that the Supreme Court had no jurisdiction to hear their grievances. Thompson had argued that the Cherokee Nation was a foreign sovereign state entitled to relief. He based his conclusion on the fact that the Cherokees had always been dealt with as such by the United States Government both before and after the adoption of the Constitution. His argument was simple but compelling. The Native Americans held the land long before the arrival of European settlers and would have been regarded by the rest of the world as a foreign nation. He failed to see how under the law of nations, the arrival of the Europeans could have altered the position when the tribes continued to live apart from the new arrivals and had been permitted the right of self-government, particularly as they had never been conquered and all wars had been concluded

---

[77] *Bank of the United States v Halstead*, 23 US 51 (1825).
[78] *Osborn v The Bank of the United States*, 22 US (9 Wheat) 738 (1824).
[79] *Jackson v Porter*, 13 F Cas 235 New York, September 1825.
[80] *Johnson v M'Intosh*, 12 US 571 (1823), in which Chief Justice Marshall giving the opinion that title to the land was in the European discovers and the Native Americans were mere tenants. For an in-depth analysis of this decision see, Lindsay G Robertson, *Conquest by Law: How the Discovery of America Dispossessed Indigenous Peoples of Their Lands* (New York: Oxford University Press, 2005).
[81] *Cherokee Nation v Georgia*, 30 US (5 Peters) 1 (1831). Newmyer writes that Marshall, whilst denying jurisdiction, treated the merits of the case in such a way as to encourage Thompson to write the dissent joined in silently by Story. Marshall had suggested that the case might be fully considered by the Court on a future occasion 'in a proper case with proper parties'. R Kent Newmyer, *John Marshall and the Heroic Age of the Supreme Court* (Baton Rouge: Louisiana State University Press, 2001), 450–51.

by peace treaties.[82] Thompson's draft manuscript dissent is an interesting insight into the working up of a final opinion. Whilst amendments of the draft in the final printed version owe more to style and emphasis than to substance, the draft contains a chronology of events and notes on the relevant provisions of the Constitution, cases, statute law and treaties absent from the delivered opinion. Thompson notes Story's concurrence in the draft.[83]

*Worcester v Georgia* (1832) was a very different proposition as the Court was able to assume jurisdiction on the ground that the missionary, Samuel Worcester, was a United States citizen. He had been imprisoned by a Georgia court for refusing to obtain a state licence permitting him to be on Cherokee lands. The Court upheld the laws and treaties of the Cherokees against Georgia enactments which included laws abrogating all Cherokee laws, abolishing their government, and confiscating land for the benefit of Georgia whites. Chief Justice Marshall, citing the provisions of 1802 Act regulating trade and intercourse with the Indian tribes, declared that the federal government, not the states, had authority over Native American affairs. His reasoning followed closely the substance of Justice Thompson's dissent in *Cherokee Nation v Georgia*.[84] In reaching his conclusion in *Worcester*, Marshall adopted the research carried out by Thompson in the earlier case and traced the many dealings between the United States and the Cherokees through the Treaties of Hopewell (1785) and Holston (1791). Both treaties had dealt with the Cherokees as a national entity separate from the State of Georgia and had explicitly recognised their right to self-government and guaranteed their right of occupation of their lands.[85] Thompson, in his *Cherokee Nation* dissent, wrote that 'the Cherokee Nation of Indians have, by virtue of these treaties, an exclusive right of occupation of the lands in question, and that the United States are bound under their guarantee, to protect the nation in the enjoyment of such occupancy'.[86] In *Worcester*, Marshall used words which were very similar to those earlier uttered by Thompson. Having rehearsed the treaties and statutes, Marshall declared that those laws:

> manifestly consider the several Indian Nations as distinct political communities, having territorial boundaries, within which their authority is exclusive, and having a right to all the lands within those boundaries, which is not only acknowledged, but guaranteed by the United States.

Thompson's dissent in *Cherokee Nation* arose from his refusal to condone Georgia's oppression of the Cherokees. He based his view on the fact that Article 3, Section 2 of the Constitution gave the Court jurisdiction because the Cherokees had been treated by the United States as a foreign nation. Whilst his agreement

---

[82] ibid, 80.
[83] Draft manuscript dissent, Smith Thompson Papers, Library of Congress. MMC 2168.
[84] *Worcester v Georgia*, 31 US (6 Peters) 515 (1832).
[85] ibid, 556–57.
[86] *Cherokee Nation v Georgia*, 30 US 1 (1831) 74–5.

with the majority view in *Worcester* at first sight seemed to contradict his long-held view of a state's right to control its internal affairs, the Court supported the Cherokee position on the ground that the Constitution expressly gave to the federal government, and not to the states, the power to control relations with the Indian tribes.

Whilst Thompson was able in both cases to show publicly his support of the Cherokees, his efforts to alleviate the suffering of the African already a slave within the United States met with little success because his hands were tied by the Constitution and laws of the United States. The problem was quite different and could not be resolved by deciding whether a distinct body of people was a 'foreign' or 'domestic dependent' nation. The African slaves were regarded in law as individual items of 'property' crucial to the economic prosperity of the South. They were not citizens. They had not the 'blessings of liberty' enshrined in the preamble to the Constitution. In fact, the Constitution endorsed the ownership of slaves and prolonged the institution by declaring that Congress had no power to prohibit, prior to 1808, the 'migration or importation of such persons as any of the States now existing shall think proper to admit'.[87] So that there could be no doubt about that prohibition, Article 5 expressly forbade any constitutional amendment to remove the ban until 1808.

The outlawing of the slave trade went a long way towards the protection of Africans in their homeland but the legal status of the slave was not finally resolved until the abolition of slavery by the Thirteenth Amendment to the Constitution on 6 December 1865. It followed, therefore, that a justice sworn to uphold the Constitution and laws of the United States faced an impossible task in attempting to influence federal law to alleviate the position of the African American. Thompson was one justice who did make the effort. Although the surviving reports do not contain any circuit opinion on slavery he may have written, he delivered three such opinions for the Supreme Court.

In *McCutchen v Marshall* (1834), a testator bequeathed his slaves to his wife and upon her death all slaves of full age were to be freed. Those under 21 were to be inherited by his brother and brother-in-law and were to be freed when they became 21. The Court dealt with the position of two children born after the testator's death whilst his wife was still alive. Thompson, writing for the Court, was constrained under the terms of the will to hold that the children remained slaves because their mother had not been freed at the dates of their birth.[88] However, in the remaining two cases, Thompson was able to demonstrate the humanitarian approach later shown in his circuit opinion in *The Amistad*.[89] In *The Emily and The Caroline* (1824) Thompson held that the offence of preparing a vessel for sail contrary to the Slave Trade Act of 1794 did not require that the vessel should have

---

[87] Article 1, Section 9, Clause 1.
[88] *McCutchen v Marshall*, 33 US 220 (1834).
[89] *The Amistad*, 40 US 518 (1841).

been completely fitted out and ready for sea. The Court affirmed the forfeiture of the vessel.[90] This case demonstrates Thompson's determination to enforce strictly the provisions designed to end further attempts to import more slaves and was much easier to achieve, whereas the sentiments in his opinion for the Court in *Lee v Lee* (1834) are remarkable given that the freedom of existing slaves was the matter in issue. The Court reversed a holding of the District of Columbia circuit court that slaves had not gained their freedom after having been moved to Washington from their birthplace in Virginia. There was a dispute as to whether they had been hired out, but the Court ordered a new trial on the basis of the justice's misdirection to the jury. A preliminary objection was made to the Court's jurisdiction and an application was made to introduce affidavits showing that the value of the two slaves was beneath the jurisdictional threshold of $1,000. Thompson gave short shrift to the application remarking, 'the matter in dispute is, therefore, the value of their freedom and this is not susceptible of a pecuniary valuation'.[91]

The most celebrated opinion on slavery delivered by Thompson was his first instance opinion in the *Schooner Amistad*. Although outside the timeline of this study, it is relevant because it is the culmination of Thompson's enlightened anti-slavery views. Africans (Mende) kidnapped from Sierra Leone were being transported by sea from Havana to plantations along the coast of Cuba. The slaves rose up and took command of the vessel, killing the captain and the cook. The ship was later intercepted off Long Island Sound by a United States revenue cutter and the slaves were taken into custody and later charged with murder and piracy. Thompson, presiding in the Connecticut circuit court upon findings of fact by the jury, dismissed all of the criminal charges against the slaves, holding that the circuit court had no jurisdiction over crimes alleged to have taken place at sea on a foreign-owned vessel. He was not able to order the release of the slaves because they were subject to a 'property' claim pending in the district court.[92] The case gave the judge an opportunity to air his views on slavery and explain how he believed his hands were tied by the Constitution. He urged the note-takers in court to report accurately the following:

> It is sufficient to say that the constitution of the Unites States, although the term slavery is not used, and the laws of the United States, do recognize the right of one man to have

---

[90] *The Emily and The Caroline*, 22 US (9 Wheat) 381 (1824).

[91] *Lee v Lee*, 33 US 44 (1834).

[92] The report in the *Southern Patriot* (Charleston, South Carolina, 26 September 1839, extracted from *The New York Journal of Commerce*) is of interest because it reveals how newspapers acquired their intelligence. The item reads, 'We learn that a member of the Grand Jury arrived in this City this morning on the steamboat from Hartford, and states that Judge THOMPSON decided that, in view of the facts presented to them, the Courts of this country had no jurisdiction in the case, and that the transaction was to us the same as if taking place in Havana. Consequently the Grand Jury found no bill against the prisoners.' The northern newspapers were generally sympathetic to the plight of the Mende and invited subscriptions to a defence fund, but the editor of *The Sun* (Baltimore) was not supportive, writing in the issue of 9 November 1839, 'THE AMISTEAD BLACKS—On the 19th ins, the second trial of these savages will take place in Hartford.'

the control of the labor of another man ... Whatever private motives the Court may have, or whatever may be their feelings, on this subject, they are not to be brought into view on this question ... It is the province and the duty of the Court to determine what the laws are, and not what it might be desirable they should be. My feelings ... are personally as abhorrent to the system of slavery as those of any man here, but I must on my oath, pronounce what the laws are on this subject

In January 1840, District Judge Andrew Judson held that the Mende were not slaves and ordered them to be delivered to the President for return to their homes.[93] On appeal to the circuit court, Thompson affirmed the opinion of the district judge *pro forma* without any findings of fact. He dismissed the claims of the Spanish government that the Mende were slaves, but allowed an appeal to be made to the United States Supreme Court. He took this course on the basis that the Supreme Court would hear the appeal within one year rather than the two years it would take if he dismissed the appeal and the Court remanded the case for further enquiry.[94] On 9 March 1841, the Court, which included Thompson, affirmed the opinions of the district and circuit courts ordered the Connecticut circuit court to free the Mende. Thompson, as the circuit judge for Connecticut, subsequently formally ordered the release of the Mende.[95]

Whilst the opinion of the Supreme Court in *Amistad* was praiseworthy, the justices were merely enforcing existing laws prohibiting the international slave trade. It is important to make the distinction between slavery and the slave trade. When it came to the position of the African already held to slavery in the United States, the justices were constrained by the Constitution and existing federal legislation. Whatever the personal views of justices such as Thompson they could do nothing to ease the suffering of the slave population. Thompson set out the difficulties facing judges in the circuit case of *In re Martin* when he refused to order the release from custody of a man alleged to have been a fugitive from labour within the meaning of the Fugitive Slave Act 1793 pending his examination by a magistrate. Feeling constrained by Article 4, Section 2 of the Constitution, which provided for the return of escaped slaves, he rejected the argument that the Act was unconstitutional, writing,

We know, historically, that [Article 4, Section 2] was a subject that created great difficulty in the formation of the Constitution, and that it resulted as a compromise not entirely satisfactory to a portion of the United States. But, whatever our private opinions on the

---

[93] For District Judge Judson's role in this case see, the lecture given on 21 April 1983 by Chief Judge Jose A Cabranes of the United States District Court for the District of Connecticut in Whitney North Seymour Jr, *United States Courts in the Second Circuit: A Collection of History Lectures Delivered by the Judges of the Second Circuit* (New York: Federal Bar Council Foundation, 1992), 48–50.

[94] The editor of *The New York Spectator* of 4 May 1840 expressed his displeasure complaining that 'The Circuit Court has contrived to slip away from the responsibility of deciding upon the appeal', describing it as 'the quasi decision'.

[95] *The United States v The Schooner Amistad*, 40 US 15 Peters, 518 (1841). The facts of the case are taken from Bruce A Ragsdale, 'Amistad: The Federal Courts and the Challenge to Slavery' (Federal Judicial Center, Federal Judicial History Office, 2002).

subject of slavery may be, we are bound in good faith to carry into execution the constitutional provisions in relation to it; and it would be an extravagant construction of this opinion in the constitution, to suppose it to be left discretionary in the states to comply with it or not, as they should think proper.[96]

# Conclusion

The defining ethos of Justice Thompson's judicial philosophy was the sovereign right of a state to determine its internal affairs. If that goal was beyond reach, he sought to advance, wherever possible, respect for both state and federal jurisdictions. The opinions examined earlier in *Livingston v Van Ingen*; *Brown v Maryland*; *Ogden v Saunders* and his dissent in *Wheaton v Peters* provide clear support for this guiding principle. He was a very political animal, as his desire for the Presidency and his unsuccessful attempt at the governorship of New York demonstrate, but those ambitions did not interfere with the performance of his judicial duties.

Despite his Republican background, Thompson realised that the survival of the Supreme Court depended upon its members presenting a united face to the nation. He toned down the views he expressed in the New York Court for the Correction of Errors case of *Livingston v Van Ingen* that New York was an independent sovereignty which had never surrendered any of its constitutional powers to the United States. His observation, in the same year in *In the Matter of Jeremiah, a Soldier*, that questions of jurisdiction between federal and state courts were 'generally nice and delicate subjects,' revealed that he was capable of moderation.

As the small number of Supreme Court dissents show, he did not set out to disrupt the Marshall Court or undermine its authority. He was prepared to modify his states' rights views in *Osborn v Bank of United States* and he also accepted in *Bank of United States v Halstead* that state laws could not frustrate the implementation of a federal circuit court order. While Dunne rightly points to Thompson as a man prepared to express dissenting views, the cases examined here do not support the view that he led a reaction to Marshall's 'federalist centralism'. Nor do those opinions confirm Hall's contention that Thompson's presence on the Court 'spelled the gradual eclipse of John Marshall's influence over the course of American law'. This investigation favours Abraham's contention that, whilst Thompson occasionally disagreed with Marshall, he generally adopted the majority view. This was not a huge political transition as the two-party system was in its infancy; political allegiances were still fluid and the responsibility of assuming high office carried with it the need to reconsider loyalties and decide upon a course best suited to the nation's interests.

---

[96] *In re Martin*, 2 Paine 348; 16 F Cas 881, 884 Circuit Court, Southern District, New York. The opinion is undated but we know that the second volume of Caines' reports covered cases decided from 1827 to 1840. The report gives the day and the month of the appearance before the magistrate but not the year.

His unwillingness to strike down state legislation stemmed from his concurrent judicial and legislative roles in New York State. Sitting as a justice and a reviewer of state legislation on the Council of Revision he was clearly conflicted by the concept that good government required the separation of the functions of the judiciary, executive and the legislature. His constitutionally incompatible functions in New York also led to an approach which sought the intention of the legislature even when the words of the statute were clear.

A firm belief in preserving the status quo and a strict adherence to precedent were elements of Thompson's judicial restraint, which preferred consistency to the occasional injustice (*Jackson v Sill*). While he furthered economic growth by settling law in cases such as *Renner v The Bank of Columbia, Bank of Columbia v Lawrence, Boyce & Henry v Edwards and Bank of Alexandria v Swann*, enabling merchants to more readily enforce promises made in bills of exchange and promissory notes, his rigid application of the doctrine of *caveat emptor* in *Seixas v Woods* and in *The Monte Allegro* did little to ensure that a purchaser received full value for money. He made no allowance for trading at arm's length with little opportunity to inspect the goods beforehand. His inflexible interpretation of a statute, as shown in *Tillman v Lansing*, is another example of the strict letter of the law triumphing over the justice of the case as is his refusal to protect from personal liability public officials acting in good faith (*Henderson v Brown; Walker v Swartout; Imlay v Sands*).

The preservation of the status quo is shown by Thompson's reluctance to overturn established land titles, particularly those granted for military service. This rigidity of judicial restraint was to some extent alleviated by his compassionate approach to the troubling issue of slavery and his efforts to alleviate the plight of the Cherokee which revealed the 'humanitarian overlay' which continued after the Marshall era in his handling, on circuit, the case of the Mende Africans in *The Amistad*.

His attitude towards juries differed from those of Washington and Story. While generally supportive of jury verdicts, Thompson made it clear in *Brewster v Gelston* that a verdict should not be permitted to stand if the judge believed it to be clearly against the weight of evidence which contrasts with Washington's pride in declaring in *Willis v Bucher et al* that he had refused to accept jury verdicts only twice in 16 years. Thompson was also quick to discharge a jury if he thought they would not be able to agree, despite the custom of discharge in cases of exhaustion, intoxication or mental illness. His robust view on the fallibility of juries was more in line with that of Livingston, from the same New York stable.

Thompson's contribution to United States law during his period on the Marshall Court did not match the expectation one would have of a justice who had the most extensive judicial experience of all of the justices before joining the Court. One would have anticipated a greater volume of opinions and some of significant impact. This is explained, only to a limited extent, by the Chief Justice's practice of reserving to himself the bulk of the Court's opinions, particularly those with a constitutional element. However, by 1823, John Marshall had begun to assign more opinions to associates and the law reports show that Justices Johnson and Story were not slow in coming forward to deliver the Court's opinion on a wide range of issues.

Thompson's place in the development of early United States law is assured by his efforts to ensure that states, whilst far from fully self-governing, had some say in their internal affairs, by his opinions which engendered confidence in commercial activity and by his endeavours to shape federal law to alleviate the plight of minorities. Hall's description of Thompson as a judge of 'modest ability' whose contribution to the court was 'mostly unremarkable' does not do him justice. His courageous stand in *Cherokee Nation v Georgia* alone removes him from the category of an also ran. In that dissent he espoused a cause unpopular to the majority of Americans and, in particular, to the State of Georgia and President Andrew Jackson. In order to take this position, he abandoned his states' rights sympathies and roundly condemned the Georgia Government for its actions. The opinions considered in this chapter establish Thompson's valuable role in the development of state and federal law at this crucial period of the life of the new Republic.

# Conclusion

This investigation into the work of four prominent justices of the United States circuit courts establishes those courts as key to the development of the federal court system in the Early Republic. It balances the approach of scholars who, when examining the rise in influence of the Supreme Court, have focused on the impact of John Marshall and the Court's landmark cases. Whilst the Supreme Court's major constitutional opinions were crucial in settling a body of United States laws, it was left to the justices on circuit, in the very early years, to construct a system of federal law which was fair, consistent and effective. The output of the Jay and Ellsworth Courts between 1798 and 1800 was so small as to be of little assistance to the justices riding circuit who, individually and collectively, had to source and fashion American law to resolve the nation's criminal and civil litigation. The justices were further hampered by the paucity of federal legislation to guide them in their task.

In short, this study maintains that a significant factor in the rise in influence of the United States Supreme Court was the shaping of law by the justices on circuit. It follows that the success of the federal court system fed up from the 'inferior' circuit courts rather than down from the Supreme Court to the lower levels. An examination of the neglected role of the federal circuit courts and a consideration of a large body of circuit reports has enabled me to look through a little-used lens to see an evolving nation; the cases tried in those courts indicating momentous issues facing the new democracy; and the ways in which the justices met those events and constructed an essential foundation of stable government.

They faced an arduous task on circuit; much more so than sitting together in the comparative comfort of a courtroom in the nation's capital and during the evenings in the same reasonable lodgings. Aside from the great physical hardship of travelling thousands of miles each year along poor roads, there was the emotional distress of separation from family and friends for months at a time; it is, therefore, not surprising that some justices refused the appointment or resigned after short periods of circuit duty. It did not end there. Once they reached their circuit destinations they had to dispense justice often without the benefit of a law library, contending with the absence of written state statutes and case citations which sometimes failed fully to record the issues and arguments. Despite these considerable problems, certainly by 1835, they had produced a system of federal justice eminently fit for purpose and it all began by the justices' exercise, often unwillingly, of the circuit court jurisdiction.

The reports examined reveal that the sheer volume of work on circuit honed the skills acquired from practice at the Bar or as a judge of a state supreme court.

It was also an ideal way of familiarising themselves with branches of the law with which they had little experience. Day-to-day exposure to all manner of legal issues endowed them with the essential expertise to conduct their business in the Supreme Court more effectively and with greater self-assurance. It also made them acutely aware when sitting on appeals of local issues and pressures encountered by justices across the circuits. The circuit experience underpinned the rise of the Supreme Court from a position of weakness to an authoritative and effective department of the federal government. Further, that the expertise and confidence gained on circuit was a factor in the federal judiciary's ability to withstand political attacks by Republican opponents during the vulnerable formative years of the Marshall Court.

This investigation contributes to our knowledge of how the law was shaped in those early years through the depth of its inquiry into the legal issues facing the justices on circuit. A total of 1854 Supreme Court, circuit court and state court opinions handed down by Justices Washington, Livingston, Story and Thompson have been examined to identify the nature of the work undertaken on circuit, analyse how the justices decided the legal issues, assess the expertise gained, and evaluate the use to which skills acquired on circuit featured in their Supreme Court contributions. The study has also shown how federal justice was received on circuit; from the acceptance with acclamation by the grand juries to the charges presented by the early justices in Pennsylvania, Delaware, Massachusetts and New Hampshire to the outright rejection by the Augusta grand jury in 1791 of the need for federal justice and of federal government interference in state affairs.[1] This examination of the nature of the litigation before the justices and the way in which each justice faced the particular problems of his circuit has revealed not only constitutional attitudes but also general jurisprudence as the circuit reports cover virtually every point of law resolving issues of national importance to opinions of interest merely to the parties of the case. The reports have also disclosed the determination of all four justices to uphold existing property rights and promote inter-state and international trade and how Justices Livingston and Thompson laid down definitive guidelines for the conduct of commercial relationships, particularly in respect of negotiable instruments, the essential currency of economic prosperity.

Washington's opinions reflect an approach to stability in the justice system based on the certainty which precedent brings to the law despite the occasional injustice caused by too-rigid an application. Story's circuit opinions have shown not only a justice comfortable with all branches of law but also one whose preoccupation was to import common law principles into criminal and civil law to supplement the few federal statutes and Supreme Court authorities in order to clarify American law and make it more readily understood.

---

[1] M Marcus, Marcus (ed), *The Documentary History of the Supreme Court of the United States, 1789–1800*, 8 vols (New York: Columbia University Press, 1985–2007) vol 2, Grand Jury Responses: Pennsylvania (45); Delaware (53); Boston (61); New Hampshire (113) and Georgia (224).

A justice's circuit opinion is generally a more reliable indicator of his jurisprudence than his opinion for the Supreme Court. Whilst a justice on circuit sometimes sat with a district judge, the justice's view of the law or facts usually prevailed and the opinion occasionally expressed his personal and political views on the issues before him. This was not always the case with the Supreme Court opinion, which often required the compromise of strongly held views for unanimity. Hence, Justice Story's assessment that his character as a judge would be more accurately reflected in his circuit rather than his Supreme Court opinions.[2]

Chapter two, by examining the debates of the Constitutional and Ratification Conventions and the fierce arguments in Congress over the Judiciary Bill 1789, has highlighted the deep divisions between Federalist and Anti-Federalists. A common theme running through all debates was the Anti-Federalists' fear that a federal judicial system would undermine the authority of state courts and legislatures. They were also afraid that the Republic, under the Federalists, would be modelled on the British monarchy with government by an elite minority. The Federalists were deeply concerned that the United States was under threat of a French-style revolution because of widespread popular support within the United States for the French wish for freedom from oppression if not for the means by which they sought to achieve it. The Alien and Sedition Acts of 1798 were a knee-jerk reaction by the Federalists to the perceived possibility of civil disobedience. The justices' conduct of the criminal trials of prominent Republicans under legislation which criminalised criticism of officers of the federal government left much to be desired. The Sedition Act was a clear infringement of the right to the freedom of speech and of the press guaranteed by the 1791 First Amendment to the Constitution. Justices Paterson and Chase refused to hear arguments as to the constitutionality of the acts and their partisan conduct of the trials denied Republicans facing loss of liberty the due process of law guaranteed by the Fifth Amendment. This controversial legislation produced not only the Virginia and Kentucky Resolutions of 1798 but also adversely affected the standing of the Federalist Party in the country and was a factor in Jefferson's success in the 1800 presidential election.

These deep divisions caused by the emergence of the two political parties added to the burden of the justices on circuit. It meant that those early circuits were both legal and political experiments; legal in the sense of establishing federal justice across the nation and political in securing public support for the concept of federal justice and government. The justices' main task was the resolution of criminal cases and civil disputes between individual citizens or a citizen against a state. However, they were expected to, and did, promote the concept of a strong federal government by use of the charge to the grand jury at the commencement of each circuit sitting. Those messages were generally well received but not in those states

---

[2] Letter, Joseph Story to District Judge Hopkinson, 16 February 1840 from the Hopkinson Papers cited in R Kent Newmyer, *Supreme Court Justice Story: Statesman of the Old Republic* (Chapel Hill: University of North Carolina Press, 1985), 318.

opposing the very concept of a national government and a federal judiciary. The political element of the grand jury charge is best illustrated by the fact that Chief Justice Jay's charge to a jury in 1793 explaining why the United States refused to be drawn into European conflicts was later sent to Europe as an explanation for neutrality.[3]

Such overtly politically motivated grand jury charges in the Court's first decade gradually disappeared with the advent of John Marshall and the emerging concept of an independent judiciary; the justices confined themselves to handing down instructions on aspects of the law relevant to the grand jury's duty to issue presentments (indictments) or to those cases which the petty juries were likely to try during the current session of the court. The falling into disuse of the grand jury charge as a political tool was due, in the first instance, to the justices' fears of further impeachments of state and federal judges by the Republicans and, when that threat had disappeared by 1807, to the fact that the new federal institutions began to gain a general acceptance and there was no need to hammer home the virtues of central government.

Justices Livingston, Story and Thompson, all politically active in the Republican Party before appointment, disappointed their respective nominating presidents by failing to vigorously defend states' rights from federal encroachment. This study offers explanations for the justices' pragmatic political shifts. First, whatever political party allegiance had been formed by class and family ties, the justices came from very similar backgrounds and shared the same fundamental values. Justice Washington, the favourite nephew and heir to the President's estate, inherited his uncle's vision of future prosperity and political stability under a strong central authority. Livingston was an active politician who, despite having served as a Federalist in the New York Assembly, supported the opposition and conducted a vigorous campaign which helped carry New York for Thomas Jefferson in the 1800 presidential election. Thompson sought high political office as a member of a Republican administration. Story was a New England Republican whose commitment to the Jeffersonian vision was not as strong as that of the President's Virginian followers. The nation was finding its way, experimenting with democratic government and allegiances were fluid. Political support might waver if expectations were not met and the justices were not the only people dealing with change as shown by James Madison's political manoeuvres described in the Introduction to this volume.

Second, the federal bench and Federalist state judges were under constant threat of impeachment by Republicans under the direction of President Jefferson who lost no opportunity to undermine the judiciary both privately and in public. These attacks had the effect of uniting the Supreme Court justices, whatever their political persuasion, against all opponents. The Court at the beginning of

---

[3] Gordon S Wood, *Empire of Liberty: A History of the Early Republic, 1789–1815* (New York: Oxford University Press, 2009), 412–13.

the nineteenth century was the weakest department of government facing a ruling party which had suspended its sittings for over a year in the Judiciary Act 1802. Not only did Jefferson attack the judiciary in private correspondence at every available opportunity, he also attacked Marshall publicly in his Second Inaugural Address for his conduct of the trial of Aaron Burr for treason. He was the instigator of impeachment against state and federal court judges and connived with Republican supporters to attack the federal judiciary in the press. One can, therefore, understand why the justices united and felt the need to tread carefully in politically sensitive cases. *Marbury v Madison* is evidence of a compromise to avoid a direct confrontation with the Jefferson administration. *Stuart v Laird* is further proof of compromise when the justices, despite serious privately expressed opposition, meekly submitted to the reintroduction of circuit riding under the Judiciary Act 1802, refusing to challenge its constitutionality.[4] The Court feared retaliation from a Republican-dominated Congress.[5] The task of developing a federal judicial system was made much more difficult by this constant sniping at the judiciary. Marshall believed that the Court was the final arbiter of the meaning and intent of the Constitution and Jefferson felt strongly that it was usurping the function of executive and legislature to undermine state sovereignty.

Third, the convention of the single opinion of the Court had the effect of achieving unanimity through compromise because of the need for unity in the face of a determined opposition, resulting in all members of the Court being more amenable to the general view. The fact that, for the greater part of the Marshall era, the justices conducted their deliberations in the same lodging house in which they all resided during term time, made lasting friendships and facilitated unanimity is apparent from Story's description of judicial conferences. Whilst a justice may still have maintained the same views he held as an advocate or state justice, he was less strident in expressing them through the medium of a dissent. The relaxed and friendly atmosphere of lodging house conferences appears from a conversation Story had with a Harvard graduate in 1826 describing their convivial spirit. Story spoke of the justices' general rule that they would take wine only when it rained. Marshall would make the following request, 'Brother Story, step to the window and see if it does not look like rain'. Story added that if the sun was shining brightly the Chief Justice would sometimes reply, 'All the better; for our jurisdiction extends over such a large territory that it must be raining somewhere.'[6]

---

[4] *Stuart v Laird*, 5 US 299 (1803).
[5] Chief Justice Marshall doubted the constitutionality of Supreme Court Justices sitting as circuit judges and Justice Chase was firmly against it. However Justices Cushing, Paterson and Washington felt that as it had been the practice for a number of years, it was too late to object (see letters of the justices between April and June 1802 in Hobson, *Papers of John Marshall*, vol 6, 108–21). The extremely short opinion handed down by Justice Paterson in *Stuart v Laird* did not touch upon any constitutional issues and expressly stated that because the justices had been acting as circuit judges for so long, it was an established practice which could not be challenged.
[6] Josiah Quincy, *Figures of the Past from the Leaves of Old Journals* (Boston: Roberts Bros, 1883), 189–90.

Whilst the justices each held firmly in mind the need for consistency across circuits, they approached the task in different ways. The circuit reports examined in chapter three establish that Justice Washington's judicial philosophy was dominated by the need for a uniformity of law and procedure flowing from strict adherence to the doctrine of legal precedent. He searched English law and state authorities to find grounds for an opinion, expressing anxiety if he was obliged to deliver an opinion devoid of past authority. He believed that a strict following of past decisions was essential to preserving existing land titles and the sanctity of contracts and, if this approach resulted in occasional injustices, it was for government to solve the problem.

Livingston's attitude towards precedent, as chapter four demonstrates, was markedly different. Whilst he believed that precedent was essential for stability, his reported circuit cases show less enthusiasm for the doctrine than those of Washington. Wherever possible, Livingston preferred state supreme court opinions to the English authorities, taking pride in the emerging body of United States law. One detects an antipathy towards the English authorities. He had less reason than the other justices to admire England because of his capture and imprisonment by the British on the voyage home from Spain in 1782 and the later condemnation by the British of two vessels with cargo in which he had a heavy financial interest. Livingston, like John Marshall, preferred to found his opinions on general principles of law rather than the culmination of an exhaustive study of the citing of past cases.

Whilst on federal circuit, Thompson drew heavily on state supreme court authorities of which he had great experience given his 16-year tenure as a New York Supreme Court Justice. He was more willing than Livingston to import English precedents into the growing body of American law. Story's circuit opinions have revealed a readiness to mine any source of law which would enhance the authority of his decisions. He, therefore, looked to state law, the works of European jurists and had the highest regard for the decisions of English judges and textbook writers. His circuit opinions were erudite, reviewed every relevant authority and were held in high regard by his brother justices.

Wherever possible, the justices followed the opinions of state supreme courts. Washington was prepared to follow a state opinion even though he was not sure it was correct because of his desire for harmonious federal and state jurisdictional relationships.[7] Livingston and Thompson were kindly disposed to guidance from that quarter, having sat as state supreme court justices. When Thompson handed down his opinion in the federal circuit court case of *Vermont v The Society for the Propagation of the Gospel* he cited no fewer than 24 New York State supreme court opinions.[8] Story circuit opinions cite numerous state court decisions. His approach arose not only for the sake of comity but also from the perspective of

---

[7] *Mott v Maris*, 17 F Cas 905 (1808).
[8] *Vermont v The Society for the Propagation of the Gospel*, 28 F Cas 1155 (1827).

public policy and public interest in avoiding conflicting opinions of federal and state judges.[9] When delivering the Supreme Court's opinion in *Bell v Morrison*, Story followed his practice on circuit and declared that the local rules of interpretation of state statutes must be presumed to be founded on a more just and accurate view of the local jurisprudence.[10] He was arguing that state courts and legislatures were best placed to identify and provide solutions to local problems and, therefore, ought to be considered with respect. However, with the advent of an increasing body of federal legislation and Supreme Court authorities, the need to look elsewhere for guidance diminished.

The advent of the professional law reporter made the justice's task much easier, but the reports whether at circuit or Supreme Court level, had to be full and accurate. Story emphasised this when writing to the Supreme Court law reporter, Henry Wheaton, who had failed to record that Livingston and Story had dissented in *Mutual Assurance Society v Taylor*. Story was concerned lest the case be later treated as a unanimous holding.[11]

The justices' letters, particularly those of Joseph Story, reveal that when they met in Washington, either on the Court or in their lodging house, they conferred and exchanged experiences of particular problems, how they had been resolved and sought advice on future cases in their circuit lists. They wrote letters seeking advice on unfamiliar topics. The exchange of semi-annual reports between Justices Washington and Story of interesting cases they had decided on their respective circuits is particularly important in the quest for consistency.[12]

A further means of achieving uniformity was the use of the certificate of division of opinion when there was a disagreement between the justice and the district judge as to the applicable law. In this way the circuit court was able to send the case to the Supreme Court for a definitive ruling on a troublesome issue which regularly faced the circuit courts. This device was so useful that, on occasion, the justices feigned disagreement to have the law clarified. Thus, in *DeLovio v Boit*, Story and District Judge Davis agreed to disagree on the extent of the federal courts' jurisdiction in admiralty matters.[13] In the event, Story was disappointed because the parties accepted his view and did not take the matter further. He adopted the same ploy in *Dartmouth College v Woodward*.[14]

A comparison of circuit and Supreme Court opinions has revealed that some justices, because of local issues or the location of their circuit centres, achieved

---

[9] *United States v Slade*, 27 F Cas 1125 (1820).

[10] *Bell v Morrison*, 26 US 351 (1828).

[11] Letter, Story to Wheaton, 31 August 1816 in Story, WW (ed), *Life and Letters of Joseph Story*, 2 vols. (London: John Chapman, 1851), vol 1, 153.

[12] Letters, Bushrod Washington to Joseph Story of 19 June 1821 and 4 December 1821 in Joseph Story Papers. Massachusetts Historical Society, Boston, cited in G Edward White, *History of the Supreme Court of the United States, vols III–IV, The Marshall Court and Cultural Change, 1815–1835* (New York: Cambridge University Press, 2010, originally published by Macmillan, 1988), 348.

[13] *DeLovio v Boit*, 7 F Cas 441.

[14] *Trustees of Dartmouth College v Woodward*, 64 New Hamp 473 (1817).

expertise in certain branches of the law which affected the Chief Justice's opinion assignment practice. Provided a justice's view of a case coincided with that of the majority, the Chief Justice considered him a candidate for authorship of the majority opinion. The opinions of the Court assigned to each justice reveal a great disparity; for example, Justice Story positioned himself as a frequent volunteer for the task, whilst Justices Todd and Duvall maintained a very low profile. A factor just as important as a willingness to write was John Marshall's awareness of the special expertise gained by his associates on circuit. That he knew his associates' strengths has been established in his letters to Justices Washington and Story requesting guidance on unfamiliar branches of law.

There is a definite correlation between circuit expertise and opinion assignment practice. The state and federal circuit court opinions of Livingston reveal a preponderance of maritime or commercial opinions. On the Supreme Court, out of a total of 36 majority opinions he was asked to write, all but one concerned maritime or commercial law. Thompson's state and federal circuit opinions demonstrate his specialities as commercial and land law. On the Court he was asked to write 59 opinions, 13 of which concerned commercial disputes and ten involved the disposition of lands. Of the commercial disputes nine covered his practice of setting guidelines for the regulation of promissory notes and bills of exchange. The majority of the remaining opinions related to procedural and jurisdictional issues.

An analysis of Washington's 520 circuit cases shows he sat on 215 admiralty cases and land disputes. On the Supreme Court he handed down 80 opinions of the Court of which 35 involved admiralty and wills, far more than any other branch of law he dealt with on the Court. Story presided over many admiralty, land and commercial cases on circuit but admiralty disputes in the busy port of Boston constituted his main source of work. His authority in admiralty cases was reflected in the large number of Supreme Court opinions he was chosen to deliver. Out of a total of 252 admiralty opinions, the Chief Justice reserved 90 to himself, which meant that Story wrote 35 per cent of the remainder. It follows, therefore, that circuit expertise was the major factor in deciding who had the Chief Justice's confidence to draw other justices together, not just to join in the result but also to persuade them to accept the reasoning behind the holding. The circuit experience meant that the Court's authority was enhanced by a justice writing the opinion who was expert in the relevant branch of law.

The remaining chapters examined the day-to-day workload of a justice on circuit to gain an insight into the events and problems of the Early Republic. Each chapter has also examined the value of circuit experience to the Supreme Court opinion as well as focusing on particular aspects of each justice's jurisprudence and the part his specialities played in shaping United States law. Story's assessment of Washington as 'a good old fashioned Federalist' with 'a cautious mind' who was 'distinguished for his moderation', has been confirmed on numerous occasions by his circuit court and Supreme Court opinions which also reveal his view that interests of individual states were secondary to those of the nation as a whole.

Evidence of his conservative Federalism has also emerged from his preservation of existing property rights and the formulation of rules facilitating interstate and international trade in manufactured goods as the means of achieving economic prosperity as opposed to the Republican desire for national wealth through agrarian self-sufficiency.[15]

Despite the occasional injustice resulting from a rigid adherence to the doctrine of precedent, it is generally accepted that a system which enables a reasonably reliable prediction of the outcome of litigation is far preferable to attempting to forecast the whims of particular judges. Counsel in Philadelphia and Trenton who researched the authorities would be well placed to advise their clients appearing in Washington's circuit courts of the prospects of success because of his strict application of precedent. The research has also revealed how Washington's view of his own slaves, as items of personal property to be disposed of as and when he saw fit, influenced his judicial stance on slavery when he expressed himself unable to comprehend that removing a slave from one 'owner' to another in a far distant land did not worsen the slave's plight.

Even if Justice Washington had had a more enlightened view of slavery it is unlikely he would have made an impression on this troubled issue as the other justices felt constrained both by the Constitution and the Fugitive Slave Act 1793 to endorse the status quo. The cases show that the justices rigorously enforced the 1808 prohibition on the international slave trade but apart from freeing a slave who had accompanied his owner to a non-slave state and resided there beyond a permitted period, the justices made no impact whatsoever on the institution of slavery within the United States which was not formally abolished until the Thirteenth Amendment in 1865.[16]

Livingston's politics reflected the fluidity of party allegiances in the early Republic as did his approach to the delicate balancing of state sovereignty and the powers of the federal government. His state and federal circuit opinions on commercial law underpinned the status of partnership and inspired confidence in the commercial world by setting out the rights and responsibilities of drawers, indorsees and payees of bills of exchange and promissory notes, the cornerstone of trade payments. Before Story arrived on the scene, Livingston was the Court's leading authority in maritime law dealing mainly with breaches of embargo and forfeiture of vessels for contravening licensing regulations.

Story mastered every branch of law to which he turned his hand, but among the most important aspects of his shaping of United States law were his repeated efforts to import English common law into federal law. He was firmly of the view

---

[15] Thomas Jefferson, 'Notes on the State of Virginia, Query XIX, The Present State of Manufactures, Commerce, Interior and Exterior Trade, 1787 in Merrill D Peterson (ed), *Thomas Jefferson: Writings* (New York: Library of America, 1984), 290–91. Jefferson believed that the United States should import manufactured goods from Europe and that Americans should farm as 'those who labour on the land are the chosen people of God'.

[16] *Prigg v Pennsylvania*, 41 US 539 (1842); Constitution, Article IV, Section 1, Clause 3.

that a common law of federal crime was necessary because of the government's failure to enact laws covering all aspects of criminality on land and at sea.[17] Whilst his efforts on circuit and on the Supreme Court to establish a common law jurisdiction failed in respect of criminal and admiralty matters, he was successful in realising his ambition when he established in *Swift v Tyson* a federal common law in commercial disputes in diversity cases where the parties to an action came from different states.[18] He overcame the rejection of his plan for a federal common law of crime by drafting a criminal code which later saw life as the Crimes Act 1825 which set out comprehensively and clearly the federal criminal law then in force.

Thompson's state, federal circuit and Supreme Court opinions highlight the pressures facing a justice attempting to balance the powers of the federal government with the right of a state to control its own affairs. His approach stemmed from a lack of separation of powers in New York State where he sat as a judge and also on the Council of Revision where he was tasked with the approval of state legislative bills. Generally unwilling to strike down such legislation, he promoted state sovereignty wherever possible or at least attempted to achieve concurrent powers. However, with so few dissents, he did not fulfil President Monroe's expectations and, all too often, succumbed to the collegiate unanimity of the Court.

From time to time a public figure will challenge mainstream opinion and speak as the nation's conscience for an oppressed minority, despite determined opposition to such humanitarian views. Justice Thompson was one such person. The federal government, led by President Andrew Jackson and the State of Georgia were determined to drive the Cherokees from their homeland in Georgia across the Mississippi to the wastelands of Oklahoma. The majority of the nation either agreed with this 'removal' policy or were indifferent to the fate of this, the most 'civilized' tribe of Native Americans. Thompson's endeavour to shape federal law to protect minorities is demonstrated by his powerful dissent in favour of the Cherokees in *Cherokee Nation v Georgia* and constituted the foundation of the Court's enlightened approach towards the Cherokees in the later opinion of *Worcester v Georgia*.[19] The Cherokee cases are noteworthy not only as evidence of a humanitarian side to Thompson's jurisprudence but also as an example of a justice setting aside his belief in state sovereignty in an attempt to halt a state's oppression of a particularly vulnerable minority group.

In addition to identifying the sources from which federal law was fashioned and highlighting particular aspects of each justice's part in the law's development, the circuit opinions shed light on the way in which the nation was changing in this period and how emerging issues were faced. The opinions have revealed how the circuit justices formulated commercial law in an expanding economy.

---

[17] Letter, Story to Nathaniel Williams, 3 August 1813 complaining about the 'deficiencies of our criminal code' and requesting Williams to put pressure on his representative in Congress and to use the press to remedy the lack of legislative diligence. WW Story, *Life and Letters*, vol 1, 246–47.

[18] *Swift v Tyson*, 41 US 1 (1842).

[19] *Cherokee Nation v Georgia*, 30 US 1 (1831). *Worcester v Georgia*, 31 US 515 (1832).

The opinions of Justices Washington, Story and Thompson have also disclosed how they promoted an important aspect of trade by protecting the working conditions, pay, health and general well-being of seamen, making it clear that fully manned vessels were essential for interstate and international commerce and for the protection of the Union.[20]

Challenges to land titles arising from the need to accommodate a rapidly increasing population formed an appreciable part of Washington's circuit docket where the absence of man-made boundaries or failure to survey or register land led to numerous possession actions. The opinions of all four justices reveal a determination to uphold existing property rights in land.[21]

The numerous embargo and non-intercourse circuit court opinions expose the vulnerability of the United States during the period of hostile relations with Britain prior to and during the War of 1812. The cases show how rigorously the justices enforced the trade prohibitions by handing down opinions forfeiting the vessel and cargo of any owner or master who ventured to disregard the regulations. They were obliged by the nature of their office to take such draconian action despite the fact that the legislation had little impact apart on Britain and severely damaged United States trade interests.

The circuit opinions also reveal extremely politically volatile cases which aroused great local public agitation such as Justice Washington's criminal trial of the Pennsylvanian general who, on the orders of his state governor, had by force of arms prevented a United States marshal from serving a federal court writ.[22] Washington's consideration of the right of a state to protect its natural resources from outsiders also had far-reaching consequences.[23] A most troublesome and politically sensitive circuit case was the trial of President Jefferson's former Vice-President Aaron Burr for treason. Chief Justice Marshall, presiding, declared it the most difficult case he had ever met when he called upon his associates for assistance on the relevant law.[24] Whilst some of the work of the justices on circuit was mundane, on occasion they faced issues of national importance which prepared them for duty on the Supreme Court.

The examination of this large number of state, federal circuit and Supreme Court opinions of four prominent Marshall associate justices reveals many important factors in the development of law in the Early Republic. It has demonstrated the sources from which the justices on circuit established a uniform system of law across the nation to resolve everyday disputes and inspire confidence in the federal court system. The justices' opinions, however, reveal much more than that because they are windows on those crucial events in the nation's history such as

---

[20] *The George*, 10 F Cas 205 (1832). *United States v Hatch*, 26 F Cas 220 (1824).
[21] *Milligan v Dickson et al*, 17 F Cas 376 (1817). *Barker v Jackson*, 2 F Cas 811 (1826).
[22] *United States v Bright*, 24 Fed Cas 1232 (1809).
[23] *Corfield v Coryell*, 6 Fed Cas 546 (1823).
[24] *United States v Burr*, 25 F Cas 30 (1807). Letter Marshall to Justice Cushing, 29 June 1807, in Hobson, *Papers of John Marshall*, vol VII, 60–2.

its vulnerability to hostile European powers, the expansion of commerce, and the thirst for land to accommodate a rapidly expanding population, one aspect of which was the displacement of the Cherokees. The continued struggle for power between the federal government and the demand of the states to govern their own affairs constantly features in the circuit and Supreme Court law reports.

There have been a number of questions addressed in this study which firmly establishes its main argument that the federal circuit courts were the foundation of United States law because it was in that jurisdiction that the justices shaped every aspect of federal law and procedure. This detailed examination of so many circuit court opinions has demonstrated how they managed that difficult task and the benefit of that experience to their Supreme Court functions. The day-to-day work of the circuit court gave the justices the expertise and authority to better perform their duties on the Supreme Court and the confidence to resist those who, in its formative years, sought to restrict its powers.

Whilst this study acknowledges the enormous contribution of Chief Justice John Marshall to the development of United States law, it begins the long overdue process of evaluating the circuit courts' role in the general acceptance of and rise in influence of the United States federal court system. The examination of the opinions of four prominent Marshall Court associate justices establishes the circuit court as vital to the federal court system because, in those very early years, it was the circuit experience and not the Supreme Court which shaped United States law and prepared each justice for a more informed discharge of his duty on the nation's highest tribunal. These justices found American law a skeleton at the beginning of the nineteenth-century. Their work in the circuit courts at the very beginning of the federal court experiment and later in their duties on the Supreme Court as that tribunal's workload increased, left a fully formed body of federal law to which later generations have added. That structure is still recognisable today and it is the legacy of which the circuit work of Justices Washington, Livingston, Story, and Thompson is a crucial and central part.

# APPENDIX A: REVERSAL RATES

An analysis of the reversal rates by the United States Supreme Court cases during the chief justiceship of John Marshall between 1801 and 1835 of appeals and writs of error from state courts and federal district and circuit courts with the reversal rates of individual justices and the number of division of opinions between the justices and their district judges.

These figures are based on the opinions contained in volumes 1–34 of the United States Reports. During this period the Court heard 1,236 applications, appeals or writs of error, reaching final opinions in 990 cases. The remaining hearings involved interlocutory procedural applications or were continued by the court for further proof. The opinions of the Court ranged from cases of great constitutional import to decisions of little consequence beyond the parties involved. It must be borne in mind that the appeals constituted only a minute proportion of the workload of the 'inferior' federal courts and state courts.

## Reversal rates

The Court reversed 421 state and federal court opinions out of its 990 final opinions, a reversal rate of 45.52 per cent. This seems rather high but it must be remembered that there was little to guide the judges by way of US Statute Law or Supreme Court precedents in those early days. Furthermore, the quality of the judges varied and the absence of law reporting and the dearth of law libraries on circuit would not help matters. Fresh evidence would, from time to time, come to light on appeal vitiating the original opinion but this did not often occur.

## District of Columbia Circuit Courts

Established by Congress in 1801, they had the same jurisdiction as the US Circuit Courts but were staffed by circuit judges not Supreme Court justices. Appeals from these courts accounted for just over one quarter of the Supreme Court's business, 323 of the 1,236 hearings. Of the 323 cases, four were jurisdictional points dependent upon the amount in issue or the status of the parties and three related to a certificate of divided opinion between the judges requesting guidance from the Court on the applicable law. Of the remaining 316 appeals, 131 were reversed, a reversal rate of 41.45 per cent.

## State Courts

64 cases, 23 reversals (35.93%)

## Federal District Courts

This category includes those district courts exercising the jurisdiction of a circuit court. The district judges did not fare well on average having been reversed more times than they were affirmed, a reversal rate of 58.2 per cent from a total of 91 appeals.

## Federal Circuit Courts

These courts, staffed by a local district judge and a Supreme Court justice sitting as a circuit judge, accounted for 519 appeals with 211 reversals (40.46%). The marked difference between the reversal rates of the federal district courts and circuit courts must be accounted for by the greater experience of the justices and their awareness, because of the nature of their duties, of the precedents of the Court and of trends in their colleagues' circuit opinions.

# Reversal rates of 15 Supreme Court justices between 1801 and 1835

**Alfred Moore. 6th Circuit. Georgia and South Carolina 1802–1804**

3 appeals, 2 reversals (66.66%).

**William Cushing. 1st Circuit. Massachusetts, Maine, Rhode Island and New Hampshire. 1801–1810**

10 appeals, 6 reversals (60%).

**William Johnson. 6th Circuit. 1804–1834**

54 appeals, 31 reversals (57.4%).

**Samuel Chase. 4th Circuit. Delaware and Maryland 1802–1811**

17 appeals, 8 reversals (47.06%).

**Thomas Todd. 7th Circuit. Kentucky, Ohio & Tennessee 1807-1826**

97 appeals, 42 reversals (43.3%).

**Gabriel Duvall. 4th Circuit. 1811–1835**

74 appeals, 31 reversals (41.89%).

**Robert Trimble. 7th Circuit. 1826–1828**

27 appeals, 11 reversals (40.74%).

**John McLean. 7th Circuit. 1829–1835**

46 appeals, 18 reversals (39.13%).

**Joseph Story. 1st Circuit. 1811–1835**

60 appeals, 23 reversals (38.33%).

**Henry Baldwin. 3rd Circuit. New Jersey, Philadelphia. 1830–1835**

8 appeals, 3 reversals (37.5%).

**H. Brockholst Livingston. 2nd Circuit. Connecticut, New York & Vermont. 1808-1823**

16 appeals, 6 reversals (37.5%).

**Bushrod Washington. 2nd Circuit. 1802–1803; 3rd Circuit. 1803–1829**

27 appeals, 8 reversals (29.63%).

**Chief Justice John Marshall. 5th Circuit. North Carolina & Virginia. 1801–1835**

39 appeals, 10 reversals (25.64%).

**Smith Thompson. 2nd Circuit. 1823–1835**

17 appeals, 3 reversals (17.65%).

**William Paterson. 2nd Circuit. 1803–1806**

No appeals. Just one division of opinion.

**The Court considered 99 certificates of division of opinion from the following justices:-**

Marshall (18); Todd (15); Story (14); Duvall (9); Washington (8); Johnson (7); Livingston (7); Thompson (7); McLean (6); Baldwin (3); Trimble (2): Chase (1); Paterson (1); Cushing (1).

# APPENDIX B: MAJORITY OPINIONS DELIVERED BY THE JUSTICES

## Chief Justice John Marshall

**1801–1803**. 15 of (24); **1804**, 10 (14); **1805**, 8 (14); **1806**, 19 (24); **1807**, 19 (28); **1808**, 11 (19); **1809**, 24 (32); **1810**, 32 (46); **1811**, 24 (39); **1812**, 20 (40); **1813**, 17 (46); **1814**, 15 (48); **1815**, 15 (48); **1816**, 19 (43); **1817**, 16 (42); **1818**, 12 (32); **1819**, 14 (33); **1820**, 11 (27); **1821**, 12 (42); **1822**, 15 (31); **1823**, 8 (30); **1824**, 20 (41); **1825**, 10 (28); **1826**, 12 (33); **1827**, 14 (47); **1828**, 25 (55); **1829**, 17 (44); **1830**, 19 (42); **1831**, 11 (42); **1832**, 22 (56); **1833**, 14 (41); **1834**, 33* (66); **1835**, 11 (33).

* A higher figure because Marshall had reserved to himself 13 Florida land cases.

The total number of majority opinions delivered by Marshall is 537 in 34 years.

It may be that Marshall's total should be higher as it is more likely than not that he would have delivered the opinions or decided a procedural point when the reporter has either named no judge or states the opinion was by 'the Court', as the reporter did on the following occasions:

**1801–1803**, 6; **1804**, 5; **1805**, 3; **1806**, 6; **1807**, 7; **1808**, 4; **1809**, 6; **1810**, 8; **1812**, 6; **1813**, 6; **1814**, 2; **1815**, 1; **1816**, 1; **1817**, 1; **1818**, 3; **1819**, 1; **1820**, 1; **1821**, 8; **1822**, 2; **1823**, 2; **1824**, 0; **1825**, 1; **1826**, 2; **1827**, 3; **1828**, 1; **1829**, 2; **1830**, I; **1831**, 1; **1832**, 4; **1833**, 3; **1834**, 0; **1835**, 1.

If one were to give him the benefit of these extra 98 cases, Marshall's total would increase to 635 which is just over half of the 1,236 cases reported during his 34 years in office. Marshall also took the lion's share of the prerogative writs. He gave the opinion in eight of the nine applications for *mandamus*, the ninth reported as a decision of the court. He dealt with the sole application for *certiorari* and he shared the eight applications for *habeas corpus* equally between himself and Associate Justice Joseph Story. As befitting the office of chief justice, Marshall reserved to himself the majority opinion in the more important constitutional cases such as *Marbury v Madison*, 5 US 137 (1803) the Court's power of judicial review; *Fletcher v Peck*, 10 US 87 (1810) contracts clause obligation and fraudulent sales of Georgia lands; *Trustees of Dartmouth College v Woodward*, 17 US 518 (1819) contracts clause obligation; *McCulloch v Maryland*, 17 US 316 (1819) validity of state tax on banks incorporated by Congress; *Cohens v Virginia*, 19 US 264 (1821) state lotteries; *Gibbons v Ogden*, 22 US 1 (1824) steamboat licences; *Ogden v Saunders*,

Appendix B

25 US 213 (1827) bankruptcy discharges; and the two Cherokee cases, *Cherokee Nation v Georgia*, 30 US 1 (1831) and *Worcester v Georgia*, 31 US 515.

## Majority opinions delivered by the associate justices

### William Paterson

1 opinion in *Stuart v Laird*, 5 US 299 (1803), Marshall did not take part as he gave the opinion in the circuit court.

### William Johnson

**1805**, 2; **1806**, 0; **1807**, 1; **1808**, 2; **1809**, 0; **1810**, 2; **1812**, 3; **1813**, 4; **1814**, 7; **1815**, 3; **1816**, 7; **1817**, 8; **1818**, 4; **1819**, 5; **1820**, 5; **1821**, 7; **1822**, 2; **1823**, 5; **1824**, 4; **1825**, 5; **1826**, 4; **1827**, 6; **1828**, 5; **1829**, 6; **1830**, 6; **1831**, 4; **1832**, 0; **1833**, 4; **1834**, 0.

112 majority opinions in 29 years. He dissented on 34 occasions. All of the other justices together dissented only 40 times.

### William Cushing

**1801-1803**, 0; **1804**. 1; **1805**, 0; **1806**, 0; **1807**, 0; **1808**, 1; **1809**, 2; **1810**, 0.

Four majority opinions in ten years.

### Joseph Story

**1812**, 2; **1813**, 7; **1814**, 10; **1815**, 7; **1816**, 9; **1817**, 8; **1818**, 4; **1819**, 9; **1820**, 3; **1821**, 7; **1822**, 6; **1823**, 9; **1824**, 11; **1825**, 7; **1826**, 5; **1827**, 9; **1828**, 7; **1829**, 11; **1830**, 3; **1831**, 7; **1832**, 13; **1833**, 8; **1834**, 7; **1835**, 10.

179 opinions in 24 years.

### Bushrod Washington

**1809**, 1; **1810**, 2; **1812**, 5; **1813**, 4; **1814**, 7; **1815**, 4; **1816**, 3; **1817**, 8; **1818**, 4; **1819**, 2; **1820**, 3; **1821**, 0; **1822**, 2; **1823**, 3; **1824**, 6; **1825**, 3; **1826**, 4; **1827**, 3; **1828**, 1; **1829**, 5.

70 majority opinions in 20 years.

### H. Brockholst Livingston

**1807–1808**, 0; **1809**, 1; **1810**, 3; **1812**, 1; **1813**, 6; **1814**, 4; **1815**, 5; **1816**, 1; **1817**, 0; **1818**, 4; **1819**, 1; **1820**, 3; **1821**, 6; **1822**, 3; **1823**, 1.

39 Majority opinions in 16 years.

## Smith Thompson

**1824**, 3; **1825**, 2; **1826**, 4; **1827**, 4, **1828**, 6; **1829**, 2; **1830**, 5; **1831**, 4; **1832**, 9; **1833**, 6; **1834**, 8; **1835**, 4.

57 majority opinions in 12 years.

## Henry Baldwin

**1830**, 6; **1831**, 4; **1832**, 1; **1833-34**, 0; **1835**, 1.

12 majority opinions in six years.

## Samuel Chase

**1801–1811**. Only one majority opinion in 11 years (in 1810).

## Gabriel Duvall

**1812**, 2; **1813**, 2; **1814**, 2; **1815–16**, 0; **1817**, 1; **1818**, 1; **1819**, 1; **1820–1822**, 0; **1823**, 1; **1824**, 1; **1825**, 0; **1826**, 1; **1827**, 0; **1828**, 3; **1829**, 1; **1830–1834**, 0.

16 majority opinions, less than one of each of the 24 years on the Court. There were 11 years when he delivered no majority opinions.

## Alfred Moore

**1801–1804**. No majority opinions, but this was during a period when Marshall delivered virtually all such opinions.

## Thomas Todd

**1812**, 1; **1813**, 0; **1814**, 1; **1815**, 0; **1816**, 3; **1817**, 0; **1818**, 2; **1819**, 0; **1820**, 1; **1821**, 2; **1822**, 1; **1823**, 0; **1824**, 1; **1825-26**, 0.

He was five years on the Court before he delivered his first majority opinion and that was on a certificate of division between himself and the district judge on circuit.

12 majority opinions in 15 years.

## Robert Trimble

**1827**, 7; **1828**, 7.

14 majority opinions in just two years.

John McLean

**1829**, 0; **1830**, 6; **1831**, 7; **1832**, 8; **1833**, 5; **1834**, 11; **1835**, 7.

44 majority opinions in seven years.

# Seriatim opinions during the Marshall years

During the chief justiceships of John Jay (1789–1795) and Oliver Ellsworth (1796–1800) opinions were generally delivered seriatim commencing with the most junior associate. However, the Jay Court occasionally used the device of the opinion of the Court.[1] The Ellsworth Court delivered a single opinion more often.[2] Although John Marshall did not initiate the single opinion of the Court, he made it his opinion delivery method of choice. There were very few seriatim opinions in the early years of his office as he took the view that a single opinion of the Court would carry much more weight with Congress, the administration and the general public than conflicting seriatim views. Seriatim opinions prevailed on the rare occasions when Marshall recused himself because he had presided over the circuit court to which the writ of error was directed[3] or when he had a personal interest in the outcome.[4] The reports demonstrate that Marshall dominated the opinion delivery of the Court although, of necessity, when he was unable to attend Court the senior associate justice would deliver the opinion of the Court.[5]

---

[1] Examples are: *Glass v The Sloop Betsey*, 3 US 6 (1794), 'Mr Chief Justice Jay delivered a unanimous opinion; *United States v Lawrence*, 3 US Reports, 42 (1795), Opinion 'By the Court' (*mandamus*).

[2] Examples are: *Hills v Ross*, 3 US 184 (1796); *McDonough v Dannery*, 3 US 188 (1796); *United States v La Vengeance*, 3 US 297 (1796); *Mossman v Higginson*, 4 US Reports, 12 (1800); *Williamson v Kincaid*, 4 US 20 (1800); *Blair v Miller*, 4 US 21 (1800); *Priestman v United States*, 4 US 28 (1800).

[3] *Lambert's Lessee v Payne*, 7 US 97 (1805); *Randolph v Ware*, 7 US 503 (1806).

[4] *Marine Insurance Co of Alexandria v Wilson*, 7 US Reports, 187 (1805); *Marine Insurance Co of Alexandria v Tucker*, 7 US 357 (1806); *Hodgson v Marine Insurance Co of Alexandria*, 9 US 100 (1809). Marshall held stock in the insurance company.

[5] Justice Washington delivered three opinions of the Court in the February 1812 term. Marshall missed the arguments having been injured when his coach overturned en route to Washington. *Hudson v Guestier*, 11 US Reports, 1 (1812); *Fitzsimons v Ogden*, 11 US Reports, 2 (1812); *Brig James Wells v United States*, 11 US 22 (1812).

# APPENDIX C: LEGAL EDUCATION AND PRIOR JUDICIAL EXPERIENCE OF UNITED STATES SUPREME COURT JUSTICES 1801–1835

*The core information is taken from two volumes of the Oliver Wendell Holmes, Devise History of the Supreme Court of the United States with additional material from other credited sources.*

Volume II, Part I, *Foundations of Power: John Marshall, 1801–1815* (1981) is edited by George Lee Haskins. He deals with Cushing, Paterson, Chase, Washington, Moore and Marshall who were members of the Court in 1801 (pp 84–106), asserting that 'all were competent lawyers, and all, save for Marshall, whose judicial career had barely begun, had proved to be competent judges' (p 85).

I have been unable to ascertain any prior judicial office held by Paterson or Washington. John Marshall did have previous judicial experience. From 1785 to 1788 he was Recorder of Richmond City Hustings Court, the predecessor of the current Richmond Circuit Court.

(Available at: https://sharepoint.richmondgov.com/circuitcourt/history/default.aspx, last accessed 20 June 2011).

Herbert A Johnson in Part II of *Foundations of Power* deals with Johnson, Livingston, Todd, Duvall and Story (pp 389–94).

In the Holmes Devise History Vols III–IV, *The Marshall Court and Cultural Change, 1815–1835*, G Edward White gives the backgrounds of Justices Thompson, Trimble, McLean, Baldwin, and Wayne.

## Fifteen Justices with tenure and age upon appointment to the Court

*William Cushing 1790–1810 (57)*

Graduate of Harvard in 1751. Read law in Boston in the office of Jeremiah Gridley. Admitted to the Bar in 1755. Judge of the Massachusetts Superior Court.

*William Paterson 1793–1806 (47)*

Graduate of College of New Jersey (now Princeton University) in 1763. Studied law under Richard Stockton. Admitted to New Jersey Bar in 1769. He was

Attorney General of New Jersey and later Governor of New York. I can find no mention anywhere of prior judicial experience.

*Samuel Chase 1796–1811 (54)*

Educated in the classics by his father. Studied law in the offices of Hammond and Hall in Annapolis. Admitted to Bar in 1791. Chief Judge of the General Court of Maryland, 1791–1796.

*Bushrod Washington 1801–1829 (36).*

Graduate of the College of William & Mary in 1778. Later attended George Wythe's law lectures at the same college. Studied law in Philadelphia in the offices of James Wilson. Admitted to the Virginia Bar. No prior judicial experience.

*Alfred Moore 1800–1804 (44).*

Educated in Boston. Later studied some law under his father but seems to have acquired most of his learning on his own. Justice of the Superior Court of North Carolina.

*Chief Justice John Marshall 1801–1835 (45)*

Tutored at home and later by a local clergyman, Archibald Campbell. Attended three months of lectures by George Wythe at William & Mary in 1780. Admitted to Bar 1780. Secretary of State under President John Adams. Recorder of Richmond City Hustings Court.

*William Johnson 1804–1834 (32)*

Graduate of the College of New Jersey (Princeton) in 1790. Studied law in the Charleston law office of Charles Pinckney. Admitted to Bar in 1793. One of three judges of the Court of Common Pleas, the highest court of South Carolina.

*H. Brockholst Livingston 1807–1823 (49)*

Graduate of College of New Jersey (Princeton) in 1774. Studied law with Peter Yates in Albany. Admitted to the Bar in 1783. Judge of the New York Supreme Court 1802–1807.

*Thomas Todd 1807–1826 (42)*

Graduate of Liberty Hall, Lexington, Virginia (now Washington & Lee University) in 1783. Following graduation he was invited to live with his late mother's cousin, Harry Innes, a distinguished Virginia lawyer and later a judge. In exchange for board and lodgings and a legal education, Todd tutored Innes's daughters.

(Clare Cushman (ed), *The Supreme Court Justices: Illustrated Biographies, 1789–1999* (Washington DC: Congressional Quarterly, 1993), 77. Admitted to the Bar in 1788. Justice of Kentucky Court of Appeals, 1801–1806. (Chief Justice, 1806).

### Gabriel Duvall 1811–1835 (58)

Educated locally. Commenced study of law under the tuition of John Hall, an eminent Annapolis attorney. Judge of the Maryland General Court, 1796–1802. (Marlborough Gazette, 18 February 1857).

### Joseph Story 1811–1845 (32)

Graduate Harvard College, 1798. Read law in the offices of Samuel Sewell and Samuel Putnam. Admitted to the Bar in 1801. No prior judicial experience.

### Smith Thompson 1823–1843 (55)

Graduate. Princeton University, 1788. Read law in the Poughkeepsie office of James Kent from 1788–1792. Judge of the New York Supreme Court 1802 (Chief Justice, 1814). (Gerald T Dunne, 'Smith Thompson,' in Friedman and Israel (eds), *Justices of the United States Supreme Court, 1789–1978: Their Lives and Major Opinions* (New York: Chelsea House Publishers, 1980), 475–509.

### Robert Trimble 1826–1828 (49)

Graduate of Transylvania University. Read law in the offices of George Nicholas and James Brown. Judge of Kentucky Supreme Court, 1807. Federal District Judge for Eastern Kentucky, 1817–1826.

### John McLean 1830–1861 (43)

Neighbourhood Schools. In 1804 began two years of study with John S Gano, a Cincinnati lawyer who was also clerk of the Hamilton County Court of Common Pleas. He also studied in the office of Arthur St Clair Jnr. Admitted to the Bar in 1807. Judge of the Ohio Supreme Court 1816–1822. (Frank Otto Gatell, 'John Mclean' in Friedman and Israel, 535–67).

### Henry Baldwin 1830–1844 (49)

Graduate of Yale College, 1797. Obtained a clerkship in the office of Alexander J Dallas, a leading Philadelphia lawyer. Joined the Allegheny Bar in 1801. No prior judicial experience. (Gatell, 571–98).

### James M Wayne 1835–1867 (44)

Graduated, BA College of New Jersey in 1808. Read law with a local attorney in Savannah, with Judge Charles Chauncey of New Haven, Connecticut, and with

*Appendix C*

his brother-in-law, Richard Stites. After an examination in open court he was admitted to the Bar in January 1811. Judge of Savannah Court of Common Pleas, 1820. Judge of the Superior Court of Georgia, 1822. (Clare Cushman, (ed), *The Supreme Court Justices: Illustrated Biographies, 1789–1999* (Washington DC: Congressional Quarterly, 1993) 111–15.

# Conclusions

1. All 15 appointees were lawyers.
2. Some were educated at local schools or by family, friends or local clergymen. Others went to college and received the standard classical education. Two had the benefit of George Wythe's lectures at William and Mary College. None followed the earlier practice of study at the Inns of Court in London, no doubt due to the strained relations between the United States and Britain and/or or lack of funds.
3. All save for Paterson, Washington, Story and Baldwin had varying prior judicial experience.
4. There seems to be no ideal age for appointment which ranged from Story at 32 to Duvall at 58.
5. All apart from Moore and Marshall served an apprenticeship with a practising attorney.
6. The appointments were made on a geographic basis to ensure that all areas of the country were represented on the Court.

# BIBLIOGRAPHY

## Primary Sources

### Bushrod Washington Papers

Duke University. Legal, financial and family correspondence, 1686–1828.
Harvard Law School Library. Letters and legal opinion, 1798–1823.
Mount Vernon Ladies Association of the Union. Personal and family correspondence, 1788–1829.
Bushrod Washington letters contained in the *Papers of George Washington Digital Edition* (Charlottesville: University of Virginia Press, 2008).

### Henry Brockholst Livingston Papers

New York State Library. Brockholst Livingston and Henry Livingston Papers, 1751–1833.

### Joseph Story Papers

Library of Congress. Papers, 1807–1843.
Massachusetts Historical Society. Papers, 1797–1857.
William L. Clements Library, University of Michigan. Papers, 1794–1843.

### Smith Thompson Papers

Library of Congress. Papers, 1765–1831
New York Historical Society. Correspondence, 1796–1843
Princeton University. Selected letters, 1775–1843

### Andrew Jackson Papers

Letters passing between Andrew Jackson and Smith Thompson. Library of Congress, Series 1, General Correspondence.

## Founding Documents

Declaration of Independence 1776
Articles of Confederation 1781
United States Constitution 1788
Bill of Rights 1791

## Statutes and Treaties

Paris Peace Treaty 1783
Treaty of Hopewell 1786 (Cherokee Nation)
Judiciary Act 1789
Crimes Act 1790
Treaty of Holston 1791 (Cherokee Nation)
Fugitive Slave Act 1793
Judiciary Act 1793
Jay Treaty 1794
Alien & Sedition Acts 1798
Judiciary Act 1801
Judiciary Act 1802
Non-Intercourse Act 1809
Embargo Act 1807
Slave Act 1807
Trading with the Enemy Act 1812
Embargo Act 1813
Judiciary Act 1891 (Evarts Act)

## Law Reports

*United States Reports, 1790–1835.*
*Federal Cases, 1789–1880*, 30 vols plus index (West Publishing Company, 1894–1897).
Caines, George, *Law Reports of the New York Supreme Court, 1803–1805*, 3 vols, 3rd ed. Revised by William G Banks (New York: Banks & Bros, Law Publishers, 1883–1885).
Gallison, John (ed), *First Circuit Reports, 1812–1815*, 5 vols (Boston: Wells & Lilly, 1815–1817).
Johnson, William, *Law Reports of the New York Supreme Court*, 3 vols, 1799–1803 and 20 vols 1806–1823 (New York: Banks & Bros, Law Publishers, 1864).
Kirby, Ephraim, *Reports of Cases Adjudged in the Superior Court of the State of Connecticut, From the year 1785 to May 1788; with Some Determinations in the Supreme Court of Errors* (Litchfield: Collier & Adams, 1789).
Mason, William P (ed), *First Circuit Reports, 1816–1830*, 5 vols (Boston: Hilliard, Gray, Little & Wilkins, 1842–1845).
Paine, Elijah Jr (ed), *Reports of Cases Argued and Determined in the Circuit Court of the United States for the Second Circuit: Comprising the Districts of New York, Connecticut, and Vermont* (New York: R Donaldson, 1827).

Peters, Richard (ed), Reports of Cases Argued and Determined in the Third Circuit: Comprising the Districts of Pennsylvania and New Jersey, 1803–1827, 3 vols, vol 1 (Philadelphia William Fry, 1819; vols 2 and 3, Philip H Nicklin, 1827).

Quincy, Josiah Jr, Reports of Cases Argued and Adjudged in the Superior Court of Judicature of the Province of Massachusetts Bay, between 1761 and 1772 (Boston: Charles C Little & James Brown 1865).

Sumner, Charles (ed), First Circuit Reports, 3 vols (Boston: Charles C Little & James Brown, 1842–1845).

Wallace, John B, Reports of Cases Argued and Determined in the Circuit Court of the United States for the Third Circuit (Philadelphia: PH Nicklin and T Johnson, 1838).

Wharton, Francis, State Trials of the United States during the Administrations of Washington and Adams: With References, Historical and Professional, and Preliminary Notes on the Politics of the Times (Philadelphia: Carey & Hart, 1849).

Washington, Bushrod, Reports of Cases Argued and Determined in the Court of Appeal of Virginia, 2 vols (Richmond: Nicholson, 1798).

## Books

Bergh, Albert Ellery, *The Writings of Thomas Jefferson*, 20 vols (Washington DC: Thomas Jefferson Memorial Association, 1903).

Binney, Horace, *Bushrod Washington* (Philadelphia: C Sherman & Son, 1858). Library of Congress (MARCXML).

Blackstone, Sir William, *Commentaries on the Laws of England*, 4th ed, 4 vols (London. 1770).

Blackstone, Sir William, *Commentaries on the Laws of England*, 4 vols variorum edition of the first nine editions (Oxford: Oxford University Press, 2016).

Boyd, Julian P, Cullen, Charles T, Catanzariti, John and Oberg, Barbara B (eds), *The Papers of Thomas Jefferson*, 42 vols to date (Princeton: Princeton University Press, 1950–2016).

Coleridge, Ernest Hartley, *Life and Correspondence of John Duke, Lord Coleridge, Lord Chief Justice of England*, vol 2 (New York: D Appleton & Co, 1904).

Capon, Lester (ed), *The Adams-Jefferson Letters* (Chapel Hill: University of North Carolina Press, 1959).

De Paux, Linda, Bickford, Charlene, Bowling, Kenneth *et al.*, *Documentary History of the First Federal Congress of the United States of America, 1789–1791*, 22 vols (Baltimore: John Hopkins University Press, 1972–2017).

Farrand, Max (ed), *Records of the Federal Convention of 1787*, 4 vols (New Haven: Yale University Press, 1937).

Ford, Paul Leicester (ed), *Thomas Jefferson: The Works*, 12 vols (New York: GP Putnam's Sons, 1904).

Freeman, Joanne B, *Alexander Hamilton: Writings* (Library of America, 2001).

Freeman, Landa M; North, Louise V, and Wedge, Janet M (eds), *Selected Letters of John Jay and Sarah Livingston Jay* (Jefferson: North Carolina: MacFarland & Company Inc. Publishers, 2005).

Hall, Kermit L and Hall, Mark David (eds), *The Collected Works of James Wilson*, 2 vols (Indianapolis: Liberty Fund, 2007).

Hobson, CF *et al* (eds), *The Papers of John Marshall 1775–1835*, 12 vols (Chapel Hill, NC: University of North Carolina Press, 1974–2006).

Hobson, Charles F (ed), *St George Tucker's Law Reports and Selected Papers, 1782–1825*, 3 vols (Chapel Hill, NC: University of North Carolina Press, 2013).

Hodgson, Adam, *Letters from North America* (London: Hurst, Robinson & Co, 1824).

Hopkinson, Joseph, *In Commemoration of the Hon. Bushrod Washington. Late One of the Justices of the Supreme Court of the United States* (Philadelphia: TS Manning, 1830).

Horowitz, Valerie L, *The Unsigned Essays of Supreme Court Justice Joseph Story: Early American Views of Law* (Clark, New Jersey: Talbot Publishing/Lawbook Exchange, 2015).

Hutson, James H. (ed), *A Supplement to Max Farrand's Records of The Federal Convention of 1797* (New Haven: Yale University Press, 1987).

Israel, Fred L, *The State of the Union Messages of the Presidents, 1790–1966*, 3 vols (New York: Chelsea House/Robert Hector Publishers, 1966).

Johnson, Henry P, *The Correspondence and Papers of John Jay*, 4 vols (New York: Burt Franklin, 1890).

Kent, James, *Commentaries on American Law*, 4 vols (New York: O. Halstead, 1826–1830).

Kent, William, *Memoirs and Letters of James Kent LLD, Late Chancellor of the State of New York* (Boston: Little, Brown & Company, 1898).

Krauss, Stanton D (ed), *Gentlemen of the Grand Jury: The Surviving Grand Jury Charges from Colonial, State, and Lower Federal Courts before 1801*, 2 vols (Durham, North Carolina: Carolina Academic Press, 2012.

Lamoine, Georges, *Charges to the Grand Jury 1689–1803* (London: Royal Historical Society, 1992). Camden Fourth Series, vol 43.

Looney J. Jefferson (ed), *The Papers of Thomas Jefferson*, Retirements Series, vol 5 (Princeton: Princeton University Press, 2008).

Marcus, Maeva (ed), *The Documentary History of the Supreme Court of the United States, 1789–1800*, 8 vols (New York: Columbia University Press, 1985–2007).

Peters, Richard (ed), *The Public Statutes at Large of the United States*, vols 1–4 (Boston: Charles C Little & James Brown, 1845–1846).

Peterson, Merrill D (ed), *Thomas Jefferson: Writings* (New York: Library of America, 1984).

Ragsdale, Bruce A (ed), *Debates on the Federal Judiciary: A Documentary History, vol I: 1787–1875* (Federal Judicial Centre, History Office, 2013).

Rakove, Jack N, *Madison: Writings* (New York: Library of America, 1999).

Richardson, James D, *A Compilation of the Messages and Papers of the Presidents*, vol 1 (Washington DC: Bureau of National Literature and Art, 1905).

Rossiter, Clinton, *The Federalist Papers* (New York: Signet Classics, 2003).

Sheppard, Steve (ed), *The History of Legal Education in the United States: Commentaries and Primary Sources*, 2 vols (Pasadena, California: Salem Press Inc, 1999).

Smith, James Morton, *Republic of Letters: The Correspondence between Thomas Jefferson and James Madison*, 3 vols (New York: WW Norton and Company, 1995).

Story, Joseph, *Commentaries on the Constitution of the United States*, 3 vols (Boston: Hilliard, Gray & Co, 1833). Facsimile of third edition, 1858 edited by EH Bennett (Clark, New Jersey: Lawbook Exchange Ltd, 2 vols, 2015).

Story, Joseph, *Commentaries on the Constitution of the United States*. 1 vol (abridged) (Boston: Hilliard, Gray & Co, 1833).

Story, Joseph *A Familiar Exposition of the Constitution* (Cambridge: Marsh, Capen, Lyon & Webb, 1840).

Story, WW (ed), *Life and Letters of Joseph Story*, 2 vols (London: John Chapman, 1851).

Story, WW (ed), *The Miscellaneous Writings of Joseph Story* (Boston: Charles C Little & James Brown, 1852).

Tucker, St George, *Blackstone's Commentaries with Notes of Reference to the Constitution and Laws of the Federal Government of the United States and of the Commonwealth of Virginia*, 5 vols (Philadelphia: William Birch & Abraham Small, 1803).
Washington, Henry Augustus, *Writings of Thomas Jefferson*, vol IV (New York: Derby & Jackson, 1859).

## Newspapers and Periodicals

Albany Centinel
American Citizen
American Monthly Review
Augusta Chronicle
Baltimore Federal Republican
Boston Traveller
Boston Weekly Messenger
Daily Mail (England)
Gazette of the United States (New York)
Gazette of the United States & Daily Evening Advertiser (Philadelphia)
Marlborough Gazette
Massachusetts Centinel
National Gazette
Niles Weekly Register
Pennsylvania Gazette
Portsmouth Oracle (New Hampshire)
Providence Gazette
Providence Patriot & Columbian Phenix
Repertory (Boston)
Republican Watch Tower (New York)
Salem Gazette
San Francisco Bulletin
Southern Centinel & Gazette
Spectator (New York)
St Louis Enquirer
Sun (Pittsfield, Mass)
Times, and Hartford Advertiser
Trenton Federalist
Universalist Magazine (Boston)
Vermont Gazette
Weekly Museum (New York)
Weekly Register of Politics & News (Baltimore)

## Government, Law and Public Departmental Documents

American State Papers, 10th class, Miscellaneous, including federal courts and judges.
Continental Congress Journals and Records.
Federal Judicial Center.
United States Census Bureau.
United States Congressional Documents and Debates, 1774–1875 (Library of Congress).

## Secondary Sources

### Books

Abraham, Henry J, *Justices, Presidents, and Senators* (Lanham: Maryland: Rowman & Littlefield Publishers Inc, 1999). 1st edition, 1974).
Adams, Henry, *History of the United States of America during the Administration of Thomas Jefferson* (C Scribner's Sons, 1889. Library of America edition, Earl N Habert (ed), 1986).
Anderson, Dice Robin, *William Giles: A Study in the Politics of Virginia and the Nation from 1790–1830* (Menasha, Wisconsin: Collegiate Press at George Banta Publishing Co, 1914).

## Secondary Sources

Arlidge, Anthony QC, *The Lawyers Who Made America: From Jamestown to the White House* (Oxford & Portland, Oregon: Hart Publishing, 2017).

Ashmore, Ann, *Dates of Arguments and Delivery of Opinions of Supreme Court Cases between 1791 and 1882* (Washington DC: Library of the Supreme Court of the United States, August 2006).

Bailyn, Bernard (ed), *The Debate on the Constitution*, 2 vols (New York: Library of America, 1993).

Baker, Sir John H. QC, *An Introduction to English Legal History* (Oxford: Oxford University Press, 4th ed. 2002).

Baker, Leonard, *John Marshall: A Life in the Law* (New York: Macmillan Publishers, 1974).

Balleisen, Edward J, *Navigating Failure: Bankruptcy and Commercial Society in Antebellum America* (Chapel Hill: University of North Carolina Press, 2011).

Bartlett, Richard A, *The New Country: A Social History of the American Frontier, 1776–1890* (New York: Oxford University Press, 1974).

Bassett, John Spencer (ed), *Correspondence of Andrew Jackson*, vol IV (Washington DC: Carnegie Institution of Washington, 1926).

Beeman, Richard, *Plain Honest Men: The Making of the American Constitution* (New York: Random House, 2009).

Bernstein, R B, *Thomas Jefferson* (New York: Oxford University Press, 2003). Folio Society edition, with emendations, 2008.

Beveridge, Albert J, *The Life of John Marshall*, 4 vols (Cambridge, Mass: Riverside Press, 1916).

Bickford, Charlene Bangs and Bowling, Kenneth R, *Birth of the Nation: The First Federal Congress, 1789–1791* (Lanham, MD: Madison House Publishers Inc, 1989).

Bilder, Mary Sarah; Marcus, Maeva, and Newmyer, R Kent, *Blackstone in America: Selected Essays of Kathryn Preyer* (New York: Cambridge University Press, 2009).

Blaustein, Albert P and Mersky, Roy M, 'Bushrod Washington' in Friedman and Israel, *The Justices of the United States Supreme Court, 1789–1969* (New York: Chelsea House Publishers, 1969).

Bourguignon, Henry J, *The First Federal Court: The Federal Appellate Prize Court of the American Revolution, 1775–1787* (Philadelphia: American Philosophical Society, 1977).

Broadwater, Jeff, *George Mason: Forgotten Founder* (Chapel Hill: University of North Carolina Press, 2006).

Carlisle, The Rt Hon Earl of (Lord Morpeth), *Travels in America* (New York: GP Putnam, 1851).

Casper, Scott E, *Sarah Johnson's Mount Vernon* (New York: Hill & Wang, 2008).

Casto, William R, *The Supreme Court in the Early Years of the Republic: The Chief Justiceships of John Jay and Oliver Ellsworth* (Columbia: University of South Carolina Press, 1995).

Chernow, Ron, *Alexander Hamilton* (New York: Penguin Press, 2004).

——, *Washington: A Life* (London: Allen Lane, 2010).

Chiorazzi, Michael and Most, Marguarite, *Prestatehood Legal Materials: A Fifty-State Research Guide: Including New York City and the District of Columbia*, 2 vols (New York: Haworth Information Press, 2005).

Corwin, Edward S *John Marshall and the Constitution: A Chronicle of the Supreme Court* (Akron: Ohio: Summit Classic Press, 2013, a reprint of the 1919 1st ed).

Commission on the Bicentennial of the United States Constitution, *The Supreme Court of the United States; Its Beginnings and its Justices, 1790–1991* (Washington DC, 1992).

Cushman, Clare (ed), *The Supreme Court Justices: Illustrated Biographies, 1789–1993* (Washington DC: Congressional Quarterly, 1993).

Darbyshire, Penny, *Sitting in Judgment: The Working Lives of Judges* (Oxford and Portland, Oregon: Hart Publishing Ltd, 2011).

Dewey, Frank L., *Thomas Jefferson, Lawyer* (Charlottesville: University of Virginia Press, 1986).

Domnarski, William, *In the Opinion of the Court* (Urbana and Chicago: University of Illinois Press, 1996).

Dunne, Gerald T, *Justice Joseph Story and the Rise of the Supreme Court* (New York: Simon & Schuster, 1970).

Duxbury, Neil, *The Nature and Authority of Precedent* (Cambridge: Cambridge University Press, 2008).

Egerton, Douglas R, *Gabriel's Rebellion: The Virginia Slave Conspiracies of 1800 and 1802* (Chapel Hill: University of North Carolina Press, 1993).

Ellis, Joseph E, *His Excellency: George Washington* (New York: Alfred A Knopf, 2004).

Ellis, Richard E, *The Jeffersonian Crisis: Courts and Politics in the Young Republic* (New York: Oxford University Press, 1971).

Epstein, Lee, Segal, Jeffrey A, Spaeth, Harold J and Walker, Thomas G (eds), *The Supreme Court Compendium: Data, Decisions & Developments* (Washington DC: CQ Press, 2003).

Frank, John F, *Justice Daniel Dissenting: A Biography of Peter V. Daniel, 1784–1860* (Cambridge: Harvard University Press, 1964).

Frankfurter, Felix, *The Commerce Clause under Marshall, Taney & White*, (Chapel Hill: University of North Carolina Press, 1937).

Frankfurter, Felix and Landis, James M, *The Business of the Supreme Court: A Study in the Federal Judicial System* (New Brunswick, New Jersey: Transaction Publisher, 2007 facsimile reprint of original publication, New York: Macmillan & Co, 1928).

Friedman, Lawrence M, *A History of American Law* (New York: Simon & Shuster, 1973).

Friedman, Leon and Israel, Fred E, *The Justices of the United States Supreme Court, 1789–1969*, vol 1 (New York: Chelsea House Publishers, 1969).

Garrison, Tim Alan, *The Legal Ideology of Removal: The Southern Judiciary and the Sovereignty of Native American Nations* (Athens: University of Georgia Press, 2002).

Goebel, Julius, Jr, *History of the Supreme Court of the United States: Antecedents and Beginnings to 1801* (New York: The Macmillan Company, 1971).

Graham, D Kurt, *To Bring Law Home: The Federal Judiciary in Early National Rhode Island* (DeKalb, Illinois: Northern Illinois University Press, 2010).

Gunther, Gerald (ed), *John Marshall's Defence of McCulloch v Maryland* (Stanford: Stanford University Press, 1969).

Hall, Kermit L and Ely, James W, *The Oxford Guide to United States Supreme Court Decisions* 2nd ed (New York: Oxford University Press, 2009).

Haskins, George and Johnson, Herbert A, *History of the Supreme Court of the United States, vol II, Foundations of Power: John Marshall, 1801–1815* (New York: Cambridge University Press, 2010, originally published by Macmillan, 1981).

Haw, James, Beirne, Francis, Beirne, Rosamund and Jett, Samuel R, *Stormy Patriot: The Life of Samuel Chase* (Baltimore: Maryland Historical Society, 1980).

Henderson, Dwight D, *Courts for a New Nation* (Washington DC: Public Affairs Press, 1971).

Heubner, Timothy S, *The Southern Judicial Tradition: State Judges and Sectional Distinctiveness, 1790–1890* (Athens: University of Georgia Press, 1999).

Hobson, Charles F, *The Great Chief Justice: John Marshall and the Rule of Law* (Lawrence: University Press of Kansas, 1996).

Hoffer, Peter Charles and Hull, NEH, *Impeachment in America, 1635–1805* (New Haven: Yale University Press, 1984).
Hoffer, Peter Charles, Hoffer, William James and Hull, NEH, *The Federal Courts: An Essential History* (New York: Oxford University Press, 2016).
Holdsworth, William S, *The Historians of Anglo-American Law* (New York: Columbia University Press, 1928. Lawbook Exchange facsimile reprint, 2014).
Holmes, Oliver Wendell, *Collected Legal Papers* (New York: Peter Smith, 1952).
Horwitz, Morton J, *Transformation of American Law, 1780–1860* (Cambridge, MA: Harvard University Press, 1977).
Hughes, Jonathan and Cain, Louis P, *American Economic History*, 5th ed (Addison, Wesley, Longman, 1998).
Isenberg, Nancy, *Fallen Founder: The Life of Aaron Burr* (New York: Viking Penguin, 2007).
Johnson, Herbert A, *The Chief Justiceship of John Marshall* (Columbia: University of South Carolina Press, 1997).
Kerber, Linda K, *Federalists in Dissent: Imagery and Ideology in Jeffersonian America* (Ithaca: Cornell University Press, 1970).
Killenbeck, Mark R, *McCulloch v Maryland: Securing a Nation* (Lawrence: University Press of Kansas, 2006).
Kutler, Stanley I, *Privilege and Creative Destruction: The Charles River Bridge Case* (Philadelphia: JB Lippincott Company, 1971).
Lind, Michael, *Land of Promise: An Economic History of the United States* (New York: Harper Collins, 2012).
McClellan, James, *Joseph Story and the American Constitution* (Norman: University of Oklahoma Press, 1971, Second Printing, 1990 with a Foreword by Stephen B Presser).
McGarvie, Mark Douglas, *Law and Religion in American History: Public Values and Private Conscience* (New York: Cambridge University Press, 2016).
Maier, Pauline, *Ratification: The People Debate the Constitution, 1787–1788* (New York: Simon & Schuster, 2010).
Mann, Bruce H, *Republic of Debtors: Bankruptcy in the Age of American Independence* (Cambridge, MA: Harvard University Press, 2002).
Meacham, Jon, *American Lion: Andrew Jackson in the White House* (New York: Random House, 2008).
——, *Thomas Jefferson: The Art of Power* (New York: Random House, 2012).
Morgan, Donald G, *Justice William Johnson: The First Dissenter* (Columbia: University of South Carolina Press, 1954).
Morison, SE, *Maritime History of Massachusetts, 1783–1860* (Boston: Houghton Mifflin Company, 1921).
Morpeth, Lord, see Carlisle, The Rt Hon Earl of.
Morris, Jeffrey B, *Federal Justice in the Second Circuit: A History of United States Courts in New York, Connecticut & Vermont, 1789–1987* (New York: Second Circuit Historical Committee, 1987).
Munger, Donna Bingham, *Pennsylvania Land Law: A History and Guide to Researchers* (Lanham, MD: S R Books, 1991).
Newmyer, R Kent, *The Supreme Court under Marshall and Taney* (Wheeling, Illinois: Harlan Davidson Inc, 1968).
——, *Supreme Court Justice Story: Statesman of the Old Republic* (Chapel Hill: University of North Carolina Press, 1985).
——, *John Marshall and the Heroic Age of the Supreme Court,* (Baton Rouge: Louisiana State Universary Press, 2001).

——, *The Treason Trial of Aaron Burr: Law, Politics, and the Character Wars of the New Nation* (New York: Cambridge University Press, 2012).

North, Douglass C, *The Economic Growth of the United States, 1790–1860* (New York: WW Norton & Co Inc, 1966. Originally published, New Jersey: Prentice-Hill Inc., 1961).

O'Connor, John E, *William Paterson: Lawyer and Statesman, 1745–1806* (New Brunswick, NJ: Rutgers University Press, 1979).

Parker, Kunal M, *Common Law, History, and Democracy in America, 1790–1900: Legal Thought Before Modernism* (New York: Cambridge University Press, 2011).

Parsons, Theophilus Jnr, *Memoir of Theophilus Parsons, Chief Justice of the Supreme Judicial Court of Massachusetts* (Boston: Ticknow and Fields, 1859).

Petrie, Donald A, *Lawful Looting on the High Seas in the Days of Fighting Sail* (Annapolis: Naval Institute Press, 1999).

Pfeffer, Leo, *This Honorable Court* (Boston: Beacon Press, 1965).

Pfister, Jude M, *Charting an American Republic: The Origins and Writing of the Federalist Papers* (Jefferson: North Carolina: McFarland & Co, Inc, Publishers, 2016).

Presser, Stephen B, Foreword to 1990 reprint of James McClellan, *Joseph Story and the American Constitution* (Norman: University of Oklahoma Press, 1971).

——, *Studies in the History of the United States Courts of the Third Circuit* (Washington DC: US Government Printing Office, 1982).

Quincy, Josiah, *Figures of the Past From the Leaves of Old Journals* 4th ed (Boston: Roberts Bros, 1883).

Ragsdale, Bruce A, *Debate on the Federal Judiciary: A Documentary History, Volume 1, 1787–1875* (Washington DC: Federal Judicial Center, 2013).

Remini, Robert V, *Andrew Jackson and His Indian Wars* (New York: Viking Penguin, 2001).

Ritz, Wilfred J, (ed by Holt, Wythe and Larue, LH), *Rewriting the History of the Judiciary Act 1789* (Norman: University of Oklahoma Press, 1990).

Robarge, David A, *A Chief's Progress: From Revolutionary Virginia to the Supreme Court* (Westport, Conn: Greenwood Press, 2000).

Roper, Donald Malcolm, *Mr Justice Thompson and the Constitution* New York: Garland Publishing Inc, 1987).

Rossiter, Clinton (ed), *The Federalist Papers* (New York: Signet Classic, 2003).

Rustein, Michael H, *The Privateering Stroke: Salem Privateers and the War of 1812* (Salem: Create Space Independent Publishing Platform, 2012).

Scott, James Brown, *Prize Cases Decided in the United States Supreme Court, 1789–1918*. Vol 1, (Oxford: Clarendon Press, 1923).

Seculow, Jay Alan, *Witnessing Their Faith: Religious Influence on Supreme Court Justices and their Opinions* (Lanham, Maryland: Rowman & Littlefield Publishers Inc, 2006).

Snell, Stephen L, *Courts of Admiralty and the Common Law: Origins of the American Experiment in Concurrent Jurisdiction* (Durham, NC: Carolina Academic Press, 2007).

Seymour, Whitney North Jr, (ed), *United States Courts in the Second Circuit: A Collected of History Lectures Delivered by the Judges of the Second Circuit* (New York: Federal Bar Council Foundation, 1992).

Sharp, James Roger, *American Politics in the Early Republic: The New Nation in Crisis* (New Haven: Yale University Press, 1993).

Simon. James F, *What Kind of Nation: Thomas Jefferson, John Marshall and the Epic Struggle to Create a United States* (New York: Simon & Schuster, 2002).

Smith, Jean Edward, *John Marshall: Definer of a Nation* (New York: Henry Holt & Company Inc, 1996).
Snell, Steven L, *Courts of Admiralty and the Common Law: Origins of the American Experiment in Concurrent Jurisdiction* (Durham, NC: Carolina Academic Press, 2007).
Spaeth, Harold J and Segal, Jeffrey, *Majority Rule or Minority Will* (Cambridge: Cambridge University Press, 1999).
Sutherland, Arthur E, *The Law at Harvard: A History of Men and Ideas, 1817–1967* (Cambridge, MA: Harvard University Press, 1967).
Stahr, Walter, *John Jay* (New York: Hambledon & Continuum, 2005).
Street, Alfred Billings, *The Council of Revision of the State of New York: Its History. A History of the Courts with which its Members were Connected, Biographical Sketches of its Members, and its Vetoes* (Albany: William Gould, 1859).
Stockdale, His Honour Eric and Holland, Justice Randy J, *Middle Temple Lawyers and the American Revolution* (Eagan, Minnnesota: Thomson West, 2007).
Surrency, Erwin C, *History of the Federal Courts* (New York: Oceana Publications Inc, 2002).
Tachau, Mary K Bonsteel, *Federal Courts in the Early Republic: Kentucky 1789–1816* (Princeton: Princeton University Press, 1978).
Urofsky, Melvin I, *A March of Liberty: A Constitutional History of the United States*, Vol 1, 3rd ed (New York: Oxford University Press, 2011).
Wallace, Anthony F C, *Thomas Jefferson and the Indians: The Tragic Fate of the First Americans* (Cambridge, MA: The Belknap Press of Harvard University Press, 1999).
Warren, Charles, *The Supreme Court in United States History*, 2 vols, Revised edition (Boston: Little Brown & Co, 1926).
Watts, Steven, *The Republic Reborn: War and the Making of Liberal America, 1790–1820* (Baltimore: John Hopkins University Press, 1987).
Weisenburger, Francis P *The Life of John McLean: A Politician on the United States Supreme Court* (Columbus: The Ohio University Press, 1937).
Wexler, Natalie, *A More Obedient Wife: A Novel of the Early Supreme Court* (Washington DC: Kalorama Press, 2006).
Wheelan, Joseph, *Jefferson's Vendetta: The Pursuit of Aaron Burr and the Judiciary* (New York: Carroll and Graff Publishers, 2005).
White, G Edward, *History of the Supreme Court of the United States, Vols III–IV, The Marshall Court and Cultural Change, 1815–1835* (New York: Cambridge University Press, 2010), originally published by Macmillan, 1988).
——, *Law in American History*, Vol 1 (New York: Oxford University Press, 2012).
White, Jonathan W, *Guide to Research in Federal Judicial History* (Washington DC: Federal Judicial Center, Federal Judicial History Office, 2010).
Winsor, Justin (ed), *The Memorial History of Boston including Suffolk County, Massachusetts, 1630–1880*. 4 vols (Boston: James R Osgood and Company, 1881).
Wonders, Peter A, (compiler) *Directory of Manuscript Collections Related to Federal Judges, 1789–1997* (Washington DC: Federal Judicial Center, 1998).
Wood, Gordon S, *Empire of Liberty: A History of the Early Republic, 1789–1815* (New York: Oxford University Press, 2009).

## Articles and Essays

Austin, Joshua M, 'The Law of Citations and Seriatim Opinions: Were the Ancient Romans and the Early Supreme Court on the Right Track?' (2010) 31(1) *Northern Illinois University Law Review* 19–36.

Baker, H Robert, 'A Better Story in *Prigg v Pennsylvania*' (2014) 10(2) *Journal of Supreme Court History* 169–89.

Balleisen, Edward J, 'Bankruptcy and Entrepreneurial Ethos in Antebellum American Law' (2004) 8 *Australian Journal of Legal History* 61–82.

Bozzo, Peter, Edwards, Shimmy and Christine, April A, 'Many Voices, One Court: The Origin and Role of Dissent in the Supreme Court' (2011) 36(3) *Journal of Supreme Court History* 193–215.

Briceland, Alan V, 'Ephraim Kirby: Pioneer of American Law Reporting, 1789' (1972) XVI *American Journal of Legal History* 297–319.

Coquillette, Daniel R, 'First Flower—The Earliest American Law Reports and The Extraordinary Josiah Quincey Jr (1744–1775)' (1996) XXX(1) *Suffolk University Law Review* 1–34.

Dunne, Gerald T, 'Brockholst Livingston' in Friedman, L and Israel, FE, *The Justices of the United States Supreme Court, 1789–1969*, vol 1 (New York: Chelsea House Publishers, 1969), 387–403.

——, 'Smith Thompson' in Friedman, L and Israel, FE, *The Justices of the United States Supreme Court, 1789–1969*, vol 1 (New York: Chelsea House Publishers, 1969), 475–92.

——, 'The Story-Livingston Correspondence' (1966) 10 *American Journal of Legal History* 224–36.

Faber, David A, 'Bushrod Washington and the Age of Discovery in American Law' (2000) 102 *West Virginia Law Review* 735–807.

Fede, Andrew T, 'Not the Most Insignificant Justice: Reconsidering Justice Gabriel Duvall's Slavery Law Opinions Favoring Liberty' (2017) 42(1) *Journal of Supreme Court History* 7–27.

Forbes, John D, 'European Wars and Boston Trade, 1783–1815' (1938) 11(4) *New England Quarterly* 709–30.

Finkelman, Paul, 'Story Telling on the Supreme Court: *Prigg v Pennsylvania* and Justice Story's Judicial Nationalism' (1994) *The Supreme Court Review* 247–94.

Gatell, Frank Otto, 'Henry Baldwin' in Friedman & Israel, *Justices of the Supreme Court, 1789–1969* (New York: Chelsea House Publishers, 1969).

Hall, Kermit L, 'The Courts, 1790–1920' in Michael Grossberg and Christopher Tomlins (eds), *The Cambridge History of Law in America, Volume II, The Long Century, 1789–1920* (New York: Cambridge University Press, 2008), 106–32.

Hall, Timothy L, 'Brockholst Livingston' in *Supreme Court Justices: A Biographical Dictionary* (New York: Facts on File Inc., 2001), 55–8.

Hall, Timothy L, 'Smith Thompson' in *Supreme Court Justices: A Biographical Dictionary* (New York: Facts on File Inc., 2001), 70–3.

Heaney, Howell J, 'The Letters of Joseph Story in the Hampton L Carson Collection of the Free Library of Philadelphia' (1958) 2(1) *The American Journal of Legal History* 68–86.

Hickey, Donald R, 'American Trade Restrictions during the War of 1812' (1981) 68(3) *The Journal of American History*, 517–38.

Hobson, Charles F, 'Defining the Office: John Marshall as Chief Justice' (2006) 154(6) *University of Pennsylvania Law Review* 1421–61.

——, 'St George Tucker's Papers (2006) 47(4) *William & Mary Law Review* 1245–78.
Holt, Wythe, 'To Establish Justice: Politics, the Judiciary Act of 1789, and the Invention of the Federal Courts' (1989) 6 *Duke Law Journal* 1421–1531.
Johnson, Herbert A, 'Judicial Institutions in Emerging Federal Systems: The Marshall Court and the European Court of Justice' (2000) 33 *John Marshall Law Review* 1063–1108.
——, 'Bushrod Washington' (2009) 62(2) *Vanderbilt Law Review* 447–90.
Kadish, Mark, 'Behind the Locked Doors of an American Grand Jury: Its History, Its Secrecy, and its Process' (1996) 24(1) *Florida State University Law Review* 1–77.
Kaufman, Paul W, 'Disbelieving Non-Believers: Atheism, Competence, and Credibility in the Turn of the Century' (2003) 15(2) *Yale Journal of Law and the Humanities* 395–433.
Kelsh, John P, 'Opinion Delivery Practices of the United States Supreme Court, 1790–1945' (1999) 77 *Washington University Law Quarterly* 137–82.
LaCroix, Alison L, 'Federalists, Federalism, and Federal Jurisdiction (24 February 2010). Final revised version of 8 November 2012 in (2012) 30 *Law and History Review* 205–44: University of Chicago Public Law Working Paper, no 297. Available at https://ssrn.com/abstract=1558612. Accessed 28 January 2017).
Langbein, John H, 'Chancellor Kent and the History of Legal Literature' (1993) *Columbia Law Review* 547–94.
——, 'Blackstone, Litchfield, and Yale' in Anthony T Kronan (ed), *History of Yale Law School: The Tercentennial Lectures* (New Haven: Yale University Press, 2004), 17–52.
Lee, Thomas R, 'Stare Decisis in Historical Perspective: From the Founding Fathers to the Rehnquist Court' (1999) 52 *Vanderbilt Law Review* 647–735.
MacGill, Hugh C and Newmyer, R Kent, 'Legal Education and Legal Thought, 1790–1920' in Michael Grossberg and Christopher Tomlins, *The Cambridge History of Law in America*, vol II (New York: Cambridge University Press, 2008), 36–67.
Mead, Joseph E, 'Stare Decisis in the Inferior Courts of the United States' (2012) 12 *Nevada Law Journal* 787–830.
Morris, Richard B, 'The John Jay Court: An Intimate Portrait' (1979) 5 *Journal of Contemporary Law* 163.
Newmyer, R Kent, 'Justice Joseph Story on Circuit and a Neglected Phase of American Legal History' (1970) XIV *The American Journal of Legal History* 112–35.
Paulson, Michael Stokes, 'Abrogating Stare Decisis by Statute' (2000) 109 *Yale Law Review* 1535–1602.
Pfister, Jude, 'The Legacy of John Jay' (2016) 38(4) *Supreme Court Historical Society Quarterly* 6–9.
Presser, Stephen B, 'Resurrecting the Conservative Tradition in American Legal History' (1985) 13 *Reviews in American History* 526–33.
Preyer, Kathryn, 'Jurisdiction to Punish: Federal Authority, Federalism, and the Common Law of Crimes in the Early Republic' (1986) IV *Law and History Review* 223–65.
Ragsdale, Bruce A, 'Amistad: The Federal Courts and the Challenge to Slavery' (2002) Federal Judicial Center, Federal Judicial History Office 1–92.
——, 'The Sedition Act Trials' (2005) (Federal Judicial Center, Federal Judicial History Office) 1–83.
Roper, Donald M, 'Judicial Unanimity and the Marshall Court: A Re-appraisal' (1965) 9(2) *American Journal of Legal History* 118–34.
Stonier, James R Jr, 'Heir Apparent: Bushrod Washington and Federal Justice in the Early Republic' in Gerber, Scott (ed) *Seriatim: The Supreme Court before John Marshall* (New York: New York University Press, 1998), 322–49.

Surrency, Edwin C, 'Law Reports in the United States' (1981) 25(1) *The American Journal of Legal History* 48–66.

Surrency, Edwin C, 'Federal District Court Judges and the History of their Courts' (1966) *History of the Federal Courts, Pamphlet No 1* 1–172.

Schwartz, Helen L, 'Demythologizing the Historic Role of the Grand Jury' (1972) 10 *American Criminal Law Review* 701.

Traynor, William Michael, 'Judicial Review before *Marbury*' (2005) 58(2) *Stanford Law Review* 455–562.

Turner, Charles C, Wat, Lori Beth, and Maveety, Nancy, 'Beginning to Write Separately: The Origins and Development of Concurring Judicial Opinions' (2010) 35(2) *Journal of Supreme Court History* 93–109.

Van Hook, Matthew, 'Founding the Third Branch: Judicial Greatness and John Jay's Reluctance' (2015) 40(1) *Journal of Supreme Court History* 1–19.

Warren, Charles C, 'The Story Marshall Correspondence (1812–1831)' (1941) 21(1) *William & Mary Quarterly*, Second Series, 1–26.

Washington, Bushrod C, 'The Late Mr Justice Bushrod Washington' (1897) IX(8) *The Green Bag* (Boston, August) 329–35.

Wheeler, Russell, 'Extrajudicial Activities of the Early Supreme Court' (1973) *Supreme Court Review* 123, 135–39.

Wolford, Thorp Lanier, 'Democratic-Republican Reaction to the Embargo of 1807' (1942) 15(1) *The New England Quarterly* 35–61.

Yurs, Dale, 'The Early Supreme Court and the Challenge of Circuit Riding' (2011) 36(3) *Journal of Supreme Court History* 181–92.

Zobel, Hiller B, 'Pillars of the Political Fabric: Federal Courts in Massachusetts, 1789–1815' (1989) 74 *Massachusetts Law Review* 197–205.

## *Unpublished Theses*

Annis, David L, *Bushrod Washington* (University of Notre Dame, August 1974). (PhD.)

Taylor, Glenn Forrester, *Jurisdiction in the 7th Circuit, District of Kentucky, 1807–1817* (University of Louisville, 1989). (MA Dissertation.)

# INDEX

*Note*: author names only include an initial or forename if needed for disambiguation. Chief justices, justices, district and probate judges are distinguished by 'CJ', 'J', 'DJ' and 'PJ'. Other names have initial or first name with an indication of office as appropriate. Law Reports listed at pp 207–8 are indexed under 'law reports (as listed at pp 207–8)' rather than under the reporter. References are included in the index only when something of substance is said about the reports or the reporter.

Abraham (1974), 159, 180
Adams, H (1889), 28–9
Adams (US President 1797–1801): *see also* Judiciary Act 1801
  Alien & Sedition Acts 1798 and, 49, 90
  appointment of Federalist judges, 26, 40
    Washington J, 56
  Jefferson's defeat of, 91, 113
  Livingston J's opposition to, 91
admiralty law: *see also* embargo laws; embargo laws, jurisprudence (Story J); embargo laws, jurisprudence (Washington); marine insurance; maritime, prize and marine insurance, jurisprudence; seamen, protection of
  Court of Appeals in Prize Cases, 74, 131n99
  district court jurisdiction, 41
  English common law and, 21, 45, 46, 59–60, 152
  Johnson J and, 137
  jurisdiction, 40–1
    seamen on board ship, 128–9
  Livingston J and, 45, 93–4, 95, 96
  Marshall CJ and, 137, 138, 139
  Peters J and, 29n27
  Story J and: *see* admiralty law (Story J)
  Thompson J and, 46, 137, 164
  Washington J and, 59–60, 63, 74–5, 77–8, 190
admiralty law (Story J)
  attempts to import English common law, 21, 111, 131, 152, 153–4
  customs law enforcement, 115–17, 125–8, 146, 153–4
    case-list, 146n162
    *Harden v Gordon*, 154
    *Orne v Townsend*, 154
    *The Pizarro*, 123, 138
    *Ruggles*, 154
  embargo laws: *see* embargo laws, jurisprudence (Story J)
  as major contributor to, 3, 137, 155
  strict enforcement of, 153–4

Alien & Sedition Acts 1798, 28, 36n65, 49, 90–1, 185
  Chase on, 185
  free speech (Constitution, First Amendment), 185
  Patterson on, 185
  political abuse of, 90
Anderson (1914), 26
Annis (1974), 55, 120
appeals
  admiralty cases, 41
  circuit court to Supreme Court
    availability of judge from state from which appeal came, xi, 25
    binding effect of decision, 169
    Judiciary Act 1789, 39
    rarity, xi, 2, 5
    uniformity and, 2
    Washington J's concerns, 59, 83
  Court of Appeals in Prizes Cases, 74, 131n99
  Court for the Correction of Errors, 92, 93, 172, 180
  district court to circuit court, 39, 41, 167–9
    limitation to civil maritime and admiralty cases, 122
    participation of district judge, 39, 41, 131–2
  limitation to matters of law, 38, 84, 122
  New York Supreme Court judges' role, 92–3
  participation of judge previously involved in the case, 39, 46, 82, 92–3, 131–2, 146, 201
  reversal rates
    by court, 195–6
    by justice, 196–7
  Story J's rulings on, 122
  writ of error, 2, 93, 122, 124, 143, 201
Arlidge (2017), 53n5
Articles of Confederation 1781
  drafters, 53n5
  prize courts, 74
Ashmore (2006), 144

associate judges
  Judiciary Act 1789 provisions, 39
  significance, xiii, 4, 8, 10–11, 120, 193–4
  Washington G's considerations when
    appointing, 24–5, 49
Austin (2010), 11n41

Bailyn (ed) (1993), 38
Baker, HR (2014), 121
Baker, L (1974), 8
Baldwin J, judicial experience and legal
  education, 204
Balleisen (2001), 101
bankruptcy/debt
  Bankruptcy Act 1841, 101
  bills of exchange/promissory notes as
    discharge, 104, 164–5
  English authorities and, 61
  imprisonment for debt, 162, 169
  Johnson J and, 158n8
  jurisprudence
    *Adams v Story*, 98, 100
    *Carpenter v Butterfield*, 163–4
    *Mason v Haile*, 80, 173–4
    *Mott v Morris*, 63–4
    *Ogden v Saunders*, 64, 82, 98, 158, 173
    *Sturges v Crowninshield*, 100–1, 144
    *Tillman v Lansing*, 162
    *US v Dugan*, 107
    *US v Giles*, 107
    *US v Morris*, 170–1
  Livingston J and, 47, 98, 100–1, 107
  Marshall CJ and, 101, 199
  remission of forfeiture, 170–1
  states' rights and, 47, 59, 82, 100–1
  statutory interpretation, 63
  Story J and, 98, 101, 115, 144, 158n8
  Thompson J and, 158, 162, 167, 169, 173–4
  Washington and, 59, 61, 67, 80, 82, 158n8
Beeman (2009), 38
Bernstein (2003), 27–8
Beveridge (1916), 7–8
Bickford and Bowling (1989), 24n2, 37, 39
bills of exchange/promissory notes: *see also*
  commercial law/trade promotion
  Livingston J on, 21, 104–5, 108, 110, 191
  Story J on, 118, 147, 150
  Thompson J on, 70–1, 84
  Washington J on, 70–1, 84
Blackstone's *Commentaries*, 20, 44, 57–8, 93,
  112–13, 135, 165–6: *see also* Tucker's *Blackstone*
Blaustein and Merskey (1969), 54, 59
Bourguignon (1977), 131n99
Bozzo et al, 11n41
Briceland (1996), 97n47
Burr, A (US Vice-President/trial for treason),
  9–10
  Hamilton's attacks on, 88n10
  Jefferson's aggression towards, 26n15, 29, 31
  Livingston J and, 88
  Marshall CJ and, 37, 139, 193

Capon (ed) (1939), 28
Casper (2008), 54–5
Catanzaritu (2000), 53
*caveat emptor*, 163, 170, 181
certainty of the law, 164, 169, 170
certificate of division of opinion, use of, 79, 92,
  131–2, 168, 195–6, 200
  as aid to uniformity, 3, 136, 189
Chase J
  abuse of grand jury charge, 4, 33–4, 35,
    36–7, 49
  on the Alien & Sedition Acts, 185
  a 'boorish Federalist', 10
  circuit riding and, 187n5
  on crime and the common law, 151–2
  education and legal experience, 203
  impeachment, 4, 28–9, 31, 33–4,
    36–7, 49
  majority opinions, 200
  reversal rates, 196
Chernow (2004), 88n10
Chernow (2010), 25
*Cherokee Nation v Georgia*: *see* Native American
  rights
Chiorazzi and Most (2005), 42
circuit courts: *see also* grand jury charge;
  political tensions; Supreme Court
  appeals from: *see* appeals, circuit court to
    Supreme Court
  constitutionality of Supreme Court justices as
    judges, 187
  as forums to hone skills/gain experience, 3, 4,
    183–4
  jurisdiction, 39–41
  seamen on board ship, 128–9
  key issues considered by, 2–3
  local ties, importance/disadvantages, 3–5, 6–7,
    21, 23–5, 34, 38, 49, 74–7, 100–1, 121, 136,
    146, 183–4, 189–90, 193
  modernization under Story J, 121–5
  political function/promotion of federal
    system, 1, 6–7, 494
  role in the development of federal law, xi, xiii,
    1, 2, 5, 46–8, 185–6
  workloads of circuit courts and Supreme
    Court compared, 1–2, 3–4
circuit riding
  abolition, 5–6, 27
  English practice, 6–7
  importance to the federal system of justice,
    6, 21
  physical and emotional hardships, 5–7, 27, 96,
    122, 183
collegiality, 48

commercial law/trade promotion: see also
  bills of exchange/promissory notes; marine
  insurance; seamen, protection of
  commerce clause (Constitution I(8)(3)), 72,
    75–6, 100, 103, 144–5
  expanding economy, influence, 192–3
  New York, importance of, 17–18
commercial law/trade promotion, jurisprudence
  (including cases on contract and negotiable
  instruments), 84
  Carpenter v Butterfield, 163–4
  Casey v Brush, 94
  Corser v Craig, 70
  Craig v Brown, 71, 84
  Dartmouth College, 66, 81
  Dugan v US, 107
  Gallagher v Roberts, 70
  Gibbons v Ogden, 103
  Grant & Swift v M'Lachlin, 164
  Green v Beals, 94
  Henderson v Brown, 94
  Humphries v Blight's Assignees, 70, 84
  Keene v US, 105
  Lee v Munroe & Thornton, 107
  Lennox v Prout, 110
  Livingston v Van Ingen, 103
  McMurtry v Jones, 70, 84
  Mandeville v Welch, 147
  Marshall v Beverley, 110
  Mumford v M'Pherson, 164
  The New York, 106
  Otis v Watkins, 106–7
  Perry v Crammond, 70, 84
  Riggs v Lindsay, 108, 110
  Seaman v Patten, 94
  Seixas v Woods, 163
  Smith v Barker, 104
  Stevens v Columbian Insurance Company, 64
  Swift v Tyson, 152
  Tittle v Beebee, 164
  US v Barker, 105
  US v Giles, 107
  US v Hoxie, 102
  Van Ingen, 103
  Young v Grundy, 108, 110
commercial law/trade promotion (Livingston J)
  bills of exchange/promissory notes, 21, 104–5,
    110, 184, 191
  commerce clause (Constitution I(8)(3)), 103
  maritime cases, 102–3, 108
  partnerships, 94, 109–10, 191
  significance of/frequency of opinions on, 3,
    21, 86–7, 92, 94, 96, 104–8, 109–10, 190, 191
commercial law/trade promotion (Marshall CJ),
  103, 106–7
commercial law/trade promotion (Story J)
  applicability of state/English common law to
    federal cases, 21, 147, 152–3, 155, 163, 191–3

contract obligations, emphasis on
  sanctity of, 66
diversity cases, 152–3
embargo laws, 115–17
negotiable instruments, 147
partnerships, 133
promotion of certainty, 70–3
protection of seamen and, 192–3
significance of/frequency of opinions on, 19,
  133, 137, 190
commercial law/trade promotion (Thompson J),
  169–72, 181, 182, 184, 190, 192–3
  bills of exchange/promissory notes, 170,
    181, 184
  caveat emptor, 163, 170, 181
  contract obligations, emphasis on sanctity
    and clarity, 162–5, 166
  evaluation, 169–72, 190
  frequency of opinions on, 169–70
  inflexibility, 181
  partnerships, 167, 170
  protection of seamen and, 167, 192–3
commercial law/trade promotion (Washington J),
  190, 192–3
  bills of exchange/promissory notes, 70–1, 84
  contracts clause (Constitution I(10)(1)), 66,
    67, 69–70, 80–1, 100, 144, 173, 198
  as federalist, 57
  limited experience, 53–4
  protection of seamen and, 72–3, 192–3
  protection of vested commercial rights/
    sanctity of contract, 66
Commission of the Bicentennial of the United
  States (1992), 5, 172
common law (state/English)
  commercial law, 21, 147, 152–3, 155, 191–3
  copyright law, 171–2
  criminal law, 21, 151–2
  limitations of state common law/importance
    of federal system, 152–3
  Livingstone J, 93, 109
  as means of clarifying American law (Story),
    21, 111, 154, 184
  modification of English common law to meet
    American needs, 151, 154
  New York State practice, 44, 93
  Story J, 3, 21, 45–6, 111, 112–13, 127, 131,
    135–6, 151–3, 191–2
common law (state/English), jurisprudence
  Clark, 152, 154
  Coolidge, 154
  Hudson, 151–2, 154
  Leroy v Lewis, 93, 109
  Penny v New York Insurance Company,
    93, 109
  Swift v Tyson, 152–3, 154, 192
  Van Ness v Pacard, 151
  Worrall, 151

## Index

consistency: *see* uniformity/consistency, need for/aids to achieving
Constitution by article
  I(8) (powers of Congress), 171–2
  I(8)(1) (power of Congress to provide for general welfare of the US), 144–5
  I(8)(3) (commerce clause), 72, 75–6, 100, 103, 144–5
  I(9)(1) (ban on Congress amendment of right to trade in slaves), 2–3, 177
  I(10)(1) (contracts clause), 66, 67, 69–70, 80–1, 100, 144, 173, 198
  I(10)(2) (power to levy import and export duties), 100
  III(1) (courts/judges), 91
  III(2) (jurisdiction over disputes between different states), 176–7
  IV(1)(3) (recapture of person held to service), 149–50
  V (ban on constitutional amendment of Constitution I(9)(1)), 177
Constitution (Amendments) by article
  First (freedom of speech), 185
  Fifth
    5 (grand jury charge), 32
    6 (due process including protection of property rights), 66
  Thirteenth (abolition of slavery), 179, 193
constitutional rights and freedoms, 76
contracts clause (Constitution I(10)(1)), 66, 67, 69–70, 80–1, 100, 144, 173, 198
contractual law: *see also* commercial law/trade promotion
  applicable law, strict compliance with, 163–4
  Thompson J and, 163–4
Coquillette (1996), 97
Court for the Correction of Errors, 92, 93, 172, 180
Crimes Act 1790, 42, 129, 152
Crimes Act 1825, 152, 154, 192
criminal jurisdiction
  Crimes Act 1825, 152
  seamen on board ship, 128–9
criminal law
  applicability of state/English common law, 21, 48, 151–2
  codification, 21
  Story J and, 21, 132–3, 147
  uniformity and consistency problems, 48
criminal law (Story J)
  codification (later Crimes Act 1825), 21, 152, 154, 192
  common law and, 21, 151–2, 184
  interest in/rarity of opinions, 147
cross-circuit consistency, 169
Cushing J
  circuit riding, 5–6

constitutionality of Supreme Court Judges as circuit court judges, 187
  death/succession to, 32, 117, 118, 122
  grand jury charges, 4, 35n56
  illness, 122
  judicial experience and legal education, 202
  judicial record, 15–16
    certificates of division, 197
    majority opinions, 199
    reversal rates, 196
  Marshall CJ's approach for advice, 9–10, 139, 193
customs law enforcement, 94, 100–1, 128
  Livingston J on, 102, 167
  Story J on, 128, 145

Darbyshire (2007), 6–7
Declaration of Independence 1776
  'Life, Liberty, and the Pursuit of Happiness', 76
  signatories, 25, 33, 53
Dewey (1986), 112n3
dispute resolutions, desiderata
  certainty of the law, 164, 169
  speedy resolution of disputes, 165
dissents: *see also* opinions
  advantages of system, 187
  data relating to, 159
  identification of dissenting judges, 139n131, 152
  increase in, 12, 140
  Johnson J, 10, 48, 97, 148, 159, 171, 189, 199
  Livingston J, 10, 92, 99, 100–1, 108, 189, 199
  Marshall CJ, 58, 106, 107–8, 139, 158–9
    dislike of, 12, 140
  in the Marshall courts, 12, 140, 187
    subsumption within CJ's opinion, 14–15
  record of, 139n131
  seriatim opinions distinguished, 11
  Story J, xi, 139, 153–4, 175, 189
  Thompson J, 12, 47, 158–9, 171–2, 173–4, 175–80, 182, 192
  value of, 12
  Washington J as reluctant dissenter, 59, 80–1, 83
  as weakening of the Court's authority, 11, 59, 80–1, 83, 122
district court jurisdiction, 40–1
diversity jurisdiction, 21, 41, 152–3, 154, 192
  *Swift v Tyson*, 152–3, 154, 192
Domnarski (1996), 2, 13–14
Dunne (1966), 86, 121
Dunne (1969), 18, 86–7, 96, 97, 108, 120–1, 132, 157–9, 171–2, 180
Dunne (1970), 120–1, 157–9
Duvall J, life and career
  judicial experience and legal education, 204

judicial record, 8, 10, 15, 16, 117, 118–19, 137, 158, 172, 190
  certificates of division of opinion, 197
  majority opinions, 200
  reversal rates, 197
Duxbury (2008), 59

Egerton (1993), 55
Ellis, JE (2004), 37
Ellis, RE (1971), 26n15
Ellsworth CJ (1796–1800), seriatim vs single opinions, 11, 201
embargo laws: *see also* maritime, prize and marine insurance, jurisprudence
  assessment of impact, 116–17
  Embargo Act 1807, 77, 102, 115–16, 125n68
  Embargo Act 1808, 106
  Embargo Act 1813, 117, 125n68
  Livingston J and, 105–7
  Non-Intercourse Act 1809, 77
  Story J and, 115–17, 125–8
  Trading with the Enemy Act 1812, 125
  Washington J on, 77–8
embargo laws, jurisprudence (Story J)
  *The Argo*, 126
  *The Boston*, 153–4
  *The Bothnea; The Janstoff*, 127, 153–4
  *Cross*, 126–7
  *The George*, 127, 153–4
  reversals, 127
  *Robinson v Hook*, 128, 153–4
  *The Rosalie and Betty*, 127
  *The St Lawrence*, 126, 146
  *The Sally*, 125–6, 146
  *The Short Staple*, 126, 127, 153–4
  *Ten Hogsheads of Rum*, 126, 153–4
  *Two Hundred Chests of Tea*, 147
  *Webber*, 126
embargo laws, jurisprudence (Washington J)
  *Parker v US*, 78
  *The Paul Sherman*, 77–8
  *US v Dixey*, 78
  *US v Morgan*, 78
English law: *see* sources of law, English authorities
Epstein et al (2003), 25, 44
Evarts Act 1891, 5–6

Faber (2000), 18
Farrand (ed) (1937), 37–8
Fay PJ, Story J's letters to, 13, 48, 119, 123, 137, 138
Fede (2017), 15
federal law, supremacy of (including in particular Story-related jurisprudence), 143–7
  *Green v Biddle*, 146
  *McCulloch v Maryland*, 144–5

*Marbury v Madison*, 143–4
*Martin v Hunter's Lessee*, 143, 144
*Mills v Duryee*, 143
*Prigg*, 119, 121, 149–50
*Sturges v Crowninshield*, 59, 83, 100–1, 108, 115, 144
federal system of justice: *see also* Jefferson (US President, 1801–9); Judiciary Act 1789; Judiciary Act 1801; Judiciary Act 1807; states' rights/state sovereignty
  Anti-Federalist opposition, 23–4, 48–9
  circuit court vs district court judge, value of opinions, 5
  circuit/district court jurisdiction, 39–41
  Constitutional Conventions, 1787 and 1788 debates, 37–8, 48–9
  cost issue, 39
  difficulties of reconciling federal and state jurisdictions, 34
  promotion of
    appointment of Federalist judges, 24
    appointment of justices from different states/regional diversity, 25, 49
    charges to the jury, 33–7: *see also* grand jury charge
    circuit riding, importance, 6, 21
    state courts' jurisdiction
      concern about independence as reason for limiting, 39
      Judiciary Act 1789 and, 38–9
    'the keystone of our political fabric' (President Washington), 24
    uniformity, importance: *see* uniformity/consistency, need for/aids to achieving
Finkelman (1994), 121, 127
Forbes (1938), 116n26
Ford (ed) (1904), 28, 30, 32n39
Frank (1964), 13
Frankfurter, Landis and Tachau (1928), xi–xii
Freeman et al (2005), 87, 89
Friedman LM (1973), 44
Fugitive Slave Act 1793, 121, 150, 179, 191

Garrison (2002), 165–6
Goebel (1971), 1n1
Graham (2010), xii, 3–4
grand jury charge, 32–7
  criticised charges
    Chase J, 4, 33–4, 35, 36–7, 49
    Iredell J, 35–6
  effectiveness/demise, 36–7, 49
  English practice, 33
  Fifth Amendment, 32
  impeachment threat as disincentive, 186
  judicial independence, effect, 186
  as means of promoting the federal cause, 3–4, 32, 49, 186–7

model charges
  Cushing J, 4, 35n56
  Jay CJ, 34–5, 186
  Story J, 35n60
  Story J's 1812 charges, 4
  Walton J, 33
  Wilson J, 34–5
modern and 17th/18th century charges distinguished, 32–3
promotion of the federal system and, 33–7
publication of charges, 33
Gunther (ed) (1969), 145

Hall, KL and Hall, MD (eds) (2007), 25
Hall, TI (2001) ('Henry Brockholst Livingstone'), 89
Hall, TI (2001) ('Smith Thompson'), 158–9, 180, 182
Hamilton, A
  death in duel, 88
  *Federalist Papers*, 7n20, 27
  Livingston J and, 88
  separation of powers and, 25–6
  views on precedent, 58
Haskins and Johnson (1926), 1n1
Haw et al (1980), 19, 33–4, 35, 121
Heaney (1958), 121
Henderson (1971), 2, 32–3
Heubner (1999), 147n167
Hickey (1981), 116–17
Hobson (1996), 8–9, 37n66, 140, 150
Hobson (2006) (articles), 8–9, 20n28, 57
Hobson (2006) (edited version of Johnson's 1974 *Papers of John Marshall*), 2, 8, 37, 140, 142, 155, 187, 193
Hobson (2013), 155
Hodgson (1824), 54
Hoffer, Hoffer and Hull (2016), 150
Hoffer and Hull (1984), 28, 30
Holdsworth (1928), 156
Holmes (*Collected Legal Papers* (Smith)), 150–1, 155
Holt (1989), 46
Horwitz (1977), 67, 70n93, 153, 170
Hudson (ed) (1987), 38
Hughes and Cain (1998), 67

impeachment
  of Chase J, 4, 28–9, 31, 33–4, 36–7, 49
  as deterrence to grand jury charges, 186
  Jefferson's policy of, 20, 28–32, 186–7
  for judicial misbehaviour, 30
  Pennsylvania Republican party's campaign, 30–1
  of Peters DJ, 29
  of Pickering DJ, 28–9, 30
Indian rights: *see* Native American rights
Iredell J

circuit riding, 6n17
grand jury charge and, 35–6
Isenberg (2007), 31, 88
Israel (1966), 31

Jay CJ, legal attitudes
  grand jury charges, 34–5, 186
  separation of powers, 25–6
  seriatim opinions, 11, 201
Jay CJ, life and career
  circuit riding, 5–6, 7n20, 39, 80, 89
  diplomatic role
    as envoy to Great Britain, 7n20
    Jay Treaty (1794), 89
    Minister to Spain, 87–8
    Paris Treaty (1783), 88
  as Federalist, 34, 87–8
  *Federalist Papers*, 7
  as first Chief Justice (1789–95), 87–8
  Governor of New York State (1795–1801), 89
  political and judicial career, 87–8
  relations with Livingstone J (brother-in-law), 87–8, 89, 98
  resignation (1789)/refusal to return (1801), 7, 89
Jefferson (US President, 1801–9): *see also* political tensions
  common law and, 117
  federalist Supreme Court, suspicion of/attacks on, 24–32
    appointment of Anti-Federalist judges as intended remedy, 96, 97–8
    impeachment policy, 20, 28–32, 186–7
    Jefferson's Vendetta, 26–32
    Judiciary Act 1802, 26
    *Marbury v Madison*, 20, 27–8, 49, 143–4, 187, 198
    separation of powers issues, 25–6
  hatred of Britain, 89
  Johnson J and, 97–8
  Livingston J and, 96
  views on
    Marshall CJ, 9, 27–8, 186–7
    Story J, 116, 117
    Washington J, 53
Johnson (1974) (edited by Hobson (2006)) (*Papers of John Marshall*), 2, 8, 37, 140, 142, 155, 187, 193
Johnson (1997), xii, xiii, 4, 8n27, 9
Johnson (2000), 11
Johnson (2009), 4, 11
Johnson J, legal attitudes
  bankruptcy/debt, 158n8
  precedent, 48
  state rights, 171
Johnson J, life and career
  admiralty cases, 137
  circuit riding, 5–6

# Index

dissents, 10, 48, 97, 148, 159, 189, 199
Jefferson J and, 97–8
judicial experience prior to appointment to the Supreme Court, 8, 171
judicial record
   certificates of division of opinion, 197
   reversal rates, 196
Judicature Act 1891 (Evarts Act), 5–6
judicial independence: see also separation of powers
   federal courts' contribution to, 3–4
   grand jury charge and, 185
   tenure during good behaviour (Constitution III(1)), 91
judicial review (including *Marbury v Madison*), 1–2, 27–8, 198
Judiciary Act 1789
   circuit court provisions, 39–41
   constitutionality (*Marbury v Madison*), 27–8, 143–4, 187
   Federalists vs Anti-Federalists/Republicans, 23–4, 27–8, 39–40, 185
   legislative history/sticking points, 38–9
   number of Supreme Court justices, 169n58
   uniformity/consistency of decision-taking and, 46
   Washington and, 46–7
Judiciary Act 1789 by section
   1 (relaxation of circuit riding requirement), 39
   2 (districts), 39
   3 (district courts), 39
   17 (oaths and affirmations), 135n117
   22 (appeals from district court), 65
   25 (appellate jurisdiction), 143
   30 (depositions), 135n117
   34 (applicability of state laws), 42
Judiciary Act 1801
   number of Supreme Court justices, 169n58
   political manoeuvring against President Jefferson, 39–40
   relief of circuit riding duties (s 3), 39–40
   repeal, 27
Judiciary Act 1802
   Chase J's attack on, 35
   dismissal of newly appointed federal circuit judges/reintroduction of circuit riding (s 4), 26, 40, 49, 187
   *Stuart v Laird*, 187
   suspension of Supreme Court proceedings, 49, 186–7
Judiciary Act 1807, 169n58
jury system
   criminal cases and, 132–3
   Livingston J on, 21, 93–5, 102, 110, 165
   Story on, 132–3
   Thompson J and, 164–5, 168
   Washington J on, 65–6, 83, 95

Kadish (1996), 33
Kaufman (2003), 135
Kelsh (1999), 12
Kent J
   *caveat emptor* and, 163
   choice of reporter, 97n5
   *Commentaries on American Law*, 155–6
   Eerie Canal Bill and, 161
   Livingston J and, 91
      as possible successor to, 199
   Story J and, 155–6
   Thompson J and, 160, 173, 204
   Washington J and, 61
Kerber (1970), 40
Killenbeck (2006), 145
Krauss (2012), 33
Kutler (1971), 66, 67

LaCroix (2012), xii, 23
Lamoine (ed), 33
land titles: see property rights/vested interests
Langbein (1993), 97
Langbein (2004), 112
law reports (as listed at pp 207–8)
   *Note*: references are included in the index only when something of substance is said about the reports or the reporter.
   Caines (*Reports of the New York Supreme Court, 1803–1805*), 92, 93n27, 94, 97, 165, 180n96
   *Federal Cases, 1789–1880*, xii–xiii, 15–16, 17, 43–4, 45, 46, 47–8, 96–7, 119, 122, 124n65, 130, 166–7
   Gallison (*First Circuit Reports, 1812–1815*), 64, 119
   Johnson (*Law Reports of the New York Supreme Court*), 43–4, 92, 93n27, 97, 165–6
   Kirby (*Reports of Cases Adjudged in the Superior Court of Connecticut*), 42
   Mason, WP (*First Circuit Reports*), 17, 119, 141
   Paine (*Second Circuit Reports*), 17, 96–7, 166–7
   Peters (*Reports of the Third Circuit*), 16n61, 17, 61, 171–2
   Quincy (*Massachusetts Reports*) (1865), 42, 97n47
   Story (*First Circuit Reports*) (1842–1845), 17, 119
   Sumner (*Reports of Cases*), 17, 119
   *United States Reports 1790–1835*, 12, 15–16, 80, 109–10, 119, 137, 138, 149, 159n11, 174n76, 195
   Wallace (*Third Circuit Reports*) (no references in the text)
   Wharton (*State Trials during the Administrations of Washington and Adams*) (no references in the text)

## Index

law reports (general): *see also* sources of law
  establishment of precedent/importance of quality, 47, 62, 165, 189
  paucity of federal cases/Supreme Court reports/slowness to appoint official reporter, 96–7, 102
  Wheaton, appointment, 97
Lee (1999), 58–9
Lind (1930), 117
Livingston J (1808–23), legal attitudes
  admiralty law/marine insurance, 45, 93–4, 96
  bankruptcy/debt, 47, 98, 100–1, 107
  bills of exchange/promissory notes, 21, 104–5, 110, 191
  commercial law/trade promotion: *see* commercial law/trade promotion (Livingston)
  criminal cases, 102
  customs law enforcement, 102
  embargo laws, 105–7
  jury system, 21, 93–4, 102, 110, 165
  key features, 3
  marine insurance, 93–4
  precedent, 98–9, 100, 109
  slavery/slave trade, 1007
  sources of law
    circuit opinions, 47
    English common law/authorities, view of, 45, 93, 109
  states' rights: *see* states' rights/state sovereignty (Livingston)
  uniformity/consistency/dependence on precedent, 47, 98–9, 100, 109, 188
Livingston J (1808–23), life and career
  appointment to New York Supreme Court (1802), 91
  appointment to the Supreme Court (1807), 96
  Burr and, 88
  candidates to succeed, 159n13
  characteristics
    fiery temper/duelling record, 87, 88–9
    flexibility, 109
    self-assurance, 98
  circuit riding, 96
    district judges, 99–100
    geographical range, 99–100
  death, 110
  dissents, 10, 92, 99, 100–1, 108, 189, 199
  education and early career, 87
  family connections, 87, 89, 91
  judicial record
    certificates of division of opinion, 197
    evaluation, 109–10
    majority opinions, 199
    paucity of federal case reports, 96–7, 102
    reversal rates, 197
    specialisms, 105–6, 109–10
  Kent J and, 91

legal studies under Yates, 88
loss of the *Diana* (*Livingston & Gilchrist v Maryland Insurance*), 88
low profile, 86–7
Marshall CJ's respect for, 105, 109
New York Supreme Court (1802–6), 91–6
  tally and scope of opinions, 92
opinions
  brevity and plain language, 98–9
  humour, 99
political affiliations
  fluidity, 87–91, 191
  reversion to federalist principles, 98
relations with Jay CJ (brother-in-law), 87–8, 8998
Story J and, 98, 108
Looney (ed) (2008), 112n3

McClellan (1971), 18–19, 114, 118, 120–1, 151, 155
McGarvie (2016), 135
MacGill and Newmyer (2008), 165–6
McLean J, judicial experience and legal education, 204
McMaster (1883–1913), 116n28
Madison (US President, 1809–17)
  Alien & Sedition Acts 1798, 90–1
  *Federalist Paper No. 10* (property rights), 57
  *Marbury v Madison*, 20, 27–8, 49, 143–4, 187, 198
  political affiliations, 90–1
majority opinions: *see* opinions
Mann (2002), 101n61
Marcus (1985–2007), 1n1, 4, 6n,17, 7n20, 24n5, 33, 34n49, 35–6, 184
marine insurance: *see also* maritime, prize and marine insurance, jurisprudence
  jurisdiction, confusion over, 131–2
  Livingston J on, 93–4
  Story J on, 122, 130–2, 154
  Thompson J on, 164
  Washington J on, 67, 71–2, 77, 80, 84
maritime, prize and marine insurance, jurisprudence
  *The Active*, 103, 110
  *Armroyd v Williams*, 78
  *Bayard et al v Massachusetts Fire & Marine Ins Co*, 130, 154
  *Coles et al v Marine Insurance Co*, 71
  *Cruder v Pennsylvania Ins Co*, 71
  *Delaware Insurance Company v Hogan*, 71, 84
  *Delovio v Boit*, 131–2, 154, 189
  *The Elizabeth*, 103
  *Glidden v Manufacturers[x2019] Ins Co*, 130, 154
  *Goyon v Pleasants*, 71
  *Harden v Gordon*, 154
  *Insurance Co v Dunham*, 132, 154

*The James Wells*, 102, 110
*The Jerusalem*, 131
*Kohne v Insurance Company of North America*, 72
*McGregor v Insurance Company of Pennsylvania*, 71, 84
*Ninety-Five Bales of Paper v US*, 110
*Odlin v Insurance Company of Pennsylvania*, 84
*Penny v New York Insurance Company*, 93
*Ross v The Active*, 72
*Tidmarsh v Washington Fire & Marine Insurance Co Inc*, 130, 154
*US v Five Packages of Linen*, 110
*Vale v Phoenix Insurance Co*, 72, 84
Marshall CJ, legal attitudes
  admiralty law, 137, 138, 139
  bankruptcy/debt, 101, 199
  circuit riding, 187n 5
  commercial law/trade promotion, 103
  Indian/Native American rights, 175n81, 176
  personal liability for public contract, 162
  precedent, 58–9
  uniformity/consistency, need for/aids to achieving, 9, 46–7, 138–43, 154–5
Marshall CJ, life and career
  Burr and, 37, 139, 193
  decision-making process: *see* opinions
  Jefferson's views on, 9, 11
  judicial experience and legal education, 8, 203
  judicial record
    admiralty expertise, 10
    certificates of division of opinion, 197
    circuit opinions, importance, 10
    dissents, 58, 106, 107–8, 139, 158–9
    majority opinions, 12, 198–9
  Story J and, 10, 12, 32, 114, 138, 139–42, 187
  Virginia Ratifying Convention (1788), 38
  Washington J and, 52–3
Mason, G's opposition to the federal judicial system (1788), 38, 171
Meacham (2008), 149n174
Meacham (2012), 29
minority rights: *see* Native American rights; slavery/slave trade
Moore J, judicial experience and legal education, 203
Morgan (1954), 13–14, 55, 120, 159
Morison (1921), 116n26
Morris, J.B. (1987), 6
Morris, R.B. (1979), 6n18
Munger (1991), 67–8

Native American rights
  Constitution 3(2), 176–7
  Indian Removal Act, 149n174
  jurisprudence

*Cherokee Nation v Georgia*, 12, 148, 174, 175–7, 182, 192, 229
*Johnson v M'Intosh*, 175
*Worcester v Georgia*, 12, 148–9, 176–7, 192
Marshall CJ on, 176
Story J on, xi, 147–9, 175n81, 176, 189
Thompson J on, 175–7
Treaties of Hopewell (1785) and Holston (1791), 176
New York Constitution 1777, applicability of British statute and common law, 93
New York Council of Revision, 161, 192
  'hard law', 159–66
New York Supreme Court
  applicability of British statute and common law (New York Constitution 1777), 44, 93
  equally divided court, handling of, 91–2
  'hard law', 159–66
  law reports, 97, 165–6
  Livingston J's tenure (1802–6), 91–6
  participation in appeal by judge previously involved in the case, 92–3
  Thompson J's tenure (1802–18), 159–66
  workload, 92
Newmyer (1970), xi, 4–5
Newmyer (1985), 8, 9, 18–20, 120–1, 122, 185
Newmyer (2001), 175n81
Newmyer (2012), 31n35
Non-Intercourse Act 1809: *see* embargo laws
North, 116n28
Novak (1966), 2

O'Connor (1979), 19, 120
opinions: *see also* dissents
  circuit opinion as indicator of justice's opinion, 185
  decision-making process (Marshall Court), 11–15
    compromise, 9, 12, 20, 27–8, 101, 137, 185, 187
    congeniality/collegiality, 11–13, 48, 49–50, 140, 154–5, 187, 189
    European Court of Justice compared, 11
    'king on a throne' or collaborative team-worker?, 7–11
    opinion assignment, xiii, 3, 14–15, 82, 105, 109, 138, 146, 189–90
    preference for the single opinion/delivery of majority of opinions himself, 11, 12, 140
    small group dynamics, 11
  drafting practice (Story J), 132n105
  drafting practice (Thompson J), 175–6
  formality of deliberations (*Hudson and Smith*), 107–8
  from seriatim to single/majority opinion, 11–12, 13–14, 32n39, 80, 201

single opinion
  as counter to Republican opposition, 11, 14–15, 187
  as Marshall's preferred option, 11, 12, 140
  time taken to prepare, 132n105, 144n156

Paris Peace Treaty (1783), 60, 69, 88, 100
partnerships, 94–110, 133, 167, 170, 191
patents
  Story J, 133
  Washington J, 46, 61–2, 67–8, 69, 80, 82
Paterson J, life and career
  Alien & Sedition Acts 1798, 185
  circuit riding, 187n5
  judicial experience and legal education, 202–3
  majority opinions, 199
Pauw and Bickford (eds) (1972–2017), 24n2
personal property rights: *see* property rights/vested interests
Peters (ed) (*The Public Statutes at Large of the United States*), 42
Peters J
  admiralty law and, 29n27
  on Washington J, 79
Peterson (ed) (1984), 9, 32, 90n20, 191
Pfister (2016) (*Charting an American Republic*), 7
Pfister (2016) ('The Legacy of John Jay'), 7
political parties, emergence of, 24n2, 185
political tensions: *see also* impeachment; Jefferson (US President, 1801–9); Judiciary Act 1789; Judiciary Act 1801; Judiciary Act 1807; states' rights/state sovereignty
  Alien & Sedition Acts 1798, political abuse of, 90–1, 185
  political fluidity, 87–91, 191
  Republican Congress vs Federalist Supreme Court, 2, 20, 21, 118, 187–8
  single opinion/consistency of Supreme Court decisions as defence, 11, 14–15
  shared backgrounds of Supreme Court justices, 57, 108, 186
  Story J, impact on, 113
precedent
  Blackstone on, 57–8
  circuit opinions, 46–8
  decision-taking in the absence of, 166
  English authorities: *see* sources of law, English authorities
  Hamilton on, 58
  Johnson J and, 48
  Kennedy J (*House v Mayo/Hohn*), 58
  Livingston J and, 98–9, 100, 109, 188
  Marshall CJ on, 58–99
  non-binding effect, 46–7
  reliable law reports, dependence on, 47, 62, 165, 189
  risks of over-dependence on, 59–60, 85, 172, 184
  as stabilizing factor, 52, 57–9, 84, 85, 184, 188
  Story J, 47, 131n99, 138–43, 154–6
  striking the balance, 58–9
  Thompson J and, 47–8, 160–1, 165–6, 169, 172, 181, 188
  Thurgood Marshall CJ (*Payne*), 58
precedent (Washington J)
  collection of, 57
    *Anton v Fisher*, 60
    *Barnes v Billingham*, 43, 60, 61, 83
    *Bobyshall v Oppenheimer*, 60, 83
    *Campbell v Claudius*, 61
    *Craig*, 61
    *Crawford v The William Penn*, 60, 62
    *Croudson v Leonard*, 59–60
    *Ferguson v Zepp*, 60–1, 83
    *Hurst v Hurst*, 61
    *Krumbar v Burt*, 61
    *Ricord v Bettenham*, 60
  English jurisprudence and, 59–61, 188
  jurisprudence
    *Bank of the US v Northumberland Union and Columbia Bank*, 46–7
    *Beach v Woodhull*, 62
    *Croudson v Leonard*, 59–60, 83
    *Dartmouth College*, 81
    *Evans v Hettick*, 46, 62
    *Hurst v Hurst*, 63
    *Hylton v Brown*, 64
    *Kirkpatrick v White*, 59, 83
    *Martin v The Bank of the US*, 46, 62
    *Metcalf v Hervey*, 64
    *Mott v Morris*, 63–4, 188
    *Odlin v Insurance Co of Pennsylvania*, 62
    *Ogden v Saunders*, 59–60
    *Schooner Exchange*, 62–3
    *Scriba v Insurance Co of North America*, 59, 83
    *Sturges v Crownshield*, 59
    *Treadwell v Bladen*, 46, 62
    *US v Bright*, 56–7, 83
    *US v Moses*, 46, 62
    *Walter v Perrine*, 62
  key feature of judicial record, 46–7, 51–2, 83–5, 184, 188
  lack of confidence, as solution to, 62–6, 83–4
  law reports, quality requirement, 62
  rigidity/caution, 58–9, 184
  statutory interpretation and, 59
Presser (1982), 29, 52n3
Presser (1990), 114, 155
Preyer (1986), 152
Prize Court of Appeals in Prize Cases, 131n99: *see also* embargo laws; embargo laws, jurisprudence (Story J); embargo laws, jurisprudence (Washington J); marine insurance; maritime, prize and marine insurance, jurisprudence; seamen, protection of

# Index

procedural matters
  certificate of division of opinion, 3, 79, 92, 131–2, 168, 189, 195–6, 200
  cross-circuit consistency, 169
  death of party, 168–9
  discharge of jury, 168
  dissents: *see* dissents
  efficient despatch of business, 169
  opinions: *see* opinions
  Thompson J and, 168–9
promissory notes: *see* bills of exchange/promissory notes; commercial law/trade promotion
property rights/vested interests
  contracts clause (Constitution I(10)(1)) and, 66, 67, 69–70, 80–1, 100, 144, 173, 198
  due process (Constitution, Fifth amendment), 66
  *Federalist Paper No. 10* (Madison), 57
  jurisprudence
    *Bleeker v Bond*, 69–70
    *Charles River Bridge*, 66–7
    *Dartmouth College*, 66
    *Fletcher v Peck*, 69–70, 118, 198
    *Golden v Prince*, 70
    *Gordon v Holiday*, 84
    *Griffith v Tunckhouser*, 69, 84
    *Huidekoper v Burrus*, 84
    *Milligan v Dickson*, 84
    *Torrey v Beardsley*, 69, 84
    *Willis v Bucher*, 69, 84
  justices' determination to preserve, 24, 57, 66, 184
  military bounty-land, 167–8
  public benefit as object, 66–7
  Thompson J and, 164, 166, 167–8
  Washington J and, 66–70, 84
    preservation of titles as a priority, 69
    recognition of public interest obligation, 70

Quincy (*Figures of the Past*) (1883), 187

Rakove (ed) (1999), 90
real property: *see* property rights/vested interests
Remini (2001), 149
reports: *see* law reports (as listed at pp 207–8); law reports (general)
Richardson (1905), 28
Ritz (1990), 42
Robarge (2000), 9–10
Roper (1963/1987), 18, 120, 157–8, 159, 162
Rossiter (2003), 58
Rustein (2012), 125

Schwartz (1972), 33
seamen, protection of
  jurisprudence
    *Barnewell v Church*, 164–5

*Girard v Ware*, 73
*Ketland v Lebering*, 73
*Smith v Jackson*, 73
*US v Smith*, 72–3
Story J and, 129–30, 192–3
Thompson J and, 167, 192–3
Washington J and, 72–3, 192–3
Sedition Act 1798: *see* Alien & Sedition Acts 1798
separation of powers: *see also* judicial independence
  Jay Courts, 25–6
  judicial vs Congress responsibility for defining the law, 82
  New York Council of Revision and, 161, 192
seriatim opinions: *see* opinions
Sewall J, 112–13
Seymour (1992), 179
Sheppard (ed) (2010), 25, 112
single opinions: *see* opinions
slavery/slave trade
  constitutional provisions, 2–3, 177, 178–80
    Constitution IV(1)(3) (recapture of person held to service), 149–50
    Thirteenth Amendment (abolition of slavery), 179, 193
  as a fact of American life, 2–3, 55–6
  Judson DJ on, 179n93
  legislation
    Fugitive Slave Act 1793, 121, 150, 179, 191
    Slave Trade Act 1794, 78–9, 81–2, 177–8
    Slave Trade Act 1807, 149
    Slave Trade Act 1810, 81–2
  Livingston J on, 107
  Story J on, 4n6, 121, 133–5
  Thompson J on, 177–80
  Washington J on: *see* slavery/slave trade (Washington J)
slavery/slave trade, jurisprudence
  *The Alexander*, 133
  *The Amistad*, 149, 177, 178–9, 181
  *Butler v Hopper*, 79
  *The Emily and The Caroline*, 177–8
  *Fales v Mayberry*, 133
  *The Joseph Segunda*, 107
  *La Jeune Eugenie*, 134
  *Lee v Lee*, 178
  *McCutchen v Marshall*, 179
  *Re Martin*, 179–80
  *The Plattsburgh*, 149
  *Prigg*, 121, 149–50, 191
  *Ex parte Simmons*, 79
  *Tryphenia v Harrison*, 78–9
slavery/slave trade (Washington J), 54–6, 78–9, 81–2
  respect for rights of owners of slaves already in the US, 56, 78–9, 85, 191
Snell (2007), 131
sources of law: *see also* law reports (general)

absence of precedent, 42: *see also* precedent
circuit opinions, xi, xiii, 1, 2, 5, 46–8
constitutional gap/paucity, xiii, 41–2, 49–50, 183
English authorities: *see also* Blackstone's *Commentaries*; common law (state/English); common law (state/English), jurisprudence; precedent (Washington J), English jurisprudence and; Tucker's *Blackstone*
  common law, 20, 23, 37, 44–5, 49–50, 93, 112–13, 165–6, 184, 191–2
  English statutory law, 44, 46, 61
  Jefferson on, 117
  Livingston J on, 44, 109
  as means of clarifying American law (Story), 21, 111, 154, 184
  Story on, 21, 45–6, 111, 112–13, 127, 131, 135–6, 151–3, 184, 191–2
  Thompson J on, 46, 163, 165–6, 171–2
federal statutes, 23
New York Constitution 1777, 93
Story J, 45–6, 135–6, 165–6
Story J on, 21, 45–6, 112–13, 127, 135–6, 191–2
Story J's emphasis on the importance of, 132
Supreme Court opinions, paucity, 1, 3, 5, 11, 20, 49–50, 184
'the laws of the several states' (Judiciary Act 1789, s 34), 42, 43–4
uniformity of decision making, importance to, 23
sovereignty of states, 2–3, 20, 21–2, 24, 172
*Augusta Chronicle*, 35–7
Spaeth and Segal (1999), 58
Stahr (2005), 91
state sovereignty: *see* states' rights/state sovereignty
states' rights/state sovereignty: *see also* federal system of justice
  Anti-Federalists' opposition to interference, 3, 23, 24, 35–6, 48–9
  bankruptcy/debt, 47, 59, 82, 100–1
  Constitution I(8), 100, 144–5, 171
  divergence between state and federal law, effect, 171–2
  failure of judicial appointees to live up to Republican presidents' expectations, 90, 100, 101, 186
  striking a difficult balance, 20, 21, 24, 100, 172
  taxation powers, 144–5, 174–5
states' rights/state sovereignty (Johnson J)
  failure to live up to Republican presidential expectations, 90
  jurisprudence
    *Adams v Story*, 101
    *Ogden v Saunders*, 101
    *Sturges v Crowninshield*, 100–1

states' rights/state sovereignty (Livingston J)
  balancing act, 191
  failure to live up to Republican presidential expectations, 90, 100, 101, 186
  jurisprudence
    *Adams v Story*, 47, 100
    *Fisher v Harnden*, 100
    *Sturges v Crowninshield*, 100–1
states' rights/state sovereignty (Marshall CJ), jurisprudence, *Sturges v Crowninshield*, 100–1
states' rights/state sovereignty (Story J), 136, 144–6
  failure to live up to Republican presidential expectations, 90, 186
  jurisprudence
    *Bell v Morrison*, 136
    *Dartmouth College*, 144
    *Harding v Wheaton*, 123
    *McCulloch v Maryland*, 144–5
    *Swift v Tyson*, 152–3
states' rights/state sovereignty (Thompson J)
  attitude as New York Supreme Court Justice, 157, 171–5
  attitude towards Marshall CJ's federalist centralism, 158–9
  disposition to uphold state laws/sovereignty, 21–2, 160–1, 180, 192
  failure to live up to Republican presidential expectations, 90, 186
  jurisprudence
    *Brown v Maryland*, 173–4
    *Gibbons v Ogden*, 172
    *Jeremiah Ferguson*, 173
    *Livingston v Van Ingen*, 172
    *Mason v Haile*, 174
    *Ogden v Saunders*, 173
    *Osborn v Bank of the US*, 174–5
    *The Robert Fulton*, 173
    *Ward v Arrendo*, 173
    *Wheaton v Peters*, 171–2
  'states' rights mercantilism … with a humanitarian overlay', 171–2
states' rights/state sovereignty (Washington J), 73–7
  jurisprudence
    *Corfield v Coryell*, 76–7
    *US v Bright*, 74–5
    *US v Lowry*, 75
statutory interpretation
  consistency of interpretation, importance, 47–8, 169
  jurisprudence, *Mann*, 124
  legislators' intention, role, 161–2
  Spencer J and, 161–2
  Story J and, 124–5, 136, 147
  strict interpretation/precedent, 59, 162–4
  Thompson J and, 161, 347–8
  Washington J and, 59, 64

Stockdale and Holland (2007), 53n5
Stonier (1998), 18, 64–5
Story J (1811–45), legal attitudes, xi, 147–9, 175n81, 176, 189
  account/evaluation of contribution, 125–33
  admiralty law: *see* admiralty law, Story J; embargo laws, jurisprudence (Story J)
  appeals from district courts, 122
  bankruptcy/debt, 98, 101, 115, 144, 158n8
  bills of exchange/promissory notes, 118, 147, 150
  commercial law: *see* commercial law/trade promotion (Story J)
  criminal law: *see* criminal law (Story J)
  diversity jurisdiction, 21, 41, 152–3, 154, 192
  federal law supremacy, 143–7: *see also* federal law, supremacy of (including in particular Story-related jurisprudence)
  grand jury charge, 35n60
  jury system, 132–3
  key features, 3
  marine insurance, 122, 130–2, 154
  Native American rights, xi, 175n81, 176, 189
  participation in appeal from case in which he had previously participated, 146
  patents, 133
  seamen
    jurisdiction over crimes on board ship, 128–9
    protection of, 129–30, 192–3
  slavery/slave trading, 4n6, 121, 133–5
  sources of law
    emphasis on importance of, 132
    English authorities/English common law, 21, 45–6, 111, 112–13, 127, 135–6, 151–4, 191–2
    state laws/precedent, 43–4
  states' right: *see* states' rights/state sovereignty (Story J)
  statutory interpretation, 136, 147
  uniformity/consistency/dependence on precedent, 47, 138–43, 154–6
Story J (1811–45), life and career
  admittance to the Bar (1801), 113
  appointment to the Supreme Court (1811), 118
    independence, 115–17
    meticulous professionalism, 111, 114, 118
    nationalism, 126
  characteristics, capacity to carry a huge workload, 142–3
  circuit riding, 26n14
  evaluation, 153–6
    Kent J, 155
    scholars' assessment, 119–20
  Jefferson's hostility towards, 116, 117
  judicial experience and legal education, 8, 111–13, 204

judicial record (circuit court), 121–5
  certificates of division of opinion, 134, 197
  circuit riding demands, 122
  inheritance of backlog, 122–3
  specialisms, 122
  Story's attachment to the circuit court, 121–2
judicial record (Supreme Court)
  dissents (including *Cherokee Nation v Georgia*), xi, 127, 139, 153–4, 175, 176, 189
  majority opinions, 199
  reversals, 153–4, 197
  tally of Marshall Court opinions, 137–8
Kent J and, 155–6
legal apprenticeship
  Putnam J, 113
  Sewall J, 112–13
letters to Jay PJ, 13, 48, 119, 123, 137, 138
Livingston J and, 98, 108
Marshall CJ's relationship with, 10, 12, 32, 114, 138, 139–42, 187
opinions other than on admiralty law, 133
political affiliations
  nationalism, 126, 145
  Republican beliefs, 113, 114
  support for strong federal state, 114–18, 143–7
  tension between, 115–18
practicality and efficiency, 122–5
  impatience with statutory drafting, 124–5
religious beliefs, 134–5
views on
  *Blackstone's Commentaries*, 112–13
  *Coke on Littleton*, 112
  fellow justices, 119, 137
Washington, cooperation with, 138–43
working methods
  certificate of division of opinion as means to secure definitive opinion, 136
  drafting practice, 132n105
  *Juniores ad Labores*, 138
  willingness to seek advice, 135–6
Story J (writings)
  *Abbott on Shipping*, 118
  *Autobiography*, 111, 113, 150
  *Chitty*, 118, 150
  *Commentaries on*, 155
    *Agency and Maritime Jurisprudence*, 150–1
    *Conflict of Laws*, 150–1
    *Equity Jurisprudence*, 150–1
    *Equity Pleadings*, 150–1
    *Promissory Notes*, 150–1
    *the Constitution of the United States*, 17, 26n14, 38, 119–20, 150–1
    *the Law of Nations*, 150–1
  *Constitutional Class Book*, 120

*Discourse on Past History, Present State & Future Prospects of Law*, 150–1
*Encyclopaedia Americana* essays, 120
*A Familiar Exposition of the Constitution*, 120
Kent J's *Commentaries* compared, 155
*Selection of Pleadings in Civil Actions*, 114
Story, WW (ed) (*Life and Letters*) (1851), 4, 12, 17, 51, 80, 110–56 *passim*, 192
Story, WW (ed) (*Miscellaneous Writings of Joseph Story*) (1852), 17, 112n3, 113, 119, 133, 152
Supreme Court justices: *see also* appeals, circuit court to Supreme Court; circuit courts; opinions; *and under individual justices*
 judicial experience and legal education, 44, 202–5
 quality, 8, 10
 salaries, 115
 shared backgrounds, 44, 57, 108, 186
 small workload/delivered opinions, 1, 3, 5, 11, 20, 49–50, 184
Surrency (1981), 17n66, 97
Surrency (1996), 99
Surrency (2002), 33
Sutherland (1967), 112, 150

Tachau (1978), x–xi, xii
Taney J (successor to Marshall CJ), 13
 *Charles River Bridge*, 67
 Story J and, 140
 Thompson J and, 169, 174
Thompson J (1823–43), legal attitudes, xii
 bills of exchange/promissory notes, 163–4, 166, 170, 181, 190
 *caveat emptor*, 163, 170, 181
 certainty of the law, 164, 169, 170
 commercial law/trade promotion: *see* commercial law/trade promotion (Thompson J)
 conservatism/preservation of the *status quo*, 161, 168, 181, 191
 contractual law, 163–4
 cross-circuit consistency, 169
 decision-taking in the absence of precedent, 166
 jury system, 164–5, 168
 key features, 3, 158–9, 180–1
 marine insurance, 164
 Native American rights (*Cherokee Nation*), 47, 175–7: *see also* Native American rights
 New York 'hard law', 159–66
 personal liability for public contract, 162–3
 precedent, 160, 165–6, 169, 181, 188
 procedural matters, 168–9
 property rights/vested interests, 164, 166, 167–8
 seamen, protection of, 167, 192–3
 separation of powers, 161, 192
 slavery/slave trade, 177–80
 sources of law
  circuit opinions, 47–8
  English authorities, 46, 163, 165–6
  state laws/precedent, 43
 speedy resolution of disputes, 164
 states' rights: *see* states' rights/state sovereignty (Thompson J)
 statutory interpretation, 47–8, 161–3
Thompson J (1823–43), life and career
 admiralty law, 46, 137
 as Associate/Chief Justice of the New York Supreme Court (1802–18), 159–66
 dissents (including *Cherokee Nation v Georgia*), 12, 47, 158–9, 171–2, 173–4, 175–80, 182, 192
 drafting practice, 175–6
 judicial experience and legal education, 166, 167, 169–71, 181–2, 188, 204
 as Justice of the Supreme Court (1823–43), 166–80
 Kent J and, 160, 173, 204
 legal appointments, 159–60
 as Naval Secretary, 159–60
 note-taking skills, 160
 political aspirations, 157–8
 record of decisions, 166–7
 scholars' assessment of performance as judge, 158–9
 Story J, Thompson's respect for, 169
 Taney J and, 169, 174
Thorp et al (1942), 116
Todd J, life and career
 circuit riding, xii
 judicial experience and legal education, 203–4
 judicial record, 8, 10, 15, 16, 40, 46–7, 117, 137, 158, 172, 190
  appeals/divisions of opinion., 197
  majority opinions, 200
Trading with the Enemy Act 1812: *see* embargo laws
Treaty of Holston (1791), 176
Treaty of Hopewell (1785), 176
Trimble J, judicial experience and legal education, 204
Tucker's *Blackstone*, 1, 20n78, 155: *see also* Blackstone's *Commentaries*
Turner, Way and Maveety, 14

uniformity/consistency, need for/aids to achieving
 appeals, 2
  certificate of division of opinion, 3, 135, 189
 criminal law: *see* criminal law
 exchanges of experience and advice between justices on circuit, 37, 48, 49–50, 138–43
 importance for the survival of the federal judicial system, 26, 37
 judicial review and, 2
 Judiciary Act 1789, 46

law reports, 189
Livingston J and, 47
Marshall CJ and, 26, 46–7, 138–43, 154–5
non-binding precedent, 46–8: *see also* precedent
sources of law including English common law, 20, 23, 37, 46, 49: *see also* sources of law
Story J and, 47, 138–43, 154–6
  *Martin v Hunter's Lessee*, 141
Thompson J and, 47–8
Washington J and, 46–7, 138–43, 154–5
Urofsky and Finkelman (2011), 25, 39

Van Hook (2015), 7n20, 39
vested interests: *see* property rights/vested interests

Wallace, AFC (1999), 29n29
War of 1812, 2, 19, 74, 116–17, 153–4, 161, 193
Warren (1911), xiin7, 1n1, 29n27, 98n48
Warren (1926), 1n1, 29, 98
Warren (1941), 121
Washington J (1803-23), legal attitudes: *see also* seamen, protection of
  admiralty law, 59–60, 63, 74–5, 77–8, 190
  appointment to the Supreme Court, 56–7
  bankruptcy/debt, 59, 61, 64, 67, 80, 82, 158n8
  bills of exchange/promissory notes, 70–1, 84
  constitutional rights and freedoms, 76
  constitutionality of Supreme Court justices as circuit court judges, 187
  embargo laws, 77–8: *see also* embargo laws, jurisprudence (Washington J)
  jury system, 65–6, 83, 95
  key features, 3
  law reports, importance, 62
  marine insurance, 67, 71–2, 77, 80, 84
  patents, 46, 61–2, 67–8, 69, 80, 82
  precedent: *see* precedent (Washington J)
  property rights/vested interests, 66–70, 84
    preservation of titles as a priority, 69
    Washington J and, recognition of public interest obligation, 70
  seamen, protection of, 72–3, 192–3
  slavery/slave trade: *see* slavery/slave trade (Washington J)
  sources of law
    English authorities, 59–61, 64
    state laws/precedent, 43
  states' rights: *see* states' rights/state sovereignty (Washington J)
  statutory interpretation, 64
  uniformity/consistency/dependence on precedent, 46–7
Washington J (1803–23), life and career
  characteristics
    conservatism/preservation of the *status quo*, 57, 59–60, 69, 84
    lack of confidence/caution, 18, 51, 59, 62–6, 76, 83, 93–4, 190
    plaintiff discourse, 98

religious beliefs, 54–5
willingness to seek advice, 79, 135–6, 138–43
circuit riding, 51–2
death, 85
family background and connections, 5257
as Federalist, 51
financial difficulties, 54
Jefferson J and, 53
judicial experience and legal education, 80, 203
  education, 52
  study with Wilson J, 53
  Third Circuit experience (1803-29), 8, 51–2, 80
judicial record
  certificates of division of opinion, 79, 197
  evaluation, 83–5
  majority opinions, 80, 199
  a reluctant dissenter, 59, 80–1
  reversals, 63
  subject matter of opinions, 67, 77
  Supreme Court opinions, 17, 80, 199
Marshall CJ and, 52–3
Peters J on, 79
specialisms (chancery and land disputes), 53–4
Story J, relationship with, 51, 59–60, 135–6, 138–43
writings
  *Life of George Washington*, 52–3
  *Virginia Court of Appeals Reports*, 53
Washington (US President, 1789–97)
  appointment of justices, 24–5
    from different states/regional diversity, 25, 49
  political role of Supreme Court and, 25
Watts (1987), 24
Wayne J, life and career, judicial experience and legal education, 204–5
Weisenburger (1937), 19, 120
Wexler (2006), 6, 36
Wheelan (2005), 26
Wheeler (1973), 26
White (1988/2010), 1n1, 16n61, 87, 157–8, 189, 201, 234
White (2012), 120–1
Wilson J, life and career
  appointment as associate justice, 25
  on circuit riding, 5–6, 36
  debt and early death, 25n10
  enforcement of payment to British subjects, 38
  grand jury charge, 34–5
  Washington J and, 53
Winsor (ed), 123n56
Wood (2007), 25, 106, 186
writ of error, 2, 93, 122, 124, 143, 201

Zobel (1989), 118, 122, 132